THE ESSENCE OF
ISLĀM
VOLUME III

Extracts from the Writings, Speeches,
Announcements and Discourses of the

Promised Messiah
Ḥaḍrat Mirzā Ghulām Aḥmad
of Qādiān
[May peace be upon him]

Published under the auspices of
Ḥaḍrat Mirzā Masroor Aḥmad
Fifth Successor to the Promised Messiah
[May Allah be his help]

The Essence of Islām Volume III

A rendering into English of Extracts from the writings, speeches, announcements and discourses of Ḥaḍrat Mirzā Ghulām Aḥmad of Qādiān, the Promised Messiah and Founder of the Aḥmadiyyah Muslim Community.

First Edition (2005):
Islām International Publications Limited
Translated into English by:
Chaudhry Muḥammad Ẓafrullāh Khān
Revised by:
Munawar Aḥmed Sa ʻeed

Published by:
Islām International Publications Ltd.
'Islamabad' Sheephatch Lane,
Tilford, Surrey GU10 2AQ
United Kingdom

Printed in UK at:
Clays Ltd, St Ives plc

ISBN: 1 85372 756 3

SUMMERY OF CONTENTS, VOL. I, II, & III

VOLUME I

INTRODUCTION
1. ISLĀM, THE TRUE AND LIVING FAITH
2. ALLAH THE EXALTED
3. THE HOLY PROPHET[sa]
4. THE HOLY QUR'ĀN

VOLUME II

1. ARABIC, THE MOTHER OF TONGUES
2. REVELATION, INSPIRATION, VISION AND DREAM
3. HADITH AND SUNNAH OF THE HOLY PROPHET[sa]
4. ANGELS
5. PRAYER
6. REPENTANCE AND SEEKING FORGIVENESS
7. SALVATION
8. THE PILLARS OF ISLĀM
9. FIGHTING IN THE CAUSE OF ALLAH
10. DIVINE DECREES AND DETERMINATION
11. RIGHTEOUSNESS
12. ARROGANCE
13. THINKING ILL OF OTHERS
14. PUNISHMENT IN THIS WORLD
15. THE SOUL
16. RESURRECTION
17. HEAVEN AND HELL
18. THE PURPOSE OF CREATION

VOLUME III

1. THE NATURAL, MORAL AND SPIRITUAL STATES OF MAN
2. FAITH, CERTAINTY AND INSIGHT
3. EFFORT AND NATURAL APTITUDE
4. THE NEED OF PROPHETS
5. PROPHETHOOD IN ISLĀM
6. JESUS[as] AND THE ADVENT OF THE MESSIAH

CONTENTS VOLUME III

PUBLISHER'S NOTE XI

NATURAL, MORAL AND SPIRITUAL STATES OF MAN......1

The Three Human States 1
The First Source—the Self that Incites to Evil....................1
The Second Source: The Self-Reproaching Self 2
The Third Source: The Soul at Rest 3
Natural and Moral States of Man 5
Three Methods of Reform 8
Khalq [Creation] and *Khulq* [Morals] 8
Natural States Become Moral by Proper Regulation......10
True Morals..11
Moral State of Man 13
Moral Qualities Related to Discarding Evil......................13
Moral Qualities Related to Doing Good 20
True Courage..28
Patience 30
Truthfulness 33
Change in Moral Qualities 35
The Reality of Love..36

FAITH, CERTAINTY AND INSIGHT 43

Faith in the Unseen Taught by Prophets..............................43
Faith and Certainty 46
Salvation Depends on Faith..50
Progressive Stages of Faith...52
Blessings of Divine Recognition...54
Three Categories of the Faithful 55
The Soul at Rest 68
A Lovely Prayer 72
Steadfastness in Faith 73
Personal Merit and Relationship with God.........................75
Stages of Spiritual Fulfilment 78
Excellences of the Men of God 93
Comprehension of the Divine...94

EFFORT AND NATURAL APTITUDE 107

THE NEED FOR PROPHETS...111

PROPHETS ARE A MANIFESTATION OF DIVINE UNITY 111
PROPHETS DEMONSTRATE GOD'S EXISTENCE 114
BLESSINGS OF OBEDIENCE TO THE HOLY PROPHET[SA] 116
BELIEF IN GOD CANNOT BE PERFECT WITHOUT BELIEF IN PROPHETS 116
WHY DO PROPHETS HAVE NEEDS LIKE OTHER PEOPLE? 122

PROPHETHOOD IN ISLĀM 125

MEANINGS AND SIGNIFICANCE OF THE SEAL OF PROPHETHOOD .125
EXCELLENCE OF THE HOLY PROPHET[SA] 127
THE SEAL OF PROPHETHOOD AS THE PERFECT MAN 129
PROPHETHOOD BY WAY OF REFLECTION 130
FREQUENT CONVERSE WITH GOD—THE ONLY CLAIM OF THE PROMISED MESSIAH 146
NEED FOR REFORMERS AFTER THE PERFECTION OF FAITH 154
NEED OF THE COMPANY OF THE RIGHTEOUS 158
NEED FOR TEACHERS AND FRESH EXPOSITION OF THE HOLY QUR'ĀN 160
FULFILLING THE NEED OF SAFEGUARDING THE HOLY QUR'ĀN...162
DIVINE PROMISE OF KHILĀFAT..165

THE MESSIAH AND HIS SECOND COMING............................169

POPULAR BELIEFS ABOUT THE ASCENSION.................................169
AḤMADIYYAH BELIEF ABOUT THE MAHDĪ 171
CONTRADICTIONS IN THE POPULAR BELIEFS 174
TRUE MEANING OF THE ASCENSION AND SECOND COMING OF JESUS 179
MISGUIDANCE ABOUT JESUS CAUSED BY THE ANTICHRIST..........184
CORRECT MEANINGS OF *NUZŪL* 185
EVIDENCE REGARDING THE DEATH OF JESUS 193
TRUE STATUS OF JESUS 210
OBJECTIONS AGAINST JESUS...213
MIRACLES OF JESUS 218
THE TRUE CLAIM OF JESUS 228
REVIEW OF THE CHRISTIAN FAITH...229
JESUS DID NOT CLAIM TO BE GOD 231
CONFESSION OF HUMAN WEAKNESSES BY JESUS 234
TRUE MEANING OF 'SON OF GOD'...236
CHRISTIAN DOCTRINE ABOUT THE SON OF MARY 237

Jesus as a Prophet 242
Absurdity of the Doctrine of Trinity 243
Jesus not Accursed 246
Ointment of Jesus 261
Jesus in Search of the Lost Sheep 263
Jesus in Kashmir 263
Evidence from Buddhist Scriptures 267
Breaking of the Cross by the Promised Messiah 272
Divine Mystery of Jesus' Second Coming 273

DAJJĀL OR THE ANTICHRIST 279

Dajjāl and Satan 279
The Word Dajjāl Signifies a Group 280
Christian Priests as Dajjāl 281
Dajjāl and the Misguided Maulavīs 284
The Meaning of Dajjāl Circuiting the Ka'bah 287

DHULQARNAIN 295

Prophecy about the Promised Messiah in Sūrah Al-Kahf 295
Time of the Promised Messiah 301

GOG AND MAGOG 305

Religious Disputes at the Time of Gog and Magog 306
European Powers are Gog and Magog 307

WOMEN 311

Extreme Attitudes about Women 311
Kind Treatment of Women 311
A Man's Right to Divorce 314
A Woman's Right to Divorce 316
Propagation of the Human Race through Marriage 317
Polygamy 318
Equal Treatment of Wives 320
Islām and the Rights of Women 322
Importance of Inculcating Piety in Ahmadi Women 323
Noble Example of the Wives of the Holy Prophet[SA] 325

THE VEIL 327

Wisdom behind the System of Veil 327
Remedies for Unchastity 330

EXTREME ATTITUDES ABOUT THE VEIL 332

PROPER UPBRINGING OF CHILDREN 335

PRAY FOR CHILDREN INSTEAD OF PUNISHING THEM 335

REPEATED CHALLENGES 337

MY OPPONENTS ARE DOOMED TO FAIL 337
DIVINE SUPPORT FOR THE RIGHTEOUS 338
INVITING ALL TO COME AND WITNESS THE SIGNS 341
APPEAL TO GIVE UP VILIFICATION AND ABUSE...........................346
BESEECHING ALLAH FOR A HEAVENLY SIGN AND DECREE 348
EVIDENCE IN THE FORM OF DIVINE BLESSINGS 353
O YE WHO DOUBT! COME TO THE HEAVENLY VERDICT!............354
AN INVITATION TO PĪR MEHR 'ALĪ SHĀH OF GOLRAH 358
KNOWLEDGE OF ARABIC AND THE HOLY QUR'ĀN AS SIGNS OF DIVINE SUPPORT..360
IN THE NAME OF ALLAH THE GLORIOUS, A PLEA TO MAULAVĪ SAYYED NADHĪR ḤUSSAIN, FOR A DEBATE ON THE LIFE OR DEATH OF JESUS SON OF MARY 371
A MISGUIDED ASSERTION OF ḤĀFIẒ MUḤAMMAD YŪSUF CHALLENGED 377
SUBMITTING THE MATTER TO THE JUDGE OF JUDGES..................378
CHALLENGE TO REACH A CONCLUSIVE SETTLEMENT 381
A SINCERE APPEAL TO ALL MUSLIMS OF INDIA..........................382
CHALLENGE TO THOSE WHO CLAIM DIVINE REVELATION...........387
HOLY QUR'ĀN — A SIGN OF THE LIVING GOD 387
FOR FOLLOWERS OF REVEALED BOOKS WHO DENY THE TRUTH OF THE HOLY QUR'ĀN..391
EVIDENCE IN THE FORM OF COUNTLESS SIGNS 393
MANIFESTATION OF THE POWER OF THE LIVING GOD, HONOUR OF THE HOLY PROPHET[SA], AND TRUTH OF THE HOLY QUR'ĀN 395
REFUTATION OF THE ĀRYĀS' FALSE DOCTRINES 397
ANNOUNCEMENT FOR A FORTY DAY PRAYER VIGIL 399
FOR THE CAREFUL ATTENTION OF SARDĀR RĀJ INDAR SINGH ...401
ANNOUNCEMENT ON THE DEATH OF LEKH RĀM 403
REAL TEST BETWEEN ISLĀM AND CHRISTIANITY 404
AN INVITATION TO ALL GOOD PEOPLE 407
A PROPOSAL TO SEEK DIVINE SETTLEMENT 409
CONCLUSIVE ARGUMENTS FOR REVEREND WHITEBRECHT.........410
LACK OF RIGHTEOUSNESS AMONG CHRISTIANS 413

Open Challenge to All Christians 415
Invitation to Christians for *Mubāhalah* 416
Prophecy about Ātham and its Fulfilment 419
An Easy *Mubāhalah* for the Christians 430
Invitation to Her Majesty the Queen of England 431
A Test for Disclosing the Unseen 431
Divine Permission for *Mubāhalah* against Maulavīs 435
Open Invitation to All who Seek a Sign 442
Peace is Best 450
Six Signs of Divine Support 451
Prayer for a Divine Decree 453

INDEX OF REFERENCES OF THE HOLY QUR'ĀN............457

SUBJECT INDEX 459

INDEX OF TERMS...471

PUBLISHER'S NOTE

"The Essence of Islām" is an English rendering of extracts from the writings, speeches, announcements and discourses of the Promised Messiah, Ḥaḍrat Mirzā Ghulām Aḥmad of Qādiān (peace be on him). Ḥaḍrat Mirzā Ghulām Aḥmad[as] claimed that he was the same Messiah and Imām Mahdī whose advent had been prophesied for latter days, not only in Islām but also in other faiths.

The original compilation, in Urdu, Arabic and Persian, from which these extracts have been rendered into English, was collated with great care and diligence by the late Syed Mīr Dāwūd Aḥmad, may Allah reward him for his great labour of love. He published his selection in the form of a book, *Ḥaḍrat Mirzā Ghulām Aḥmad Qādiāni, alaihis-salāto wassalām, apnī tehrīroṅ kī rū sei,* or 'Ḥaḍrat Mirzā Ghulām Aḥmad[as] of Qādiān, according to his writings'.

The original English translation was done by Ḥaḍrat Chaudhry Muḥammad Zafrullāh Khān[ra], a companion of the Promised Messiah (peace be on him) who achieved great distinction as a statesman, jurist and scholar of comparative religious studies. Volume I and II were published by the London Mosque in 1979 and 1981 respectively during the lifetime of the revered translator. He also prepared the manuscripts of volumes three and four but these could not be published during his lifetime.

Second editions of volume one and two were published in 2004. We are now happy to present the third volume of "The Essence of Islām," which is being published for the first time. This volume sets out an English rendering of the words of Ḥaḍrat Mirzā Ghulām Aḥmad[as] himself, in exposition of these important topics:

- NATURAL, MORAL AND SPIRITUAL STATES OF MAN
- FAITH, CERTAINTY AND INSIGHT
- EFFORT AND NATURAL APTITUDE
- THE NEED FOR PROPHETS
- PROPHETHOOD IN ISLĀM
- THE MESSIAH AND HIS SECOND COMING
- DAJJĀL OR THE ANTICHRIST
- DHULQARNAIN
- GOG AND MAGOG
- WOMEN
- THE VEIL
- PROPER UPBRINGING OF CHILDREN
- REPEATED CHALLENGES

Under the direction of Vakālat-e-Taṣnīf, London, the translation was compared with the original text and compiled by Mr. Munawar Aḥmed Sa'eed with the support of the translation team working in Masjid Baitur Raḥmān in USA. In addition to those listed in the Publishers' Note of Volume I, three members who rendered valuable services for this volume are: Aḥmad Ṭāriq, Ḥāris Aḥmad and Nāṣir M. Malik.The publishers would like to express their appreciation for the help and support provided by Maulānā Munīr-ud-Dīn Shams, Additional Vakīl-ut-Taṣnīf, who supervised the project and provided the vital link for seeking guidance from Ḥaḍrat Mirzā Ṭāhir Aḥmad, Khalifatul Masīḥ IV[rh] and Ḥaḍrat Mirzā Masroor Aḥmad, Khalīfatul Masīḥ V (May Allah be his help). In

Rabwah, Vakālat-e-Taṣnīf, headed by Professor Chaudhry Muḥammad 'Alī reviewed the document, helped in incorporating the verses of the Holy Qur'ān and Urdu and Persian texts, and provided guidance in translating some difficult parts.

The system used for references is the same as adopted in Volumes I and II. All references, unless otherwise noted, are from the Holy Qur'ān. In the text, the references to the Holy Qur'ān are given exactly as they were given in the original writings. In the footnotes, references are given in the modern numerical system. In these references, we have counted *Bismillāhir Raḥmānir Raḥīm* as the first verse and have used the numerical system in which the first number refers to the *Sūrah* (chapter) and the second number refers to the *Āyah* (verse).

References to the Books of the Promised Messiah[as] are based on the London Edition of the Rūḥānī Khazā'in published in 1984. References to Malfūẓāt and Majmū'ah Ishtihārāt are also based on the London edition.

The following abbreviations have been used in this booklet, Readers are requested to recite the full salutations when reading the book:

sa. An abbreviation for *ṣal-lallāhu 'alaihi wa sallam*, meaning "May peace and blessings of Allah be upon him," is written after the name of the Holy Prophet Muḥammad[sa].

as. An abbreviation for *'alaihis salām*, meaning "May peace be upon him," is written after the name of Prophets other than the Holy Prophet[sa].

ra. An abbreviation for raḍi-Allāho ‘anhu/‘anhā/‘anhum meaning, “May Allah be pleased with him/her/them,” is written after the names of the Companions of the Holy Prophet[sa] and of the Promised Messiah[as].

rh. An abbreviation for *raḥimahullāh*, meaning, “May Allah have mercy on him,” is written after the names of deceased pious Muslims who are not Companions.

In transliterating Arabic words we have followed the following system adopted by the Royal Asiatic Society.

ا	at the beginning of a word, pronounced as a, i, u preceded by a very slight aspiration, like h in the English word ‘honour’.
ث	*th*, pronounced like *th* in the English word ‘thing’.
ح	*ḥ*, a guttural aspirate, stronger than h.
خ	*kh*, pronounced like the Scotch ch in ‘loch’.
ذ	*dh*, pronounced like the English th in ‘that’.
ص	*ṣ*, strongly articulated s.
ض	*ḍ*, similar to the English th in ‘this’.
ط	*ṭ*, strongly articulated palatal t.
ظ	*ẓ*, strongly articulated z.
ع	‘, a strong guttural, the pronunciation of which must be learnt by the ear.
غ	*gh*, a sound approached very nearly in the r ‘*grasseye*’ in French, and in the German r. It requires the muscles of the throat to be in the ‘gargling’ position whilst pronouncing it.
ق	*q*, a deep guttural k sound.

ئ ', a sort of catch in the voice.

Short vowels are represented by *a* for —َ— (like *u* in 'bud'); *i* for —ِ— (like *i* in 'bid'); u for —ُ— (like *oo* in 'wood'); the long vowels by *ā* for —ٰ— or آ (like *a* in 'father'); ī for ی —ِ— or —ٖ— (like *ee* in 'deep'); *ai* for ی —َ— (like *i* in 'site')♦; *ū* for و —ُ— (like *oo* in 'root'); *au* for و —َ— (resembling *ou* in 'sound').

Please note that in transliterated words the letter 'e' is to be pronounced as in 'prey' which rhymes with 'day'; however the pronunciation is flat without the element of English diphthong. If in Urdu and Persian words 'e' is lengthened a bit more it is transliterated as 'ei' to be pronounced as 'ei' in 'feign' without the element of diphthong thus 'کے' is transliterated as 'Kei'. For the nasal sound of 'n' we have used the symbol 'ń'. Thus Urdu word 'میں' would be transliterated as 'meiń'.*

The consonants not included above have the same phonetic value as in the principal languages of Europe.

Please also note that the words in the text in normal brackets ( ) and in between the long dashes — are the words of the Promised Messiah[as] and if any explanatory words or phrases are added by the publisher for the purpose of clarification, they are put in square brackets [ ].

♦ In Arabic words like شیخ (Shaikh) there is an element of diphthong which is missing when the word is pronounced in Urdu.

* These transliterations are not included in the system of transliteration by Royal Asiatic Society. **[Publisher]**

May Allah accept our humble efforts and make this blessed task a source of guidance for many. Āmīn.

The Publishers

بِسۡمِ اللّٰہِ الرَّحۡمٰنِ الرَّحِیۡمِ

1

NATURAL, MORAL AND SPIRITUAL STATES OF MAN

The Holy Qur'ān has bestowed a singular favour on the world by distinguishing between the natural state of man and his high moral qualities. It does not rest content with transporting man from the natural state to high moral qualities, but it further opens the doors to pure insight which lead to the stage of spiritual states. Indeed, it has helped millions of people reach that stage.

[Islāmī Uṣūl kī Philosophy, Rūḥānī Khazā'in, vol. 10, pp. 367-368]

The Three Human States

The first question is about the distinction between the natural, moral and spiritual states of man. The Holy Qur'ān has so distinguished between them that it has indicated three separate sources for each of them. In other words, it has pointed out the three springs from which these states respectively flow.

The First Source—the Self that Incites to Evil

The first spring, which is the source of all natural states, is designated by the Holy Qur'ān as *Nafs-e-Ammārah* [the self that incites to evil], as it says:

إِنَّ النَّفْسَ لَأَمَّارَةٌ بِالسُّوءِ [1]

This means that it is a characteristic of *Nafs-e-Ammārah* that it incites man to evil—which is contrary to his excellence, and goes against his moral condition—and seeks to lead him to undesirable and sinful ways. Thus, to be drawn towards intemperance and evil is the natural state which dominates man until the moral state takes over and he begins to be guided by reason and understanding. Until that happens, he continues to follow his natural instincts in eating, drinking, sleeping, walking, anger and emotion etc. When, under the direction of reason and understanding, he begins to control his natural states and creates a balance, it is at this point that the three states cease to be natural and come to be known as moral, as we shall elaborate later.

The Second Source: The Self-Reproaching Self

The source of moral state, according to the Holy Qur'ān , is *Nafs-e-Lawwāmah* [the self-reproaching self.] Allah says in the Holy Qur'ān:

وَلَآ أُقْسِمُ بِالنَّفْسِ اللَّوَّامَةِ [2]

This means that: 'I call to witness the self which reproaches itself over misdeeds and all acts of intemperance.'

Nafs-e-Lawwāmah [the self-reproaching self] is the second source of human states; it gives birth to moral conditions and, at this stage, man is emancipated from his resemblance to animals. In the above verse, *Nafs-e-Lawwāmah* has been called to witness for the purpose of

---

[1] Yūsuf, 12:54 **[Publisher]**

[2] Al-Qiyāmah, 75:3 **[Publisher]**

dignifying it. Which means that because of his progress from *Nafs-e-Ammārah* to *Nafs-e-Lawwāmah*, a person becomes worthy of being admitted to Divine presence. It is called 'self-reproaching' because it rebukes man on vice and does not approve of him following his natural inclinations and leading the life of animals. It desires that he should adopt good conduct, exhibit good morals, display no intemperance and that his natural emotions and desires should be manifested under the direction of reason. As it rebukes man over vice, it is called the self-reproaching self. But although it does not approve of natural desires and rebukes itself, it does not have complete power to do good and is at times overcome by natural passions; hence it is likely to fall and stumble. It is very much like a frail child who does not want to fall, but falls because it is weak, and it is ashamed of its weakness. In short, this is the moral state which seeks to attain high moral qualities and is disgusted with being self-willed, yet it cannot assert itself completely.

The Third Source: The Soul at Rest

Then there is a third source, which signifies the beginning of the spiritual state. The Holy Qur'ān describes it as *Nafs-e-Muṭma'innah* [the soul at rest]; it says:

يٰۤاَيَّتُهَا النَّفْسُ الْمُطْمَئِنَّةُ ○ ارْجِعِيْۤ اِلٰى رَبِّكِ رَاضِيَةً مَّرْضِيَّةً ○
فَادْخُلِيْ فِيْ عِبٰدِيْ ○ وَادْخُلِيْ جَنَّتِيْ ○[3]

(Part 30, Rukū' 14)

This means that: 'O tranquil soul that has found peace in God, return to thy Lord well pleased with Him as He is well pleased with thee. Join My chosen servants and

---

[3] Al-Fajr, 89:28-31 **[Publisher]**

enter My Paradise.'

This is the stage at which the soul, having been delivered from all weakness, is filled with spiritual strength and has such a relationship with God Almighty that it cannot live without Him. Just as water flows downwards and rushes forth because of its sheer volume, and removes all obstacles in its way, so does the soul flow towards God. It is to this state that the Divine injunction refers: 'O soul that has found peace in God, return to Him.' It brings about a great transformation, not only after death, but also in this very life, and is granted a paradise in this world even before the hereafter. As indicated in the above verse, such a soul is directed to return to its Lord the Nourisher, for He nurtures it. His love becomes its sustenance, and it drinks from the same life-giving spring. Thus it is delivered from death, as Almighty Allah says in the Holy Qur'ān:

قَدْ أَفْلَحَ مَنْ زَكّٰهَا ۝ وَقَدْ خَابَ مَنْ دَسّٰهَا ۝[4]

That is, He who cleanses his self of earthly passions shall be saved and will not perish, but he who is lost in such sensual desires shall lose hope in life.

In short, these are the three states, which may be called the natural, moral and spiritual states. Since natural urges become dangerous when aroused and very often destroy morality and spirituality, they have been described in the Holy Book of God Almighty as *Nafs-e-Ammārah* [the self that incites to evil.] If it is asked how the Holy Qur'ān affects these natural states of man and what guidance it furnishes about them, and to what extent it

---

[4] Al-Shams, 91:10-11 **[Publisher]**

seeks to retain them, then let it be known that, according to the Holy Qur'ān, the physical states of man are closely related to his moral and spiritual states. Even a man's habits and his way of eating and drinking affect his moral and spiritual states. If the physical states are exercised under the direction of Divine law, then, just as everything becomes salty in a salt mine, these natural states become moral states and have a deep impact on spirituality. That is why the Holy Qur'ān has placed so much stress on physical cleanliness, proprieties and temperance in connection with all kinds of worship, as well as on inner purity for the purpose of attaining righteousness and humility.

When we ponder over it, it becomes clear that physical conditions deeply affect the soul. We can see that our outward actions, though apparently physical in nature, have a great effect on our spiritual condition. For instance, when our eyes shed tears, even if by way of affectation, the tears immediately affect the heart, which becomes sorrowful. In the same way, when we laugh, even if for show, the heart begins to feel cheerful. It is also observed that physical prostration generates humility in the soul, and when we strut about with our head raised and chest pushed out, this attitude generates a kind of arrogance and vanity. These illustrations demonstrate how physical conditions directly affect spiritual ones.

[Islāmī Uṣūl kī Philosophy, Rūḥānī Khazā'in, vol. 10, pp. 316-320]

Natural and Moral States of Man

As indicated by the Holy Word of God Almighty, natural states, the source of which is *Nafs-e-Ammārah* [the self that incites to evil] are not something separate from moral states. The Holy Word of God has placed all physical faculties, desires and urges under the category of natural states. These natural states, when consciously regulated, tempered and employed at the right time and place, become moral. In the same way, moral states are not something entirely distinct from spiritual states. Moral states become spiritual when they are combined with absolute devotion to God, complete purification of the self, cutting asunder from the world, turning wholly to God with perfect love, complete devotion, full serenity, contentment, and complete accord with Divine Will.

Natural states alone do not make man worthy of praise until they take on a moral complexion, because these states can also be found in other animals and even in physical matter. In the same way, adopting good morals does not bestow spiritual life upon man. A person who denies the existence of God can also exhibit good morals. To be meek or humble or peace loving or shunning evil or avoiding the evildoer, are all natural states. Even an unworthy person, who is entirely unacquainted with the true source of salvation, can attain these states. Many animals are pliable and through conditioning and training do learn to behave peacefully, so much so that they do not retaliate even after being badly beaten; yet you cannot call them human, let alone humans of a higher order. Likewise, a person who holds the worst of views and is even guilty of misconduct can also exhibit these qualities. It is possible that a person may learn to be merciful to such an extreme that he may not even permit himself to kill the germs that infest his own wounds; or he may be so mindful of preserving life that he may not wish to harm the lice in his hair or the worms that are generated in the stomach, intestines, or the brain. I can even imagine that a person may be moved by pity so much so that he may even give up eating honey because it is obtained by destroying many lives and by driving away the poor bees from their hives. I can also conceive that a person may avoid using musk, as it is the blood of a poor deer and is obtained by killing the animal and separating it from its young. I would also not deny that a person might stop using pearls or wearing silk because they are both obtained by killing innocent worms. I can even concede that a person suffering from pain may choose to avoid using leeches; he may be prepared to suffer rather than kill the leech. Whether others accept it or not, I can also accept that a person might carry pity so far as to spare even the water worms and risk dying of thirst. I can accept all this, but I can never accept that these natural states could be called moral, or that these alone can wash out a person's inner impurities, the presence of which is an obstacle in the path of meeting God Almighty.

I can never believe that to be meek and harmless in this manner, in which even some animals and birds excel, could become the means of acquiring a high degree of humanity. In my view, this is opposed to the cardinal virtue of seeking God's pleasure and it amounts to fighting the law of nature and rejecting the bounties that nature has bestowed upon us. Spirituality can be attained only through the exercise of each moral quality at its proper time and place, treading faithfully in the way of God, and being wholly devoted to Him. He who truly becomes God's cannot exist without Him. A person who truly understands God is like a fish offered unto the hand of God. Its water is the love of God.

[Islāmī Uṣūl kī Philosophy, Rūḥānī Khazā'in, vol. 10, pp. 325-327]

Three Methods of Reform

I have mentioned that there are three sources of human states, namely, *Nafs-e-Ammārah* [the self that incites to evil], *Nafs-e-Lawwāmah* [the self-reproaching self] and *Nafs-e-Muṭma'innah* [the soul at rest.] Similarly, there are three methods of reform.

The first method of reform is that savages should be trained in rudimentary morals so that they follow the etiquette pertaining to social matters like eating, drinking, marriage, etc. They should not go about naked, nor eat carrion, nor exhibit any other ill manners. This is the elementary stage of reform of the natural state. It is the type of reform that should be adopted, for example, when teaching proper manners to a wild savage of Port Blair whom one should start instructing in basic morals and manners.

The second method of reform is that, after a person has acquired basic human manners, he should be instructed in higher moral qualities and taught to exercise all human faculties on their proper occasion and place.

The third method of reform is that those who have formally learned to exercise morals should be taught to relish the taste of true Love and Communion. These are the three reforms mentioned in the Holy Qur'ān.

[Islāmī Uṣūl kī Philosophy, Rūḥānī Khazā'in, vol. 10, pp. 327-328]

Khalq [Creation] and *Khulq* [Morals]

People commonly take *Khulq* [morals] to means meekness, courtesy and humility. They are wrong. The truth is that corresponding to every physical action there is an inner quality which is called *Khulq* [moral]. For instance, a person sheds tears through the eyes and, corresponding to this action, there is an inner quality called tenderness which takes on the character of a moral quality when exercised on its proper occasion and under the control of God-given wisdom. In the same way, a person defends himself against the attack of an enemy with his hands, and corresponding to this physical action there is an inner quality called bravery. When a person shows bravery on its proper occasion, it becomes a moral quality. In the same way, sometimes a person tries to save the oppressed from the oppressors, wishes to make some provisions for the indigent and the hungry, or seeks to serve humanity in some other way, and corresponding to such an action there is an inner quality called mercy. Sometimes a person punishes a wrongdoer, and corresponding to this action there is an inner quality called retribution. Sometimes a person is attacked, but he does not want to retaliate in kind and condones the wrong of a wrongdoer, and corresponding to this action there is an inner quality called forgiveness and forbearance. Sometimes a person uses his hands or feet, or employs his head or heart or his wealth to promote the welfare of his fellow beings, and corresponding to this action there is an inner quality called generosity. When a person exercises all these qualities at their proper time and place, they are called moral qualities. Addressing our Holy Prophet (peace and blessings of Allah be upon him), Allah the Glorious, says:

إِنَّكَ لَعَلٰى خُلُقٍ عَظِيْمٍ [5]

That is, 'Yours is indeed the most exalted moral station.'

[Islāmī Uṣūl kī Philosophy, Rūḥānī Khazā'in, vol. 10, pp. 332-333]

---

[5] Al-Qalam, 68:5 **[Publisher]**

Natural States Become Moral by Proper Regulation

Natural states are not something apart from moral states. When employed temperately on their proper place and occasion, and regulated by reason, natural states acquire the character of moral states. When exercised without the control and advice of reason and understanding, they are not truly moral; however much they may resemble them, they are no more than the involuntary exercise of natural impulses. For instance, if a dog or a goat shows love or docility towards its master, the dog will not be considered moral nor will the goat be called civilized, nor, for that matter, will we describe a wolf or a tiger as immoral on account of its savage nature. As we have already said, a moral quality emerges only when reflection and regard for the appropriate time and occasion come into play. A person who does not exercise reason and prudence is like the suckling whose mind and intellect are not yet governed by reason, or like the insane who have lost their reason and intelligence.

Sometimes a suckling or an insane person does appear to act in a manner which looks ethical, but no sensible person would call them moral as such behaviour does not spring from discretion and propriety but is a natural response to stimuli. For example, a human baby seeks its mother's breast immediately after it is born; a chicken runs to pick up grain as soon as it is hatched; a newly hatched leech behaves like a leech; a baby snake acts like a snake; and a tiger cub conducts itself like a tiger. Particularly, one should carefully observe a human baby to see how, immediately after it is born, it begins to behave like humans, and these natural habits become more pronounced after a year or so. For instance, its crying becomes louder, its smile turns into laughter, and its vision becomes more volitional. At this stage, it reveals another natural trait by displaying its pleasure or displeasure through gestures and tries to strike someone or desires to give something to someone. But all these movements are natural impulses. Indeed a savage too is like a child whose share of human reason is very meagre. He too displays natural impulses in his words, actions and movements, and is subject to his natural drives. But nothing proceeds from him in consequence of reflection and deliberation. Whatever takes place inside him continues to issue forth in response to the external stimuli. It is quite possible that his natural impulses, which are exhibited as a reaction to the external stimuli, may not be all bad. Some may look like moral actions, but they are devoid of rational reflection and choice and, even if they seem to some degree so motivated, they cannot be relied upon on account of the domination of natural impulses.

True Morals

In short, we cannot truly attribute morals to a person who is subject to natural impulses like animals or infants or the insane, and who lives more or less like savages. In the true sense, the time of morals, whether good or bad, begins when a person's God-given reason ripens and he is able to distinguish between good and bad and the degree of good and evil. And he begins to feel sorry when he misses an opportunity of doing good and is remorseful when he has done something wrong. This is the second stage of man's life, which is designated as *Nafs-e-Lawwāmah* [the self-reproaching self] in God's Holy Word.

It should, however, be remembered that mere advice is

not enough to lead a savage to the stage of the self-reproaching self. It is necessary that he should become conscious of the existence of God to a degree at which he should not consider his own creation as meaningless and without purpose, so that an understanding of the Divine should create true morals in him. That is why God Almighty has drawn attention to the need of understanding the True God and has given the assurance that every action and moral quality has a consequence, which becomes the source of spiritual comfort or spiritual torment in this life and the consequences of which would be fully apparent in the hereafter. In short, at the stage of the self-reproaching self, a person partakes so much of reason and understanding and good conscience that he reproaches himself over evil and is willing and eager to do good. That is the stage at which a person acquires the high moral qualities.

[Islāmī Uṣūl kī Philosophy, Rūḥānī Khazā'in, vol. 10, pp. 330-332]

Addressing the Holy Prophet (peace and blessings of Allah be upon him), God, the Glorious, says:

إِنَّكَ لَعَلَىٰ خُلُقٍ عَظِيمٍ [6]

That is, 'Yours is indeed the most exalted moral station.' This means that all high moral qualities, such as generosity, bravery, justice, mercy, benevolence, sincerity, courage, etc., were combined in the Holy Prophet[sa].

In short, all modes of behaviour found in the human person, like courtesy, modesty, integrity, politeness, righteous indignation, steadfastness, chastity, temperance, moderation, sympathy, bravery, generosity, forgiveness,

---

[6] Al-Qalam, 68:5 **[Publisher]**

patience, benevolence, sincerity, loyalty, etc., when they find expression at their proper time and place, under the guidance of reason and reflection, are designated moral. All such qualities are in reality the natural states and emotions of the human person and they are designated as such only when exercised at their proper time and place.

[Islāmī Uṣūl kī Philosophy, Rūḥānī Khazā'in, vol. 10, p. 333]

Moral State of Man

Moral qualities are of two kinds. First, those moral qualities that enable a person to discard evil and, secondly, those moral qualities that enable him to do good. Discarding evil includes those moral qualities through which a person tries that he should cause no harm to the person, property, honour or life of another person by his tongue, hand, eyes or any other organ, nor should he intend to cause any harm or humiliation. Doing good comprises all those morals through which a person tries to benefit the property or honour of another person through his tongue or hand or property or knowledge or through other means, or even intends to do so. Or he overlooks if anyone had done him any harm, for which the perpetrator deserved to be punished, and thus saves him from suffering physical torment, or financial loss; or tries to award him the punishment which in reality proves to be a blessing in disguise for the culprit.

[Islāmī Uṣūl kī Philosophy, Rūḥānī Khazā'in, vol. 10, pp. 339-340]

Moral Qualities Related to Discarding Evil

It should be clear that the moral qualities that the True Creator has prescribed for discarding evil are known by four names in Arabic, which has a specific name for all human ideas, actions and morals.

The first moral quality for discarding evil is known as *Iḥṣān*. This term connotes the particular kind of chastity which relates to the procreative power of man and woman. *Muḥṣin* and *Muḥṣinah* respectively connote the man or woman who abstains from illicit sex or its preliminaries, the consequence of which for both is disgrace and curse in this world and torment in the hereafter; and for their relatives it is quite damaging, as well as a source of disgrace….

Remember, the moral quality of *Iḥṣān* or chastity or sexual purity, can be called moral only when a person, who is capable of ogling or fornicating restrains himself from it. If a person lacks manhood, on account of immaturity, impotence, being a eunuch or because of old age, we cannot credit him with this particular moral quality known as chastity….

God Almighty has not only commanded chastity, but has also prescribed five remedies to safeguard it, namely, abstaining from looking at those whom we are not allowed to, or hearing their voices, or listening to stories about them and avoiding participating in all those occasions which are likely to lead to evil, and fasting, if one is unmarried.

We can confidently claim that this excellent teaching with all its details, as set out in the Holy Qur'ān, is peculiar to Islām alone….

Of the various forms of discarding evil, the second is the virtue known as *Amānat* and *Diyānat* [honesty and integrity], which is the indisposition to harm anyone by taking possession of his property mischievously and dishonestly. It should be clear that honesty and integrity constitute a natural human condition. That is why a child, which is by nature simple and naïve, and, because of its young age, has not yet acquired any bad habits, dislikes what belongs to others; so much so that it is with great difficulty that it allows a strange woman to breastfeed it. If a wet-nurse is not appointed early enough, it becomes very difficult for another woman to suckle the baby, and in such a case the child suffers so much that its very life is endangered. It is naturally averse to the milk of another woman. What is the secret of this aversion? Only that it has an innate aversion to leave its mother and turn to what belongs to a stranger.

When we reflect deeply upon this habit of the infant it becomes clear that this characteristic of disliking what belongs to a stranger, and even suffering because of it, is the source of honesty and integrity. No one can be credited with the quality of integrity unless, like the infant, he develops in his heart a deep dislike and abhorrence for the possession of another person's property. But an infant does not employ this habit on its proper occasion and often suffers a great deal on account of its ignorance. This habit is a natural mode of behaviour, which it exhibits involuntarily; it cannot, therefore, form part of its morals, though in human nature this is the root cause of the moral values of honesty and integrity. Just as an infant cannot be described as faithful and trustworthy on account of this unconscious habit, similarly a person who does not employ this natural state on its proper occasion, cannot be said to possess this moral quality.

To be honest and trustworthy is a very delicate matter and a person cannot be honest and trustworthy unless he fulfils all aspects of it. In the following verses God, by way of illustration, teaches us how to be honest:

وَلَا تُؤْتُوا السُّفَهَآءَ اَمْوَالَكُمُ الَّتِيْ جَعَلَ اللّٰهُ لَكُمْ قِيٰمًا وَّ ارْزُقُوْهُمْ فِيْهَا وَ
اكْسُوْهُمْ وَقُوْلُوْا لَهُمْ قَوْلًا مَّعْرُوْفًا ۝ وَابْتَلُوا الْيَتٰمٰى حَتّٰٓى اِذَا بَلَغُوا النِّكَاحَ
فَاِنْ اٰنَسْتُمْ مِّنْهُمْ رُشْدًا فَادْفَعُوْٓا اِلَيْهِمْ اَمْوَالَهُمْ ۚ وَلَا تَاْكُلُوْهَآ اِسْرَافًا
وَّ بِدَارًا اَنْ يَّكْبَرُوْا ۭ وَمَنْ كَانَ غَنِيًّا فَلْيَسْتَعْفِفْ ۚ وَمَنْ كَانَ فَقِيْرًا فَلْيَاْكُلْ
بِالْمَعْرُوْفِ ۭ فَاِذَا دَفَعْتُمْ اِلَيْهِمْ اَمْوَالَهُمْ فَاَشْهِدُوْا عَلَيْهِمْ ۭ وَكَفٰى بِاللّٰهِ حَسِيْبًا ۝ [7]

وَلْيَخْشَ الَّذِيْنَ لَوْ تَرَكُوْا مِنْ خَلْفِهِمْ ذُرِّيَّةً ضِعٰفًا خَافُوْا عَلَيْهِمْ
فَلْيَتَّقُوا اللّٰهَ وَلْيَقُوْلُوْا قَوْلًا سَدِيْدًا ۝ اِنَّ الَّذِيْنَ يَاْكُلُوْنَ اَمْوَالَ الْيَتٰمٰى
ظُلْمًا اِنَّمَا يَاْكُلُوْنَ فِيْ بُطُوْنِهِمْ نَارًا ۭ وَسَيَصْلَوْنَ سَعِيْرًا ۝ [8]

Translation: 'If there is a rich person among you who is not mentally fit, e.g., an orphan, or a minor, and there is a risk that he will waste his property due to imbecility, take charge of the property (as court of wards) and do not hand over the property which can be used for trade and commerce to the feeble-minded. But feed them and clothe them properly as required and speak to them appropriately, that is, teach them things that add to their understanding and skills until they are no longer ignorant and inexperienced. If they are the progeny of a trader, teach them trade, and if their parents belonged to another profession, train them accordingly. In short, train them and keep testing them to make sure that your training is not in vain, until they reach the marriageable age, i.e., the age of 18. Then if you find them capable of managing their own property, hand it over to them. Do not squander away their property. Nor, for that matter, should you hasten to consume their belongings fearing that they will come asking for it when they grow up. A person who is rich should not take any compensation for

---

[7] Al-Nisā', 4:6-7 **[Publisher]**

[8] Al-Nisā', 4:10-11 **[Publisher]**

managing the property, but one who is needy can do so only to the extent allowed by custom.' It was customary among the Arabs that they only accepted a part of the profits of the property of orphans and left the principal intact. The same in indicated here.

Then it is said: 'When you deliver their property to them, do so in the presence of witnesses. And if a person dies, leaving behind weak and minor children, he should not make a will that does injustice to the children. Those who devour the property of orphans in a manner unjust to the orphans do not devour property, rather they swallow fire and they shall be cast into a blazing fire'.

In these verses, Allah the Most High has listed comprehensively all the ways of being dishonest, and no type of dishonesty has been left out. God did not merely forbid stealing, lest an ignorant one should think that theft alone was unlawful for him and that all other improprieties were permitted. Declaring all dishonest acts unlawful is true wisdom.

In short, if a person does not possess the qualities of integrity and honesty with full awareness of their implications, even if he does appear to exercise integrity and honesty in certain matters, this behaviour of his will not be considered moral. Instead it will be a natural state lacking rational awareness and insight.

The third moral quality in the context of renouncing evil is called *Hudnah* and *Haun* in Arabic, which means not to inflict physical suffering on anyone wrongfully, to be harmless, and to live peacefully. Peacefulness is undoubtedly a high moral quality and is a must for mankind. The natural faculty corresponding to this moral quality possessed by a child, the regulation of which produces this moral quality, is affection, or malleability. In his natural state, when man is deprived of reason, he can neither understand the subject of peace nor the concept of making war. At that time the impulse of attachment found in him is the root of peacefulness. But, as it is not exercised because of reason, reflection and choice, it cannot be called moral. It would become moral only when a person chooses to be harmless and employs the moral quality of peacefulness on its proper occasion and refrains from employing it out of place. In this context the Divine teaching is:

وَأَصْلِحُوا ذَاتَ بَيْنِكُمْ [i] وَالصُّلْحُ خَيْرٌ [ii] وَإِنْ جَنَحُوا لِلسَّلْمِ فَاجْنَحْ لَهَا [iii]
وَعِبَادُ الرَّحْمٰنِ الَّذِيْنَ يَمْشُوْنَ عَلَى الْأَرْضِ هَوْنًا [iv] وَإِذَا مَرُّوْا بِاللَّغْوِ مَرُّوْا
كِرَامًا [v] اِدْفَعْ بِالَّتِيْ هِيَ أَحْسَنُ فَإِذَا الَّذِيْ بَيْنَكَ وَبَيْنَهُ عَدَاوَةٌ كَأَنَّهُ
وَلِيٌّ حَمِيْمٌ [vi] [9]

That is: 'Try to promote accord among yourselves.'

'Goodness lies in reconciliation.'

'If they incline towards peace, incline thou also towards it.'

'The true servants of the Gracious Lord are those who walk upon earth in peace.'

'When they happen to hear anything impertinent which portends argument or spells trouble, they pass on with quiet dignity and do not pick up fights on minor matters.'

This means that, unless faced with extreme repression, they do not like to protest. These indeed are the

---

[9] [i] Al-Anfāl, 8:2 [ii] Al-Nisā', 4:129 [iii] Al-Anfāl, 8:62 [iv] Al-Furqān, 25:64 [v] Al-Furqān, 25:73 [vi] Ḥā Mīm Al-Sajdah, 41:35 **[Publisher]**

proprieties of peacefulness that one should ignore trivialities and be ready to forgive. The term '*laghv*', according to Arabic lexicon, means the certain kind of behaviour, for instance, when a mischief monger indulges in loose talk or does something to cause harm, but in fact is unable to cause harm or create trouble; hence it is the sign of peacefulness to condone such senseless misdemeanour.

The fourth form of renouncing evil consists in *Rifq* and *Qaul-i-Ḥasan* [gentleness and politeness] and the natural state that gives birth to this quality is called *Talāqat*, or cheerfulness. Until a child learns to speak, it displays cheerfulness in place of courtesy and politeness. This shows that the root of courtesy is cheerfulness. Cheerfulness is a natural faculty and courtesy is a moral quality that is generated by the proper use of this faculty. In this context the teaching of God Almighty is:

وَقُولُوا لِلنَّاسِ حُسْنًا (i) لَا يَسْخَرْ قَوْمٌ مِّن قَوْمٍ عَسَىٰ أَن يَكُونُوا خَيْرًا مِّنْهُمْ وَلَا
نِسَاءٌ مِّن نِّسَاءٍ عَسَىٰ أَن يَكُنَّ خَيْرًا مِّنْهُنَّ ۖ وَلَا تَلْمِزُوا أَنفُسَكُمْ وَلَا تَنَابَزُوا
بِالْأَلْقَابِ (ii) اجْتَنِبُوا كَثِيرًا مِّنَ الظَّنِّ إِنَّ بَعْضَ الظَّنِّ إِثْمٌ ۖ وَلَا تَجَسَّسُوا
وَلَا يَغْتَب بَّعْضُكُم بَعْضًا ..... وَاتَّقُوا اللَّهَ ۚ إِنَّ اللَّهَ تَوَّابٌ رَّحِيمٌ (iii) وَلَا تَقْفُ
مَا لَيْسَ لَكَ بِهِ عِلْمٌ ۚ إِنَّ السَّمْعَ وَالْبَصَرَ وَالْفُؤَادَ كُلُّ أُولَٰئِكَ كَانَ عَنْهُ مَسْئُولًا (iv) [10]

Translation: 'Say to people that which is really good.'

'Let not one people laugh at another people; it may well be that those who are laughed at are really praiseworthy. Let one group of women not deride other women; it is possible that those who are mocked at are really good. Do not cast aspersions and do not address your fellow

---

10 (i)Al-Baqarah, 2:84 (ii)Al-Ḥujurāt, 49:12 (iii)Al-Ḥujurāt, 49:13 (iv) Banī Isrā'īl, 17:37 **[Publisher]**

men with offensive names.'

'Do not spread doubts and suspicions, nor should you be curious about other people's faults. Do not complain or grumble.

'Do not accuse anyone without proof. Remember, every organ of the body will be called to account. The ear, the eye and the heart shall all be answerable.'

Moral Qualities Related to Doing Good

Of the moral qualities that are related to doing good, the first one is *'Afw,* or forgiving people's sins. Forgiving someone who causes harm and deserves to be punished, imprisoned, fined, or handled directly, provided such forgiveness is appropriate, would amount to doing him good. In this context, the teaching of the Holy Qur'ān is:

وَالْكٰظِمِيْنَ الْغَيْظَ وَالْعَافِيْنَ عَنِ النَّاسِ [11]

جَزٰٓؤُا سَيِّئَةٍ سَيِّئَةٌ مِّثْلُهَا ۚ فَمَنْ عَفَا وَاَصْلَحَ فَاَجْرُهٗ عَلَى اللّٰهِ [12]

This means that: 'The righteous are those who control their anger when the occasion so demands and pardon sin when the situation requires.'

'The recompense of an injury is a penalty in proportion thereto, but whoso forgives—and effects thereby a reform in the offender and no harm is apprehended, that is to say, he exercises forgiveness on its proper occasion—will have his reward with Allah.'

The above verse shows that the Qur'ān does not teach non-resistance to evil on all occasions, or that mischief

[11] Āl-e-'Imrān, 3:135 **[Publisher]**

[12] Al-Shūrā, 42:41 **[Publisher]**

makers and wrongdoers should never be punished. What it teaches is that one must consider whether the occasion demands forgiveness or punishment and to adopt the course which would be in the best interest of both the offender and the community at large. At times, an offender might repent if he is forgiven, but at times he may become even more daring. Therefore, God Almighty says: Do not cultivate the habit of forgiving blindly; consider carefully wherein lies the real good—in forgiveness or in punishment—and do what is appropriate considering the time and the circumstances.

A study of the human race reveals that some people are by nature highly vindictive: they preserve in their minds all the wrongs done to their fathers, and there are others who carry forbearance and forgiveness even to the extent of shamelessness and are guilty of condoning and forgiving such shameless acts as are contrary to self-respect, honour, dignity and chastity, and tarnish the image of good morals. As a result, the entire society is outraged. That is why the Holy Qur'ān has enjoined the condition of proper time and occasion for the exercise of every moral quality and does not approve of such moral quality as is not in keeping with the prerequisites of the occasion....

We have repeatedly stressed that the difference between a moral quality and natural state is that a moral quality is always in keeping with the requirements of the place and time and a natural state finds expression regardless of such conditions.

[Islāmī Uṣūl kī Philosophy, Rūḥānī Khazā'in, vol. 10, pp. 340-352]

All scholars are agreed that the highest moral station is not merely dependent on exercising forgiveness and forbearance on every occasion. Had man been told merely to exercise forgiveness and forbearance, hundreds of moral acts that depend upon indignation and retribution would have become impossible. Human nature, which makes man what he is, is that God has invested man as much with the faculty of forgiveness and forbearance as with the sentiment of indignation and revenge. God has placed reason over all these faculties as the arbiter. Therefore, man realizes his true humanity when both these types of faculties are exercised under the control of reason. That is to say, these faculties should be like the subjects and reason should, like a just ruler, be occupied with fostering them, enhancing their beneficence, settling their conflicts and resolving their difficulties.

For instance, on occasion one gets angry whereas it is gentleness that is really called for. On such occasions, reason intervenes to restrain the anger and activates gentleness. And at times the occasion demands anger but gentleness takes hold instead. On such an occasion, reason rouses anger and quells gentleness. In short, in-depth research shows that man has been sent into this world well equipped with a variety of faculties; perfection of his nature lies in exercising every faculty on its proper occasion; there should be anger when anger is called for and mercy when mercy is needed and not that there should be only gentleness and all other faculties should remain suspended and inactive. The display of gentleness on its proper occasion is an excellence, but the tree of man's nature which has many branches would not be considered perfect by the flourishing of only one branch. It would only be considered complete when all its branches flourish and no branch exceeds or falls short of its appropriate norm.

Reason undeniably shows that to condone the wickedness of a wicked person always and on all occasions cannot possibly be considered moral. The law of nature too exposes the defect of such a notion. We observe that the True Planner has so ordained that in the order of the universe sometimes tenderness is required and severity is required at others; sometimes forgiveness is required and sometimes punishment is required. Tenderness alone or severity alone would upset the system of the universe. Therefore, it proves that to forgive always and on all occasions is not a true virtue and that to consider such teaching as perfect is an error which is being committed by those whose insight into human nature is not deep enough and whose eyes remain closed to all the faculties that have been bestowed upon man for use on appropriate occasions. A person who continues to exercise the same faculty on all occasions, allowing all other faculties to fall into disuse, seeks, as it were, to change his God-given nature and, on account of his short-sightedness, declares the act of the All-Wise God to be objectionable. Would it be commendable if we were to keep overlooking the offences of the offenders all the time, regardless of the requirement of the situation and propriety, and were never to have such sympathy with the offender that, by remedying his mischief, we should reform him?

Clearly, just as it is objectionable and unethical to punish or take revenge over trifles, it is likewise contrary to goodwill to make it a point always to forgive whenever a person commits an offence. Whoever allows an offender to go unpunished is as much an enemy of law and order as he who is always ready to malign and take revenge. The ignorant would like to condone and forgive at every occasion. They just do not realize that forgiveness on every occasion disrupts the order of the world. Also, it is against the best interests of the culprit, for he becomes more and more hardened in his evil ways and the tendency to do mischief gets even more entrenched. Let a thief go unpunished and see what he does the next time! That is why God Almighty said in His Book, which is full of wisdom:

وَلَكُمْ فِي الْقِصَاصِ حَيٰوةٌ يّٰاُولِي الْاَلْبَابِ [13]

مَنْ قَتَلَ نَفْسًا بِغَيْرِ نَفْسٍ اَوْ فَسَادٍ فِي الْاَرْضِ فَكَاَنَّمَا قَتَلَ النَّاسَ جَمِيْعًا [14]

This means that: 'O men of understanding! Your life lies in killing the killer; and award punishment proportionate to the crime.'

'Whosoever kills a person unjustly and without cause is virtually guilty of killing the whole of mankind.'

اِنَّ اللّٰهَ يَاْمُرُ بِالْعَدْلِ وَالْاِحْسَانِ وَاِيْتَآئِ ذِي الْقُرْبٰى [15]

That is: 'God enjoins that you must exercise justice, benevolence, and *Ītā'i dhil Qurbā* [graciousness towards all as between kindred] on their proper occasions.'

Let it be known that the teaching of the Gospels is inferior to and falls short of the perfection that sustains and regulates the order of the universe; rather, it is a grave error to regard this teaching as perfect and complete. Such a teaching can never be perfect. It belongs to the period in which the Children of Israel had been left with the minimal sentiment of compassion, whereas ruthlessness, cruelty, brutality, hard-heartedness and maliciousness

---

[13] Al-Baqarah, 2:180 **[Publisher]**

[14] Al-Mā'idah, 5:33 **[Publisher]**

[15] Al-Naḥl, 16:91 **[Publisher]**

had exceeded all limits. Since they were excessively given to vengefulness, God so willed that they should be made to incline towards compassion and forgiveness. But this teaching of mercy and forbearance was not a teaching that could stand forever, as it was not based on an absolute value. Instead, it was like a local law, which was expediently designed, with a view to reforming the headstrong Jews, and it was meant for a limited duration.

Jesus was only too well aware that God would soon abolish this provisional teaching and would send the Perfect Book for the guidance of mankind, which would invite the whole world to real virtue and open the door of truth and wisdom to the servants of God. This is why he had to say that there were so many things which still remained to be taught which they were unable to bear at the time, and that someone else would come after him who would explain everything and raise religion to perfection. Consequently, Jesus was seated in heaven leaving the Gospels incomplete, and it was the same incomplete book that remained with the people for such a long time. Then, in keeping with the prophecy of the same innocent prophet, God sent down the Holy Qur'ān and revealed a comprehensive law, which neither—like the Torah—laid down that the principle of 'Tooth for a tooth' be practiced in all circumstances, nor did it ordain—like the Gospels—that one must be always ready to be hit by an aggressor. Instead, the Perfect Book has abolished all the provisional injunctions. It invites us to true virtue, and enjoins that which results in genuine benefit, be it hard or soft.

The Holy Qur'ān says:

وَجَزٰٓؤُا سَيِّئَةٍ سَيِّئَةٌ مِّثْلُهَا فَمَنْ عَفَا وَاَصْلَحَ فَاَجْرُهٗ عَلَى اللّٰهِ [16]

(Part Number 25)

This means that: In principle, the evildoer deserves retribution proportionate to his crime, but he who forgives in order to reform, provided forgiveness does not result in further mischief, will have his reward with Allah.

[Brāhīn-e-Aḥmadiyyah, Rūḥānī Khazā'in, vol. 1, pp. 409-434, subnote. 3]

The second moral quality for doing good is *'Adl* [equity], the third is *Iḥsān* [benevolence] and the fourth is *Ītā'i dhil Qurbā* [graciousness towards all as between kindred.] In this context Allah the Glorious says:

اِنَّ اللّٰهَ يَاْمُرُ بِالْعَدْلِ وَالْاِحْسَانِ وَاِيْتَآئِ ذِي الْقُرْبٰى
وَيَنْهٰى عَنِ الْفَحْشَآءِ وَالْمُنْكَرِ وَالْبَغْيِ [17]

This means that: 'Almighty Allah enjoins you to return good for good, and should the occasion call for benevolence, to be benevolent, and if the occasion calls for spontaneous graciousness for all, quite like the next of kin, then to be gracious with natural compassion. However, God forbids that you should exceed the proper limits in one direction or the other and should be benevolent contrary to reason and should fail to be benevolent when the occasion demands or that you should fail to be gracious when the occasion demands or should be over gracious beyond that is needed. This noble verse discusses all the three stages of doing good.

The first stage is that we should do good in return for

---

[16] Al-Shūrā, 42:41 **[Publisher]**

[17] Al-Naḥl, 16:91 **[Publisher]**

good. This is the lowest level and even an average person can attain it by doing good to those who do him good.

The second level is relatively more difficult to attain. It consists of taking the initiative in doing good to someone *ex gratia*, when he is not entitled to it. This moral quality is of an intermediate grade. Most people are benevolent towards the poor, but there is a hidden deficiency in such benevolence. The person who acts benevolently is conscious of it and at least desires either gratitude or prayer in return. If on any occasion the beneficiary should turn against him, the benefactor dubs him ungrateful. Sometimes, he puts too heavy a price on the beneficiary on account of his benevolence or reminds him of his kindness. God Almighty warns the benevolent as follows:

لَا تُبْطِلُوْا صَدَقٰتِكُمْ بِالْمَنِّ وَ الْاَذٰى [18]

That is: 'O benevolent ones! Render not vain your charitable acts, which should be based on sincerity, by reminding the recipients of your generosity and hurting their feelings.'

The term *Ṣadaqah* [charity] is derived from *Ṣidq* [sincerity], and thus if the heart is devoid of sincerity and integrity, charity ceases to be charity and becomes ostentation….

The third level of doing good, according to God Almighty, implies that at this stage, the good action is done spontaneously and without consciousness of doing good or expecting gratitude in return. Instead, the good action is done under the upsurge of spontaneous emotion, quite like to the next of kin, for instance, a mother does good

---

[18] Al-Baqarah, 2:265 **[Publisher]**

to her son out of pure sympathy. This is the highest grade of doing good, which cannot be surpassed.

God Almighty has made all these categories of doing good contingent upon the demands of time and occasion and has clearly laid down in the above verse, that if these good acts are not done on their proper occasion, they will become vices. *'Adl* [fairness] will become *Faḥshā'* [foul], or in other words, crossing limits will result in an undesirable situation. And *Iḥsān* [right] would become *Munkar* [wrong] which reason and conscience reject. And *Ītā'i dhil Qurbā* [spontaneous compassion] will turn into transgression, that is, this ill-placed sympathy would create an ugly situation. Actually, *Baghī* means such excessive rain as destroys the harvest; hence exceeding the appropriate limits is also *Baghī*.

In short, any of these three qualities, exercised out of place, would deteriorate in character; that is why these are made contingent upon the due observance of occasion and place. Here it should be remembered that justice, benevolence or graciousness as between kindred are not by themselves moral qualities. These are man's natural states and faculties, which are found even in children before their reason is developed. To become moral, the exercise of reason is the condition precedent. Another requirement is that every natural faculty should be exercised in its proper occasion and place.

[Islāmī Uṣūl kī Philosophy, Rūḥānī Khazā'in, vol. 10, pp. 353-354]

True Courage

Of all the natural states of man is one that resembles courage. For example, a suckling sometimes tries to put its hand into the fire because of this natural faculty. Before being exposed to various frightening experiences, a human being does not fear anything due to his natural fearlessness. In this condition, he fearlessly fights tigers and wild beasts, and sets out alone to challenge a multitude of men, and people consider him to be very brave. But this is only a natural state, which is also found in wild beasts and even in dogs. True courage, which is one of the high morals, is contingent on place and occasion. These places and occasions are mentioned in the Holy Word of God Almighty as follows:

وَالصّٰبِرِيْنَ فِي الْبَأْسَآءِ وَالضَّرَّآءِ وَحِيْنَ الْبَأْسِ [19]

وَالَّذِيْنَ صَبَرُوا ابْتِغَآءَ وَجْهِ رَبِّهِمْ [20]

اَلَّذِيْنَ قَالَ لَهُمُ النَّاسُ اِنَّ النَّاسَ قَدْ جَمَعُوْا لَكُمْ فَاخْشَوْهُمْ
فَزَادَهُمْ اِيْمَانًا ۖۗ وَّقَالُوْا حَسْبُنَا اللّٰهُ وَنِعْمَ الْوَكِيْلُ [21]

وَلَا تَكُوْنُوْا كَالَّذِيْنَ خَرَجُوْا مِنْ دِيَارِهِمْ بَطَرًا وَّرِئَآءَ النَّاسِ [22]

These verses mean that: ‘The brave are those who do not run away from battle or adversity’;

‘Their steadfastness in battle and hardship is to win the pleasure of God. They do not intend to display their bravery but to please Him’;

‘They are threatened that people have mustered against them and that they should be afraid of them. Threats only reinforce their faith and they declare: God is Sufficient for us. That is, their courage is not like that of dogs and wild beasts, which is based only on natural passions and is one-sided. Their courage has two dimensions. Some-

---

[19] Al-Baqarah, 2:178 **[Publisher]**

[20] Al-Ra‘d, 13:23 **[Publisher]**

[21] Āl-e-‘Imrān, 3:174 **[Publisher]**

[22] Al-Anfāl, 8:48 **[Publisher]**

times they fight their selfish desires and conquer them with their personal courage; and at times, when they see that the appropriate thing would be to confront and fight the enemy, they do so not only due to their natural passion, but also to help the truth. They display bravery by putting their trust in God rather than their own selves.'

'Their courage is free from ostentation and vanity, nor is it for self-aggrandizement, rather God's pleasure is their supreme object.'

These verses illustrate that the source of true courage is patience and steadfastness. Courage means to remain steadfast and not to run away like cowards when assailed by a selfish motive or some other affliction. Therefore, there is a great difference between the courage of a man and that of a predator. A predator's fierceness and fury is only one-sided when it is roused, but a person who possesses true courage, chooses between confrontation or non-resistance, whichever may be more appropriate.

[Islāmī Uṣūl kī Philosophy, Rūḥānī Khazā'in, vol. 10, pp. 358-360]

Patience

Ṣabr [Patience] is one of the natural human states. One has to exercise it in the face of calamities, ailments and hardships which constantly befall him. Man comes to practise patience in the end, albeit after a great deal of moaning and crying. But it should be clearly understood, that, according to the Holy Book of God, such steadfastness is not part of morals, instead it is a state that follows exhaustion as a matter of course. After all, it is quite natural for man to cry and bewail in the face of a calamity, but, in the end, after venting his feelings, he recovers and after the climax he begins to relax. Both these states are natural and have nothing to do with morals. On the contrary, the moral part of it would be that after losing something, considering it to be a trust from God Almighty, one should not complain about it. Rather, one should affirm that God has taken back what belonged to Him in the first place, and should accept the will of God. Regarding this particular moral quality, God Almighty's Holy Word, the Glorious Qur'ān, says:

وَلَنَبْلُوَنَّكُمْ بِشَيْءٍ مِّنَ الْخَوْفِ وَالْجُوْعِ وَنَقْصٍ مِّنَ الْأَمْوَالِ وَالْأَنْفُسِ
وَالثَّمَرٰتِ ؕ وَبَشِّرِ الصّٰبِرِيْنَ ○ الَّذِيْنَ إِذَآ أَصَابَتْهُمْ مُّصِيْبَةٌ ۙ قَالُوْٓا
إِنَّا لِلّٰهِ وَإِنَّآ إِلَيْهِ رٰجِعُوْنَ ○ أُولٰٓئِكَ عَلَيْهِمْ صَلَوٰتٌ مِّنْ رَّبِّهِمْ وَ
رَحْمَةٌ ۟ وَأُولٰٓئِكَ هُمُ الْمُهْتَدُوْنَ ○ [23]

This means that: 'O believers! We shall keep trying you. Thus, at times you will be overtaken by fear; sometimes you will be visited by adversity and starvation or you will suffer financially; sometimes your lives will be endangered, sometimes your toil will be fruitless and your efforts will not yield the desired results; and sometimes your dear children will die. Therefore, convey glad tidings to those, who, when they are visited by a calamity, affirm: We belong to God and we are His trust and vassals. The truth is that trust should return to its owner. These are the people who are the recipients of Divine grace and these are the people who have found their way to God.'

In short, the name of this moral quality is steadfastness or, in other words, willing submission to the Divine will. From another perspective, this quality may also be called *'Adl* [equity or justice.] Throughout a believer's life, God Almighty does so many things to his liking and manifests

---

[23] Al-Baqarah, 2:156-158 **[Publisher]**

thousands of matters in accord with his wishes, and He has blessed him with so many bounties in keeping with his needs, that he cannot even count them. Therefore, if God ever desires that man should comply with His will, it would be unfair and improper not to submit to His will, to find excuses, or to lose faith and go astray.

[Islāmī Uṣūl kī Philosophy, Rūḥānī Khazā'in, vol. 10, pp. 361-362]

Ṣalāt [Prayer] and *Istighfār* [seeking forgiveness] are excellent remedies for apathy and indifference. One should supplicate in *Ṣalāt*: O Allah, alienate me from my sins. If a person continues to pray sincerely, it is certain that his prayer would be answered sometime. It is not good to be in a hurry. A farmer does not harvest the crop immediately after sowing. One who is impatient is unfortunate. The sign of a pious one is that he is not impatient. Lack of patience has resulted in many a known case of failure. If a person digs a well to the depth of twenty arms length, and stops short of just one due to his impatience, he would waste his entire labour. Were he to dig the remaining arm length with patience, he would achieve his purpose.

It is the way of God Almighty that He bestows the blessings of love, eagerness and understanding after sufferings. A bounty that is easily acquired is not appreciated. It is well said by Sa'dī:

گر نہ باشد بدوست راہ بردن
شرط عشق است در طلب مُردن [24]

[Malfūẓāt, vol. 4, p. 245]

---

[24] *Even if it is not possible to reach the Friend;*
Love demands that one should die seeking. **[Publisher]**

Truthfulness

Of all the natural states of man, one that is an essential part of his nature is truthfulness. Normally, unless a person is moved by some selfish motive, he does not wish to tell a lie. He is naturally averse to falsehood and is reluctant to have recourse to it. That is why, he dislikes a person whom he knows to be a liar and looks down upon him with contempt. But this natural state by itself cannot be considered moral. Even children and the insane exhibit this quality. The fact is that so long as a person does not renounce such selfish motives as prevent him from telling the truth, he cannot be considered truthful. If a person tells the truth only when he stands to lose nothing but tells a lie when his honour, property or life are threatened, how then can he be considered better than children and the insane. Do minors and the insane not speak this kind of truth? There is hardly anyone in the world who would tell a lie without any motive. Truth that is abandoned at a time of risk can never form part of the true morals. The real occasion of telling the truth is when one apprehends loss of life or property or honour. In this context, the Divine teaching is:

فَاجْتَنِبُوا الرِّجْسَ مِنَ الْأَوْثَانِ وَاجْتَنِبُوا قَوْلَ الزُّورِ [25]

وَلَا يَأْبَ الشُّهَدَاءُ إِذَا مَا دُعُوا [26]

وَلَا تَكْتُمُوا الشَّهَادَةَ وَمَنْ يَكْتُمْهَا فَإِنَّهُ آثِمٌ قَلْبُهُ [27]

وَإِذَا قُلْتُمْ فَاعْدِلُوا وَلَوْ كَانَ ذَا قُرْبَىٰ [28]

---

[25] Al-Ḥajj, 22:31 **[Publisher]**

[26] Al-Baqarah, 2:283 **[Publisher]**

[27] Al-Baqarah, 2:284 **[Publisher]**

[28] Al-An‘ām, 6:153 **[Publisher]**

كُونُوا قَوَّامِينَ بِالْقِسْطِ شُهَدَاءَ لِلَّهِ وَلَوْ عَلَىٰ أَنفُسِكُمْ أَوِ الْوَالِدَيْنِ وَالْأَقْرَبِينَ [29]

وَلَا يَجْرِمَنَّكُمْ شَنَآنُ قَوْمٍ عَلَىٰ أَلَّا تَعْدِلُوا [30]

وَالصَّادِقِينَ وَالصَّادِقَاتِ [31]

وَتَوَاصَوْا بِالْحَقِّ وَتَوَاصَوْا بِالصَّبْرِ [32]

لَا يَشْهَدُونَ الزُّورَ [33]

Translation: 'Keep away from idol worship and lying', because falsehood too is an idol; one who relies upon it ceases to rely upon God. Hence, by telling lies, one loses God.

'When you are summoned to testify to the truth, do not refuse to do so.'

'Do not conceal true testimony; and he who conceals it, his heart is certainly sinful.'

'And when you speak, speak only what is absolutely true and fair, even when you testify against a close relative.'

'Hold fast to the truth and justice, and bear witness only for the sake of Allah. Never utter a lie even if telling the truth may endanger your lives or your parent's lives or other loved ones like your children.'

'Let not hostility towards a people prevent you from giving true testimony.'

'Truthful men and truthful women will earn great reward.'

---

[29] Al-Nisā', 4:136 **[Publisher]**

[30] Al-Mā'idah, 5:9 **[Publisher]**

[31] Al-Aḥzāb, 33:36 **[Publisher]**

[32] Al-'Aṣr, 103:4 **[Publisher]**

[33] Al-Furqān, 25:73 **[Publisher]**

'They are accustomed to counselling truth.'

'They do not keep company with the untruthful.'

[Islāmī Uṣūl kī Philosophy, Rūḥānī Khazā'in, vol. 10, pp. 360-361]

Change in Moral Qualities

There are two schools of thought regarding the possibility of moral reform. There are those who believe that man is capable of moral reform, and others who believe that he is not. The truth of the matter is that morals can be changed if one is not complacent, and makes an effort to do so.

This reminds me of a story. It is said that once a man came to see the famous Greek philosopher Plato and sought permission to enter. It was Plato's habit that he only allowed visitors to enter after studying their facial features and physiognomy. This helped him to judge the personality of the visitor. This time too his servant described to him the features of the visitor. Plato said: "Tell him that since he is a man of low morals, I will not see him." The visitor heard Plato's remark and said that what he had said was true, but he had given up his evil ways and was a reformed man. Plato agreed that such a change was possible. The visitor was then shown in and was received with much respect and honour.

Philosophers who believe that moral reform is not possible are mistaken. We know of some civil servants who were given to taking bribes, repented of it and thereafter would not accept a bribe even of the highest amount.

Repentance, in reality, is very vital and helpful to bring about moral reform and makes a man perfect. In other words, if a person seeks to shed his bad habits for good ones, he must first repent with sincerity and full resolve.

[Malfūẓāt, vol. 1, pp. 137-138]]

The Reality of Love

The fourth objection is that Islamic teaching never enjoins love for the followers of other religions; it only enjoins love for Muslims.

In reply, let it be clear that all this is the unfortunate outcome of the New Testament which is neither complete nor perfect, and because of which Christians digressed from the truth and reality. If one reflects deeply on what love is, when it should be exercised, and what hatred is and when it should be exercised, then not only does one comprehend true philosophy of the Holy Qur'ān, but the soul also achieves the perfect light of true understanding.

Remember, love is not pretence or affectation. It is one of the human faculties. The essence of love is to have sincerity for something and to be drawn irresistibly towards it. Just as the real characteristics of an object are only truly perceived when it reaches perfection, the same is the case with love, in that its qualities are openly revealed when it is extreme and reaches perfection. Referring to this, Allah the Almighty says:

أُشْرِبُوْا فِيْ قُلُوْبِهِمُ الْعِجْلَ [34]

That is: 'They loved the calf as if their hearts were permeated with it.'

In point of fact, when a person falls in love with someone and his love is total, it becomes his food and his drink, as it were. Indeed he takes on the complexion of the character and lifestyle of the beloved. The greater the love, the more a person is involuntarily drawn towards the qualities of the loved one, so much so, that he becomes his

[34] Al-Baqarah,2:94 **[Publisher]**

very reflection. That is why, consistent with his capacity, a person who loves God acquires, metaphorically speaking, God's light. Similarly, those who love Satan acquire the darkness which belongs to Satan. This being the reality of love, how can a true Scripture, which is from God, ever permit that you should love Satan as you love God, or love the successors of Satan the way you ought to love the successors of the Gracious One.

The pity of it is that we had hitherto held the New Testament to be false only because it deifies a humble mortal. But now we can also prove that various other teachings of the Gospels are also impure. How can a teaching be pure which requires one to love Satan as he ought to love God? It would be an exercise in futility to contend that these sayings were a slip of the tongue on the part of Jesus because he was ignorant of the philosophy of the Divine. If this was so, why did he claim to be the reformer of his people? Was he a child? Did he not even know that true love demands that the lover should sincerely love the habits, morals and religious practices of the beloved, and should endeavour heart and soul to be lost in them, so that he may attain through the beloved the life that belongs to him. The true lover loses himself in the beloved. He becomes the manifestation of the beloved and reflects in himself the image of the beloved to the extent that it becomes part and parcel of his person. After acquiring his complexion and by standing with him, he demonstrates to the people that for a fact he is totally lost in love for his beloved.

Muḥabbat [love] is an Arabic word which literally means 'to be filled'. The well-known Arabic idiom تَحَبَّبَ الْحِمَارُ is used when an Arab wants to say that a donkey's belly is full of water. When he wants to say that the camel drank water to its full capacity, he says: شَرِبَتِ الْإِبِلُ حَتّٰى تَحَبَّبَتْ. *Ḥub*, meaning grain, is also derived from the same root, meaning that it is full of the qualities of the grain. Similarly, *Iḥbāb* also means to sleep, for he who is filled with something else loses himself as if he had gone to sleep and he had been deprived of all consciousness of his own self. If this is the reality of love, the Gospel, which teaches to love Satan and his followers, in other words it teaches that you too should partake of their wickedness. What a teaching! How can such a teaching be attributed to God Almighty. On the contrary, it seeks to convert man into Satan. May God save all from this teaching of the Gospel.

If it is asked that since it is forbidden to love Satan and his ilk, what kind of treatment should be meted out to them? The answer is that the Holy Word of God Almighty enjoins that they should be treated with great kindness and compassion, just as a kind-hearted person is kind to the lepers, the blind, the crippled and the lame, etc. However, the difference between compassion and love is that a lover admires all the words and deeds of his beloved and desires that he too should become like his beloved; but a compassionate person looks at the recipient of his compassion with concern and is afraid lest the sufferer should perish in his pitiable state. The sign of a truly compassionate person is that he is not always gentle to his object of pity. Rather, he deals with him in accordance with the demands of time and occasion. At times he is gentle and at times he is harsh. Sometimes he offers him drink and sometimes, like a wise doctor, considers the amputation of his hand or foot to save his life. Sometimes he operates upon his limb, and sometimes he applies balm. If you happen to visit a big hospital, which is frequented by hundreds of patients of all kinds, and observe the daily tasks of an experienced doctor, you will then hopefully come to understand the meaning of compassion.

The Holy Qur'ān teaches us to love the virtuous, the pious and righteous, and also to have compassion for the wicked and the disbelievers. Almighty Allah says:

عَزِيْزٌ عَلَيْهِ مَا عَنِتُّمْ حَرِيْصٌ عَلَيْكُمْ [35]

That is: 'O disbelievers, this Prophet is so compassionate that he cannot stand the sight of your suffering and is highly solicitous for your safety from these hardships.'

لَعَلَّكَ بَاخِعٌ نَّفْسَكَ اَلَّا يَكُوْنُوْا مُؤْمِنِيْنَ [36]

That is: 'Will you die worrying why they do not believe?' This means that, your compassion has reached the limit where your anguish for them has brought you close to death.

تَوَاصَوْا بِالصَّبْرِ وَتَوَاصَوْا بِالْمَرْحَمَةِ [37]

That is: 'The faithful are those who counsel patience and compassion to one another,' i.e., they advise patience in adversity and compassion towards God's creatures. Here too *Marḥamah* means compassion, for this is what the word *Marḥamah* implies in Arabic.

In short, the true meaning of the Qur'ānic teaching is that love, which in reality means to reflect in one's person the qualities of the beloved, is not permissible except for God Almighty and for the righteous ones. Indeed it is

---

[35] Al-Taubah, 9:128 **[Publisher]**

[36] Al-Shu'arā', 26:4 **[Publisher]**

[37] Al-Balad, 90:18 **[Publisher]**

strictly forbidden for all others. For instance, the Holy Qur'ān says:

وَالَّذِيْنَ اٰمَنُوْٓا اَشَدُّ حُبًّا لِّلّٰهِ[38]

It also says:

يٰٓاَيُّهَا الَّذِيْنَ اٰمَنُوْا لَا تَتَّخِذُوا الْيَهُوْدَ وَالنَّصٰرٰٓى اَوْلِيَآءَ[39]

At another place it says:

يٰٓاَيُّهَا الَّذِيْنَ اٰمَنُوْا لَا تَتَّخِذُوْا بِطَانَةً مِّنْ دُوْنِكُمْ[40]

That is to say, do not love the Jews and Christians, nor those who are not righteous.

Reading these verses, the uninformed Christians are misled. They think that Muslims are enjoined not to love Christians and other non-believers, but they do not realize that every word is used with reference to the context. What constitutes love can be entertained for evildoers and the disbelievers only when one partakes of their disbelief and impiety. Ignorant indeed would be the person who enjoined love for the enemies of his faith. We have pointed out several times that love means to look with pleasure on the words, actions, habits, morals, and faith of the beloved, to be pleased with them, and to accept his influence. But this is not possible on the part of a believer with regard to a disbeliever.

A believer will, however, have compassion for the disbeliever and will have full sympathy for him and will

---

[38] 'And those who believe are stronger in *their* love for Allah.'—Al-Baqarah, 2:166 **[Publisher]**

[39] 'O ye who believe! take not the Jews and the Christians for friends.'—Al-Mā'idah, 5:52 **[Publisher]**

[40] 'O ye who believe! take not *others* than your own people as intimate friends.'—Āl-e-'Imrān, 3:119 **[Publisher]**

seek to help him in his physical and spiritual ailments. Allah the Almighty has repeatedly admonished that we should have sympathy for people regardless of their religion, should feed the hungry, procure freedom for slaves, pay off the debts of those burdened with them, and have true sympathy for the whole of mankind. He says:

إِنَّ اللّٰهَ يَأْمُرُ بِالْعَدْلِ وَالْإِحْسَانِ وَإِيْتَآئِ ذِي الْقُرْبٰى [41]

This means that: 'God commands you to be just or, even more than just, to be benevolent like a mother to her child, or like a person who is kind to another because of the feelings of kinship.'

لَا يَنْهٰكُمُ اللّٰهُ عَنِ الَّذِيْنَ لَمْ يُقَاتِلُوْكُمْ فِي الدِّيْنِ وَلَمْ يُخْرِجُوْكُمْ مِّنْ دِيَارِكُمْ
أَنْ تَبَرُّوْهُمْ وَتُقْسِطُوْٓا إِلَيْهِمْ إِنَّ اللّٰهَ يُحِبُّ الْمُقْسِطِيْنَ [42]

That is: 'The fact that Allah forbids you from loving the Christians and others should not be taken to mean that He forbids you from doing good or showing compassion and sympathy. No. Be compassionate, sympathetic and just to those who have not fought to kill you, nor have they driven you out of your homes, whether they are Jews or Christians, for Allah loves the people who do so.'

إِنَّمَا يَنْهٰكُمُ اللّٰهُ عَنِ الَّذِيْنَ قَاتَلُوْكُمْ فِي الدِّيْنِ وَأَخْرَجُوْكُمْ مِّنْ دِيَارِكُمْ وَظَاهَرُوْا
عَلٰٓى إِخْرَاجِكُمْ أَنْ تَوَلَّوْهُمْ ۚ وَمَنْ يَّتَوَلَّهُمْ فَأُولٰٓئِكَ هُمُ الظّٰلِمُوْنَ [43]

That is: 'Allah forbids you from being friendly and intimate with only those who have waged religious wars

---

[41] Al-Naḥl, 16:91 **[Publisher]**

[42] Al-Mumtaḥinah, 60:9 **[Publisher]**

[43] Al-Mumtaḥinah, 60:10 **[Publisher]**

against you and have driven you out of your homes, and have aided others in driving you out of your homes. Friendship with them is forbidden, because they are bent upon destroying your faith.'

It is worth remembering that the reality of friendship is sympathy and well wishing. A believer can, therefore, have friendship, sympathy and goodwill for Christians, Jews, and Hindus and can exercise benevolence towards them, but cannot love them. **This is a fine distinction, which should always be kept in mind.**

[Nūr-ul-Qur'ān part 2, Rūḥānī Khazā'in, vol. 9, pp. 429-436]

2

FAITH, CERTAINTY AND INSIGHT

As far as the belief in God Almighty, the question of metaphors, and the phenomena of here and the hereafter is concerned, the approach of philosophers is very different from that of Prophets.

Faith in the Unseen Taught by Prophets

The main principle followed by the Prophets is that faith proves fruitful only if the unseen is accepted as unseen, and the self-evident testimony of physical senses and absolute mathematical proof is not insisted upon inasmuch as all spiritual merit and worthiness of nearness to the Divine depends upon righteousness, and he alone possesses true righteousness who safeguards himself against the extremes of investigation, multiple denials, and testing every little detail, and is prepared to accept a way that appears safer and preferable to other ways as the truth, out of a sense of precaution. This is faith, and this is what helps open the door of Divine grace and becomes the means of acquiring good fortune here and in the hereafter. When a person establishes himself firmly on faith and then seeks to foster his knowledge through prayer, worship, reflection and observation, God Almighty Himself becomes his Guardian, and, taking him by the hand, leads him from the stage of faith to that of *'Ain-ul-Yaqīn* [certainty by sight.] But all this is achieved only through steadfastness, striving, effort and purification of the ego. He who seeks clarification of all details at the very first stage, and is not prepared to abandon his false doctrines and evil ways before such clarification, prevents himself from treading upon the path of righteousness and achieving merit. Faith demands belief in certain matters which are still unseen to some degree, that is to say, they are still in a condition which is not established fully by reason, nor has it been perceived through spiritual vision, but is accepted on the basis of probability.

This is the true philosophy of the Prophets by following which, millions of God's creatures have procured heavenly blessings and countless people have arrived at the stage of perfect understanding and many more continue to do so. The perfect certainties which the philosophers sought to achieve hastily and daringly, and failed to achieve, have not only all been achieved with the utmost ease by the faithful ones, but they have reached the stage of that perfect understanding which has not been heard or seen or conceived by any philosopher. As against this the false and deceptive philosophy, of which the newly educated are so fond, and the ill consequences of which have ruined so many of the simple-minded, demands, that until the root and branch of everything is fully established and is clearly revealed, it should never be acknowledged, whether it be God or anything else. The greater philosophers among them who held fast to these principles, called themselves research scholars, and they are also known as atheists. The doctrine of these great philosophers, resulting from their basic principle, is that whereas the existence of God cannot be established undeniably through reason, nor is the being of God visible to the eye, belief in such a God is utterly contrary to the established philosophic doctrine. Thus at the very first step they set God Almighty aside, and repudiate the angels as they too, like God Almighty, are not visible. Then these philosophers turned their attention to the existence of souls and expressed the view that there was no satisfactory proof that the soul survives death, for it cannot be seen, nor does it disclose its existence in any perceptible manner. On the contrary, souls, after their separation from the body, leave no sign behind, nor do they produce any effect, and belief in their existence is equally contrary to reason. Thereafter, the penetrating sight of the learned philosophers discovered that the limitations of the law and the distinction between lawful and unlawful are contradictory to the basic philosophical principle and express the view that there is no philosophical reason to support the distinction between mother and sister and wife, or the distinction between that which is lawful and that which is unlawful, except in cases in which the harmfulness of something is established by the harm it does. They also opine that nudism is not in any way opposed to reason, and is hygienically beneficial in some respects.

These philosophers have set forth other doctrines also but the sum or the substance of their philosophy is that they do not accept anything without conclusive proof. In their philosophical view no type of misconduct need be discarded, unless it is proved to be hygienically harmful or socially disturbing. These are the superior philosophers. But those of a lower degree, being apprehensive of condemnation by the community, have, to some degree, softened their principles and profess a somewhat doubtful acceptance of God and the hereafter and other concepts of this kind. The superior philosophers regard them as utterly foolish and cowardly, and a source of disgrace, since they claim to be philosophers but do not adhere strictly to the basic principles of philosophy. Therefore the superior ones do not consider them worthy of the honourable appellation of a philosopher.

[Surmah Chashm-e-Āryā, Rūḥānī Khazā'in, vol. 2, pp. 83-88, footnote]

I desire to lead these theoretical philosophers, who are unaware of the love for the Divine and are negligent in their appreciation of His Exalted Being, to the straight path through such persuasive arguments as I am capable of. I have observed that their spiritual condition has become very weak, and unwarranted freedom and weakness of faith have seriously undermined their sincerity, religious resolve, and spiritual condition. They have confused truth with falsehood in an odd manner. The roots of the blessings of religion are faith, confidence, goodwill, obedience of true spiritual guides, and the Divine word, but these people misunderstand religion on account of their wrong philosophy.

It is, therefore, incumbent upon them to discard prejudice and self-approval, and reflect in a simple way upon the question: What is faith and why is it expected to confer any benefit?

Faith and Certainty

Be it known, therefore, that faith means a sincere declaration of the acceptance of the message of a Prophet, out of righteousness and as a matter of wise precaution, purely on the basis of goodwill. That is to say, to proclaim acceptance whole-heartedly, finding that certain reliable factors point in that direction, without waiting for perfect and conclusive proof. The stage when perfect reasons and conclusive arguments become available in support of the truth is designated the stage of certainty through knowledge. When God Almighty, out of His special bounty, should in an extraordinary manner bestows the lights of guidance, and should acquaint a creature of His with His favours and bounties, and should bestow reason and knowledge from Himself, and opening the doors of visions and revelation should disclose the wonders of Divinity, and should reveal His beauty as the Beloved, that stage is designated understanding, or in other words, certainty by sight and is also called guidance and insight.

When, in consequence of the profound effect of all these experiences, the heart of a lover of God is surcharged with love and devotion to a degree where his whole being is saturated with delight, and heavenly light totally envelops his heart and excludes all darkness and constraint, so that, on account of the perfection of his love and devotion and the climax of his sincerity and loyalty, misfortunes and calamities become a source of delight and sweetness for him, that stage is designated as the stage of being at rest. It is also called salvation, deliverance or certainty by realization.

All these ranks are granted after arriving at the stage of faith. One who is firm in one's faith progressively achieves these ranks. But one who does not adopt the way of faith and demands conclusive, certain, and patent proof of every verity before accepting it, has no relationship with the way of faith and can never become the recipient of the grace of that Almighty and Self-Sufficient Being.

It has ever been the way of Allah—and this is a fine point of the appreciation of the Divine over which the fortunate ones should reflect—that merit and heavenly grace follow only upon faith. The true philosophy of this way is that in the primary stage of faith a person should avoid a long series of doubts and denials regarding the acceptance of the Absolute Self-Sufficient One, and His power and His promise, and His warning, and His revelations, and His mysteries. For the maintenance of the condition of faith, on which all merit depends, it is necessary that God Almighty should not display all matters of faith as plainly as other realities become apparent to everyone.

[Surmah Chashm-e-Āryā, Rūḥānī Khazā'in, vol. 2, pp. 70-80]

Faith means acceptance at a stage when knowledge is not yet complete, and the struggle with doubts and suspicions is still in progress. He who believes, that is to say, has faith, on the basis of probability and likelihood and despite weakness and the lack of perfect means of certainty, is accounted righteous in the estimation of the Supreme One. Thereafter, perfect understanding is bestowed on him as a bounty, and he is given to drink of the cup of understanding after partaking of faith. When a pious one, on hearing the call of a Messenger, a Prophet or a commissioned one of God, does not just go about criticizing, but takes that portion which he can recognize and understand on the basis of clear proof the means of acceptance and faith, and considers that which he is unable to understand as metaphorical or allegorical, and thus removing all contradiction out of the way, believes simply and sincerely, then God Almighty, having pity on him and being pleased with his faith, and hearing his supplications, opens the gates of perfect understanding for him and leads him to perfect certainty through visions, revelation and other heavenly signs.

[Ayyām-uṣ-Ṣulḥ, Rūḥānī Khazā'in, vol. 14, p. 261]

The Word of God directs us: Have faith and you will be delivered. It does not tell us: Demand philosophical reasons and conclusive proofs in support of the doctrines that the Holy Prophet (peace and blessings of Allah be upon him) has presented to you, and do not accept them until they are established like mathematical formulae. It is obvious that if the teaching of a Prophet is to be accepted only after being tested by the canons of current knowledge, that would not be faith in the Prophet; inasmuch as every verity when it is established clearly, becomes binding, whether it is set forth by a Prophet or by anyone else. Even if expounded by a vicious person it has to be accepted. That which we would accept by putting our trust in a Prophet, and by affirming his righteousness, must be of a nature which possesses a probability of truth in the estimation of reason and yet leaves room for a foolish person to incline towards its rejection as false; so that by taking the side of truth and affirming the righteousness of a Prophet we may be rewarded for our well-thinking, penetrating intelligence, respectfulness and faith. This is the purport of the teaching of the Holy Qur'ān that we have set forth. But thinkers and philosophers have never followed this way and have always been heedless of faith. They have always been in search of the kind of knowledge which is demonstrated to them as being immediate, incontrovertible and certain.

It should be remembered that God Almighty, by demanding faith in the unseen, does not wish to deprive the believers of certainty of understanding the Divine. Indeed, faith is a ladder for arriving at this certainty of understanding, without which it is in vain to seek true understanding. Those who climb this ladder surely experience for themselves the pure and undefiled spiritual verities. When a sincere believer accepts Divine commands and directions for the only reason that God Almighty has bestowed them upon him through a righteous bearer, he becomes deserving of the bounty of understanding. That is why God Almighty has established a law for His servants that they should first acknowledge Him by believing in the unseen, so that all the problems they face may be resolved through the bounty of true understanding. But it is a pity that a hasty one does not adopt these ways. The Holy Qur'ān contains the promise of God Almighty that if a person, who accepts the call of the Holy Prophet (peace and blessings of Allah be upon him) on the basis of faith, seeks to comprehend its reality and strives after such comprehension, the reality will be disclosed to him by means of visions and revelations and his faith will be elevated to the stage of the understanding.

[Ā'īna-e-Kamālāt-e-Islām, Rūḥānī Khazā'in, vol. 5, pp. 251-253, footnote].

Salvation Depends on Faith

I affirm repeatedly and emphatically that if religious doctrines had been self-evident like philosophical propositions and mathematical equations, they would certainly not have been considered the basis for achieving salvation. Dear brethren, rest assured that salvation depends upon faith, and faith is related to the unseen. If the underlying reality of things had not been concealed, there would have been no faith, and without faith there would be no salvation. It is faith alone which is the means of winning Divine pleasure. It is a ladder for achieving nearness to God, and a spring for washing away the rust of sin. We are dependent upon God Almighty, and it is faith that discloses this dependence. We are dependent on God Almighty for our salvation and our deliverance from every ill. Such deliverance can be achieved only through faith. The remedy for the torments of this life and the hereafter is faith. When, through the power of faith, we find that a difficulty is not impossible of resolution, it is resolved for us. It is through the power of faith that we are able to achieve that which appears to be impossible and contrary to reason. It is through the power of faith that miracles and extraordinary events are witnessed, and what is considered impossible happens.

It is through faith that we are convinced of the existence of God. He remained hidden from philosophers, and thinkers could not discover Him; but faith leads to God even a humble one who is clothed in rags, and enables him to converse with Him. The power of faith is the means of contact between a believer and the True Beloved. This power leads a poor humble one who is rejected of mankind to the palace of holiness, which is the throne of Allah and, gradually removing all intervening obstructions, reveals the countenance of the Eternal Beloved.

Arise then, and seek faith and burn the dry and useless tomes of philosophy; only through faith shall you achieve blessings. One particle of faith is better than a thousand volumes of philosophy.

Faith is not only the means of achieving salvation in the hereafter, but also provides deliverance from the torments and curses of this life. We find deliverance from soul-melting sorrows through the blessings of faith. It is faith through which a perfect believer finds comfort and joy in the midst of anxiety, agony, torment and sorrow, and when he is confronted with failure in all directions and all the familiar doors appear locked and barred. Perfect faith removes all feeling of distance and separation. There is no wealth that can be compared to faith. In this world everyone, with the exception of the believer, is overwhelmed with grief. In this world everyone is afflicted with the agony of loss and unfulfilled desires, except a believer.

Faith! how sweet are your fruits and how fragrant are your flowers; praise be to Allah, how wonderful are your blessings and what beautiful lights shine in you. No one can reach the Pleiades unless he is inspired by you. It has pleased God Almighty that now you should arrive and philosophy should depart. *Nothing can stop His grace.*

[Ā'īna-e-Kamālāt-e-Islām, Rūḥānī Khazā'in, vol. 5, pp. 270-273, footnote].

Progressive Stages of Faith

It is obvious that the primary task and important step we have to undertake is to recognize God. If our recognition of God is defective, doubtful and befogged, our faith cannot be bright and shining. So long as we have no true experience of the recognition of God, through His attribute of *Raḥīmiyyat*, we cannot drink the fresh water of the spring of true comprehension. If we do not deliberately deceive ourselves, we will have to confess that we need our doubts and hesitations to be removed through the Divine attribute of *Raḥīmiyyat*, and we need our hearts to be so powerfully affected by the experience of Divine mercy, grace and power, as to rescue us from the passions that overpower us on account of the weakness of our faith, and turn us to the opposite direction. Is it not true that on arriving in this fleeting world, man becomes involved in a dangerous darkness because his heart is not illumined by the powerful rays of Divine recognition? He is not inspired by the search for the joys of the hereafter and of true prosperity as much as he is attracted to the world and its appendages: wealth, powers, and governance. If he were to find some prescription that would enable him to abide in this world forever, he would be ready to affirm that he has no desire for heaven and for the bounties of the hereafter. What is the reason for this? Is it not that there is no true faith in the existence of God Almighty, His power, His mercy and His promises?

Thus it is necessary for a seeker after truth to continuously occupy himself with the search for true faith and not to deceive himself by thinking that he is a Muslim who believes in God and His Messenger, and reads the Holy Qur'ān, and shuns associating anything with God, and observes prayer and avoids evils and improprieties.

In the hereafter, only that person will achieve perfect salvation, true prosperity and real happiness who has gained in this life that living and true light which turns a person, together with all his faculties and capacities and designs, towards God Almighty and whereby his lower life dies altogether, and his soul undergoes a righteous change. What is that living and true light? It is the Divinely bestowed capacity, which is designated certainty or perfect comprehension. This is the power that pulls a person with its strong hand out of a dark and fearful pit and places him against a bright and peaceful background.

Before this light is acquired, all righteous actions are by way of habit, and a person is likely to stumble when confronted with the least trial. Without perfect certainty no one's relationship with God is duly adjusted. He who is granted certainty flows like water and rushes like the wind towards God. He consumes everything else like fire and, in trials and misfortunes, displays a firmness like that of the earth. Recognition of God renders a person insane in the eyes of the world, but sane and wise in the estimation of God. This drink possesses a sweetness which renders the whole body sweet; it is a delicious milk, which relieves him who drinks it of all desire for other bounties. It can be achieved only through such prayers as are offered at the risk of one's life. It is not acquired through the sacrifice of another's blood but through true sacrifice of the ego. How difficult is this task. Ah! how difficult!

[Ayyām-uṣ-Ṣulḥ, Rūḥānī Khazā'in, vol. 14, pp. 244-246]

Blessings of Divine Recognition

Those who truly seek God know well that comprehension of God can be achieved only through God Himself, and God alone can bestow full recognition of Himself. This is not a matter of man's own choice. By no contrivance can man discard sin and achieve nearness to God unless he is granted full comprehension. No atonement can be of help, nor is there any way of being purified from sin, except through that perfect comprehension which generates perfect love and perfect fear. These two alone provide a barrier against sin. When the fire of the love and fear of Allah is set ablaze, it reduces all causes of sin to ashes. This holy fire and the foul fires of sin can never coexist. Man cannot desist from evil, nor can he advance in love, until he is blessed with full comprehension, and that does not happen until God Almighty sends down living blessings and miracles.

[Brāhīn-e-Aḥmadiyyah, part V, Rūḥānī Khazā'in, vol. 21, p.7]

Humbleness is like a seed for faith. By discarding all that is vain, faith begins to sprout. When one spends one's wealth in the cause of Allah, the plant of faith brings forth shoots which strengthen it to a degree. By exercising control over carnal passions, these branches acquire strength and firmness. By safeguarding all branches of one's trusts and covenants, the tree of faith is enabled to stand firm on its trunk. Then, at the time of bringing forth fruit, the grace of a new capacity is bestowed on it, without which it can bring forth neither fruit nor flowers.

[Brāhīn-e-Aḥmadiyyah, part V, Rūḥānī Khazā'in, vol. 21, p. 209, footnote]

Remember, it is never possible to get rid of sin without the certainty of faith. Without certainty, it is not possible to live the life of angels; without it, it is not possible to discard debauchery; without it, it is not possible to undergo a holy change and to be drawn towards God in an extraordinary manner; without it, it is not possible to leave the earth and climb to heaven; without it, it is not possible to have perfect fear of God; without it, it is not possible to tread along the delicate paths of righteousness and to purify one's conduct of all traces of ostentations. Similarly, it is not possible without this certainty to reject worldly riches and honour, and be heedless of the favour of kings and to believe in God alone as one's treasure.

[Nuzūl-ul-Masīḥ, Rūḥānī Khazā'in, vol. 18, pp.469-470]

Three Categories of the Faithful

Those who submit to God are, in fact, of three types. First, those who, on account of the obstruction of worldly means, are not able to see God's beneficence clearly, and are not inspired by that eagerness which is generated by an appreciation of the grandeur of Divine beneficence; nor are they moved by the love which is inspired by a concept of the greatness of the Benefactor's favours. They casually acknowledge God Almighty as the Creator, but do not contemplate the details of Divine beneficence which would impress a true concept of the Divine Benefactor upon their minds, inasmuch as the dust of exaggerated regard for material means creates a veil which prevents them from observing the full countenance of the Creator of the means. They are thus unable to appreciate the full beauty of the Bountiful. Their defective comprehension is confused by their regard for the means, and, as they are not able to estimate duly the bounties of God, they do not pay as much attention to Him as would be generated in their minds by a proper appreciation of His favours. Thus, their comprehension is somewhat misty because they put their trust in their own efforts and in the means that are available to them. They also acknowledge formally their obligation towards God on account of His being the Creator and the Provider. As God Almighty does not require of anyone that which is beyond the limits of his intellectual capacity, He only requires of them an expression of gratitude for His favours. In the verse:

إِنَّ اللّٰهَ يَأْمُرُ بِالْعَدْلِ [44]

'justice' implies only this kind of obedience.

But above this there is another grade of comprehension which is reached when a person, disregarding the means, clearly observes God's gracious and beneficent hand and emerges completely out of the veils of material means. At that stage, he realizes the futility and falsity of expressions like: 'I obtained this success through proper irrigation of my fields;' or 'I obtained this success through my own efforts;' or 'I achieved my purpose through the favour of X;' or 'I was saved from ruin by the care of Y.'

---

[44] 'Verily, Allah enjoins justice.'—Al-Naḥl, 16:91 **[Publisher]**

Rather, he beholds only one Being and one Power and one Benefactor and one Hand. Then he views the favours of God Almighty clearly without the least obstruction resulting from associating means with the Benefactor. This view is so clear and certain that in his worship of the true Benefactor he does not contemplate Him as being absent but conceives Him as being present. Such worship is designated by the Holy Qur'ān as *Iḥsān*. The Holy Prophet (peace and blessings of Allah be upon him) has himself attributed this meaning to *Iḥsān,* as reported in *Bukhārī* and *Muslim*.

There is yet another grade above this, which is:

إِيْتَآئِ ذِي الْقُرْبٰى [45]

It means that when a person continues to view Divine favours, without the association of material means, and worships God conceiving Him to be present and to be the direct Benefactor, he begins to have personal love for God.

The continuous contemplation of beneficence necessarily generates in the heart of the beneficiary love for the Benefactor, Whose unlimited favours surround him on all sides. In such a situation he does not worship the Benefactor merely out of an appreciation of His bounties, but out of personal love for Him like the love of an infant for its mother. At this stage he not only views God at the time of his worship but is also filled with delight like a true lovers. This is the grade which God Almighty has designated to be like beneficence between kindred, and this is the grade which is indicated in the verse:

فَاذْكُرُوا اللّٰهَ كَذِكْرِكُمْ اٰبَآءَكُمْ اَوْ اَشَدَّ ذِكْرًا [46]

---

[45] 'Giving like to the next of kin.'—Al-Naḥl, 16:91 **[Publisher]**

which throws light on the verse:

إِنَّ اللّٰهَ يَأْمُرُ بِالْعَدْلِ وَالْإِحْسَانِ وَإِيْتَآئِ ذِي الْقُرْبٰى [47]

Here God Almighty sets out the three grades of comprehension of the Divine. The third grade is that of personal love, at which all personal desires are consumed, and the heart becomes so filled with love as a crystal vial is filled with perfume. This grade is also referred to in the verse:

وَمِنَ النَّاسِ مَنْ يَّشْرِيْ نَفْسَهُ ابْتِغَآءَ مَرْضَاتِ اللّٰهِ ۚ وَاللّٰهُ رَءُوْفٌ ۢ بِالْعِبَادِ [48]

This means that: ‘Of the believers there are some who sell their lives in return for the pleasure of Allah. These are the ones upon whom Allah is Most Compassionate.’

Again it is said:

بَلٰى مَنْ أَسْلَمَ وَجْهَهٗ لِلّٰهِ وَهُوَ مُحْسِنٌ فَلَهٗٓ أَجْرُهٗ عِنْدَ رَبِّهٖ
وَلَا خَوْفٌ عَلَيْهِمْ وَلَا هُمْ يَحْزَنُوْنَ [49]

That is:‘The truly delivered are those who commit themselves wholly to God and, recalling His favours, worship Him as if they behold Him. Such have their reward with God and they have no fear, nor do they grieve.’

That is to say, God and His love become their whole purpose, and their reward is Divine favours. At another place it is said:

يُطْعِمُوْنَ الطَّعَامَ عَلٰى حُبِّهٖ مِسْكِيْنًا وَّيَتِيْمًا وَّأَسِيْرًا ۝

---

[46] ‘Celebrate the praises of Allah as you celebrated the praises of your fathers, or even more than that.’—Al-Baqarah, 2:201 **[Publisher]**

[47] ‘Verily, Allah enjoins justice, and the doing of good to others and giving like kindered.’—Al-Naḥl, 16:91 **[Publisher]**

[48] Al-Baqarah, 2:208 **[Publisher]**

[49] Al-Baqarah, 2:113 **[Publisher]**

إِنَّمَا نُطْعِمُكُمْ لِوَجْهِ اللّٰهِ لَا نُرِيْدُ مِنْكُمْ جَزَآءً وَّلَا شُكُوْرًا ۝[50]

That is: 'Believers are those who, out of their love for God, feed the needy, the orphans and the captives saying: We feed you in order to win the pleasure of Allah; we do not desire anything in return or any expression of gratitude from you.'

These verses show clearly that the Holy Qur'ān has described the highest grade of Divine worship and righteous action as that which is inspired by true love of God and sincere seeking of His pleasure. This excellent teaching, which is set out so clearly in the Holy Qur'ān, is not explained with such clarity and detail in the Gospels. God Almighty has designated this religion as Islām, so as to indicate that man should worship God not out of selfish motives, but out of spontaneous eagerness.

Islām means discarding all desires and submitting to Divine will. In this world, no religion other than Islām lays down such objectives. There is no doubt that for the demonstration of His mercy God has promised the believers diverse types of bounties; but He has instructed those believers who are eager to achieve the highest grade that they should worship Him out of spontaneous personal love.

[Nūr-ul-Qur'ān, No. II, Rūḥānī Khazā'in, vol. 9, pp. 437-441]

Remember, the verse:

بَلٰى مَنْ اَسْلَمَ وَجْهَهٗ لِلّٰهِ وَهُوَ مُحْسِنٌ فَلَهٗٓ اَجْرُهٗ عِنْدَ رَبِّهٖ
وَلَا خَوْفٌ عَلَيْهِمْ وَلَا هُمْ يَحْزَنُوْنَ[51]

---

[50] Al-Dahr, 76:9-10 **[Publisher]**

[51] 'Nay, whoever submits himself completely to Allah, and is the doer of good, shall have his reward with his Lord. No fear *shall*

indicates the three grades of the perfection of good fortune, namely *fanā* [extinction of the self], *baqā* [revival] and *liqā'* [communion.] *'Complete submission to Allah'* means to surrender to Him all human faculties and organs, and whatever belongs to oneself, and to dedicate everything to the cause of God. This condition is described as *fanā* [extinction of the self.] When a person, conforming with the purpose of this verse, submits the whole of his being and his faculties to God Almighty, and dedicates himself to His cause, and wholly refrains from all personal moves and rests, then undoubtedly he experiences a type of death. The Sufis designate such death as *fanā*.

Then, the expression, *'and acts righteously'*, points to the stage of *baqā* [revival.] When a person, after complete surrender and abandonment of all personal desires and the cessation of all personal movement, begins to move in obedience to Divine direction, such revival is called *baqā*. Then follows the verse:

فَلَهٗٓ اَجْرُهٗ عِنْدَ رَبِّهٖ وَلَا خَوْفٌ عَلَيْهِمْ وَلَا هُمْ يَحْزَنُوْنَ [52]

This signifies affirmation, acceptance and reward and negates fear and grief. This condition refers to *liqā'* [communion.] For, when a person achieves such a high grade in his comprehension of the Divine, certainty, trust and love as to exclude all imagination and fancy and doubt concerning the reward of his sincerity and faith and loyalty, which becomes so certain and absolute and visible and perceptible as if he is already enjoying it, and

---

come upon such, neither shall they grieve.'—Al-Baqarah, 2:113 **[Publisher]**

[52] Ibid.

his belief in the Being of God Almighty becomes so certain as if he is beholding Him, and he loses sight of all fear and grief, past or present, which disappear altogether and every spiritual bounty appears present before him, that condition which is free from all constraint and is secure against every doubt and apprehension and is free from all anxiety of waiting, is designated *liqā'* [communion.] This grade of *liqā'* is clearly indicated by the word *Muḥsin*, inasmuch as according to the interpretation of the Holy Prophet (peace and blessings of Allah be upon him) *Iḥsān* is the condition in which a worshipper establishes such a relationship with God Almighty as if he is beholding Him. The grade of *liqā'* is achieved perfectly when Divine reflection completely covers the humanity of the seeker as iron is covered by the fire in which it is heated, so much so, that the physical eye perceives nothing but the fire. This is the stage at which some seekers have stumbled and have conceived the symbolic relationship as the physical union of the two beings.

Some Sufis have designated the saints who have arrived at the stage of *liqā'* or who have partaken of it to a degree, as children of God. On account of their having been completely covered by certain Divine attributes, just as a child has some resemblance to his father in respect of his form and features, in the same way, they too, in consequence of having adorned themselves reflectively with certain Divine attributes, acquire some resemblance to the beautiful attributes of God Almighty. Such titles are not commonly used in the idiom of the Shariah, but those invested with the quality of spiritual comprehension have derived them from the Holy Qur'ān; as Allah the Exalted has said:

فَاذۡکُرُوا اللّٰہَ کَذِکۡرِکُمۡ اٰبَآءَکُمۡ اَوۡ اَشَدَّ ذِکۡرًا[53]

That is: 'Remember Allah with the eagerness with which you remember your fathers.'

It is obvious that if the metaphorical use of these expressions had been forbidden by Shariah, God Almighty would have safeguarded His Word against such use of the expressions as might have allowed others to use them.

At this stage of *liqā'* [communion], a person sometimes does bear some characteristics which appear to be beyond human capacity and have the colour of Divine power. For instance, our lord and master, the Chief of the Prophets, Ḥaḍrat Khātam-ul-Anbiyā' (peace and blessings of Allah be upon him) threw a handful of gravel at the enemy during the battle of Badr, not with any prayer but only with his spiritual power, and that handful of gravel exhibited Divine power and affected the hostile forces in such an extraordinary manner that not a single one was left who's eyes were not affected by it…

In the same way, another miracle of the Holy Prophet (peace and blessings of Allah be upon him), which relates to the splitting of the moon, was manifested by Divine power. It was not the consequence of any prayer. It was manifested by the mere pointing of his finger, which was charged with Divine power. There are many other miracles of the Holy Prophet (peace and blessings of Allah be upon him), which were not accompanied by any prayer but were manifested through his person as the symbol of Divine power….

---

[53] Al-Baqarah, 2:201 **[Publisher]**

My purpose in stating all this is that when a person arrives at the grade of *liqā'*, he manifests Divine powers on the occasions of the upsurge of this grade. Anyone who spends some time in the intimate company of such a person witnesses some of these manifestations, inasmuch as during the upsurge of this condition, such a one reflectively manifests Divine attributes, so much so that his mercy becomes the mercy of God, and his wrath becomes the wrath of God. Very often when he says, even without a prayer, that such and such should happen, it happens. If he looks upon anyone with anger such a person is afflicted with some calamity, and if he looks upon someone with compassion, that person becomes the object of Divine mercy. Just as the Divine command: 'Be', always produces the desired result, in the same way, when such a person says, 'Be', in the state of the upsurge of *liqā',* it does not fail to produce the desired result. The reason for the manifestation of these extraordinary happenings is that such a person, on account of his strong relationship with God, takes on reflectively a Divine complexion and passes completely into the control of Divine manifestations, and the True Beloved takes him into His embrace and removes all intervening obstructions on account of his closeness to Him; and as He Himself is Blessed, He blesses that person's words, deeds, movement, rest, food, dress, house, time, and all his belongings. In such a state everything that comes in contact with him is blessed even without prayer. Blessings that he observes, and whose fragrance he perceives, descend upon his house and upon the doors of his house. When he travels, God Almighty keeps him company with all His blessings, and when he comes home he brings with him an ocean of light. In short, he becomes a wonderful person whose true condition is known only to God Almighty.

In this context, it should be clearly understood that once the condition of:

آَسْلَمَ وَجْهَهُ لِلّٰهِ [54]

is fully established, which the Sufis designate as *fanā*, and which the Holy Qur'ān describes as steadfastness, the grade of *baqā* and *liqā'* follow immediately upon it. In other words, when a person empties himself completely of his condition as a creature and altogether discards desire and design and arrives at the stage of perfect surrender, he immediately experiences the stage of *baqā*. But until the condition of *fanā* is fully established, and leaning wholly towards God Almighty becomes a natural characteristic, the stage of *baqā* cannot be reached. That stage is reached only when obedience ceases to be an effort, and the green and waving branches of obedience sprout forth from the heart like a natural growth and all that is considered one's own truly becomes God's, and just as other people delight in indulgence, such a person's whole delight centres on worship and remembrance of God, and the pleasures of God take the place of his personal desires.

When this condition of *baqā* is fully established and saturates the being of the seeker, and becomes his permanent characteristic, and he witnesses a light descending from heaven which removes all obstructions, and a fine, sweet and delicious feeling of love which had not been perceived before is generated in the heart, and a coolness

---

[54] 'He who submits himself completely to Allah.'—Al-Baqarah, 2:113 **[Publisher]**

and a contentment and a peace and a delight are experienced like the experience of suddenly meeting and embracing a long separated friend, and the bright, delicious, blessed, comforting, eloquent, fragrant and gladdening words of God begin to descend at all times, whether sitting, standing, asleep or awake, like a cool, pleasant and fragrant breeze which comes across a garden of flowers and begins to blow in the morning and brings with it a delight and intoxication, and the seeker is so drawn towards God Almighty that he finds it impossible to live without a lover-like contemplation of Him, and not only is he ready to sacrifice his wealth, life, honour, children and all he has, but has already sacrificed all of it in his heart, and he feels such a strong pull the nature of which he is not able to determine; and he perceives a brilliant light illumining his inner self like the dawning of the day; and he observes streams of devotion, love and loyalty flowing mightily through himself and feels every moment **as if God Almighty has descended upon his heart;** when this condition is experienced in all its aspects it is then that a seeker should be happy and should express his gratitude to the True Beloved, for that is the ultimate stage which is called *liqā'*.

At this stage, the seeker feels as if he has been washed in many holy waters, and has been created anew by casting out every trace of his ego, and the throne of the Lord of the worlds has been set inside him, and that God's shining countenance with all its winning beauty has appeared before him.

It should, however, be remembered that the last two stages, *baqā* and *liqā'*, are not achieved through one's own effort but are Divine bounties. Effort is confined to the stage of *fanā* and the journey of all righteous seekers terminates at that stage, and the circle of human excellences is thus completed. When the pure minded seeker traverses the stage of *fanā* as it should be traversed, it is Divine practice that the breeze of Divine bounty immediately conveys him to the stage of *baqā* and *liqā'*.

It is thus obvious that all the travails and labours of this journey are up to the stage of *fanā*, and thereafter no scope is left for human effort, labour and striving. A bright flame of Divine love thereafter falls upon the pure love of the seeker after God, the Noble and Exalted. Through the union of the two, a bright and perfect reflection of the Holy Spirit is generated in the human heart. At the stage of *liqā'* the light of the Holy Spirit is very bright and the extraordinary manifestations to which we have already referred proceed from the seeker because the light of the Holy Spirit always attends upon him and dwells within him. He is never separated from this light, nor does it ever depart from him. It issues from him with every breath, falls with his glance upon everything and manifests its illumination in his words. This light is called the Holy Spirit. But this is not the real Holy Spirit. The real Holy Spirit is in heaven. This Holy Spirit is a reflection which dwells permanently in the bosom, heart and brain of the holy person and does not leave him even for a moment.

[Ā'īna-e-Kamālāt-e-Islām, Rūḥānī Khazā'in, vol. 5, pp. 63-72]

Every true seeker naturally wishes to know what he should do to achieve this high stage of converse with the Divine. The answer is that this stage is a new existence at which one is given new faculties, new powers and a new life. This new existence cannot be achieved without the surrender of the previous existence. When the previous existence is wholly discarded through a true and real sacrifice, which means the sacrifice of life, honour and wealth and all other trappings of the ego, this second existence immediately takes its place.

The signs of the discarding of the previous existence are that previous characteristics and emotions are replaced by new characteristics and new emotions, and one's nature undergoes a tremendous change. All states of existence, relating to morals, faith and worship, are so transformed that they appear to take on a new colour.

In short, one becomes a new person and God Almighty also appears anew. New delights, previously unknown, are experienced in gratitude, steadfastness and remembrance of God. One feels clearly that he has full trust in his Lord and cares the least for everything other than Him. The contemplation of the Being of God Almighty overwhelms the heart to such a degree that every being other than Him disappears altogether and all material means appear useless and contemptible. Devotion and loyalty surge up to such a degree that every calamity appears light, and even the experience of calamities and misfortunes is perceived as a delight. When all these signs are perceived, it should be realized that the previous existence has suffered a total death.

Such a death invests a seeker with wonderful powers to exercise in the cause of God. He is given the power to perform all those heavy tasks which others only talk about but cannot perform, and to carry the burdens that others only estimate but cannot lift. He does all this, not of his own strength, but with the assistance of a great Divine power, which renders him firmer than the mountains, and bestows upon him a faithful heart. He is then able, for the glory of God Almighty, to do such things and manifest such devotion as is beyond the power of man. He cuts asunder from all besides Allah, and removes all intervening barriers and obstructions. He is tested and persecuted and encounters diverse types of trials and is afflicted with such calamities and misfortunes as would have destroyed mountains and darkened the sun and the moon; but he remains steadfast and endures all hardships cheerfully. Even if he is ground to dust by the mortar and pestle of calamities, no sound proceeds from him except: *'I stand with God'*. When a person arrives at this stage, he rises above the conditions of this world and is given, by way of reflection, all of the guidance and high status that were bestowed upon previous Prophets and Messengers, and he becomes their heir and their deputy.

[Ā'īna-e-Kamālāt-e-Islām, Rūḥānī Khazā'in, vol. 5, pp. 233-237]

The Soul at Rest

The third question is: what are the spiritual states?… According to the Holy Qur'ān, '*Nafs-e-Muṭma'innah*' [the Soul at Rest] is the source of spiritual states that conveys a person from the stage of a moral being to that of a godly being, as Allah the Exalted, has said:

يَٰٓأَيَّتُهَا ٱلنَّفۡسُ ٱلۡمُطۡمَئِنَّةُ ۝ ٱرۡجِعِيٓ إِلَىٰ رَبِّكِ رَاضِيَةً مَّرۡضِيَّةً ۝
فَٱدۡخُلِي فِي عِبَٰدِي ۝ وَٱدۡخُلِي جَنَّتِي ۝ [55]

That is: 'O Soul at Rest with thy Lord, return to thy Lord, He is well pleased with thee and thou are well pleased with Him. So join My true servants and enter My garden.'

The highest spiritual condition man can achieve in this

---

[55] Al-Fajr, 89:28-31 **[Publisher]**

life is to be at peace with God Almighty and all his comfort, joy and delight should be centred in God. This is the condition called the heavenly life, whereby a person is granted heaven in return for his perfect devotion and loyalty. Other people await the promised heaven but such a person enjoys heaven in this very life. Arriving at this stage, a person realizes that the worship which is prescribed for him is truly a nourishment for the soul upon which his spiritual life largely depends, and that to arrive at that condition he need not wait for another life; rather he can attain it in this very life. At this point we come to realize that all the reproof that '*Nafs-e-Lawwāmah*' [the reproaching self] administers to him on his unclean life, and yet fails to rouse fully his longing for virtue and to generate real disgust against his evil desires and to bestow full power of adherence to virtue, is transformed by this urge which is the beginning of the development of the Soul at Rest. On arriving at this stage, a person becomes capable of achieving complete prosperity. All passions of the self begin to wither and a strengthening breeze begins to blow upon the soul, so that the person concerned looks upon his previous weaknesses with remorse. At that time nature and habits experience a complete transformation and the person is drawn far away from his previous condition. He is washed and cleansed, and God inscribes love of virtue upon his heart and casts out from it the impurity of vice with His own hand. All the forces of truth enter the citadel of his heart, and righteousness occupies all the battlements of his nature, and truth become victorious and falsehood lays down its arms and is put to flight. The hand of God governs his heart and he walks under God's shadow. God Almighty has indicated all this in the following verses:

أُولَٰئِكَ كَتَبَ فِي قُلُوبِهِمُ الْإِيمَانَ وَأَيَّدَهُم بِرُوحٍ مِّنْهُ [56]

وَزَيَّنَهُ فِي قُلُوبِكُمْ وَكَرَّهَ إِلَيْكُمُ الْكُفْرَ وَالْفُسُوقَ وَالْعِصْيَانَ ۚ أُولَٰئِكَ
هُمُ الرَّاشِدُونَ ۝ فَضْلًا مِّنَ اللَّهِ وَنِعْمَةً ۚ وَاللَّهُ عَلِيمٌ حَكِيمٌ ۝ [57]

جَاءَ الْحَقُّ وَزَهَقَ الْبَاطِلُ ۚ إِنَّ الْبَاطِلَ كَانَ زَهُوقًا [58]

These verses mean that: ‘These are the ones in whose hearts Allah has inscribed faith with His own hand and whom He has helped with the Holy Spirit.’

‘O believers, Allah has made faith attractive to you and has instilled its beauty and grace in your hearts. And He has made your hearts averse to disbelief, wickedness and disobedience and has impressed upon your hearts the repugnance for evil ways. All this has come about through the grace and favour of Allah.’

‘Truth has arrived and falsehood has fled. How could falsehood ever stand up to truth.’

All this pertains to the spiritual states which a person attains at the third stage. No one can acquire true insight unless he arrives at this condition. The fact that God inscribes faith on their hearts with His own hand and helps them with the Holy Spirit means that no one can achieve true purity and righteousness without His help. At the stage of ‘the reproaching self’, a person repents time and again, yet he keeps falling down, and begins to despair and to consider his condition beyond remedy. He remains in this situation for a period and when the appointed time comes, a light which possesses Divine power descends upon him at night or during the day. With the descent of

---

[56] Al-Mujādalah, 58:23 **[Publisher]**

[57] Al-Ḥujurāt, 49:8-9 **[Publisher]**

[58] Banī Isrā’īl, 17:82 **[Publisher]**

that light, he undergoes a wonderful change and he perceives the control of a hidden hand, and beholds a wonderful world. At that time he realizes that God exists, and his eyes are filled with a light they did not possess before.

The question is, how shall we discover that path and how shall we acquire that light? Be it known that in this world every effect has a cause and behind every move there is a mover. For the acquisition of every type of knowledge there is an appointed way, called the straight path. Nothing can be achieved in this world without conformity to the rules that nature has laid down in this respect from the very beginning. The law of nature teaches us that to achieve any objective there is a straight path and that the objective in question can be achieved only by following that path. For instance, if we are sitting in a dark room, the straight path for obtaining the light of the sun is for us to open the window that faces the sun. When we do that, the light of the sun instantly enters the room and illuminates it. Thus it is obvious that for the acquisition of God's love and real grace there must be some window, and there must be an appointed method for the acquisition of pure spirituality. That way is that we should seek the straight path which leads to spirituality, just as we seek a straight path for the achievement of all other purposes. Does that method consist in seeking to meet God only through the exercise of our reason and by following our self-appointed ways? Can the doors that can only be opened by His powerful hands yield to our logic and philosophy? Can we find the Ever-Living and Self-Subsisting God through our own devices? Certainly not. The only straight path for the achievement of this purpose is that we should first devote our lives, together with all our faculties, to the cause of God Almighty, and should then occupy ourselves with supplication for meeting Him, and should thus find God through God Himself.

A Lovely Prayer

The most lovely prayer which instructs us concerning the time and occasion of supplication, and depicts before us the picture of spiritual zeal is the one that God, the Beneficent, has taught in the opening chapter of the Holy Qur'ān.

بِسۡمِ اللّٰہِ الرَّحۡمٰنِ الرَّحِیۡمِ ○ اَلۡحَمۡدُ لِلّٰہِ رَبِّ الۡعٰلَمِیۡنَ ○ [59]

'Every possible praise belongs to Allah alone, Who is the Creator and Sustainer of all the worlds.'

الرَّحۡمٰنِ الرَّحِیۡمِ ○ [60]

'He provides for us out of His mercy before any action proceeds from us, and after we have acted He rewards our actions out of His mercy.'

مٰلِکِ یَوۡمِ الدِّیۡنِ ○ [61]

'He alone is the Master of the Day of Judgement. He has not committed that day to anyone else.'

اِیَّاکَ نَعۡبُدُ وَ اِیَّاکَ نَسۡتَعِیۡنُ ○ [62]

'O You Who comprehends all these attributes, we worship You alone and seek Your help in all our affairs.'

The use of the plural pronoun 'we' in this context indicates that all our faculties are occupied in His worship

---

[59] Al-Fātiḥah, 1:1-2 **[Publisher]**

[60] Al-Fātiḥah, 1:3 **[Publisher]**

[61] Al-Fātiḥah, 1:4 **[Publisher]**

[62] Al-Fātiḥah, 1:5 **[Publisher]**

and are prostrate at His threshold. Every person by virtue of his inner faculties is a community and a nation. The prostration of one's entire faculties before God constitutes the condition referred to as Islām.

اِهْدِنَا الصِّرَاطَ الْمُسْتَقِيْمَ ۝ صِرَاطَ الَّذِيْنَ اَنْعَمْتَ عَلَيْهِمْ [63]

'Guide us along the straight path and establish us firmly on it; show us the path of those on whom You have bestowed Your bounties and favours.'

غَيْرِ الْمَغْضُوْبِ عَلَيْهِمْ وَلَا الضَّآلِّيْنَ ۝ [64]

'And save us from the paths of those who incur Your wrath, and could not reach You and lost their way.'

Āmīn. O Allah, accept our supplication.

These verses tell us that Divine bounties and favours are bestowed only upon those who offer their lives as sacrifice in the cause of God and, devoting themselves wholly to and being occupied entirely with His pleasure, continue to supplicate so that they might be granted all the spiritual bounties that a human being can receive by way of nearness to God, meeting Him and hearing His words. With this supplication they worship God through all their faculties, eschew sin and remain prostrate at His threshold. They safeguard themselves against all vice and shun the ways of God's wrath. As they seek God with high resolve and perfect sincerity, they find Him and are filled with the cups of Divine knowledge....

Steadfastness in Faith

The true and perfect grace that conveys a person to the

---

[63] Al-Fātiḥah, 1:6-7 **[Publisher]**

[64] Al-Fātiḥah, 1:7 **[Publisher]**

spiritual world depends upon absolute steadfastness, by which is meant the degree of sincerity and faithfulness that cannot be shaken by any trial. It means a relationship with the Divine, which should be so strong that it cannot be cut by a sword or consumed by fire or damaged by any other calamity. The death of dear ones or separation from them should not interfere with it, nor should fear of dishonour affect it, nor should a painful death move the heart away from it in the least degree. Thus this door is very narrow and this path is very hard. Alas, how difficult this is! Alas, how very difficult!!

This is indicated by Allah the Glorious in the following verse:

قُلْ إِنْ كَانَ آبَاؤُكُمْ وَأَبْنَاؤُكُمْ وَإِخْوَانُكُمْ وَأَزْوَاجُكُمْ وَعَشِيرَتُكُمْ
وَأَمْوَالٌ اقْتَرَفْتُمُوهَا وَتِجَارَةٌ تَخْشَوْنَ كَسَادَهَا وَمَسَاكِنُ تَرْضَوْنَهَا
أَحَبَّ إِلَيْكُمْ مِنَ اللّٰهِ وَرَسُولِهِ وَجِهَادٍ فِي سَبِيلِهِ فَتَرَبَّصُوا حَتَّى يَأْتِيَ اللّٰهُ
بِأَمْرِهِ ۗ وَاللّٰهُ لَا يَهْدِي الْقَوْمَ الْفَاسِقِينَ ۝ [65]

Meaning that: 'Tell them: If your fathers and your sons and your brethren and your wives and your kinsfolk and the wealth that you have acquired with great effort, and the trade the dullness of which you apprehend, and the dwellings that you fancy, are dearer to you than Allah and His Messenger and striving in His cause, then wait until Allah pronounces His Judgement. Allah will never guide the disobedient people.'

This verse clearly shows that people who put aside the will of God and give preference to their relatives and their properties, are evildoers in the estimation of God. They will surely be ruined because they preferred

---

[65] Al-Taubah, 9:24 **[Publisher]**

something to God.

This is the third stage in which a person becomes godly who welcomes thousands of calamities for the sake of God, and leans towards Him with such sincerity and devotion, as if he has no one related to him except God, and all others have died. The truth is that until we submit ourselves to death we cannot behold the Living God. The day our physical life undergoes death is the day of the manifestation of God. We are blind until we become blind to the sight of all besides God. We are dead until we become like a corpse in the hand of God. It is only when we face God completely that we acquire the steadfastness that overcomes all passions of the self; and such steadfastness brings about the death of the life which is devoted to selfish purposes.

[Islāmī Uṣūl kī Philosophy, Rūḥānī Khazā'in, vol. 10, pp. 377-383]

Personal Merit and Relationship with God

There are three types of people who partake of heavenly signs. First there are those who possess no merit in themselves and have no relationship with God Almighty. On account of their intellectual appropriateness they experience true dreams and visions that are not characterized by any sign indicating their acceptability to God and their being loved by Him, nor are they of any benefit for them. Thousands of wicked and vicious people share such experiences with them. It is often observed that despite such dreams and visions their conduct is not praiseworthy and their faith is very weak, so much so that they do not have the courage to bear true witness and they do not fear God as much as they fear the world and they cannot separate themselves from the wicked. They dare not bear such true testimony as might offend a person of high status. They are slothful and lazy in respect of religious obligations and are wholly preoccupied with worldly anxieties and grief. They deliberately support falsehood and abandon truth. They are guilty of dishonesty at every step and some of them do not even restrain themselves from vice and sin and have recourse to every unlawful device for the purpose of acquiring worldly benefits. The moral condition of some of them is deplorable and they are riddled with envy, miserliness, self-conceit, arrogance and pride. They have recourse to every meanness and are characterized with diverse types of shameful ills. Some of them see only evil dreams, of which a number come true, as if their brains have been fashioned only for evil and ill-omened dreams. They are not capable of having dreams that benefit them or indicate something good for another person. Their dreams are of a category which might be described as resembling the experience of a person who perceives smoke from a distance but sees neither the light of the fire nor feels its warmth. Such people have nothing to do with God and spiritual matters; they have been given only smoke which yields no light.

The second category of people who see true dreams or receive revelations are those who have some relationship with God but that relationship is not perfect. Their dreams and revelations resemble the experience of a person who perceives the light of fire from a long distance in a dark and cold night, which enables him to avoid potholes, thorns, rocks, serpents and wild beasts, but which cannot save him from dying of cold. If such a person does not arrive within the warm circle of the fire, he is also destroyed in the same manner as the one who walks in the dark.

The third category of people who experience true dreams

and revelations can be compared to a man, who, on a dark and cold night, is not only guided by the bright light of a fire, but actually enters its warm circle, and is fully safeguarded against the effects of the cold. Only those people arrive at this stage who burn up the garment of low passions in the fire of love for the Divine and adopt a life of bitterness for the sake of God. They perceive death ahead of them and run forward to meet it. They accept every torment in the cause of God. For the sake of God, they become enemies of their ego and exhibit such a degree of strength of faith against it that even angels marvel at it. They are spiritual champions and all satanic assaults prove utterly ineffective against their spiritual strength. They are truly faithful and devoted. Scenes of worldly pleasures cannot mislead them nor can they be turned away from their True Beloved by their love of wife and children. In short, no bitterness can frighten them nor can any physical pleasure bar their approach towards God. No relationship can disrupt their relationship with God.

There are three spiritual grades, of which the first is called certainty by inference, the second is called certainty by sight, and the third blessed and perfect condition is called certainty by experience. Human comprehension cannot become perfect nor can it be washed clean of all impurities until it arrives at the stage of certainty by experience, since this stage does not depend only on observation, but envelops the human heart as an immediate experience; and the seeker, plunging into the flaming fire of Divine love, totally negates his ego. At this stage human comprehension moves from theory to experience and the lower life is utterly consumed. Such a man is seated in the lap of God Almighty. Just as a piece of iron, when heated in fire, assumes the appearance and qualities of fire, in the same way, a seeker who has arrived at this stage is invested reflectively with Divine attributes. He surrenders himself so completely to the pleasure of God that he speaks under the direction of God, sees under the direction of God, hears under the direction of God, and moves under the direction of God, as if there is only God inside his mantle. His humanity is completely subordinated to Divine manifestations. This subject is delicate and is above common understanding; I shall, therefore, not explore it further.

[Ḥaqīqat-ul-Waḥī, Rūḥānī Khazā'in, vol. 22, pp. 22-25]

Stages of Spiritual Fulfilment

The word *Aflaḥa* is repeated six times in these verses[66]. In the first verse its use is explicit as is said:

قَدْ اَفْلَحَ الْمُؤْمِنُوْنَ ۝ الَّذِيْنَ هُمْ فِيْ صَلَاتِهِمْ خٰشِعُوْنَ ۝ [67]

In the other verses it is expressed through the conjunctive. In the lexicon the meaning of *Aflaḥa* is اُصِيْرَ اِلَى الْفَلَاحِ i.e., one was turned towards his object of success and made to move towards it. According to this meaning, the first move of a believer towards achieving his objective is humility in his prayer, an act that involves the abandonment of pride and arrogance. The objective attained thereby is that the self adopts the habit of humbleness and becomes ready and attuned to establishing a relationship with God.

The second step towards fulfilment is the abandonment

---

[66] The reference is to the opening verses of Sūrah Al-Mu'minūn, the twenty-third chapter of the Holy Qur'an. **[Publisher]**

[67] 'Surely, success does come to the believers, who are humble in their Prayers.'—Al-Mu'minūn, 23:2-3 **[Publisher]**

of vain thinking and pursuits, for until a believer acquires the strength to abandon vain pursuits for the sake of God, which is not a difficult matter, it is unreasonable to expect that he will be able to turn away from such pursuits from which he derives some benefit or pleasure, and which are difficult to abandon. This shows that after the abandonment of pride the next step is the giving up of vain pursuits in consequence of which some relationship is established with God Almighty and, as a result, faith becomes stronger than before. This relationship is feeble because the relationship with vain pursuits is also feeble and by discarding a weak relationship one is rewarded with a relationship which is also weak.

The third step towards spiritual fulfilment is to spend one's wealth in the cause of Allah, which is a greater sacrifice than turning away from vain pursuits, as wealth is earned with effort and is something useful, and is also a source of prosperity and comfort. This sacrifice requires stronger faith than the giving up of vain pursuits. Consequently, faith is strengthened further and the relationship with God is likewise fostered. This purifies the self because the sacrifice of wealth for the sake of God is not possible without such purification.

The fourth step is the restraint of passions against unlawful indulgence, which is a stronger attachment than attachment to wealth, for wealth is spent in the pursuit of one's passions. To control passion for the sake of God is a greater sacrifice than the sacrifice of wealth. Consequently, the abandonment of the pursuit of passions strengthens relationship with God, for whatever a person gives up for the sake of God, he is granted something better in its place.

لطف او ترك طالباں نه كند　　كس به كار ہش زیاں نه كند
ہر كه آں راه جست یافته است　　تافت آں رو كه سر نتافته است [68]

The fifth step is to discard the ego altogether in the cause of God. This means to render back to God that which has been committed to one as a trust. At this stage a believer is required to modify his relationship to everything that is bestowed upon him as if all of it were a trust to be devoted to the cause of God. This is the meaning of the verse:

وَالَّذِيْنَ هُمْ لِاَمٰنٰتِهِمْ وَعَهْدِهِمْ رٰعُوْنَ ۝ [69]

A person's life and wealth and all his sources of comfort are trusts committed to him by God; rendering them back is obligatory on the trustee. The sacrifice of the ego, therefore, means that the trust should be rendered back to God Almighty, and also that one's covenant of faith with God should be duly fulfilled and the obligations that one owes to his fellow beings should be fully discharged as a true sacrifice, inasmuch as the complete fulfilment of all aspects of righteousness also amounts to a type of death. In this context fulfilment means that when a believer spends his life in the cause of God and carries into effect all aspects of righteousness, Divine lights envelop his being and invest him with spiritual beauty, as the bones are rendered beautiful by being clothed in flesh.... Both

---

[68] His grace does not forsake the seekers;
In His path no one suffers loss.
Whoever seeks this path, finds it;
Bright becomes the face that does not turn away from Him.
[Publisher]

[69] 'And who are watchful of their trusts and their covenants.'—Al-Mu'minūn, 23:9 **[Publisher]**

these states have been described by God Almighty as garments. Righteousness too has been described as a garment, as Allah says:

لِبَاسُ التَّقْوٰى[70]

The flesh with which the bones are clothed has also been described as a garment, as Allah says:

فَكَسَوْنَا الْعِظٰمَ لَحْمًا[71]

…. It should be remembered that the fifth stage is the final stage of the spiritual journey. When that stage reaches perfection, it is followed by the sixth stage, which is a pure bounty, and is bestowed upon the believer without any further effort or toil. Effort has nothing to do with it. In other words, just as the believer forsakes his self for the sake of God, and is granted a new soul….; in the same way, a believer who dedicates his life to the cause of God out of personal love for God, is honoured with the spirit of God's personal love which is accompanied by the Holy Spirit. God's personal love is a spirit and the Holy Spirit is not something apart from it; there is no separation between God's love and the Holy Spirit. That is why we have mostly mentioned God's personal love without mentioning the Holy Spirit, inasmuch as the two are essential to each other. When this spirit descends upon a believer, worship ceases to be a burden, and he is invested with such strength and pleasure that it prompts him to worship and remember God out of the eagerness of love and not through conscious effort. Such a believer continuously attends upon

---

[70] 'Raiment of Righteousness.'—Al-A'rāf 7:27 **[Publisher]**

[71] 'Then We clothed the bones with flesh.'—Al-Mu'minūn.—23:15 **[Publisher]**

the threshold of God, like the angel Gabriel, and is granted permanent nearness of the Lord of Honour, as God Almighty has said:

وَالَّذِيْنَ هُمْ عَلٰى صَلَوٰتِهِمْ يُحَافِظُوْنَ ۝[72]

That is: 'The perfect believers are those who are ever present before God and themselves guard their prayers.'

At that stage a believer deems his prayer essential for nurturing his spiritual life without which he cannot survive. This stage cannot be achieved without the spirit which descends from God Almighty upon a believer. When a believer discards his life for the sake of God Almighty he deserves to be given a new life.

All this shows that according to sane reason, these are the six stages which have to be traversed by a believer who seeks the perfection of his spiritual being, and even cursory reflection would show that a believer must pass through six conditions during the course of his spiritual journey. The reason for this is that until a person succeeds in establishing a perfect relationship with God, his imperfect ego loves five vicious conditions, and the discarding of the love of each condition requires a motive which should enable him to overcome that love so that a new love may take its place.

The first condition which a person loves is one of heedlessness in which he is at a distance from God Almighty. His ego is in a sort of disbelief, and he is drawn towards arrogance and hard-heartedness and does not at all partake of humility and meekness and lowliness. He loves this condition and regards it as the best for himself.

---

[72] Al-Mu'minūn, 23:10 **[Publisher]**

When Divine favour designs his reform, some event or calamity impresses the grandeur and fear and power of God Almighty upon his heart, in consequence of which he becomes humble and his love of pride, arrogance and heedlessness is altogether wiped out. It is often observed that when the whip of Divine terror strikes in a fearful manner, it bends down the necks of even daring evildoers; it awakens them from the slumber of heedlessness and makes them humble and meek. This is the first stage of turning to God available to a fortunate one through observing Divine grandeur and awe or through some other means. Although he loved his heedless and unrestrained life, he has to give it up as it yields to a stronger and opposite influence.

The second condition is that though such a believer does turn towards God Almighty in some measure, this change is still affected by the impurity of vain talk, actions and pursuits that he loves. He sometimes experiences humility in prayer but vain pursuits and associations and indulgences continue to preoccupy him. In a sense he oscillates between two states.

واعظاں کیں جلوہ بر محراب و ممبر مے کنند

چوں بخلوت مے روند آں کار دیگر مے کنند [73]

Thereafter, if Divine favour wishes to save him from ruin, another greater manifestation of Divine grandeur, awe and power descends upon his heart which strengthens his faith and consumes all his vain thoughts and tendencies. It generates in his heart such love for the Lord of Honour as overcomes his love for vain pursuits

---

[73] *The preachers who put up a great show on the pulpit;*
Indulge in different kinds of activity in privacy. **[Publisher]**

and preoccupations and displaces them with the result that his heart becomes disgusted with such deeds.

A third evil condition which still afflicts the believer and which is dearer to him than the second, is his natural love of wealth, which he considers the support and comfort of his life and which he conceives as having been achieved through his own effort and striving. For this reason, he finds it very difficult and bitter to part from his wealth in the cause of God.

When Divine favour desires to rescue him from this tremendous involvement, he is given knowledge of the providence of God and the seed of trust in God is sown in his heart. This is supplemented by the awe of the Divine, and these two manifestations of beauty and glory take possession of his heart; in consequence the love of wealth departs from his heart and the seed of the love of the Bestower of wealth is sown in its place. Thereby his faith is further strengthened beyond the degree of faith which he enjoyed in the previous stages, inasmuch as at this stage he not only discards all things vain, but also gives up the wealth on which he thinks his present life depends. If his faith had not been strengthened with the support of trust in God, and his eyes had not been directed towards the True Providence, he could not have been cured of the malady of miserliness. Thus this power of faith not only rescues him from indulgence in all vanity, but also creates a strong faith in the providence of God and illumines the heart with the light of trust in God. He can now spend his wealth, of which he had been enamoured, very easily and cheerfully in the cause of God, and the weakness which results from the despair of miserliness is totally replaced by eager hope in God Almighty; and the love of wealth is overcome by the love of the Bestower of wealth.

This is followed by the fourth condition which is so dearly loved by *Nafs-e-Ammārah* [the self that incites to evil] and which is much worse than the third condition in which only wealth had to be discarded. In this condition, the unlawful passions of the ego have to be eschewed. The sacrifice of wealth is naturally easier for a person than the discarding of his carnal passions. Therefore this condition is more terrible and dangerous than the previous one. Witness the verse:

وَلَقَدْ هَمَّتْ بِهٖ وَهَمَّ بِهَا لَوْلَآ اَنْ رَّاٰ بُرْهَانَ رَبِّهٖ [74]

This means that carnal passion is so fierce an urge that its restraint needs a strong sign. Thus it is obvious that the power of faith in the fourth stage is much stronger than it is in the third stage, and the manifestation of Divine grandeur, awe and power is also greater. At this stage it is also necessary that the prohibited pleasure should be substituted by a spiritual pleasure. As strong faith in the providence of God Almighty is needed to cure miserliness, and a strong feeling of trust is required when the pocket is empty so that miserliness may be repelled and hope may be fixed on the opening of hidden sources, in the same way, for deliverance from carnal passions and the extinguishing of the fire of lust, it is necessary to have strong faith in the fire which affects both body and soul with severe torment. Also needed is a taste of the spiritual delight which renders these murky pleasures unattractive and dispensable.

---

[74] 'And she made up her mind with regard to him, and he made up his mind with regard to her. If he had not seen a manifest sign of his Lord, *he could not have shown such determination.*'—Yūsuf, 12:25 **[Publisher]**

A person who is in the grip of carnal passion is, as it were, caught in the mouth of a most poisonous serpent. Thus, as the malady of miserliness is graver than the malady of indulgence in vain pursuits, in the same way being caught in the grip of carnal passions is graver than the malady of miserliness, and is a severer calamity than all other calamities, and needs the special mercy of God Almighty to be delivered from it. When God Almighty designs to deliver someone from this calamity, He visits him with such a manifestation of His grandeur, awe and power, as grinds down all carnal passions and invests his heart with eagerness for His own love along with a manifestation of beauty. Just as a suckling baby, on being weaned, passes a restless night or two, and soon forgets its mother's milk and turns away from suckling even if the mother presents her breast to him, in the same way, a righteous one is disgusted with carnal passions when he is weaned away from the milk of desire and is granted spiritual nourishment in its place.

This is followed by the fifth condition, the disorders of which are dearly loved by the self that incites to evil. At this stage only one struggle is left and the time approaches near when the angels of God would conquer the whole territory of the ego and would bring it under their complete control, and, disrupting the whole system of the ego, would ruin the territory of carnal faculties and humiliate its chieftains and destroy their kingdom. For that is what happens when a kingdom is destroyed, as it is said:

إِنَّ الْمُلُوكَ إِذَا دَخَلُوا قَرْيَةً أَفْسَدُوهَا وَجَعَلُوا
أَعِزَّةَ أَهْلِهَا أَذِلَّةً ۚ وَكَذَٰلِكَ يَفْعَلُونَ ۝ [75]

---

[75] 'Surely, kings, when they enter a country, despoil it, and turn the

This is the last trial for a believer and is the last struggle with which all stages of his journey come to an end. His progress, through his effort and striving, arrives at its climax and human effort completes its operation up to its last limit. Thereafter, there is only bounty and grace, which is described as a new creation. This fifth condition is even more difficult than the fourth. In the fourth condition the believer has to discard unlawful passions but in the fifth condition he has to surrender his self altogether and to restore it to God Almighty as a trust which had been committed to his care. Devoting himself wholly to the work of God, he should make his ego serve on His behalf, be determined to spend it in the cause of Allah, and strive to negate his self altogether, for, as long as the self persists, sinful tendencies also continue—a condition which is inconsistent with righteousness. Besides, so long as the self persists, it is not possible for man to tread along the finer paths of righteousness or to discharge fully the trusts and covenants of God and His creatures. But as miserliness cannot be discarded without trust in God and faith in His providence, and deliverance cannot be achieved from illicit passions without the supremacy of Divine awe and grandeur and the substitution of spiritual delights, in the same way this grand rank where the self is discarded and all trust restored to God Almighty, cannot be attained until a fierce wind of the love of God begins to blow and renders a person madly devoted to the cause of Allah. These are, in truth, the pre-occupations of those who are inebriated with the love of God. These are not the pursuits of the worldly wise.

---

highest of its people into the lowest. And thus will they do.'—Al-Naml, 27:35 **[Publisher]**

آسماں بارامانت نتوانست کشید
قرعهٔ فال بنام من دیوانه زدند [76]

Almighty Allah points towards this, saying:

إِنَّا عَرَضْنَا الْأَمَانَةَ عَلَى السَّمٰوٰتِ وَالْأَرْضِ وَالْجِبَالِ فَأَبَيْنَ أَنْ يَحْمِلْنَهَا
وَأَشْفَقْنَ مِنْهَا وَحَمَلَهَا الْإِنْسَانُ إِنَّهُ كَانَ ظَلُومًا جَهُولًا ۝ [77]

'We presented Our trust, which must be rendered back to Us, to all those who dwell in the earth and in heaven but all of them refused to accept it, out of apprehension lest a default should ensue, but man accepted this trust as he was *ẓalūm* [firm] and *jahūl* [oblivious of consequences.]'

The two terms (*ẓalūm* and *jahūl*) are used for man as a compliment and not in a derogatory sense. They signify that man had been endowed with the capacity of being harsh upon his own self for the sake of God and could incline towards Him and be oblivious of his own being. Therefore, he accepted the responsibility of treating his entire being as a trust to be expended in His cause.

The requirement laid down for the fifth stage in the verse is:

وَالَّذِيْنَ هُمْ لِأَمٰنٰتِهِمْ وَعَهْدِهِمْ رَاعُوْنَ ۝ [78]

This means that: 'The believers are those who are watchful of their trusts and covenants.' That is to say, in discharging their trusts and covenants they spare no effort in exercising righteousness and watchfulness.

This is an indication that man and all his faculties, the

---

[76] *The heavens could not bear the burden of the trust;*
It fell to my lot to carry it, for I cared not of the consequences.
[Publisher]

[77] Al-Aḥzāb, 33:73 **[Publisher]**

[78] Al-Mu'minūn, 23:9 **[Publisher]**

vision of his eyes, the hearing of his ears, the speech of his tongue, and the strength of his hands and feet are all but a trust committed to him by God Almighty, and He can take them back whenever He so wills. Being watchful of these trusts means devoting all the faculties of the spirit and the body to the service of God Almighty while observing all the requirements of righteousness as if they all belong not to man but to God and their movement and operation is not directed by his will but by the will of God. One should have no design of one's own, and only God's will should work through all his faculties. His self in the hands of God should be like a corpse in the hands of the living. His own will should be excluded and the complete control of God Almighty should be established over his being, so much so, that by Him should he see, and by Him should he hear, and by Him should he speak, and by Him should he move or remain passive. The minutest impurities of the ego, which cannot be observed even through a microscope, should be removed, leaving only the pure spirit. In short, the guardianship of God should envelop him and should isolate him from his own being. He should cease to direct his being and all direction should come from God. His personal desires should be wiped out and should be replaced by Divine designs. The previous governance of his being should be totally displaced by another. The habitation of the ego should be destroyed and the camp of the Divine should be established in its place. Divine awe and power should uproot all the plants that were watered from the foul spring of the ego, and replant them in the pure soil of the pleasure of God. All his desires and designs should be subordinated to God, and all the structures of the self that incites to evil should be demolished and laid in the dust, and a palace of purity and holiness should be erected in the heart which should become the habitation of the Lord of Honour. Only then could it be said that a person has restored those trusts that the Bountiful has committed to him, and has fulfilled the purpose of the verse:

وَالَّذِيْنَ هُمْ لِاَمٰنٰتِهِمْ وَعَهْدِهِمْ رٰعُوْنَ ۝ [79]

At this stage a framework is prepared and the spirit of Divine manifestation, which means the personal love of the Divine, enters into the believer together with the Holy Spirit and bestows a new life and a new power upon him. All this happens under the influence of the spirit which, at this stage, establishes a relationship with the believer but does not yet take up its abode in his heart.

This is followed by the sixth spiritual stage in which the personal love of the believer reaches its climax and draws to itself the personal love of Allah the Exalted. Thereupon the personal love of God Almighty enters into the believer and envelops him, in consequence of which he is granted a new and extraordinary power. That power generates such life in his faith as a soul creates in the lifeless body. All faculties are illumined by it, and the believer is so inspired by the Holy Spirit, that he is given access to matters and to knowledge that are above normal human conception. At this stage the believer, having traversed all stages of the progress of faith, is designated in heaven as the vicegerent of God, on account of the excellences with which he is invested and which partake of Divine qualities.

When a person stands before a mirror, all his features are

---

[79] Ibid.

reflected in it; similarly, a believer who completely discards his ego so that no part of his own being survives, becomes like a mirror and all the features and qualities of the Divine are reflected in him. It can be said that the mirror, which reflects all the features of the one standing before it, becomes his vicegerent; in the same way a believer, by reflecting Divine qualities, becomes a vicegerent of God and reflects Divine features. As God is Hidden beyond hidden and is transcendent in His Being, in the same way, a perfect believer becomes hidden and transcendent in his being. The world cannot appreciate his reality as he is placed far away from the sphere of the world. It is a wonderful thing that after this holy change in the perfect believer, when he loses his self altogether for the sake of God and emerges in a new garment of holiness, God, Who is Unchangeable and Ever-Living and Self-Subsisting, too appears to him in a new guise. This does not mean that any change takes place in the eternal attributes of the Divine. He is eternally unchangeable, but there is a new Divine manifestation for the perfect believer.

When the believer brings about a change in himself, a change manifests itself in the Divine, the nature of which we cannot fathom. This happens in such a manner that God's unchangeable Being is not affected by the dust of events. He remains unchangeable as ever.

It is a change of the type as has been mentioned, that when a believer moves towards God Almighty, the Almighty moves much more swiftly towards him, though it is obvious that as the Divine is not subject to change, He is also not subject to movement. All these expressions are metaphorical and the need for their use arises because experience testifies that as a believer assumes a new being by discarding his ego in the cause of God, God also assumes a new aspect vis-à-vis the believer, and deals with him in an exclusive manner. God reveals to him of His kingdom and mysteries that which He does not reveal to others, and displays for his sake that which He does not display for the sake of others. He helps and succours him in a manner that causes people to marvel. He manifests extraordinary happenings for such a person, and works miracles in his support and establishes his supremacy from every point of view. He invests him with a strange kind of magnetism, whereby a whole world is drawn to him and only those remain unaffected who are eternally unfortunate.

All this shows that when a true believer carries out a holy change in himself, God Almighty also appears to him with a new kind of manifestation. This is proof that God has created man for Himself, and when man turns towards God Almighty, from that very moment God turns towards him and becomes his Guardian, his Providence, his Supporter, and his Helper. If the whole world were to be on one side and a true believer on the other, it is the believer who would stand supreme, because God is true in His love and always fulfils His promises. He does not let one who becomes His to be destroyed. Such a believer when thrown into the fire finds himself in a garden; and when pushed into a whirlpool emerges in a beautiful orchard. His enemies design stratagems against him to destroy him, but God frustrates all their plans and projects, for He is with him at every step. In the end, those who seek to humiliate him die in disgrace and end in failure, but he who becomes God's with his whole heart and soul and determination, never dies without realizing his desires. His life is blessed and is prolonged till he achieves his purpose. All blessings are by virtue of sincerity and all sincerity is in seeking the pleasure of God, and all seeking of God's pleasure ensues from discarding one's own pleasure. This is the death which is followed by life. Blessed is he who partakes of this life.

[Brāhīn-e-Aḥmadiyyah, part V, Rūḥānī Khazā'in, vol. 21, pp. 230-243]

Excellences of the Men of God

The excellences of the men of God who have a relationship of love and friendship with Him are not confined to prophecies alone. Verities are disclosed to them and they are granted spiritual comprehension. The wonders and mysteries of the Shariah and proofs of the truth of Islām are revealed to them. The inner meanings of the Holy Qur'ān and the fine points of the Word of God are miraculously conveyed to them. They become heirs to miraculous wonders and heavenly knowledge both of which are bestowed directly upon those whom God loves. They are favoured with special love and are invested with devotion and sincerity like Abraham[as]. The Holy Spirit is reflected in their hearts. They become God's and God becomes theirs. Their prayers bring about extraordinary results. God's jealousy is roused in their support. They are blessed with victory over their opponents in every field. Their countenances shine with the light of Divine love. God's mercy comes down upon their dwellings like rain. Like a beloved child, they rest in the lap of God. God displays greater wrath in their support than a wild tigress whose young is threatened. They are protected against sin, attacks of the enemies, and errors of teaching. They are the kings of heaven. God hears their supplications in a wonderful manner, so much so that kings have recourse to them. The Lord of Glory resides in their hearts. They are invested with a Divine prestige and their countenances display royal self-sufficiency. They consider the world and its inhabitants to be less than a dead insect. They know only the One and melt under His fear every moment. The world falls at their feet, and it is as if God manifests Himself in human form. They are the light of the world and the pillar of this mortal universe. They are the princes of true peace and they are the sun that dispels darkness. They are hidden beyond hidden and no one truly recognizes them, except God, and no one truly recognizes God except themselves. They are not God but it cannot be said that they are distinct from God. They are not immortal but it cannot be said that they die. Can a wicked person, whose heart and thoughts and life are foul, ever resemble them? Certainly not, except for such resemblance as a shining pebble may sometimes have with a diamond.

When men of God appear in the world, a type of spirituality descends from heaven on account of the blessings that they enjoy and all temperaments are activated, and those whose hearts and minds have affinity with true dreams begins to experience such dreams and visions, as when rain brings down water from the sky the subsoil water also rises, and every kind of vegetation begin to sprout. On the contrary, if rain is held back over a period of time, the water in the wells also dries up. Thus the men of God are in fact heavenly water and with their coming the waters of the earth also swell.

[Toḥfah-e-Golarhviyyah, Rūḥānī Khazā'in, vol. 17, pp. 170-172]

Comprehension of the Divine

The fifth excellent element of *Sūrah Al-Fātiḥah* is that it comprises the complete and perfect teaching which is needed by a seeker after truth and which constitutes a perfect code of conduct for progress towards nearness to God and comprehension of the Divine. Such progress begins from the point when the seeker, purely for the sake of God, imposing a death upon his ego and submitting to hardship and pain, discards all those desires of the flesh which constitute a barrier between him and his Master. Such desires turn his face away from God, directing it towards personal enjoyments, physical emotions, habits, thoughts, designs, other creatures and involve him in their fears and hopes. The average degree of progress is that all the effort that has to be made for the suppression of the self and all the pain that has to be endured in discarding familiar habits should appear as bounties, and labour should be perceived as delight and pain should be felt as comfort, and constraint should be appreciated as cheerfulness. The higher grade of progress is that the seeker should cultivate such union, love, and accord with God and His will and designs that his self ceases to have an identity and influence of its own. The Being and attributes of God should be reflected in the mirror of his own being without any trace of darkness or suspicion through perfect surrender, which should create the utmost inconsistency between the seeker and his personal desires so that the reflection of the Being and attributes of the Divine should become clearly visible. In this statement there is not a single word that endorses the false theories of *Wujūdīs*[80], or of the Vedāntists[81], because these people do not recognize the essential and eternal distinction between the Creator and His creation.

---

[80] Those who believe that God and the material world are one and the same thing. **[Publisher]**

[81] Believers in the Vedic doctrine of the eternity of souls. **[Publisher]**

They have been grievously misled by their doubtful visions which are often experienced in a condition of imperfect progress, or result from practices which induce a type of insanity, or those who, in a condition in which they are not in full possession of their senses, overlook the difference that subsists between the Divine and the human spirit in respect of powers, faculties, qualities and holiness. It is obvious that the Almighty Whose eternal knowledge comprehends the smallest particle and to Whom no defect or default can be attributed and Who is free from every type of ignorance, stain, weakness, grief, sorrow, pain and commitment, cannot in essence be the same as one who is subject to all these deficiencies. Can man, who for his spiritual progress is subject to many contingencies which have no limit, be the same or identical with that Perfect Being Who is subject to no contingency? Can he who is mortal and whose soul suffers from the obvious deficiencies of creation, with all his stains and weaknesses and impurities and defects and shortcomings, be the equal of the Lord of glorious attributes Who is eternally perfect on account of holy excellences and qualities?

سُبْحٰنَهٗ وَتَعٰلٰى عَمَّا يَصِفُوْنَ [82]

What we mean by this third stage of progress is that in that stage the seeker surrenders himself so completely to the love of God and that Perfect Being approaches so close to him with all His perfect attributes, that the manifestations of Divinity overcome his personal desires to such a degree that he develops a complete dissociation

---

[82] 'Holy is He and exalted *far* above what they attribute *to Him*.'—Al-An'ām, 6:101 **[Publisher]**

from and enmity with his personal emotions as well as with everyone who is subject to such emotions.

The difference between this stage and the second stage is that though in the second stage also complete accord is established between the will of the seeker and the will of God and the pain that proceeds from God is felt as a bounty, yet his relationship with God is not such as to charge him with personal enmity towards everything beside God, so that the love of God should not merely be the goal of the heart but should become its characteristic. In short, in the second stage accord with God and opposition to all beside Him is the goal of the seeker and he finds pleasure in the achievement of that goal, but in the third stage of progress these two become an integral part of his being from which he cannot depart under any circumstances, because it is not possible for something to be separated from itself. On the contrary such departure is possible in the second stage. So long as the sainthood of a seeker does not arrive at the third stage it is not permanent and is not secure against peril, the reason being that so long as the love of God and opposition to all beside Him does not become characteristic of a person, some traces of wrong linger in him because he has still not fully discharged his obligations to Providence and falls short of perfect *liqā'*. But when the love of God and accord with His will saturate his being, so much so that God becomes his ears with which he hears, and becomes his eyes with which he sees, and becomes his hands with which he grips, and becomes his feet with which he walks, then there is left in him not a trace of wrong and he becomes secure against every hazard. This stage is indicated in the verse:

اَلَّذِيْنَ اٰمَنُوْا وَلَمْ يَلْبِسُوْٓا اِيْمَانَهُمْ بِظُلْمٍ

أُولَٰٓئِكَ لَهُمُ الْأَمْنُ وَهُمْ مُّهْتَدُوْنَ۝ [83]

It should be realized that these three grades of progress which are the root of all knowledge and comprehension, and indeed are the essence of faith, are set out in the *Sūrah Al-Fātiḥah* beautifully and in the most orderly manner. The first stage of progress which is the preliminary step towards nearness to God has been inculcated in the verse:

اِهْدِنَا الصِّرَاطَ الْمُسْتَقِيْمَ۝ [84]

To abandon every kind of misguidance and to turn wholly to God by adopting the straight path is to climb the steep hill which has been described as *fanā*, inasmuch as to discard at one stroke all familiar ways and habits and to abandon suddenly all personal desires to which one has been subject all one's life and to turn straight towards God, away from all considerations of repute and honour and self-esteem and showing off, deeming everything beside Allah as non-existent, is an enterprise that amounts to death. Such a death is the source of spiritual birth. Until a grain is buried in the earth and gives up its shape, it is impossible for a new grain to come into being. In the same way the body of spiritual birth is created from the death which is *fanā*. As the ego is defeated and its operation and will and its turning towards creatures are progressively obliterated, so do the limbs of spiritual birth go on being fashioned until, when complete annihilation of self is achieved, he is given the robe of the sec-

---

[83] 'Those who believe and mix not up their belief with injustice; it is they who shall have peace and who are rightly guided.'—Al-An'ām, 6:83 **[Publisher]**

[84] 'Guide us in the straight path.'—Al-Fātiḥah, 1:6 **[Publisher]**

ond being and then comes the time of:

ثُمَّ اَنْشَاْنٰهُ خَلْقًا اٰخَرَ [85]

As this complete effacement is not possible without the help and the special attention of the All-Powerful, therefore this supplication has been taught:

اِهْدِنَا الصِّرَاطَ الْمُسْتَقِيْمَ [86]

which means 'Lord! establish us along the straight path and deliver us from every type of misguidance.'

This steadfastness and treading along the straight path, which we are commanded to seek, is a hard enterprise and at first it appears to the seeker like the attack of a lion that must prove fatal. But if the seeker is steadfast and accepts this death, there is no death for him after that. God is too Noble to confront him again with the blazing fires of hell. In short this perfect steadfastness is the *fanā* [death] which completely demolishes the whole system of the being of a servant of God. He has to withdraw suddenly and totally from every type of desire, lust, design and selfish pursuit. This is the stage where human effort and human striving are in the forefront and all the labours of the saints and the seekers arrive at their climax. Thereafter follow heavenly bounties in which no human effort is involved and God Himself provides a hidden chariot and heavenly charger for viewing the heavenly wonders.

The second step in the progress towards nearness of God is indicated in the verse:

---

[85] 'Then we developed it into another creation.'—Al-Mu'minūn 23:15 **[Publisher]**

[86] Al-Fātiḥah, 1:6 **[Publisher]**

صِرَاطَ الَّذِيْنَ اَنْعَمْتَ عَلَيْهِمْ [87]

'Guide us along the path of those on whom Thou hast bestowed Thy favours.'

It should be remembered that those who are the recipients of the overt and covert bounties of God are not exempt from suffering. Indeed they are afflicted with such calamities and torments that would have destroyed altogether the faith of another. They are described as the recipients of Divine favours because on account of their overwhelming love for God they view calamities also as bounties and derive pleasure from everything that they experience at the hand of the True Beloved, whether of pain or of comfort. Thus this is the second stage of progress towards nearness in which everything that proceeds from the Beloved appears a bounty and is a source of delight. This condition results from perfect love for and sincere relationship with the Beloved. It is a special gift which has nothing to do with design and planning. It is a pure Divine favour and when it is received the seeker is relieved of all burdens and every pain is perceived as a favour, and elicits no complaint or grievance. This is a condition of revival after death, because in this condition he encounters favours from every direction and is, therefore, appropriately described as one who is the recipient of favours. This condition is also described as *baqā*, inasmuch as in this condition the seeker feels as if he has been revived after death and perceives great cheerfulness and is relieved of all the constraints of humanness and experiences the nurturing lights of the Divine descending upon him as bounties. At this stage, the door

---

[87] Al-Fātiḥah 1:7 **[Publisher]**

of every favour is opened to him and Divine favours proceed towards him in full force. This stage is also called experience of God, inasmuch as in this stage the wonders of Providence are revealed to the seeker and he experiences such Divine favours as are hidden from others. He is favoured with true visions and is honoured with the words of God and is informed of the delicate mysteries of the hereafter, and is given a large portion of knowledge and comprehension. In short, he becomes the recipient of so many overt and covert bounties that he arrives at that stage of certainty in which he feels as if he is beholding the True Designer with his eyes. Such perfect knowledge of heavenly mysteries is called experience of God. This is the stage at which a person is granted love of the Divine, but it does not yet become his characteristic.

The third stage of progress, which is the ultimate step in treading the paths of nearness to God has been described in the verse:

غَيْرِ الْمَغْضُوْبِ عَلَيْهِمْ وَلَا الضَّآلِّيْنَ ۝ [88]

This is the stage when the love of God and the enmity to all beside Him become characteristic of the seeker and dwell in him as his temperament. In this stage the seeker is naturally enamoured of Divine qualities and the personal love of God so grips his heart that any departure therefrom becomes impossible and not to be thought of. If his heart and soul are wrung in the machinery of severe tests and trials, nothing but love for the Divine emerges therefrom. At this stage the seeker experiences delight

---

[88] 'Those who have not incurred displeasure, and those who have not gone astray.'—Al-Fātiḥah, 1:7 **[Publisher]**

only in the throbbing of his love for the Divine and regards it as the true comfort of his heart. This is the stage when all progress towards nearness to God terminates and the seeker arrives at the climax that has been determined for human nature.

[Brāhīn-e-Aḥmadiyyah, Rūḥānī Khazā'in, vol. 1, pp. 586-624, footnote 11].

God Almighty is most Benevolent and Merciful. When a person turns to Him with sincerity and devotion He demonstrates even greater sincerity towards him. Such a one never perishes. God Almighty has great qualities of love, loyalty, grace and benevolence, and the power to demonstrate Divine might, but he alone witnesses them fully who is completely lost into His love. Though He is most Benevolent and Merciful yet He is Self-Sufficient and Independent, therefore he alone is blessed with a new life by Him who welcomes death in His cause. He alone is awarded heavenly bounties who discards everything for His sake.

One who establishes a perfect relationship with God resembles a person who perceives the light of fire from afar and then approaches it close and plunges into it till he is completely consumed, and there is nothing left but the fire. In the same way the one who has established a perfect relationship with God Almighty approaches Him until the fire of Divine love envelops him and the flame of light wholly consumes the framework of his ego and takes its place. This is the climax of the blessed love of God. Its principal sign is that it generates Divine qualities in him who experiences it, and he takes on a new life, entirely different from his previous life, which is generated by the burning up of the low attributes of humanness by the flame of light. A piece of iron which is thrown into fire and is wholly possessed by the fire, takes on the appearance of fire; still we cannot call it fire despite the fiery characteristics it shows. In the same way he who is enveloped from head to foot in the flame of Divine love becomes a demonstrator of Divine manifestation, but it cannot be said that he is God. He is a creature of God who has been enveloped in that fire. After he is completely possessed by that fire he demonstrates a thousand signs of perfect love so that through them he is recognized by a wise seeker after truth. One of those signs is that from time to time God, the Benevolent, causes His eloquent and delicious words to issue from his tongue, which are invested with Divine glory and blessing and the perfect demonstration of the hidden, and are accompanied by a light which indicates that they are a certainty and not a matter of doubt. They possess a Divine brilliance and are free from every impurity. Very often they comprise great prophecies which relate to vast and universal affairs. Those prophecies are matchless in quantity and quality. No one can ever produce their match. They are charged with Divine majesty. Through their perfect power they reveal the countenance of the Divine. They are not like the utterances of soothsayers but carry with them signs of the love and acceptance of their proponent, and are filled with the spirit of Divine support and help. Some of these prophecies are related to himself or to his children, or wives, or relations, or friends, or enemies, and some have a wider scope. To him are revealed matters that are not disclosed to others, and to him are opened the doors of the unseen which are not opened to others. The word of God descends upon him as it descends upon holy Prophets and Messengers of God and is certain and free from doubt. His tongue is so honoured that the words that issue from it cannot be matched by anyone both with regard to their literary excellence and their meaning. His eye is given a visionary power through which he can see hidden events. Very often written statements are presented before his eyes. He meets the dead as if they were alive. Sometimes he views things from a distance of thousands of miles as if they were lying at his feet.

His ears are also blessed with the faculty of hearing hidden sounds. He can often hear the voice of angels and finds comfort in it at times of disturbance. Even more surprisingly, he can sometimes hear the voice of inanimate objects, vegetables, and animals.

فلسفی کُو منکر حنّانہ است
از حواس انبیاء بیگانہ است [89]

In the same way his sense of smell can perceive hidden fragrance. Very often he can smell good news and can perceive the bad odour of disagreeable matters. His heart is endowed with the faculty of intuition. Many things flit across his mind and prove true. Likewise, Satan has no influence over him for Satan is left no part in him. On account of his complete surrender to God, his tongue becomes the tongue of God and his hand becomes the hand of God. Even apart from revelation, whatever issues from

---

[89] *The philosopher, who denies the phenomenon of Ḥannānah;**
Is unaware of the senses of the Prophets.

* *Ḥannānah* is the name of a tree trunk against which the Holy Prophet (peace and blessings of Allah be upon him) leaned while delivering his sermons in the mosque. Later on, a pulpit was built, and when the Holy Prophet (peace and blessings of Allah be upon him) stood on it to deliver his sermon, *Ḥannānah* started crying and its cries were heard not only by the Holy Prophet (peace and blessings of Allah be upon him) but also by his companions. **[Publisher]**

his tongue is not from him but from God, inasmuch as his own being is wholly consumed and destroyed and he is given a new and holy life which all the time reflects Divine light.

His forehead is blessed with a light which is not granted to any except the lovers of God, and sometimes its brilliance is such that even a non-believer can perceive it, particularly when he is persecuted and turns to God Almighty seeking His help. That time of devoted attention to God is a special hour and Divine light is manifested in his countenance.

His hands, feet and body are invested with a blessing in consequence of which the clothes worn by him become blessed and on some occasions touching them or handling them becomes the cause of the healing of spiritual or physical ills.

In the same way God, the Lord of Honour and Glory, invests his dwelling with a blessing, which safeguards it against calamities. God's angels watch over it.

His city or town is blessed in a special manner. Even the dust over which he treads receives a blessing.

His desires take on the colour of prophecy. When he feels an intense desire for something to eat or drink or wear or behold, that thing becomes available.

His pleasure and displeasure also presage a corresponding happening. When he is greatly pleased with someone, that is an indication of the future rise of that person; and when he is wroth with someone, that indicates the latter's decline and ruin, inasmuch as by virtue of his complete surrender to God he dwells in the mansion of truth and his pleasure and displeasure become the pleasure and displeasure of God, not in consequence of his desire but by virtue of Divine attention.

In the same way, his supplication and attention are in a different category from those of other people and are charged with special effect. There is no doubt that except in cases of absolute Divine decrees, if his attention is fully devoted towards the removal of a calamity, God Almighty averts it, whether it affects an individual or a group or a country or a sovereign. The secret of it is that such people are totally lost to their own beings; therefore, very often their will coincides with the will of God. Thus when their attention is directed intensely towards the removal of a calamity and is wholly concentrated on God it is the Divine way that in such a situation God hears them and does not reject their supplication, though sometimes their prayer is not heard so that their being the creatures of God may be demonstrated and they may not be deified by the ignorant ones.

[Ḥaqīqat-ul-Waḥī, Rūḥānī Khazā'in, vol. 22, pp. 16-20]

3

EFFORT AND NATURAL APTITUDE

There are some people who attain exalted spiritual station without effort and striving on their part. Their very nature is such that without any effort or striving, they love God and come to have such spiritual relationship with the Holy Prophet (peace and blessings of Allah be upon him) as can never be surpassed. As time passes, their inner fire of love for God continues to grow stronger and with it grows the fire of love for the Holy Prophet (peace and blessings of Allah be upon him.) In all these matters God becomes their Guardian and Provident. When that fire reaches its climax, they fervently desire that the glory of God be manifested upon the earth, and this becomes their greatest delight and their ultimate purpose. Thereupon God's signs appear for them on the earth. God Almighty does not manifest His grand signs, nor does He convey information of great future events to anyone except those who are wholly lost in His love, and are as desirous of the manifestation of His Unity and Glory as He Himself is. They are unique because special Divine mysteries are revealed to them and the unseen is disclosed to them with the utmost clarity. No one else is honoured in this unique way.

[Ḥaqīqat-ul-Waḥī, Rūḥānī Khazā'in, vol. 22, p. 68]

The Sufis have mentioned two ways of spiritual progress—effort and natural aptitude. Effort is to embark upon the way of Allah and His Messenger out of a wise choice. As God says:

قُلۡ اِنۡ کُنۡتُمۡ تُحِبُّوۡنَ اللّٰہَ فَاتَّبِعُوۡنِیۡ یُحۡبِبۡکُمُ اللّٰہُ [90]

(Part Number 3)

That is: 'If you wish to become the loved ones of Allah, then follow the Holy Prophet (peace and blessings of Allah be upon him.)'

That perfect guide is the Messenger[sa] who endured such calamities as have no equal, and did not pass one day in comfort. Only those can be counted his true followers who follow every word and action of his with the utmost effort. God does not love the slothful and those who have no desire to encounter hardship. Such people will only incur the wrath of God Almighty. In order to carry out this Divine commandment of following the Holy Prophet (peace and blessings of Allah be upon him), the seeker must first study the whole life of the Holy Prophet[sa] and then follow in his footsteps. This is the way of a seeker. It is fraught with calamities and hardships; it is only by enduring them that a person becomes a seeker.

The rank of those invested with natural aptitude is higher than that of the other seekers. God Almighty does not treat them as mere seekers but Himself exposes them to calamities and draws them towards Himself through His eternal magnetism. All Prophets were so drawn towards God. When confronted with calamities, the human soul is illumined by undergoing such hardship, just like iron and glass, which, though they have the quality to shine, but become capable of reflection only after being polished to the extent that they begin to reflect the features of anyone who stands before them. Spiritual exertion and toil act like polish. The heart too should be polished until it de-

---

[90] Āl-e-'Imrān,3:32 **[Publisher]**

velops the quality of reflection; which in other words means:

تَخَلَّقُوْا بِاَخْلَاقِ اللّٰهِ [91]

The heart of the seeker is a mirror which is so polished by calamities and hardships that he begins to reflect the qualities of the Prophet[sa]. This stage is reached when, through striving and repeated efforts at purification, all impurities are washed away. Every believer is in need of such cleansing. No believer will attain salvation without becoming a polished mirror. The seeker carries out this polish himself and endures hardships by virtue of his own pursuits, but the one with a natural aptitude is subjected to hardships. God Himself becomes his Polisher and, polishing him with diverse types of calamities and hardships, bestows upon him the qualities of a mirror. The end result of a seeker and one possessing natural aptitude is the same. Hence, righteousness has two aspects: effort, and natural aptitude.

[Malfūẓāt, vol. 1, pp. 29-28]

---

[91] Acquire the attributes of Allah. **[Publisher]**

4

THE NEED FOR PROPHETS

God Almighty has bound up belief in His own existence with belief in His Messengers. The reason for this is that man is invested with the capacity of believing in the Unity of God as stone is invested with the capacity of flaring up; and a Messenger is like the flint which elicits the spark from the stone by striking it. It is, therefore, not possible that without the flint, that is to say without a Divine Messenger, the spark of the Unity of God may be ignited in a human heart. It is only a Divine Messenger who brings down *Tauḥīd* [belief in the Unity of God] upon the earth and it is achieved only through him. God is hidden and displays His countenance only though a Messenger.

[Ḥaqīqat-ul-Waḥī, Rūḥānī Khazā'in, vol. 22, p. 131]

Prophets are a Manifestation of Divine Unity

The misconception that belief in the Unity of God is enough for the salvation of man, and that it is not necessary to believe in a Prophet, is utterly absurd. People who entertain such a belief seek to separate the soul from the body. Belief in the Unity of God can only be established through a Prophet, and is not possible without believing in him. If a Prophet, who is the source of belief in God's Unity, is excluded, Divine Unity cannot be upheld. A Prophet alone is the cause and source and father and fountain and perfect manifestation of the belief in the Unity of God. Through him alone can one behold the hidden countenance of God and realize His existence. On the one hand, the Divine is eminently Self-Sufficient and cares not whether anyone is guided or goes astray; on the other, He desires that He should be known and that His creatures should derive benefit from His eternal mercy. He, therefore, manifests Himself to him whose heart is charged to the highest degree with the natural desire of attaining nearness to the Holy One, and is also filled with utmost sympathy for mankind. God displays to him the light of His being and eternal attributes. In this manner, the person who possesses such superior nature—who, in other words, is called a Prophet—is drawn towards God. On account of the extreme eagerness with which his heart is charged with sympathy for mankind, he desires by his spiritual inclination, supplication and humility, that others too should recognize the God Who has been revealed to him so that they too may attain salvation. He sincerely offers the sacrifice of his own self and, out of the desire that mankind may be revived, strives to the utmost degree and is always ready to suffer many deaths, as is indicated in the verse:

لَعَلَّكَ بَاخِعٌ نَّفْسَكَ أَلَّا يَكُونُوا مُؤْمِنِينَ [92]

God is Self-Sufficient, and doesn't stand in need of creatures, but in view of the grief, sorrow, torment, humility, extreme devotion, truthfulness and integrity of such a person, God manifests Himself through His signs to the eager hearts of men.

As a result of the earnest supplications of such a person, which create a tumultuous uproar in heaven, Divine signs descend upon the earth like rain and extraordinary

---

[92] 'Haply thou wilt grieve thyself to death because they believe not.'—Al-Shu'arā', 26:4 **[Publisher]**

happenings are witnessed, which reveal the countenance of God and the world bears witness that God exists. Had the Holy Prophet[sa] not turned to God with so much supplication, entreaty and earnestness, and had he not offered the sacrifice of his self and accepted a hundred deaths at every step, Divine countenance would never have been revealed to the world, because God Almighty, due to His Self-Sufficiency, is completely independent. He says:

إِنَّ اللّٰهَ غَنِيٌّ عَنِ الْعٰلَمِيْنَ [93]

وَالَّذِيْنَ جَاهَدُوْا فِيْنَا لَنَهْدِيَنَّهُمْ سُبُلَنَا [94]

That is: 'Allah is independent of all the worlds;' and

'It is Our eternal law that those who strive after Us and seek Us with the utmost effort, We show them Our way.'

The first and foremost in offering sacrifices in the cause of Allah, are the Prophets. Everyone strives for himself but Prophets strive for others. People sleep, but the Prophets stay awake on their behalf. People laugh and the Prophets weep for them. They willingly bear hardship for the deliverance of mankind. They do this so that God may so manifest Himself that people should be convinced that He exists, and His existence and Unity may be clearly perceived by them and through such perception mankind might attain salvation. Thus the Prophets suffer death out of their sympathy for their enemies. And when their agony reaches its climax and heaven is filled with their tormented supplications, God Almighty exhibits the brightness of His countenance and manifests His

---

[93] Āl-e-'Imrān, 3:98 **[Publisher]**

[94] Al-'Ankabūt, 29:70 **[Publisher]**

existence and His Unity to mankind through powerful signs. Thus there is no doubt that the knowledge of God and of His Unity is gained by man only through a Prophet and cannot be achieved otherwise. The highest example in this regard was set by our Holy Prophet (peace and blessings of Allah be upon him), who lifted a whole people out of the filth in which they were steeped, and conveyed them to a garden. He provided excellent spiritual food and drink for those who were on the point of death because of spiritual starvation. He raised them from their animal condition to the condition of man, and then civilized them, and made them perfect, and exhibited so many signs that they were enabled to see God, and brought about such a change in them that they began to shake hands with angels. No other Prophet was able to bring about such a complete change in his people, for their followers did not achieve perfection.

[Ḥaqīqat-ul-Waḥī, Rūḥānī Khazā'in, vol. 22, pp. 116-118]

Prophets Demonstrate God's Existence

It should be remembered that it is the Prophets (peace be on them) who demonstrate the existence of God and teach people His Unity. If those holy ones had not appeared, it would have been impossible to discover the straight path with certainty. Though a person of sincere nature, possessing sane reason can, by reflecting on the universe and observing its perfect and well-established order, conclude that there ought to be a Creator of this well-ordered universe, however, there is a world of difference between 'Ought to be' and 'Is'. The Prophets alone (peace be on them) established through thousands of signs and miracles that the Transcendent Being Who comprises all power does in fact exist. Indeed, the degree of comprehension that the need of a Creator may be perceived by the observation of the universe is also a reflection of the rays of Prophethood. Had there been no Prophets, no one would have achieved this degree of reason. This may be understood through the contemplation that, though there is water below the surface of the earth, the maintenance of that water depends upon the water that descends from the sky. When there is a long drought, the underground water dries up and when rain descends the underground water also begins to well up. In the same way, with the advent of a Prophet, reason—which is sub-surface water—is sharpened and improved; and when over a long period no Prophet is raised the sub-surface water of reason begins to decline and becomes muddied and the worship of idols and all manner of paganism and vice abound. The eye possesses the faculty of sight, yet it needs the light of the sun to be able to see. In the same way, human reason, which resembles the eye, needs the light of the sun of Prophethood. And when that sun disappears reason becomes confused and dark; just as you cannot see with the eye alone, you cannot see without the light of Prophethood.

As the recognition of God always depends upon the recognition of a Prophet, it is not possible to recognize the Unity of God without him. A Prophet is a mirror for the observance of the Divine. God can only be seen through this mirror. When God Almighty designs to reveal Himself to the world, He raises a Prophet, who is a manifestation of Divine powers, and sends down His revelation to him and manifests His Divine powers through him. It is then that the world comes to know that God exists.

[Ḥaqīqat-ul-Waḥī, Rūḥānī Khazā'in, vol. 22, pp. 114-116]

Blessings of Obedience to the Holy Prophet[sa]

Know well that Prophets do not appear for mere ostentation or show. If people do not derive any spiritual benefit from them and they do not prove to be a source of grace, it would have to be confessed that their advent is only for show, and that it is without any meaning; but that is not so. Prophets are a source of many blessings and abundant grace. With his coming, a fountain of virtue springs forth. Just as mankind derives benefit from the light of the Sun and its benefit does not stop at any point, in this way, the Sun of the grace and blessing of the Holy Prophet (peace and blessings of Allah be upon him) continues to shine and to bestow benefits upon the fortunate ones. That is why God Almighty has said:

قُلْ اِنْ كُنْتُمْ تُحِبُّوْنَ اللّٰهَ فَاتَّبِعُوْنِيْ يُحْبِبْكُمُ اللّٰهُ [95]

This means: 'Tell them, If you want to become the loved ones of Allah, then follow me, Allah will then love you.'

True obedience to the Holy Prophet[sa] makes a person beloved of God, and becomes a means for the forgiveness of sins.

[Malfūẓāt, vol. 3, p. 55]

Belief in God cannot be Perfect without Belief in Prophets

QUESTION: Although we believe that mere verbal profession of *Tauḥīd* [Divine Unity] cannot ensure salvation and that none can attain salvation by departing from obedience to the Holy Prophet (peace and blessings of Allah be upon him), yet to dispel any possible doubt, we would like to know the true meanings of the verses cited by

---

[95] Āl-e-'Imrān, 3:32 **[Publisher]**

'Abdul Ḥakīm Khān[96], for instance:

إِنَّ الَّذِينَ آمَنُوا وَالَّذِينَ هَادُوا وَالنَّصَارَىٰ وَالصَّابِئِينَ مَنْ آمَنَ بِاللَّهِ
وَالْيَوْمِ الْآخِرِ وَعَمِلَ صَالِحًا فَلَهُمْ أَجْرُهُمْ عِنْدَ رَبِّهِمْ [97]

بَلَىٰ مَنْ أَسْلَمَ وَجْهَهُ لِلَّهِ وَهُوَ مُحْسِنٌ فَلَهُ أَجْرُهُ عِنْدَ رَبِّهِ [98]

تَعَالَوْا إِلَىٰ كَلِمَةٍ سَوَاءٍ بَيْنَنَا وَبَيْنَكُمْ أَلَّا نَعْبُدَ إِلَّا اللَّهَ وَلَا نُشْرِكَ بِهِ شَيْئًا
وَلَا يَتَّخِذَ بَعْضُنَا بَعْضًا أَرْبَابًا مِنْ دُونِ اللَّهِ [99]

ANSWER: These verses of the Holy Qur'ān do not mean that salvation can be achieved without believing in the Holy Prophet[sa]. They lay down that salvation cannot be achieved without believing in God—Who has no associate—and in the Last Day; and that belief in God cannot be perfect without belief in Prophets, inasmuch as Prophets illustrate the attributes of God and the true comprehension of God Almighty, without which belief remains imperfect. For instance, the Divine attributes that He speaks, hears, knows the unseen, has power to show mercy and to inflict punishment, cannot be understood except through a Messenger of God. If these attributes are not demonstrated through testimony, the existence of God is not positively established and belief in God has

---

[96] 'Abdul Ḥakīm Khān was a Muslim, who turned apostate. **[Publisher]**

[97] 'Surely, the believers, and the Jews, and the Christians and the Sabians—whichever party from among them truly believes in Allah and the Last Day and does good deeds shall have their reward with their Lord.'—Al-Baqarah, 2:63 **[Publisher]**

[98] 'Nay, whoever submits himself completely to Allah, while he is excellent in conduct, shall have his reward with his Lord.'—Al-Baqarah, 2:113 **[Publisher]**

[99] 'Come to a word equal between us and you—that we worship none but Allah, and that we associate no partner with Him, and that some of us take not others for Lords beside Allah.'—Āl-e-'Imrān, 3:65 **[Publisher]**

no meaning. A person who believes in God must believe in His attributes also, and for such belief he must believe in the Prophets. For instance, God's attribute of speech can only be appreciated by proof of His word and it is only Prophets who furnish proof of His word.

The Holy Qur'ān comprises two types of verses. One type is *Muḥkamāt* [fundamental and explicit], for instance the verse:

إِنَّ الَّذِيْنَ يَكْفُرُوْنَ بِاللّٰهِ وَرُسُلِهٖ وَيُرِيْدُوْنَ اَنْ يُّفَرِّقُوْا بَيْنَ اللّٰهِ وَرُسُلِهٖ وَيَقُوْلُوْنَ نُؤْمِنُ بِبَعْضٍ وَّنَكْفُرُ بِبَعْضٍ ۙ وَّيُرِيْدُوْنَ اَنْ يَّتَّخِذُوْا بَيْنَ ذٰلِكَ سَبِيْلًا ۙ اُولٰٓئِكَ هُمُ الْكٰفِرُوْنَ حَقًّا ۚ وَاَعْتَدْنَا لِلْكٰفِرِيْنَ عَذَابًا مُّهِيْنًا ۝[100]

That is: 'There are those who do not want to believe in both Allah and His Messengers and seek to make a distinction between Allah and His Messengers and say: We believe in God, but not in His Messengers; and seek to separate Allah from His Messengers. There are others who believe in Allah but not the Prophets, or they believe in some Prophets but not in others and desire to adopt a position between the two; these indeed are the confirmed disbelievers. We have prepared a humiliating punishment for such disbelievers.'…

The second type of verses are *Mutashābihāt* [allegorical] which have very subtle meanings. Their true meaning is revealed only to those who are firmly grounded in knowledge. Those whose hearts are afflicted with hypocrisy do not care to follow what is *Muḥkamāt* [fundamental] and seek to follow only that which is allegorical. The Word of God is full of *Muḥkamāt* [fundamental] verses, whose meaning is clear, and the ne-

---

[100] Al-Nisā', 4:151-152 **[Publisher]**

glect of which occasions great harm. For instance, one who believes in God but does not believe in His Messengers has to repudiate Divine attributes. This is illustrated by the new sect of Brahmus who proclaim that they believe in God but do not believe in the Prophets. They repudiate the Word of God, while it is obvious that if God hears He also speaks. If His speaking is not established, His hearing is also not proved. Thus these people become like atheists by repudiating Divine attributes.

Divine attributes are eternal and ever-lasting. They are demonstrated only by Prophets. The denial of the attributes of God invariably leads to the denial of God's existence. This shows that belief in God necessarily implies belief in the Prophets (peace be on them), without which belief in God is imperfect and incomplete. The fundamental verses not only abound in number, but are also supported by the continuous testimony of the Prophets. Anyone who studies the Holy Qur'ān and the books of other Prophets will find that they insist upon belief in the Messengers of God as much as belief in God Himself. If the allegorical verses are interpreted in a sense which is contrary to the meaning of the fundamental verses, great harm would ensue therefrom and many other verses would have to be rejected. No contradiction is possible in the Word of God; therefore the implicit must be reconciled with the explicit....In the Holy Qur'ān, the word 'Allah' has throughout been used as connoting the Being Who sends Prophets and Messengers and Books, Who is the Creator of heaven and earth and possesses such and such attributes and is One without associate. It is true that those who have had no access to God's word and are utterly unaware of it, will be judged according to their degree of knowledge, reason and intelligence, but it is not possible that they should achieve the grades and ranks which will be bestowed upon those who follow the Holy Prophet (peace and blessings of Allah be upon him.) The blind obviously cannot arrive at the high stations of those who are guided by the light of Prophethood. This is Divine grace which He bestows on whom He wills.

Now, observe the outrage that is committed by Miāń ‘Abdul Ḥakīm who disregards hundreds of verses of the Holy Qur’ān which proclaim emphatically that the profession of belief in the Unity of God alone is not enough for the achievement of salvation and that faith in the Holy Prophet[sa] is also essential; and, like the Jews, he twists the meanings of two or three concise verses and insists upon his own interpretation. Every sensible person can realize that if those verses mean what ‘Abdul Ḥakīm opines, then it is goodbye to Islām and the commandments like prayer and fasting etc., which have been taught by the Holy Prophet (peace and blessings of Allah be upon him) are rendered vain and meaningless. If it were true that everyone can attain salvation through his fancied version of the Unity of God, then the rejection of Prophets and the repudiation of faith would be no sin and would do no harm. However, there is not a single verse in the Holy Qur’ān which relieves a Muslim from obedience to the Holy Prophet (peace and blessings of Allah be upon him.) Even if these two or three verses which Miāń ‘Abdul Ḥakīm relies upon had appeared to him contradictory to hundreds of verses of the contrary import, he should have subordinated them to the large number of other verses, and should not have disregarded the latter and thus advanced towards apostasy. In truth there is no contradiction in the word of Allah. It is only a case of deficient understanding and murky disposition. We should interpret the Word of God Almighty, as He Himself has interpreted it and should not, like the Jews, place another construction upon it.

It has always been the way of the Divine Word and of His Messengers, that they seek to guide a hardened disbeliever by instructing him that if he believes in God, and loves Him, and accepts Him as One without associate, he will surely attain salvation. The purpose of this is that if such a person would believe truly in God, he would be enabled by God to accept Islām. The Holy Qur'ān, which these people ignore, clearly affirms that true faith in God leads to faith in the Holy Prophet (peace and blessings of Allah be upon him), and such a person becomes ready to accept Islām. My own method also is that when an Āryā, a Brahmu, a Christian, a Jew, or a Sikh, or any other non-Muslim persists in wrong reasoning, I tell him that such discussion will not help him in any way but that if he sincerely believes in God, He will Himself open the way of salvation to him. But by this I do not at all mean that salvation can be achieved without following the Holy Prophet (peace and blessings of Allah be upon him); what I mean is that if a person believes sincerely in God, God will open his heart to belief in the Holy Prophet[sa]....

It should be remembered that, in the first place, the true Unity of God cannot be appreciated without following the Holy Prophet (peace and blessings of Allah be upon him.) As I have just mentioned, Divine attributes, which cannot be isolated from the Being of God, cannot be observed except through the mirror of the revelation vouchsafed to a Prophet. They are illustrated in practice only by a Prophet. But even if someone should acquire an imperfect appreciation of them, it would not be altogether free from traces of polytheism till such a one is led by God into Islām by accepting His total obedience. Whatever a believer receives from God Almighty through God's Messenger is a heavenly gift which is not tainted by his own pride and self-esteem, but whatever a person achieves through his own effort is always affected by some taint of polytheism. That is why Messengers have been sent to teach the true Unity of God, and mankind has not been left dependent upon reason alone so that the Unity of God should remain pure and should not be tainted with human conceit. This is why erring philosophers have never been able to grasp the pure Unity of God, inasmuch as they are afflicted with pride, arrogance and conceit, and pure Unity demands the negation of the self. Such negation cannot be effected unless a person sincerely believes that it is a Divine gift in which his effort has no part. For instance, one farmer keeps awake throughout the night and irrigates his field with great hardship, while another one sleeps all night and a cloud arises and rain fills his field with water. Would these two be equal in their gratitude to God? Indeed not. He whose field is irrigated without his labour would be more grateful than the other. That is why the Word of God has repeatedly admonished man to be grateful to God, who sends Messengers to teach him the Unity of God.

[Ḥaqīqat-ul-Waḥī, Rūḥānī Khazā'in, vol. 22, pp. 172-179]

Why do Prophets have Needs like other People?

I wish to explain why Prophets feel the need of things like the help of other people. God Almighty has power to safeguard them against all needs. These needs arise so that they might manifest examples of dedication to God, like that of Abū Bakr[ra], and faith in the existence of God

Almighty may be generated, and such dedicated people may serve as a sign of God and the world may witness examples of that hidden delight and love for the sake of which a loved and desired thing like wealth can be easily and cheerfully sacrificed. After the sacrifice of wealth and riches, these people are granted the power and courage to complete their dedication to God by sacrificing their very lives for Him. Thus the true purpose of the Prophets, peace be on them, feeling the need of things is that they may inculcate the discarding of desire and love for mortal things and be invested with a delicious faith in the existence of God Almighty and develop the spirit of self sacrifice in the cause of the promotion of the welfare of their fellow beings. This holy group subsists under the care of the Master of the treasuries of the heaven and earth and can encounter no real need. Their needs are encountered for the perfection of their teaching and promotion of mankind's faith and high qualities.

[Malfūẓāt, vol. 2, pp. 96-97]

5

PROPHETHOOD IN ISLĀM

Meanings and Significance of the Seal of Prophethood

In Islām, the door to Prophethood which claims to be independent (of the Holy Prophet[sa]) is closed.

[Ayyām-uṣ-Ṣulḥ, Rūḥānī Khazā'in, vol. 14, p. 308]

It should be clearly understood that the door of law-bearing Prophethood is firmly closed after the Holy Prophet (peace and blessings of Allah be upon him.) There can be no book after the Holy Qur'ān which comprises new commandments or abrogates those contained in it or suspends obedience to it. The authority of the Holy Qur'ān will last to the Day of Judgment.

[Al-Waṣiyyat, Rūḥānī Khazā'in, vol. 20, p. 311, footnote]

It has been revealed to me that the door of independent Prophethood is firmly closed after the Seal of the Prophets (peace and blessings of Allah be upon him.) Now there can arise no independent Prophet, neither old nor new. Our misguided opponents do not consider this door completely closed. According to them there is a window open for the return of the Israelite Prophet, the Messiah.

[Sirāj-e-Munīr, Rūḥānī Khazā'in, vol. 12, pp. 5-6]

A Prophet is one who receives revelation from God and is honoured with converse with Him. It is not necessary that he should be the bearer of a new law or should not be the follower of a law-bearing Prophet. Thus no harm is done if a follower of the Holy Prophet[sa] is raised as such a Prophet, particularly when he receives all grace from the Holy Prophet himself (peace and blessings of Allah be upon him.) What is most harmful is to believe that the followers of the Holy Prophet (peace and blessings of Allah be upon him) are debarred from enjoying converse with God until the Day of Judgement. That religion does not deserve to be called a religion nor is that Prophet worthy of being called a Prophet, whose followers cannot come near enough to God to be honoured with His word. Accursed and detestable is the religion which teaches that human progress depends only on a few principles which are transmitted from generation to generation, that all revelation is a matter of the past and there can be no further revelation, and that hearing the voice of the Ever-Living and All-Powerful God is to be wholly despaired of.

[Brāhīn-e-Aḥmadiyyah, part V, Rūḥānī Khazā'in, vol. 21, p. 306]

In Arabic and Hebrew, the word *Nabī* [Prophet] means one who makes prophecies on the basis of revelation received from God. As the Holy Qur'ān does not close the door of Prophethood whereby a person through obedience to the grace of the Holy Prophet (peace and blessings of Allah be upon him) may be granted converse with God and may be informed of hidden matters through Divine revelation, then what is there to stop the appearance of such a Prophet among the Muslims? We do not believe that such Prophethood is barred. Only that Prophethood is barred which is accompanied by the commandments of a new Shariah, or claims to be outside the following of the Holy Prophet (peace and blessings of Allah be upon him.) But a claim to Prophethood by one whom Divine revelation describes as a follower of the Holy Prophet[sa] and who is also designated as a Prophet, is not contrary to the Holy Qur'ān, inasmuch as such Prophethood is a reflection of the Prophethood of the Holy Prophet (peace and blessings of Allah be upon him) and is not independent Prophethood.

[Brāhīn-e-Aḥmadiyyah, part V, Rūḥānī Khazā'in, vol. 21, pp. 351-352]

Excellence of the Holy Prophet[sa]

The charge advanced against me and my Jamā'at, that we do not believe in the Holy Prophet (peace and blessings of Allah be upon him) as the Seal of Prophets, is altogether false. The strength, certainty, comprehension and insight with which we acknowledge and believe in the Holy Prophet (peace and blessings of Allah be upon him) as the Seal of the Prophets, cannot even be dreamed of by the other Muslims; they do not have the capacity to comprehend the reality and the mystery comprised in the Seal of Prophethood. They have merely heard an expression from their ancestors but they are unaware of its import and do not know what it signifies and what is meant by believing in it. But we believe with full comprehension—and God Almighty knows this well—that the Holy Prophet (peace and blessings of Allah be upon him) is the Seal of the Prophets. God Almighty has disclosed the reality of the Seal of Prophethood in such a manner that we derive special delight from its contemplation which cannot be conceived of by anyone except those who have drunk deep at this fountain.

We can illustrate the Seal of Prophethood by the example of the moon, which begins as a crescent and arrives at its perfection on the fourteenth night when it is called the full moon. In the same manner the excellences of Prophethood reached their climax in the Holy Prophet (peace and blessings of Allah be upon him.) Those who believe that Prophethood has been closed compulsorily, and that the Holy Prophet (peace and blessings of Allah be upon him) should not be regarded as being superior even to the Prophet Jonas have not understood the reality of the Seal of Prophethood and do not have true knowledge of his superiority and excellences. Despite their own ignorance and lack of understanding, they charge us with denying the Seal of Prophethood. What shall I say concerning such invalids and how shall I express my pity for them!

[Malfūẓāt, vol. 1, pp. 342-343]

I wish to reaffirm that the principal connotation of the expression 'Seal of the Prophets' is that the qualities of Prophethood beginning with Adam[as] found perfection in the Holy Prophet (peace and blessings of Allah be upon him.) This is the obvious meaning. The other meaning is that the circle of the excellences of Prophethood was completed with the advent of the Holy Prophet (peace and blessings of Allah be upon him.) It is entirely true that the Holy Qur'ān brought perfection to imperfect teachings, and thereby Prophethood attained perfection and Islām became the manifestation of:

اَلْيَوْمَ اَكْمَلْتُ لَكُمْ دِيْنَكُمْ [101]

These are the signs of Prophethood. There is no need to discuss their reality and inner meanings. The principles are self-evident and clear and are known as established verities. It is not necessary for a believer to get involved in their detailed exposition. All that is needed is faith. The Finality of Prophethood is the sign of the Holy

---

101 'This day have I perfected your religion for you.'—Al-Mā'idah, 5:4 **[Publisher]**

Prophet (peace and blessings of Allah be upon him) and it is necessary for every Muslim to believe in it.

[Malfūẓāt, vol. 1, pp. 286-287]

The Seal of Prophethood as the Perfect Man

The vision of the Perfect Man, to whom the Holy Qur'ān was revealed, was not limited. His concern and sympathy for all was faultless. His self was imbued with perfect sympathy that transcended the limitations of time and space. That is why he was granted full and complete share of the manifestation of Divine Providence. Thus, he became the Seal of the Prophets. This was not because no one was to be granted any spiritual grace after him, but because no one could achieve any grace without the attestation of his seal, and that the door of converse with God would never be closed to his followers. No other Prophet has been granted this seal; he is the only one through whose seal such Prophethood can be achieved and for which it is necessary that its recipient should be a follower of his. His high resolve and deep sympathy did not desire to leave his followers in a position of disadvantage and did not tolerate that the door of revelation, which is the true basis of complete comprehension, should be closed upon them. He desired that, in order to maintain the sign of the Seal of Prophethood, the grace of revelation should be confined to his followers, and the door of revelation should be closed for those who are not his followers. It was in this sense that God made him the Seal of the Prophets. Thus it has been forever ordained that he who is not his follower, and is not completely devoted to him, can never be the recipient of perfect revelation, inasmuch as independent Prophethood came to an end with him (peace and blessings of Allah be upon him.) But

Prophethood by way of *ẓill* [reflection], which is to receive Divine revelation through the grace of Muḥammad[sa], shall continue till the Judgement Day, so that the door of spiritual perfection should not be closed on mankind and the sign which the high resolve of the Holy Prophet (peace and blessings of Allah be upon him) desired—namely, that the doors of converse with God should remain open and the comprehension of the Divine, which is the basis of salvation, should not become extinct.

[Ḥaqīqat-ul-Waḥī, Rūḥānī Khazā'in, vol. 22, pp. 29-30].

The question can be raised that as there have been many Prophets among the followers of Moses[as], it therefore follows that the status of Moses[as] was higher than that of the Holy Prophet[sa]. The answer is that these Prophets were raised by God independently of Moses[as], but there have been thousands of saints through the blessing of following the Holy Prophet (peace and blessings of Allah be upon him), and also the one who was both a follower and a Prophet. There is no other instance of such bounteous grace in the case of any other Prophet. Among the followers of Moses[as], with the exception of the Prophets, most other people were spiritually imperfect, and the Prophets themselves were raised independently of Moses[as]. But among Muslims thousands achieved sainthood by following the Holy Prophet[sa] alone.

[Ḥaqīqat-ul-Waḥī, Rūḥānī Khazā'in, vol. 22, p. 30, footnote]

Prophethood by way of Reflection

When Maulavī Ṣāḥibzādah 'Abdul Laṭīf Ṣāḥib came to Qādiān, not only did he have the advantage of listening to detailed reasons in support of my claim, but during the few months that he spent in my company in Qādiān and during my journey to Jhelum when he was with me, he observed many heavenly signs in my support. By witnessing all these lights and extraordinary events, he was filled with rare certainty and was pulled upward by superior power. On one occasion, I explained a particular point to him which pleased him greatly. The point was that, as the Holy Prophet (peace and blessings of Allah be upon him) was the like of Moses[as] and his Khulafā' are the likes of the Prophets of Israel, then why is it that the Promised Messiah has been called a Prophet in the Aḥādīth while all other Khulafā' have not been so named? I told him that as the Holy Prophet (peace and blessings of Allah be upon him) was the Seal of the Prophets and there was to be no Prophet after him, therefore, if all the Khulafā' had been named Prophets, his being the Seal of the Prophets would have been put in doubt, and if no one of his followers had been designated a Prophet, his being the like of Moses[as] would have been open to question, inasmuch as the Khulafā' of Moses[as] were Prophets. Therefore, Divine wisdom determined that a large number of Khulafā' be sent down, but out of regard for the Seal of Prophethood, not be called Prophets, nor be granted the rank of Prophethood, so as to emphasize the Seal of Prophethood. Divine wisdom also determined that the last Khalīfa, i.e., the Promised Messiah, should be designated as a Prophet, so that the two dispensations should be proved as being alike in the matter of Khilāfat. I have pointed out several times that the Prophethood of the Promised Messiah is by way of reflection, inasmuch as he has been designated a Prophet by virtue of his being the perfect reflection of the Holy Prophet (peace and blessings of Allah be upon him.) In one of my revelations God Almighty has told me:

يَا اَحْمَدُ جُعِلْتَ مُرْسَلاً

'O Aḥmad, you have been made a Messenger'; i.e., as you were held worthy of the name of Aḥmad, by way of *burūz* [second coming], while your name was Ghulām Aḥmad, in the same way you have been held worthy of the title of a Prophet by way of *burūz*, inasmuch as Aḥmad is the Prophet and Prophethood cannot be separated from him.

[Tadhkirat-ush-Shahādatain, Rūḥānī Khazā'in, vol. 20, pp. 45-46]

If anyone should ask how there can be a Prophet among the Muslims when God has put an end to Prophethood, the answer would be that God, the Lord of Honour and Glory, has named me Prophet only as proof of the perfection of the Prophethood of the best of mankind. The perfection of the Holy Prophet[sa] would be established only by the proof of the perfection of his followers, for, in the absence of such proof, the claim of the perfection of the Holy Prophet[sa] would not be substantiated in the eyes of the wise. The only meaning of the Seal of Prophethood is that all the excellences of Prophethood achieved their climax in the person of the Holy Prophet[sa]. Of the great excellences of Prophethood, is the perfection of the Holy Prophet[sa] in respect of the conveyance of spiritual grace to his followers, which cannot be established without its manifestation among them. Besides, I have mentioned several times that in the design of God, Prophethood in my case means only the frequency of converse with God and this concept is accepted by the leaders of the Ahl-e-Sunnah.

Thus the controversy is purely verbal. Therefore, O you who possess wisdom and understanding, do not hasten towards denial. Allah's curse and the curse of mankind and of the angels be upon him who makes a claim beyond this even by as much as a particle.

[Al-Istiftā, Rūḥānī Khazā'in, vol. 22, p. 637 footnote]

The Divine revelation:

خدا کی فیلنگ اور خدا کی مہر نے کتنا بڑا کام کیا [102]

means that God felt that, because of its widespread corruption, mankind was in need of a grand reformer, so the Seal of God blessed a follower of the Holy Prophet (peace and blessings of Allah be upon him) with the rank of being a follower on the one hand, and a Prophet on the other. Allah the Exalted, bestowed upon the Holy Prophet (peace and blessings of Allah be upon him) the Seal for the purpose of conveying spiritual excellence, which had not been bestowed on any other Prophet and that is why he was named the Seal of Prophets. This means that obedience to the Holy Prophet[sa] bestows the excellences of Prophethood and his spiritual attention fashions Prophets. No other Prophet has been granted such spiritual power. This is the meaning of the Ḥadīth:

عُلَمَاءُ اُمَّتِی كَاَنبِیاءِ بَنِی اِسْرائِیلَ

'The divines from among my people will be like the Prophets of Israel.'

There were many Prophets from among the children of Israel, but their Prophethood was not because of their obedience to Moses[as]; rather it was a direct bounty from God. That is why they were not designated Prophets in one aspect and the followers of a Prophet in another, but

---

[102] 'What a grand task has been accomplished by the 'feeling' of God and His Seal.' Note: This Urdu revelation contains the actual English word 'feeling'. **[Publisher]**

were called independent Prophets and the dignity of Prophethood was bestowed directly upon them. Leaving them aside, if we look at the rest of the children of Israel, we observe that they had very little guidance and righteousness. Few *Auliyā'ullāh* [friends of Allah] appeared among the followers of Moses[as] and Jesus[as]. Most of them were disobedient, vicious and worshippers of the world. That is why the Torah and the Gospel make no mention of the evidence of their spiritual influence. The Torah frequently designates the companions of Moses[as] as disobedient, hard-hearted, sinful and rebellious. The Holy Qur'ān mentions that their disobedience had reached such a degree that on the occasion of a battle, their response to Moses[as] was:

فَاذْهَبْ اَنْتَ وَرَبُّكَ فَقَاتِلَآ اِنَّا هٰهُنَا قٰعِدُوْنَ [103]

That is: 'Go thou and thy Lord and fight the enemy; here we shall sit.'

Such was the measure of their disobedience. In contrast, the hearts of the companions of the Holy Prophet (peace and blessings of Allah be upon him) were so inspired by love of God, and they were so affected by the spiritual attention of the Holy Prophet (peace and blessings of Allah be upon him), that they sacrificed themselves in the cause of God like sheep and goats. Can anyone show us followers of any previous Prophet, who demonstrated such sincerity and devotion? We have mentioned the companions of Moses[as]. Now let us turn to the Jesus' disciples. One of them, Judas Iscariot, betrayed him in return for thirty pieces of silver. Peter, to whom had been committed the keys of heaven, cursed Jesus to his face

---

[103] Al-Mā'idah, 5:25 **[Publisher]**

and the remaining disciples deserted Jesus at the time of his trial. Not one of them remained steadfast. They all turned out to be cowards. In contrast, the companions of the Holy Prophet (peace and blessings of Allah be upon him) demonstrated such steadfastness and were so reconciled to death that any mention of their devotion brings tears to one's eyes.

What was it that inspired them with such devotion? Whose hand was it that brought about such a change in them? In their pre-Islamic ignorance, there was no sin and no wrong that they did not commit. On becoming the followers of the Holy Prophet[sa], they were so drawn to God, as if God dwelt within them. I tell you truly that it was the spiritual attention of the Holy Prophet[sa] that pulled them out of a low life into a holy one. Those who later entered Islām in hosts did not do so under the threat of a sword. They did so in consequence of the sincere supplications and humble and passionate prayers which the Holy Prophet (peace and blessings of Allah be upon him) offered in Mecca for thirteen years, so that even the soil of Mecca confessed that it was under the blessed feet of him whose heart proclaimed the Unity of God so passionately that heaven was filled with his cries. God is Self-Sufficient. He does not care whether anyone is rightly guided or goes astray. The light of guidance which was so extraordinarily manifested in Arabia, and then spread to the rest of the world, was a consequence of the heartfelt desire of the Holy Prophet (peace and blessings of Allah be upon him.) Followers of every religion had digressed and strayed away from the spring of *Tauḥīd* [belief in the Unity of God] but it continued to flow in Islām. All these blessings were granted in answer to the supplications of the Holy Prophet (peace and blessings of Allah be upon him) as God Almighty has said:

لَعَلَّكَ بَاخِعٌ نَّفْسَكَ اَلَّا يَكُوْنُوْا مُؤْمِنِيْنَ [104]

Meaning that: 'Will you grieve yourself to death because they did not believe?'

The reason why the followers of previous Prophets did not achieve such a high grade in righteousness was that those Prophets did not have the same degree of concern and anguish for their followers as did the Holy Prophet[sa]. It is a pity that ignorant Muslims of this age do not appreciate the Holy Prophet[sa] as he deserves, and therefore they stumble at every step. They interpret the Seal of Prophethood in a manner that is derogatory of the Holy Prophet (peace and blessings of Allah be upon him) and does not hold him up to praise as if he had no power to bestow spiritual grace upon his followers or to help perfect them spiritually, and had been appointed merely to teach them the law. God Almighty has taught Muslims the prayer:

اِهْدِنَا الصِّرَاطَ الْمُسْتَقِيْمَ ۝ صِرَاطَ الَّذِيْنَ اَنْعَمْتَ عَلَيْهِمْ [105]

If the Muslims are not the heirs of the previous Prophets and have no share in the favours that were bestowed upon them, why were they taught this prayer? It is a pity that Muslims, on account of their bigotry and ignorance, do not reflect duly on this verse. They are too eager to see Jesus descend from heaven, while the Holy Qur'ān testifies that he is dead and was buried in Srinagar, Kashmir, as God Almighty has said:

---

[104] Al-Shu'arā', 26:4 **[Publisher]**

[105] 'Guide us along the straight path, the path of those upon whom Thou has bestowed Thy favours.'—Al-Fātiḥah, 1:6-7 **[Publisher]**

وَاٰوَيْنٰهُمَآ اِلٰى رَبْوَةٍ ذَاتِ قَرَارٍ وَّ مَعِيْنٍ[106]

That is: 'We delivered Jesus and his mother from the hands of the Jews and conveyed them to a region of high mountains which was a place of security and was watered with clear springs.'

This was Kashmir. And this is why Mary's tomb is not to be found in Palestine, and the Christians claim that she too disappeared like Jesus. How unjust it is of the ignorant Muslims to believe that the followers of the Holy Prophet (peace and blessings of Allah be upon him) are deprived of converse with God while at the same time they repeat the sayings of the Holy Prophet (peace and blessings of Allah be upon him) that among his people there will be those who will resemble the Prophets of Israel, and there will also be one who will be a Prophet in one aspect and the follower of the Holy Prophet[sa] in another. He would be the one who will be called the Promised Messiah.

[Ḥaqīqat-ul-Waḥī, Rūḥānī Khazā'in, vol. 22, pp. 99-104, footnote]

I tell you truly that Islām is so patently true that if all the disbelievers of the world were to stand in prayer on one side, and I were to stand alone on the other, in supplication before God for a particular purpose, God will support me, not because I am better than all others, but because I believe sincerely in His Messenger and know that all Prophethood ended with him and that all law is comprised in his law. Yet one type of Prophethood has not ended, that is to say, the Prophethood which is granted in consequence of complete obedience to the Holy Prophet (peace and blessings of Allah be upon him)

---

[106] Al-Mu'minūn, 23:51 **[Publisher]**

and which is illumined by his lamp. This Prophethood has not ended inasmuch as it is a reflection of his Prophethood and is given through him and is his manifestation and receives grace from him. God is the enemy of whoever regards the Holy Qur'ān as abrogated and follows a law opposed to the law of Muḥammad and seeks to put his own law in practice and does not follow the Holy Prophet[sa] and seeks to set up himself in his place. But God loves him who makes the Holy Qur'ān his code and regards the Holy Prophet (peace and blessings of Allah be upon him) as the Seal of the Prophets and knows that he is dependent upon his grace. Such a man becomes the beloved of God Almighty. God's love pulls him towards Him and honours him with His converse and displays signs in his support. When such a person's obedience to the Holy Prophet[sa] arrives at its climax, God bestows a Prophethood upon him which is a reflection of the Prophethood of Muḥammad (peace and blessings of Allah be upon him), so that Islām may continues to remain fresh and alive through such people and should remain supreme over its opponents.

A foolish one, who is in truth an enemy of the faith, does not desire that converse with God should continue as a characteristic of Islām. He rather wishes that Islām too should become a dead religion like all the others; but that is not what God desires. In the revelation vouchsafed to me, God Almighty has employed the expression Prophet and Messenger concerning me hundreds of times, but these expressions mean only frequent converse with God which comprises the unseen. Everyone is entitled to use an expression in a particular sense. God too designates frequent experience of converse with Him as Prophethood, meaning that such converse comprises a great deal of that which is unseen. Accursed is he who claims to be a Prophet, but whose Prophethood is divorced from the grace of the Holy Prophet (peace and blessings of Allah be upon him.) The Prophethood that has been bestowed on me belongs to the Holy Prophet (peace and blessings of Allah be upon him) and is not a new Prophethood. Its only purpose is to make manifest to the world the truth of Islām and to display the righteousness of the Holy Prophet (peace and blessings of Allah be upon him.)

[Chashma-e-Ma'rifat, Rūḥānī Khazā'in, vol. 23, pp. 339-341]

I believe truly and completely in God's word:

وَلٰكِنْ رَّسُوْلَ اللّٰهِ وَخَاتَمَ النَّبِيّٖنَ [107]

This verse contains a prophecy of which our opponents are not aware: God Almighty affirms in this verse that, after the Holy Prophet (peace and blessings of Allah be upon him), the door of prophecy has been closed forever and that it is no longer possible that a Hindu or a Jain or a Christian or a nominal Muslim should be able to rightfully assume the title of Prophet. All doors of Prophethood have been closed except that of complete devotion to the Holy Prophet[sa]. He who approaches God through this door is clothed, by way of reflection, in the same mantle of Prophethood that is the mantle of the Prophethood of Muḥammad. Therefore, his Prophethood is not a cause for jealousy, because he does not claim anything on his own account but acquires everything from the spring of the Holy Prophet[sa]. He is given the names Muḥammad and Aḥmad in heaven. This means

---

[107] '....but he is the Messenger of Allah and the Seal of the Prophets.'—Al-Aḥzāb, 33:41 **[Publisher]**

that the Prophethood of Muḥammad is bestowed on Muḥammad by way of reflection and on none other. The meaning of the verse:

مَا كَانَ مُحَمَّدٌ اَبَآ اَحَدٍ مِّنْ رِّجَالِكُمْ وَلٰكِنْ رَّسُوْلَ اللّٰهِ وَخَاتَمَ النَّبِيّٖنَ [108]

is that:

لَيْسَ مُحَمَّدٌ اَبَا اَحَدٍ مِّنْ رِّجَالِ الدُّنْيَا وَ لٰكِنْ هُوَ اَبٌ لِرِجَالِ الْاٰخِرَةِ
لِاَنَّهٗ خَاتَمَ النَّبِيّٖنَ وَ لَا سَبِيْلَ اِلٰى فُيُوْضِ اللّٰهِ مِنْ غَيْرِ تَوَسُّطِهٖ [109]

In short, my Prophethood and Messengership is because of my being Muḥammad and Aḥmad and not because of my own self, and I have been given this name by virtue of my utter devotion to the Holy Prophet[sa]. Thus there is no contravention of the Seal of Prophethood, but the supposed descent of Jesus from heaven would certainly amount to such contravention.

It should also be remembered that the literal meaning of '*Nabī*' is one who discloses the unseen in consequence of being informed of it by God. Therefore, wherever this connotation is established, the title of Prophet would be justified. A Prophet is necessarily a Messenger, for if he is not a Messenger, he cannot be the recipient of knowledge of the unseen as indicated by the verse:

لَا يُظْهِرُ عَلٰى غَيْبِهٖٓ اَحَدًا اِلَّا مَنِ ارْتَضٰى مِنْ رَّسُوْلٍ [110]

---

[108] 'Muḥammad is not the father of any of your men, but *he is* the Messenger of Allah and the Seal of the Prophets.'—Al-Aḥzāb, 33:41 **[Publisher]**

[109] 'Muḥammad is not the father of any man of the world, but he is the father of men of the hereafter because he is Seal of the Prophets, and there is no way of receiving Divine grace except through him.' **[Publisher]**

[110] 'He reveals not His secrets to anyone, except to him whom He

If it were held that there could be no Prophet in this connotation after the Holy Prophet (peace and blessings of Allah be upon him), it would follow that the Muslims are deprived of converse with the Divine; for he who discloses the unseen on the basis of knowledge bestowed upon him by God, would necessarily be a Prophet within the meaning of the above verse. In the same way, he who is sent by God Almighty must be designated a Messenger. The only distinction is that, after the Holy Prophet (peace and blessings of Allah be upon him), there cannot be any Prophet till the end of days who shall be the bearer of a new law, or who would be granted the title of a Prophet without having arrived at such a stage of utter devotion to the Holy Prophet (peace and blessings of Allah be upon him) wherein he is named Muḥammad and Aḥmad in heaven;

وَ مَنِ ادّعٰی فَقَدْ كَفَرَ [111]

The key to this mystery is that the true connotation of the 'Seal of the Prophets' demands that if anyone calls himself a Prophet while there is the slightest distance between him and the Holy Prophet[sa], will be guilty of contravening the Seal of Prophethood. But he who is so completely devoted to the Holy Prophet[sa] that, on account of his complete unity and the absence of any difference between them, he is given his name and reflects, like a bright mirror, the countenance of the Holy Prophet[sa], then he would be called a Prophet without contravening the Seal, because he is Muḥammad, though only by way of reflection. Thus, despite the claim of

---

chooses, namely a Messenger *of His*.'—Al-Jinn, 72:27-28 **[Publisher]**

[111] 'He who falsely claims [to be a Prophet] is an infidel.' **[Publisher]**

Prophethood by a person who is designated Muḥammad and Aḥmad, by way of reflection, our lord and master Muḥammad would still be the Seal of the Prophets inasmuch as this second Muḥammad is his reflection and bears his name. But Jesus cannot come without breaking that Seal, since his Prophethood is distinct from the Prophethood of the Holy Prophet[sa]. If no one can be a Prophet or a Messenger, even by way of reflection, then what is the purpose of the prayer:

اِهْدِنَا الصِّرَاطَ الْمُسْتَقِيْمَ ۝ صِرَاطَ الَّذِيْنَ اَنْعَمْتَ عَلَيْهِمْ [112]

I do not deny being a Prophet and a Messenger in this connotation. It is for the same reason that the Promised Messiah has been designated a Prophet in *Ṣaḥīḥ Muslim.* If one who is bestowed knowledge of the unseen by God Almighty cannot bear the title of *'Nabī'*, how then should he be designated? If you say that such a one should be called Muḥaddath, I would counter that no lexicon attributes to the word '*Taḥdīth*' the meaning 'disclosure of the unseen', but Prophethood has this connotation. The word *'Nabī'* [Prophet] is common to Arabic and Hebrew. In Hebrew it is called *Nābī* and is derived from the root *Nābā* meaning to prophesize on the basis of knowledge derived from God. *Nabī* is not necessarily law-bearing. This is a Divine gift which carries with it knowledge of the unseen.

[Eik Ghalaṭī kā Izālah, Rūḥānī Khazā'in, vol. 18, pp. 207-210]

All doors are closed except the one which has been opened by the Holy Qur'ān. Now there is no need to follow the Prophets and Books of the past, inasmuch as the

---

[112] 'Guide us in the right path–the path of those upon whom Thou hast bestowed Thy blessings.'—Al-Fātiḥah, 1:6-7 **[Publisher]**

Prophethood of Muḥammad comprises all of them and all ways are closed except the way of this Prophethood. All verities that lead to God are comprised in the Holy Qur'ān. No new verity will be disclosed after the Holy Qur'ān, nor is there any verity which was disclosed before it and is not contained in it. Therefore, all Prophethood is closed with this Prophethood and so it should have been, for everything that has a beginning must have an end. But the Prophethood of Muḥammad is not deficient in bestowing grace. Indeed it possesses this quality in a greater degree than all previous Prophethoods. By following this Prophethood a person easily attains nearness to God. Obedience to it makes one more worthy of the bounty of the love of God, and of converse with Him, than was the case with previous Prophethoods. But a perfect follower of this Prophethood cannot just be called a Prophet, for this would be an offence against the complete and perfect Prophethood of Muḥammad. He can be called a Prophet and the follower of a Prophet at the same time, for this involves no offence against the complete and perfect Prophethood of Muḥammad, but rather adds to its brightness. When converse with the Divine arrives at its climax, both quantitatively and qualitatively, and suffers from no impurity or deficiency and unequivocally comprehends the matters relating to the unseen, it is designated Prophethood. All Prophets are agreed on this.

In short, it was not possible that a people about whom it was said:

كُنْتُمْ خَيْرَ أُمَّةٍ أُخْرِجَتْ لِلنَّاسِ [113]

---

[113] 'You are the best people raised for the benefit of mankind.'—

and who were taught the prayer:

اِهْدِنَا الصِّرَاطَ الْمُسْتَقِيْمَ ○ صِرَاطَ الَّذِيْنَ اَنْعَمْتَ عَلَيْهِمْ [114]

should have been deprived of this high rank and not one of them should have achieved it. In that case, not only would the Ummah have remained inferior and imperfect and like the blind, but also the spiritual grace of the Holy Prophet (peace and blessings of Allah be upon him) would have been deemed imperfect and tainted, and the prayer that the Muslims had been taught to repeat in their five daily prayers, would have proved purposeless. On the other hand, if this rank had been bestowed upon a Muslim directly and not through his following the light of the Prophethood of Muḥammad, the significance of the Seal of Prophethood would have been obscured. Therefore, in order to safeguard the Muslims against both these contingencies, God Almighty bestowed the honour of perfect, complete and holy converse with Himself upon some individuals from among the Muslims who had arrived at the climax of devotion to the Holy Prophet[sa]. No intervening barrier remained and they illustrated in their person the meaning of being followers of the Holy Prophet[sa] in the true sense of the word, so much so that their own being gave place to the reflection of the Holy Prophet[sa] in the mirror of their devotion, and they were bestowed complete and perfect converse with God.

In this way, some individuals from among the Muslims were bestowed the title of Prophet, for such a Prophethood is not distinct from the Prophethood of

---

Āl-e-'Imrān, 3:111 **[Publisher]**

[114] 'Guide us in the right path–The path of those upon whom Thou has bestowed Thy favours.'—Al-Fātiḥah, 1:6-7 **[Publisher]**

Muḥammad (peace and blessings of Allah be upon him); but if it is viewed carefully, it is the very Prophethood of Muḥammad manifested in a new aspect. This is the meaning of the Holy Prophet (peace and blessings of Allah be upon him) having described the Promised Messiah as:

نَبِيُّ اللّٰهِ وَ اِمَامُكُمْ مِنْكُمْ

which means that he will be a Prophet but he will also be from the Ummah. No outsider can be admitted to such a rank. Blessed is he who appreciates this point and saves himself from ruin.

[Al-Waṣiyyat, Rūḥānī Khazā'in, vol. 20, pp. 311-312]

What God requires of you, in the matter of belief, is that God is One and that Muḥammad (peace and blessings of Allah be upon him) is His Prophet and the Seal of Prophets and is the greatest of them all. After him there is no Prophet except only one who is reflectively clothed in the mantle of *Muḥammadiyyat.* Inasmuch as a servant cannot be separated from his master, nor is a branch separable from its root, he who is designated Prophet by God on account of his perfect devotion to his master does not contravene the Seal of Prophethood. Just as when you look into a mirror, there are not two of you but only one, although there appear to be two: the real one and the reflection. That is what God designated in the case of the Promised Messiah. This is also the meaning of the saying of the Holy Prophet (peace and blessings of Allah be upon him) that the Promised Messiah would be buried with him in the same grave; which means that they would be completely identical.

[Kashtī-e-Nūḥ, Rūḥānī Khazā'in, vol. 19, pp. 15-16]

Remember, I am not a Messenger or Prophet by virtue of

a new law, a new claim or a new name; but I am a Messenger and Prophet by virtue of perfect reflection. I am the mirror in which the form and the Prophethood of Muḥammad are perfectly reflected. Had I been a claimant of distinct Prophethood, God Almighty would not have named me Muḥammad and Aḥmad and *Muṣṭafā* and *Mujtabā*. Nor would I have been bestowed the title of *Khātam-ul-Auliyā'* [Seal of the Elect of God], resembling the title of the Seal of the Prophets. In such a case, I would have been given a separate name. But God Almighty admitted me completely into the being of Muḥammad, so much so that He did not desire that I should have a separate name or a separate tomb, for a reflection cannot be separated from its original. Why did this come about? It came about because God had appointed the Holy Prophet (peace and blessings of Allah be upon him) as Seal of Prophets, and, in order to maintain the parallel between the Mosaic dispensation and the Muḥammadī dispensation, it was necessary that the Muḥammadī Messiah should be bestowed the dignity of Prophethood like the Mosaic Messiah, so that the Muḥammadī Prophethood should not be considered deficient in any respect when compared to the Mosaic Prophethood. Therefore, God Almighty created me as a perfect reflection, and invested me with the reflection of Muḥammadī Prophethood, so that in one aspect I should bear the title of *Nabī'ullāh* [Prophet of God], and in another aspect the Seal of Prophethood should be safeguarded.

[Nuzūl-ul-Masīḥ, Rūḥānī Khazā'in, vol. 18, pp. 381-382, footnote]

Frequent Converse with God—the only Claim of the Promised Messiah

In order to provoke the common people, my opponents allege that I lay claim to Prophethood. This is an utterly false accusation. I do not claim any Prophethood that is barred by the Holy Qur'ān. All I claim is that in one aspect I am a follower of the Holy Prophet[sa] and, in another, through the grace of the Prophethood of the Holy Prophet (peace and blessings of Allah be upon him), I am a Prophet. In my case Prophethood means only that I am frequently honoured with converse with God Almighty. The truth is as the revered reformer of Sarhind has recorded in his Maktūbāt:

> Though some individuals from among the Muslims are honoured with converse with the Divine and will continue to be so honoured, yet only he is called a Prophet who is so honoured most frequently and to whom the unseen is frequently disclosed.

There is a prophecy in the Aḥādīth that there will appear among the Muslims one who will be called 'Īsā and Ibn-e-Maryam and will be designated a Prophet, that is to say, he will be so frequently honoured with converse with God and so much of the unseen will be disclosed to him as is not possible in the case of anyone except a Prophet as God Almighty has said:

فَلَا يُظْهِرُ عَلٰى غَيْبِهٖٓ اَحَدًا اِلَّا مَنِ ارْتَضٰى مِنْ رَّسُوْلٍ [115]

This means that: 'God does not grant anyone clear and consistent ascendancy over His domain of the unseen, except him whom He chooses as His Messenger.'

It has been established that the bounty of converse with God and of disclosure of the unseen has been bestowed on me to a degree to which it has not been bestowed on anyone during the last thirteen hundred years. Should anyone challenge this, the onus of proof lies with him.

---

[115] Al-Jinn, 72:27-28 **[Publisher]**

In short, I alone have been honoured with so great a share of Divine revelation and of knowledge of the unseen as has not been bestowed on any of the *Auliyā'* and *Abdāl* and *Aqṭāb* among the Muslims before me. For this reason I alone have been bestowed the title of Prophet and no one else has deserved it because it implies frequency of revelation and repeated disclosure of the unseen, a condition which was not fulfilled by any of them.

[Ḥaqīqat-ul-Waḥī, Rūḥānī Khazā'in, vol. 22, pp. 406-407]

My critic has further objected that God Almighty has said:

اَلْيَوْمَ اَكْمَلْتُ لَكُمْ دِيْنَكُمْ وَاَتْمَمْتُ عَلَيْكُمْ نِعْمَتِيْ [116]

Therefore no reformer or Prophet is now needed. In so thinking the critic has raised an objection against the Holy Qur'ān itself, inasmuch as the Holy Qur'ān has promised the appointment of successors from among the Muslims and has said that through them faith would be strengthened, doubts would be set at rest and security would be restored after a state of fear. Thus if nothing is permissible after the perfection of the faith, then, according to the critic, the Khilāfat that continued for thirty years after the Holy Prophet[sa] would also be rendered unnecessary, as the faith had been perfected and nothing more was needed.

The citation of the verse اَلْيَوْمَ اَكْمَلْتُ لَكُمْ دِيْنَكُمْ [117] by the critic is out of place. We do not allege that a reformer or a Muḥaddath detracts anything from the faith or adds anything to it. What we say is that when, after the lapse

---

[116] 'This day have I perfected your religion for you and completed My favour upon you.'—Al-Mā'idah, 5:4, **[Publisher]**

[117] Ibid.

of time, the holy teaching of the faith is covered with the dust of wrong thinking and the pure countenance of truth becomes hidden, then reformers, Muḥaddathīn and spiritual successors appear to reveal the true and beautiful countenance of the faith.

We do not know whence our poor critic has learnt that reformers and spiritual successors arrive for the purpose of adding to or abrogating the faith. Their purpose is not to abrogate but to display the light and brilliance of the faith. The conception of the critic that there is no such need reveals that he does not have much regard for the faith. He has never reflected on what Islām is, what its progress signifies, how its real progress can be achieved, and who can be considered a true Muslim. That is why he considers it enough that the Holy Qur'ān being available, and there being a plethora of divines, the hearts of most people are automatically drawn to Islām and no reformer is needed. He does not appreciate the fact that reformers and spiritual successors are needed among the Muslims, in the same way as Prophets are needed among other people. It cannot be denied that Moses (peace be upon him) was a Prophet and a Messenger and that the Torah was a complete code for the children of Israel; and just as the Holy Qur'ān contains the verse اَلْيَوْمَ اَكْمَلْتُ لَكُمْ[118] so does the Torah contain verses to the effect that the children of Israel have been given a perfect and glorious Book. The Holy Qur'ān also describes the Torah as such. Yet hundreds of Prophets appeared among the children of Israel after the Torah, who brought no new book and whose function was to pull people who had departed

---

[118] Ibid.

from the teachings of the Torah back to it and to purify the hearts of those who had been afflicted with doubts, atheism and lack of faith. God the Exalted has affirmed in the Holy Qur'ān:

وَلَقَدْ اٰتَيْنَا مُوْسَى الْكِتٰبَ وَقَفَّيْنَا مِنْۢ بَعْدِهٖ بِالرُّسُلِ [119]

That is: 'We bestowed the Torah upon Moses[as] and thereafter sent many Messengers in its support and to testify to its truth.'

ثُمَّ اَرْسَلْنَا رُسُلَنَا تَتْرَا [120]

That is: 'Then, We sent Our Messengers one after the other.'

All these verses show that it is the way of Allah that after sending down His Book He sends Prophets in support of it. In support of the Torah sometimes as many as four hundred Prophets were sent at one and the same time; as testified by the Bible.

The reason for sending so many Prophets is that God Almighty has warned emphatically that abiding hell is the punishment for denial of His Book; as is said:

وَالَّذِيْنَ كَفَرُوْا وَكَذَّبُوْا بِاٰيٰتِنَآ اُولٰٓئِكَ اَصْحٰبُ النَّارِ ۚ هُمْ فِيْهَا خٰلِدُوْنَ [121]

This means that: 'Those who are disbelievers and reject Our signs are condemned to the fire and shall abide therein forever.'

Thus as the punishment of rejection of a Divine Book is so severe and the phenomenon of Prophethood and divine revelation is so difficult of comprehension, indeed

---

[119] Al-Baqarah, 2:88 **[Publisher]**

[120] Al-Mu'minūn, 23:45 **[Publisher]**

[121] Al-Baqarah, 2:40 **[Publisher]**

God Almighty Himself is so transcendent that unless the human eye is illumined by divine light it is not possible to achieve true and holy comprehension of Him, let alone the comprehension of Prophets and divine books, therefore, the *Raḥmāniyyat* of God demanded that his blind and unseeing creatures should be helped very greatly, and it should not be considered enough that a Messenger and a Book having been sent, thereafter, despite the passage of a long period of time, the disbelievers may be committed to the everlasting torment of hell on account of the denial of such doctrines as later generations can comprehend as merely pure and excellent statements.

It should be clear to a thoughtful person that God, Who is *Raḥmān* [Gracious] and *Raḥīm* [Merciful], cannot, without convincing explanation, prescribe so great a punishment as condemnation to everlasting hell for people of different countries who have heard of the Qur'ān and of the Holy Prophet[sa] after centuries and who, not being proficient in Arabic, cannot perceive the excellence of the Holy Qur'ān. Nor can human conscience reconcile itself to the fact that a person may be condemned without being convinced that the Holy Qur'ān is the Word of God. That is why God Almighty has promised that He will continue to appoint vicegerents so that they, being invested reflectively with the lights of Prophethood, should demonstrate the excellences of the Holy Qur'ān and its holy blessings to the people and thus make them responsible for believing in it and acting upon it.

It should also be remembered that such exposition has to adopt different forms in every age, and that a reformer is equipped with the faculties, capacities and qualities which are suited to the reform of the mischief which is current in his time. Thus God Almighty will ever continue to do so, as long as He wills, so that reform and virtue may continue to flourish. These statements are not without proof and are testified by an unbroken series of precedents.

Apart from the Prophets, Messengers and *Muḥaddathīn* who appeared at different times in different countries, if one takes into account only those who appeared in Israel, it would be discovered that in the fourteen centuries between Moses[as] and Jesus[as], thousands of Prophets and *Muḥaddathīn* appeared and occupied themselves diligently in the service of the Torah. The Holy Qur'ān and the Bible both testify to this. Those Prophets brought no new book and taught no new faith. They only served the Torah. They appeared whenever atheism, disbelief, misconduct, and hard-heartedness became prevalent in Israel.

It is a point to ponder that the Law of Moses[as] was limited in its scope and was not meant for the whole of mankind, nor was it to last forever, yet God Almighty took care to send thousands of Prophets for the revival of that law and those Prophets exhibited such signs as enabled the children of Israel to behold God afresh. Then how can it be that Muslims, who have been designated the best of people, and are attached to the Best of the Prophets (peace and blessings of Allah be upon him) be accounted so unfortunate that God Almighty looked at them with mercy only for thirty years and after exhibiting heavenly lights to them during that time, turned His face away from them. Centuries passed after the departure of the Holy Prophet[sa], and thousands of disorders arose, and great earthquakes were felt, and diverse forms of corruption spread, and a whole world mounted attacks against Islām, and all its blessings and miracles were denied, and that which was acceptable was declared unacceptable, and yet God Almighty never again looked upon the Muslims nor had mercy on them, nor did He consider that the Muslims were also weak human beings and, like the children of Israel, their plants also were in need of heavenly water. Could the Beneficent God, Who had sent the Holy Prophet (peace and blessings of Allah be upon him) to remove all corruption forever, turn away from the Muslims like this? Can we conceive that God Almighty was so merciful towards previous people and, having revealed the Torah, sent thousands of Prophets and *Muḥaddathīn* in support of the Torah and for the repeated revival of the hearts of the children of Israel, but that the Muslims were subject to His wrath and, therefore, after the revelation of the Holy Qur'ān, He forgot them and left them forever to the reasoning and deduction of clerics? God clearly stated concerning Moses[as]:

وَكَلَّمَ اللّٰهُ مُوْسٰى تَكْلِيْمًا [122]

رُسُلًا مُّبَشِّرِيْنَ وَمُنْذِرِيْنَ لِئَلَّا يَكُوْنَ لِلنَّاسِ عَلَى اللّٰهِ حُجَّةٌ
بَعْدَ الرُّسُلِ ۭ وَكَانَ اللّٰهُ عَزِيْزًا حَكِيْمًا [123]

That is to say: 'Allah spoke to Moses[as]' and 'sent Messengers bearing glad tidings as well as warnings to help him and to testify to his truth, so that people may not have any excuse after that, and, after witnessing a host of Prophets, should believe in the Torah with all their heart.'

Then He says:

---

[122] Al-Nisā', 4:165 **[Publisher]**

[123] Al-Nisā', 4:166 **[Publisher]**

وَرُسُلًا قَدْ قَصَصْنَاهُمْ عَلَيْكَ مِن قَبْلُ وَرُسُلًا لَّمْ نَقْصُصْهُمْ عَلَيْكَ [124]

That is: 'We sent many Messengers before thee, some of whom We have mentioned to thee and some We have not so mentioned.'

But God made no such arrangement for the Muslims and withheld from them the mercy and grace He had bestowed upon the people of Moses[as]! It is obvious that, with the passage of time, previous miracles and wonders became mere tales. Succeeding generations, finding themselves bereft of all such wonders, begin to entertain doubts about miracles and extraordinary happenings. Having the example of thousands of Prophets of Israel before them, the Muslims would be disheartened and, considering themselves unfortunate, would either envy the children of Israel or would consider the history of Israel also a chain of imaginary tales. It is idle to assert that, as there have been thousands of Prophets and many miracles have been shown in the past, the Muslims were in no need of extraordinary events and wonders and blessings and that is why God Almighty held everything of that kind back from the Muslims. This is the kind of thing that is asserted by those who have no regard for the faith. Man is very weak and always needs strengthening of faith. In this respect no help can be derived from self-conceived arguments. It is necessary to realize afresh that God exists. False belief, which is not effective in restraining a person from misconduct, may however continue to exist as a matter of speculation and form.

Need for Reformers after the Perfection of Faith

It should be remembered that the perfection of faith does

---

[124] Al-Nisā', 4:165 **[Publisher]**

not dispense with the need of safeguarding it. For instance, if a person builds a house, sets all its rooms in order and fills all the needs relating to its structure, and, after a long time, dust settles on it in because of rains and dust storms, and its beauty is covered up; if, at such a time, a person who inherits this house wishes to undertake its cleaning and whitewashing, would this not be the height of folly to stop him from doing so for the reason that the house had been completed long ago? These people do not reflect that the completion of a structure is one thing and its seasonal cleaning is quite another. It should be remembered that reformers do not add anything to or subtract anything from the faith. They restore to the hearts that which had been lost. To assert that it is not necessary to believe in reformers is disobedience of a Divine command. He has directed:

وَمَنْ كَفَرَ بَعْدَ ذٰلِكَ فَاُولٰٓئِكَ هُمُ الْفٰسِقُوْنَ [125]

'Whoever rejects the Khulafā', after they have been sent, is indeed from amongst the sinners.'

To summarise, it was necessary that after the death of the Holy Prophet (peace and blessings of Allah be upon him) reformers should have appeared among the Muslims at times of disorder and trials, who should have been entrusted with one of the functions of the Prophets, namely that they should call men to the true faith and remove all innovations and exhibit the truth of the faith from every point of view with the help of heavenly light and invite people to truth, love and piety by the force of their example. The reasons for this are:

Firstly, reason affirms that matters relating to God and

---

[125] Al-Nūr, 24:56 **[Publisher]**

the hereafter are very fine and imperceptible. One has to believe in the unseen and the supernatural. No one has ever seen God Almighty or observed heaven and hell, or met the angels. What is more, Divine commandments are opposed to the desires of the ego and restrain from that in which the ego delights. Therefore it is necessary that either the Prophets of God, who bring the law and the Book and possess spiritual power, should live long and continue to bless their followers in each century with their company, and should train them under their own graceful supervision and convey to them the blessing, light and spiritual comprehension which they had done in the early part of their ministry. Or, if that should not be possible, then their spiritual heirs, who are equipped with their high qualities and can set forth the verities and insights comprised in the Divine Book under the guidance of revelation, and can illustrate in practice that which is related to the past and can lead a seeker after truth to certainty, must continue to appear in times of trouble and trials so that man who is afflicted with doubt and forgetfulness should not be deprived of the true grace of the Prophets.

It is obvious that when the time of a Prophet comes to an end, and those who have witnessed his blessings pass away, their experiences become tales in the eyes of the people of the next generation. The moral qualities of the Prophet, his worship, his steadfastness, his devotion, Divine support, extraordinary events, and miracles which testified to his Prophethood and the truth of his claim becomes fictional in the estimation of subsequent generations. Therefore, the freshness of the faith and the eagerness of obedience that are the characteristics of those who are favoured with the company of the Prophet are not found in those who come after them. It is clear that the kind of sincerity and devotion with which the companions of the Holy Prophet (peace and blessings of Allah be upon him) sacrificed their wealth, lives, and honour in the cause of Islām were not to be found even among the second century Muslims, let alone Muslims of subsequent centuries. Why was this so? It was because the companions, may Allah be pleased with them, had beheld the countenance of the true one, whose love for Allah was so spontaneously testified even by the disbelieving Quraish. These people, observing his daily supplications, his loving prostrations, his condition of complete obedience, the bright signs of perfect love and devotion on his countenance, and the rain of Divine light on his face, were compelled to affirm:

عَشِقَ مُحَمَّدٌ عَلٰى رَبِّهٖ

'Muḥammad has fallen in love with his Lord.'

The companions not only observed the devotion, love and sincerity which surged up in the heart of our lord and master Muḥammad (peace and blessings of Allah be upon him) like a raging ocean, they also observed God Almighty's love for him, in the guise of extraordinary support and help. Then they realized that God exists and their hearts testified that He stood by the Holy Prophet (peace and blessings of Allah be upon him.) They had witnessed so many Divine wonders and so many heavenly signs that they were left in no doubt about the existence of a Supreme Being Who is God, Who controls everything and for Whom nothing is impossible. That is why they exhibited such devotion and made such sacrifices as are not possible for anyone until all his doubts have been resolved. They realized that to win His pleasure it was necessary to accept Islām and to obey the Holy Prophet[sa] with complete sincerity. After this absolute certainty, the kind of obedience they exhibited and the feats they performed and the manner in which they laid down their lives at the feet of their Holy Preceptor, were matters which were not possible for anyone who had not witnessed what the companions had witnessed.

Such high qualities cannot be developed and salvation cannot be truly achieved without such means. It is, therefore, necessary that the Beneficent God Who has invited everyone to salvation should make a similar arrangement in every century so that His creatures should not fail in any age to attain the stage of absolute certainty.

Need of the Company of the Righteous

The affirmation that the Holy Qur'ān and the Aḥādīth alone suffice us and that we do not need the company of the righteous is opposed to the teachings of the Holy Qur'ān, as Allah the Exalted has said:

وَكُوْنُوْا مَعَ الصّٰدِقِيْنَ [126]

The truthful are those who have recognized the truth through their spiritual insight and are devoted to it. This high grade of spiritual insight cannot be achieved unless heavenly guidance conveys a seeker to the stage of certainty by experience. In this sense the truly righteous are the Prophets, the Messengers, the Muḥaddathīn and the perfect Auliyā' who are guided by heavenly light and who behold God Almighty with the sight of certainty in this very world. The verse that we have just quoted indicates that the world is never left without the truthful, as

[126] 'And be with the truthful.'—Al-Taubah, 9:119 **[Publisher]**

the commandment كُوْنُوْا مَعَ الصّٰدِقِيْنَ[127] necessitates the presence of the truthful at all times.

Besides, observation confirms that the learning and knowledge of those who do not seek the company of the righteous does not help to rid them of their physical passions, and that they do not achieve even that minimum status in Islām which generates the certainty of belief that God does indeed exist. They do not believe in the existence of God with the same certainty as they feel with regard to their wealth, which is locked in their boxes, or about the houses which they own. They dread swallowing arsenic, as they are certain that it is a fatal poison, but they do not dread the poison of sin, though they read in the Holy Qur'ān:

إِنَّهٗ مَنْ يَّأْتِ رَبَّهٗ مُجْرِمًا فَإِنَّ لَهٗ جَهَنَّمَ ۖ لَا يَمُوْتُ فِيْهَا وَلَا يَحْيٰى[128]

The truth is that he who does not recognize God Almighty cannot recognize the Holy Qur'ān. It is true that the Holy Qur'ān has been revealed for guidance, but the guidance of the Qur'ān is bound up with the personality of the one to whom it was revealed or of one who is appointed his substitute by God. Had the Qur'ān alone been enough, God Almighty had the power to have the Qur'ān inscribed on the leaves of trees or could have made it descend from heaven in the form of a book, but this was not what He did. He did not send the Qur'ān into the world till the teacher of the Qur'ān had been sent. You will find that at several places the Holy Qur'ān affirms:

يُعَلِّمُهُمُ الْكِتٰبَ وَ الْحِكْمَةَ[129]

---

[127] Ibid.

[128] 'Verily, he who comes to his Lord a sinner—for him is hell; he shall neither die therein nor live.'—Ṭā Hā, 20:75 **[Publisher]**

That is: 'The Holy Prophet (peace and blessings of Allah be upon him) teaches the Qur'ān and its wisdom to the people.' At one place it is said:

لَا يَمَسُّهٗۤ اِلَّا الْمُطَهَّرُوْنَ [130]

This means that: 'The verities and the insights of the Qur'ān are revealed only to the purified.'

Need for Teachers and Fresh Exposition of the Holy Qur'ān

This shows clearly that for the true understanding of the Holy Qur'ān a teacher is needed who is purified by God Almighty Himself. Had a teacher of the Qur'ān not been needed, there would have been no such need from the beginning of time. It is idle to assert that in the beginning a teacher was needed for the exposition of the difficult parts of the Qur'ān, and that exposition having been made, a teacher is no longer needed. Fresh exposition is needed from time to time. The Muslims are confronted with new difficulties in every age. It is true that the Qur'ān comprises all knowledge but not all its knowledge is disclosed at one time. It is revealed as difficulties and problems are encountered. Spiritual teachers, who are the heirs of the Prophets and are reflectively invested with their qualities, are sent to resolve the difficulties that arise in every age. The reformer whose functions closely resemble the functions of a Messenger bears the name of that Messenger in the estimation of Allah.

Teachers are also needed, because some portions of the teaching of the Holy Qur'ān are matters of *ḥāl* as op-

---

[129] Al-Jumu'ah, 62:3 **[Publisher]**

[130] Al-Wāqi'ah, 56:80 **[Publisher]**

posed to *qāl*.[131] The Holy Prophet (peace and blessings of Allah be upon him), who was the first teacher of the Holy Qur'ān and the true heir of its teaching, demonstrated its teachings to his companions by his own practice and example. For instance, the Divine affirmation that He knows the unseen, accepts prayer, has power to do all that He wills, leads His seekers to the true light, sends His revelation to His sincere servants, and causes His spirit to descend upon whomsoever He wills out of His creatures, are all matters that can be understood only through the example of the teacher himself.

It is obvious that the superficial clerics, who are themselves blind, cannot illustrate these teachings. On the contrary, they teach that all these matters have been left behind and can no longer be experienced. Thus they create doubts in the minds of their disciples concerning the greatness of Islām. They teach that Islām is no longer a living faith and there is no way now to discover its true meaning. It is obvious, however, that if God Almighty designs that His creatures should always drink from the spring of the Holy Qur'ān, He would have made provisions for it as He always done. Had the teachings of the Holy Qur'ān been limited, as the teaching of an experienced and right thinking philosopher is limited, and did it not comprise the heavenly teaching which can only be demonstrated by practice, then, God forbid, the revelation of the Qur'ān was needless. But I know that if one were to reflect upon the distinction between the teaching of the Prophets and the teaching of the philosophers, assuming both to be true, the only distinction that would be

---

[131] *Ḥāl* here means the practical demonstration of faith, as opposed to *qāl*, which connotes only verbal acceptance. **[Publisher]**

discovered is that a great portion of the teaching of the Prophets is metaphysical and can only be understood and appreciated through practical demonstration, and can be illustrated only by those who have the personal experience of it....

If Allah the Glorious has so willed that this portion of the teaching of His Book should not be confined to the early ages, then He must have arranged for the teachers of that portion to be available at all times, since the portion of the teaching which relates to personal experience cannot be comprehended except through teachers who have experienced it. Therefore, if after the Holy Prophet (peace and blessings of Allah be upon him) teachers who were guided by the reflection of the light of Prophethood had not been available, it would mean that God Almighty, having removed from the world at an early stage those who understood the Holy Qur'ān truly and correctly, deliberately let the Qur'ān become useless. But this would be contrary to His promise:

إِنَّا نَحْنُ نَزَّلْنَا الذِّكْرَ وَإِنَّا لَهُ لَحٰفِظُوْنَ [132]

That is: 'It is We Who have sent down the Qur'ān and We shall continue to safeguard it.'

Fulfilling the Need of Safeguarding the Holy Qur'ān

I am unable to understand that if those with complete understanding of the Qur'ān and belief in its certainty through personal experience have all passed away, then how has the Qur'ān been safeguarded? Does safeguarding it mean that the Qur'ān, beautifully inscribed, would be preserved forever locked in safes like treasures that lie

---

[132] Al-Ḥijr, 15:10 **[Publisher]**

buried under the earth and are of no use to anyone? Can anyone imagine that this is the true meaning of this verse? If so, there is nothing extraordinary about it. Rather, such a claim is laughable and amounts to inviting ridicule from the enemies of Islām. Of what use is the safeguarding which does not serve the true purpose? It is quite possible that a copy of the Torah or the Gospel may be found which has been similarly safeguarded. There are thousands of books, which have continued to exist entirely unaltered and which are for certain the writings of a particular person. There is no particular merit in such preservation, and such safeguarding of the Qur'ān would be of no benefit to the Muslims. It is true that the safeguarding of the text of the Holy Qur'ān is greater than that of all other books and is in itself extraordinary, but we cannot imagine that God Almighty, Who always has a spiritual purpose, meant only the safeguarding of the text of the Holy Qur'ān. The very word *dhikr* [remembrance] clearly indicates that the Holy Qur'ān will be preserved forever as a remembrance, and its true *dhākirīn*[133] will always be present. This is confirmed by another verse, which says:

بَلْ هُوَ اٰيٰتٌۢ بَيِّنٰتٌ فِيْ صُدُوْرِ الَّذِيْنَ اُوْتُوا الْعِلْمَ[134]

'The Holy Qur'ān is composed of clear signs in the bosoms of those who have been bestowed knowledge.'

This verse clearly means that the believers have been bestowed knowledge of the Holy Qur'ān and they act upon it. As the Qur'ān is preserved in the bosoms of the believers, the verse:

---

[133] Those who learn the Qur'an, act according to it, and recite it to others. **[Publisher]**

[134] Al-'Ankabūt, 29:50, **[Publisher]**

إِنَّا نَحْنُ نَزَّلْنَا الذِّكْرَ وَإِنَّا لَهُ لَحٰفِظُوْنَ [135]

means that it would not cease to dwell therein….

Secondly, reason demands that for the teaching and understanding of Divine books, it is necessary that, like the advent of the Prophets, recipients of revelation and persons equipped with spiritual knowledge should also continue to appear from time to time. Similarly, when we study the Qur'ān and deliberate upon it we discover that the availability of spiritual teachers is part of the Divine design. For instance God has said:

وَأَمَّا مَا يَنْفَعُ النَّاسَ فَيَمْكُثُ فِي الْأَرْضِ [136]

(Part Number 13)

'That which benefits people endures in the earth.'

The Prophets who strengthen people's faith through miracles, prophecies, verities, insights and the example of their own righteousness, and benefit the seekers after truth, are obviously the greatest benefactors of mankind. And it is also obvious that they do not remain upon the earth for a long time and pass away after a short existence. Yet the purport of this verse cannot be contradictory to this reality. Therefore, with reference to the Prophets, this verse means that they continue their beneficence by way of reflection. God Almighty at the times of need raises a servant of His who becomes their example reflectively and thus continues their spiritual life. It is for this purpose that God has taught the prayer:

اِهْدِنَا الصِّرَاطَ الْمُسْتَقِيْمَ ۝ صِرَاطَ الَّذِيْنَ اَنْعَمْتَ عَلَيْهِمْ [137]

---

[135] 'Verily, We Ourself have sent down this Exhortation, and surely We will be its Guardian.'—Al-Ḥijr, 15:10 **[Publisher]**

[136] Al-Ra'd, 13:18 **[Publisher]**

'O Allah, guide us along the straight path, the path of those servants upon whom Thou has bestowed Thy favours….'

Not only has He taught this prayer, but has also promised in another verse:

وَالَّذِيْنَ جَاهَدُوْا فِيْنَا لَنَهْدِيَنَّهُمْ سُبُلَنَا [138]

'Those who strive in Our path—which is the right path—We will surely guide them along Our ways.'

It is clear that the ways of God Almighty are those that have been disclosed to the Prophets.

[Shahādat-ul-Qur'ān, Rūḥānī Khazā'in, vol. 6, pp.339-352]

Divine Promise of Khilāfat

There are other verses which also indicate that it is God's design that spiritual teachers, who are the heirs of the Prophets, should always continue to be available. For instance:

وَعَدَ اللّٰهُ الَّذِيْنَ اٰمَنُوْا مِنْكُمْ وَعَمِلُوا الصّٰلِحٰتِ لَيَسْتَخْلِفَنَّهُمْ
فِي الْاَرْضِ كَمَا اسْتَخْلَفَ الَّذِيْنَ مِنْ قَبْلِهِمْ [139]

وَلَا يَزَالُ الَّذِيْنَ كَفَرُوْا تُصِيْبُهُمْ بِمَا صَنَعُوْا قَارِعَةٌ اَوْ تَحُلُّ قَرِيْبًا مِّنْ
دَارِهِمْ حَتّٰى يَاْتِيَ وَعْدُ اللّٰهِ اِنَّ اللّٰهَ لَا يُخْلِفُ الْمِيْعَادَ [140]

وَمَا كُنَّا مُعَذِّبِيْنَ حَتّٰى نَبْعَثَ رَسُوْلًا [141]

Meaning: 'O True believers among the followers of Muḥammad (peace and blessings of Allah be upon him), Allah has promised those among you who believe and act

---

[137] Al-Fātiḥah, 1:6-7 **[Publisher]**

[138] Al-'Ankabūt, 29:70 **[Publisher]**

[139] Al-Nūr, 24:56 **[Publisher]**

[140] Al-Ra'd, 13:32 **[Publisher]**

[141] Banī Isrā'īl, 17:16 **[Publisher]**

righteously, that He will surely make them successors in the earth, as He made successors among those who were before them.'

'Those who disbelieve will continue to be afflicted with a calamity, physical or spiritual, or would descend close to their dwellings till the Divine promise is fulfilled. Surely Allah doeth not contrary to His promise.'

'And We send not a punishment till after We have raised a Messenger.'

If a person reflects upon these verses he will realize that God Almighty has clearly promised the Muslims a permanent Khilāfat. If this Khilāfat were not permanent there would have been no sense in describing it as resembling the Khilāfat of the Mosaic dispensation....

A Khalīfa is a reflection of a Prophet. As man is mortal, God Almighty designed that Prophets, who are more exalted and honoured than all other beings, should be reflectively preserved forever. For this purpose, God instituted Khilāfat so that the world should at no time be deprived of the blessings of Prophethood. He who limits it to thirty years, foolishly overlooks the true purpose of Khilāfat, and does not realize that God did not design that the blessings of Khilāfat be limited to thirty years after the death of the Holy Prophet (peace and blessings of Allah be upon him) and that, thereafter, the world may go to ruin....

There are many other verses in the Holy Qur'ān, which give tidings of a permanent Khilāfat among the Muslims, and there are also several Aḥādīth to the same effect. But what I have said already should suffice for those who accept established verities as great wealth.

There is no worse concept concerning Islām than to say

that it is a dead religion whose blessings were confined only to its beginning. Can the Book that opens the door of perpetual good fortune inculcate so discouraging a doctrine that there is no blessing or Khilāfat in the future and that everything has been confined to the past? True, there will be no independent Prophets among the Muslims. But if there were also to be no Khulafā' to demonstrate the proofs of spiritual life from time to time, that would spell the end of spirituality in Islām….It causes one's heart to tremble to imagine that Islām has now died and that no such people would arise in it, whose spiritual manifestations would be a substitute for miracles and whose inspiration a substitute for revelation, let alone that a Muslim should believe in any such possibility as a doctrine. May God Almighty guide those who are involved in such misguided thinking.

[Shahādat-ul-Qur'ān, Rūḥānī Khazā'in, vol. 6, pp.352-356]

6

THE MESSIAH AND HIS SECOND COMING

I solemnly believe that Jesus (peace be upon him) is dead and is in the company of the departed ones. And why should I not believe this, when God Almighty has declared him dead in His Mighty Book, the Holy Qur'ān. There is no mention anywhere in the Qur'ān of his extraordinarily long life or of his second advent. Rather the Holy Qur'ān declares him to be dead and says nothing more. I consider it an utterly false and vain notion that he is alive in his physical body and will appear in this world a second time. I believe this, not only on the basis of the revelations vouchsafed to me, but also because I know that it is opposed to the clear, conclusive and certain testimony of the Holy Qur'ān.

[Āsmānī Faiṣlah, Rūḥānī Khazā'in, vol. 4, p. 315]

Popular Beliefs about the Ascension

It is clear that Christians and the bulk of Muslims entertain the belief that Jesus (peace be upon him) ascended bodily to heaven. Both imagine that he is physically alive in heaven and will descend upon the earth sometime in the latter days. But there is one difference between the two doctrines. Christians believe that Jesus[as] died on the cross, came back to life, then ascended bodily to heaven and took his seat on the right hand of his Father and will descend to the earth to judge mankind in the latter days. They allege that Jesus is the God, the Creator and Master of the world, and that he will descend in glory at the end of the world to judge mankind. Then all those who have not accepted him or his mother as God will be seized and cast into hell where they will stay weeping and grinding their teeth. Muslims, on the one hand, allege that Jesus[as] was not crucified and did not die on the cross. He was not even nailed to the cross; rather, when he was apprehended by the Jews, an Angel of God carried him bodily to the second heaven where he abides alongside the Prophet Yaḥyā[as] or John.[142] Muslims also believe that Jesus[as] was a revered Prophet of God and was neither God nor the son of God. They believe that he will descend in the latter days leaning upon two angels, near a minaret in Damascus, or at some other place, and that he and the Imam Muḥammad Mahdī, who will have already appeared from among the descendants of Ḥaḍrat Fāṭima, will both join forces to slaughter all those who do not immediately accept Islām. In short, the Muslims who call themselves Ahl-e-Sunnah and also Ahl-e-Ḥadīth, who are commonly known as Wahābīs, say that the real purpose of the second advent of Jesus[as] is that, like the Mahadev of Hindus, he should destroy the greater part of the world. He will first warn people to become Muslims and if they resist he will put them to the sword....

As regards Christians, the Muslim divines assert that, when Jesus[as] descends from heaven, he will break all the crosses in the world and will mercilessly drown the whole world in blood....Though Jesus[as] will himself be a Mahdī, indeed he will be the principal Mahdī, yet he will not be the Khalīfa because the Khalīfa must be from among the Quraish. Muḥammad Mahdī will be the Khalīfa. According to them, both of them will together

---

[142] John the Baptist. **[Publisher]**

fill the earth with human blood and will cause bloodshed unparalleled in the annals of the world. They will start killing as soon as they appear, without any admonition and without manifesting any sign. They allege that Jesus[as] will be a counsellor or minister of Imam Muḥammad Mahdī who will be the ruler, but Jesus will constantly incite the Mahdī to bloodshed as if to make up for his previous teachings: 'Resist not evil, and, being smitten on one cheek, turn the other cheek as well.'

[Masīḥ Hindustān Meiń, Rūḥānī Khazā'in, vol. 15, pp. 5-7].

Aḥmadiyyah Belief about the Mahdī

My belief and the belief of the members of my Community is that the bulk of the Aḥādīth concerning the advent of the Mahdī and the Promised Messiah are utterly untrustworthy. These fall into three categories:

1) The Aḥādīth which are false and fabricated. They are reported on the authority of people who were considered dishonest and given to falsehood. No sincere Muslim can place any trust in them.

2) The Aḥādīth which are considered weak and which are untrustworthy on account of mutual contradictions. They are either not mentioned by the great Imāms of Ḥadīth or have been mentioned as doubtful, and the truth and honesty of their narrators is not certified.

3) The Aḥādīth which are true, and are confirmed as such, but have either been already fulfilled or they make no reference to any physical warfare and only predict the coming of the Mahdī who will have no worldly kingdom or Khilāfat and will neither fight nor cause bloodshed. He will have no army but will establish faith in the hearts of the people through his spirituality and inner attention. For instance, there is the Ḥadīth:

لَا مَهْدِى اِلَّا عِيْسٰى [143]

This is mentioned in the collection of Ibn-e-Mājah, which is known by this very name, and is also comprised in Ḥākim's *Mustadrak,* on the authority of Anas bin Mālik. This Ḥadīth has been narrated by Muḥammad bin Khālid Jundī on the authority of Abān bin Ṣāleḥ who related it on the authority of Ḥasan Baṣrī who related it on the authority of Anas bin Mālik who heard it from the Holy Prophet (peace and blessings of Allah be upon him.) This Ḥadīth means that there will be no Mahdī except the person who will appear in the spirit of Jesus[as], and whose teachings will be like those of Jesus[as], because he will not physically resist evil nor fight; he will spread the truth through his holy example and through heavenly signs, and will be both the Promised Messiah and the Mahdī. This Ḥadīth is supported by another Ḥadīth comprised in the collection of *Ṣaḥīḥ Bukhārī*, which says:

يَضَعُ الْحَرْبَ

This means that the Mahdī, whose other name will be the Promised Messiah, will put an end to all religious wars and will direct that there should be no fighting in the cause of religion and that religion should be propagated through the light of the faith, moral miracles and the signs of nearness to God. I, therefore, affirm that he who fights in this age for the sake of religion, or lends support to any such fighter, or—openly or secretly—counsels fighting, or entertains any such designs, is guilty of disobedience to God and the Holy Prophet[sa] and transgresses the limits, obligations and admonitions which are prescribed by them.

---

143 'There will be no Mahdī except 'Īsā.'—**[Publisher]**

…**I am the Promised Messiah** who is Divinely guided, and who follows the morals of the Messiah (peace be on him.) Everyone should judge me with reference to these morals and should purge his heart of all ill will concerning me. A careful consideration of the teaching that I have set forth during the last twenty years, from *Brāhīn-e-Aḥmadiyyah* to *Rāz-e-Ḥaqīqat*, should testify to my inner purity. I can prove that I have spread these books as far as Arabia, Turkey, Syria and Kabul. I utterly repudiate the doctrine that Jesus will descend from heaven to fight the battles of Islām, or that anyone who calls himself Mahdī, and appears from among the descendants of Ḥaḍrat Fāṭima, will be the monarch of the time, and that the two of them will start a reign of bloodshed. God has revealed to me that all these speculations are false. Jesus (peace be on him) died long ago and lies buried in Moḥalla Khānyār in Srinagar, Kashmir. Thus as the descent of the Messiah from heaven is disproved, the appearance of any warrior Mahdī is also falsified. Let him who thirsts for truth accept this.

[Ḥaqīqat-ul-Mahdī, Rūḥānī Khazā'in, vol. 14, pp. 429-433]

My statement concerning the Promised Messiah, whose descent from heaven and second advent into the world is awaited, which God Almighty has disclosed to me by His grace and mercy, is that there is no mention in the Holy Qur'ān of the second advent of Jesus. According to the Holy Qur'ān, Jesus has departed from this world forever. Some Aḥādīth, which are replete with metaphors, predict the second advent of Jesus. Their context indicates that they do not predict the second coming of Jesus, son of Mary, but comprise metaphorical statements which mean that in an age that would resemble the age of Jesus, son of Mary, a person will resemble Jesus, son of Mary, in his temperament, power and function. As Jesus, son of Mary, had revived the religion of Moses[as] and had set forth afresh the true teaching of the Torah, which the Jews had forgotten, in the same way this second Messiah would revive the faith of the Prophet who was like Moses[as] and was the Seal of the Prophets (peace and blessings of Allah be upon him.) This Messiah of the Prophet who was the like of Moses[as] will completely resemble the Messiah of Moses[as] in the events of his life and in all other consequences that his people will experience on account of their obedience to him or their denial of him. God Almighty has revealed to me that I am that Promised Messiah.

Contradictions in the Popular Beliefs

According to their old ideas which have taken firm root in their hearts, the Muslims' claim that Jesus, son of Mary, will descend from heaven near the eastern minaret of Damascus with his hands resting on the shoulders of two angels. Some of them say that he will descend on the minaret with the help of a ladder which the Muslims will provide for him, and the angels will then depart. He will be well dressed—he will not be naked—and will meet the Mahdī in that condition. His age will be the same as when he ascended to heaven, that is thirty-two or thirty-three years. Passage of years and months will not have affected his age or physique; nor will his hair and nails have grown; they will only become subject to change after his descent. He will not engage in fighting, but the disbelievers will die by the power of his breath alone, which, instead of reviving the dead as it formerly did, will now cause the living to die.

Here the clerics contradict themselves and assert that he

will wage wars, and the one-eyed Antichrist will die at his hands. The Jews will also be killed by his command. They assert that he will be the same Jesus, son of Mary, who was a Prophet of God and who was bestowed the Gospel through Gabriel, and yet they allege that on his descent upon earth he will have lost his status of Prophethood and will only be a follower of the Holy Prophet (peace and blessings of Allah be upon him) and will be bound by the law of the Holy Qur'ān, like the Muslims, and will join them in their prayers. Some say that he will be a follower of the great Imam Abū Ḥanīfa, but it is not specified which of the four Sufi orders, Qādrī, Chishtī, Suharwardī or Naqshbandī he will identify himself with. In short, they begin with describing him as a Prophet and then reduce him to a degree that no sensible person can ever contemplate. Then, converting his functions from their metaphorical description into physical activities, they allege that he will break crosses and slaughter swine. They do not explain what he will gain by breaking crosses. Even if he broke one or two million crosses, would the Christians, who are devoted to the worship of the cross, not make new ones in place of the broken ones? If the slaughtering of swine is also to be taken literally, will the principal occupation of the Messiah be that of hunting swine with a pack of dogs? If that is so, it will be a great day for Sikhs and some nomadic tribes like the Chamārs, Sānsīs, Gondelas, etc., who are fond of hunting swine. But this activity of his will not in any way benefit the Christians, who are already very skilful in hunting swine. There are up to a thousand shops in London that sell the flesh of swine, and up to twenty-five thousand pigs are daily sent to the outlying areas of the city. The question is: is it worthy of a

Prophet who has appeared for the reform of mankind to waste his time hunting pig, a disgusting animal, while even touching the pig is a grave sin according to Torah. A question also arises that—while hunting is a hobby of the idle—if the Messiah is still to be so fond of hunting, is there any dearth of such good animals as deer, caribou, rabbits, etc., that he should soil his hands with the blood of such a foul animal?

I have presented here a picture of the character and activities of the Messiah in his second advent, as conceived by the bulk of the Muslims. It is for sensible people to consider how unnatural, contradictory and inconsistent with the high status of Prophethood all this is. It should be remembered that none of this nonsense is mentioned in either of the two great compilations of Aḥādīth. Imam Bukhārī has given no indication that the Messiah who is to come will be the same person as Jesus, son of Mary. On the contrary, he has narrated two actual sayings of the Holy Prophet (peace and blessings of Allah be upon him), which distinguish the Second Messiah from the first. The connotation of one of these Aḥādīth is that the son of Mary will appear from among you, and it further clarifies that he will be your Imam from within you.

One should carefully consider how the Holy Prophet (peace and blessings of Allah be upon him), in order to remove any misunderstanding which may result from the name 'son of Mary', goes on to say: Do not take him to be the son of Mary himself, rather:

بَلْ هُوَ إِمَامُكُمْ مِنْكُمْ [144]

---

[144] 'He will be your Imam from among your own people.' **[Publisher]**

The other Ḥadīth, which gives the same indication, is that the Holy Prophet (peace and blessings of Allah be upon him) described the features of the first and the second Messiah differently. His description of the features of the second Messiah fits me exactly. Is the clear distinction between the features of the two not enough to prove that the first and the second Messiah are in fact two distinct personalities?

[Izāla-e-Auhām, Rūḥānī Khazā'in, vol. 3, pp. 121-125]

It would not be without interest to mention that the Promised Messiah's appearance was awaited by all Muslim sects and everyone was looking forward to the fulfilment of the prophecies predicting this event in the context of the repeated sayings of the Holy Prophet[sa]. Many who were favoured with visions had intimated, on the basis of revelation, that the Promised Messiah would appear at the beginning of the fourteenth century of the Islamic era. The advent of the Promised Messiah is only briefly referred to in the Holy Qur'ān, but it is mentioned so frequently in Aḥādīth, that it is unreasonable to deny its authenticity. Of all the prophecies made by the Holy Prophet[sa], this is the one that has been reported more than any other....

It is a pity, however, that despite its frequent occurrence, the divines of this age of ignorance have gone utterly astray in construing this prophecy correctly. In consequence of their grave misunderstanding, they have inserted shameful contradictions into the body of this doctrine. On the one hand, they are compelled to believe, in accordance with the Holy Qur'ān and true Aḥādīth, that Jesus[as] has died; and, on the other, they believe that he has not died and is alive in heaven in his physical body, and will descend to earth some time in the latter days. Again they hold, on the one hand, that the Holy Prophet (peace and blessings of Allah be upon him) was the last Prophet, and yet they also believe that a Prophet will come after him, namely Jesus[as] son of Mary. They believe on the one hand that the Promised Messiah will appear when the Antichrist has supremacy over the whole world, with the exception of Mecca and Medina. On the other, they are compelled to believe, in accordance with a true tradition narrated by Bukhārī, that the Promised Messiah will appear at the time of the supremacy of the cross, that is to say at the time when Christianity will be dominant, and the power and the wealth of Christians will be greater than all others. Again, they believe that the Promised Messiah will not be the Mahdī and the Imam, rather some other person from the descendants of the Holy Prophet[sa] will be the Mahdī. In short, they set forth so many contradictions that they have created serious doubts about the very truth of this prophecy; for a collection of contradictions cannot be true, and sensible people cannot accept it at the cost of reason. That is why the newly educated section of Muslims, who judge everything by the criteria of nature, its laws and the dictates of reason, have been compelled to reject this prophecy despite its frequent occurrence. Indeed, if this prophecy can only be interpreted in a manner that would entail so many contradictions, then human reason, failing to reconcile them, would resolve the difficulty by rejecting the prophecy altogether. That is why those who are committed to nature and reason have rejected this great prophecy despite its frequency. It is a pity, however, that these people were hasty in their rejection of the prophecy, as no sensible person should reject a prophecy that is reported with such persistence and frequency as to guarantee its accuracy. The way of fairness and support of the truth was not to reject the prophecy, but to reject the interpretations put upon it by the foolish clerics which entail all manners of contradiction. It is the faulty reasoning of the dim-witted clerics which has misinterpreted a simple prophecy in such a way that it has become a myriad of contradictions which have bewildered every research minded people.

True Meaning of the Ascension and Second Coming of Jesus

God Almighty has now disclosed the true meaning of the prophecy, which is free from all contradictions and unreasonableness. He has thus furnished every fair-minded seeker of truth the opportunity to accept the prophecy and to look for its fulfilment, thus safeguarding himself against rejecting a clear and true prophecy.

[Kitāb-ul-Bariyyah, Rūḥānī Khazā'in, vol. 13, pp. 205-211, footnote]

There are great difficulties in interpreting this prophecy literally, for this would invite all manner of objections before the Messiah even descends from heaven. There is no need for us to get involved in these difficulties. Why should we seek to bring the son of Mary down from heaven and deprive him of his Prophethood? Why should we degrade him so that someone else should be the Imam and he should be the follower; and another should take the covenant of allegiance as the Imam and Khalīfa while he should be a helpless spectator; and he should become a common Muslim, and dare not even mention his Prophethood?

[Izāla-e-Auhām, Rūḥānī Khazā'in, vol. 3, p.174]

Sensible people had no difficulty in understanding this prophecy as the holy words of the Holy Prophet (peace and blessings of Allah be upon him) clearly indicated that it did not mean the second coming of a Prophet of Israel himself; for he had repeatedly affirmed that there would be no Prophet after him. The Ḥadīth [145]لا نبی بعدی was so well-known that no one entertained any doubt about it. The Holy Qur'ān, every word of which is conclusive and final, had also confirmed it in the verse

وَلٰكِنْ رَّسُوْلَ اللّٰهِ وَخَاتَمَ النَّبِيّٖنَ [146]

that Prophethood had come to an end with the Holy Prophet (peace and blessings of Allah be upon him.) Then how was it possible that anyone, with the status of an independent Prophet, should come after the Holy Prophet[sa]? Such an event would altogether disrupt the whole pattern of Islām. To assert, on the other hand, that Jesus[as] would come a second time, bereft of his Prophethood, would be the height of impertinence and shamelessness. Can a Prophet like Jesus (peace be on him), who is accepted of God Almighty and one of His favourites, ever be deprived of his Prophethood?

[Kitāb-ul-Bariyyah, Rūḥānī Khazā'in, vol. 13, pp. 217-218, footnote]

The 'Descent' or the 'Coming' does not mean the coming of the Messiah son of Mary; it is actually a figure of speech signifying the coming of someone resembling the son of Mary; and, in accordance with Divine intimation and revelation, it is the present writer—my own humble self—to whom it applies.

I am only too well aware that as soon as this view of mine, which is based on clear and definite revelation, is

---

[145] 'There is no Prophet after me.' **[Publisher]**

[146] 'But he is the Messenger of Allah and the Seal of the Prophets.'—Al-Aḥzāb, 33:41 **[Publisher]**

made public, many a hostile pen shall come alive and there will be a public outcry full of horror and rejection....

There are two Prophets concerning whom it has been supposed, on the basis of the Bible, Aḥādīth and some scriptures, that they were raised bodily to heaven; one was John, whose name is also Elia or Elias, and the other is Jesus, son of Mary. Some of the books of the Old and New Testaments state, with regard to both of them, that they were raised bodily to heaven and will at some time be seen descending upon the earth. Some of the Aḥādīth also use similar expressions with reference to them. With regard to Elias, the Gospels state that the prophecy concerning his descent was fulfilled in the advent of John the son of Zachariah. Jesus clearly said: John is Elias who was to come. Let him, who will, accept. Thus the controversy regarding the physical ascent to heaven of one of them and his descent at some later time, was settled by a Prophet, namely Jesus, and his second coming was thus explained. The agreed Christian doctrine, in accordance with the Bible, is that Elias descended from heaven in the time of Jesus, when one possessing his power and spirit was born to Zechariah as his son and was named John. But the Jews still await his descent. They believe that he will descend physically from heaven....In any event, Jesus furnished the true interpretation of the expression 'descent from heaven' and the manner of the descent of Elias was settled. But with regard to Jesus, it is still asserted emphatically that he will descend physically from heaven wearing luxurious robes and in the company of angels. Christians and Muslims do not agree on the place of the descent, whether he will descend in Mecca, or in some church in London or the Imperial Cathedral in

Moscow. Had not the Christians been impelled by age-old mischief, they could have appreciated more easily than the Muslims that the descent of Jesus should be in accord with the interpretation of descent furnished by Jesus himself....

The Christians also believe that Jesus entered heaven after his ascent. According to Luke, Jesus tried to comfort a thief with the assurance: 'You will enter heaven with me today.' Christians also believe that a person, however low his station, who is once admitted to heaven will not be expelled from there. Muslims also believe the same, as Allah the Glorious has said:

وَمَا هُمْ مِّنْهَا بِمُخْرَجِيْنَ [147]

'Those who are granted admission into Paradise will not be expelled therefrom.'

Though there is no express mention in the Holy Qur'ān of the entry of Jesus into heaven, yet his death is mentioned at three different places. In the case of holy personages, death and entry into heaven are simultaneous, as is indicated by the verses:

قِيْلَ ادْخُلِ الْجَنَّةَ [148]

وَادْخُلِيْ جَنَّتِيْ [149]

they are made to enter paradise forthwith. It is now incumbent upon both Muslims and Christians to consider whether it is possible that a favourite of God, like Jesus, should be admitted to heaven and then be expelled from it. Would this not be contrary to the promise of God

---

[147] Al-Ḥijr, 15:49 **[Publisher]**

[148] 'It was said to *him*, Enter Paradise.'—Yā Sīn 36:27 **[Publisher]**

[149] 'And enter thou My Garden.'—Al-Fajr, 89:31 **[Publisher]**

Almighty, which is clearly set out repeatedly in all holy books?...The disbelievers of Mecca had demanded from the Holy Prophet (peace and blessings of Allah be upon him) that he should ascend to heaven and descend therefrom while they watched, and he was instructed to say:

قُلْ سُبْحَانَ رَبِّي[150]

This means that the wisdom of God Almighty does not permit the exhibition of such extraordinary signs in this world, since such exhibition would destroy the reality of faith in the unseen.

How can that which was not permissible in the case of the Holy Prophet[sa], who was the best of Prophets (peace and blessings of Allah be upon him), be permissible in the case of Jesus? It would be the height of disrespect to hold that a situation was not permissible in the case of the Holy Prophet (peace and blessings of Allah be upon him) and yet accept it as permissible in the case of Jesus. No true Muslim can be guilty of such impertinence….

Our lord and master, the Seal of Prophets, has distinguished between the first Messiah and the second Messiah by declaring not only that the second Messiah would be a Muslim who is bound by the commandments of the Holy Qur'ān, such as prayer and fasting etc., but he would be born in a Muslim home, would be the Imam of Muslims, would bring no new religion, would not claim any Prophethood apart from the Prophethood of the Holy Prophet[sa], but also has described the differences in features between the first and the second Messiah. The features of the first Messiah as observed by the Holy Prophet (peace and blessings of Allah be upon him) on

---

[150] Banī Isrā'īl, 17:94 **[Publisher]**

the night of his spiritual ascent was: medium height, rosy complexion, curly hair and a broad chest. (See *Ṣaḥīḥ Bukhārī*, p.489.) But he described the features of the second Messiah as wheatish complexion and straight hair coming down to the ears (*Bukhārī*.) Does this distinction in their features not clearly establish that the first Messiah and the second Messiah are distinct personages? The designation of both as son of Mary is a fine metaphor that has been employed to indicate resemblance in their temperaments and spiritual qualities.

[Tauḍīḥ-e-Marām, Rūḥānī Khazā'in, vol. 3, pp. 51-59]

Misguidance about Jesus caused by the Antichrist

If you do not overlook the events of today, you will realize that the prevalent misguidance has been propagated by the Antichrist against whom every Prophet has warned, and whose foundation was laid by the Christian doctrine and the Christian people. It was therefore, necessary that the reformer of the age should be designated the Messiah, inasmuch as all corruption has proceeded from the followers of the Messiah. It has been revealed to me in a vision that Jesus was made aware of the poisonous atmosphere that has been spread in the world by the Christian people, in consequence of which, his soul was moved towards a spiritual descent and in its agitation, finding his people bent upon ruin, it desired a substitute on earth who should resemble him and should possess an identical temperament. Therefore, God Almighty granted him, according to His promise, one whose soul resembled his soul, upon whom were bestowed the resolve, character and spirituality of Jesus. A close relationship was established between him and Jesus as if the two had been fashioned out of the same jewel. The spiritual attention of Jesus made the heart of the other its resting place and desired to fulfil itself through him. In this sense his being became the being of Jesus and the passionate intentions of Jesus descended upon it, a descent that was metaphorically described as the descent of Jesus. It is a spiritual mystery that sometimes so firm a spiritual relationship is established between the holy ones who have passed away and those who are living, through the reflection of their attention and the unity of their thinking, that those in heaven regard those on earth as their spiritual substitutes. The designs generated in their hearts in heaven are correspondingly generated by God's command in the hearts of their reflections on earth. A soul which is thus united with one on earth is bestowed the capacity to communicate its designs fully to that soul. This transfer takes place under Divine direction. This is the Divine way in which Prophets and the holy ones who have passed away descend upon the earth. It was thus that Prophet Elijah descended in the form of John the Baptist. This is also the true meaning of the descent of Jesus, which has been revealed to me. If anyone should still persist in denial I would be ready to enter into a *Mubāhalah* [Prayer duel] with him.

[Ā'īna-e-Kamālāt-e-Islām, Rūḥānī Khazā'in, vol. 5, pp. 254-256]

Correct Meanings of *Nuzūl*

It is asked: how can we reject the clear and obvious statements of the Aḥādīth which expressly state that Jesus, son of Mary, would descend from heaven near the eastern minaret of Damascus with his hands on the shoulder of two angels? The answer is that descent in this context does not mean descent from heaven in a physical body. The Aḥādīth do not even employ the word 'heaven'. The Arabic word *Nuzūl* [descent] is commonly used to connote arrival. A person who arrives at one place from another is described as having descended at that place. For instance, it is said that an army or a camp has descended at such and such a place. This does not mean that the army or the camp have descended from heaven. The Holy Qur'ān has also employed the expression *Nuzūl* [descent] for the Holy Prophet (peace and blessings of Allah be upon him). It is also stated in a verse that iron has descended from heaven.[151] It is thus obvious that this descent does not connote what people have imagined.

[Izāla-e-Auhām, Rūḥānī Khazā'in, vol. 3, pp. 132-133]

The word *Nuzūl* is being deliberately misinterpreted. In the idiom of scriptures, he who comes from God is described as having descended from heaven (see John 1:38.)[152] The same is indicated in the verses:

إِنَّآ أَنزَلْنَٰهُ فِي لَيْلَةِ ٱلْقَدْرِ [153]

ذِكْرًا رَّسُولًا [154]

Common people, whose thinking is earthy, interpret everything in a physical sense. They do not stop to reflect that as according to their conception Jesus will descend from heaven in the company of angels, in the same way they also believe that the Holy Prophet (peace and blessings of Allah be upon him) had ascended to heaven in the company of angels, indeed there was also a *burrāq* at his service. But did anyone observe the ascent and descent of

---

[151] The reference is to Al-Ḥadīd, 57:26. **[Publisher]**

[152] John 1:30 in the New King James Version. **[Publisher]**

[153] 'Surely, We sent it down on the Night of Destiny.'—Al-Qadr, 97:2 **[Publisher]**

[154] '*Allah has sent down to you* a Reminder—A Messenger.'—Al-Ṭalāq, 65:11-12 **[Publisher]**

the Holy Prophet (peace and blessings of Allah be upon him) or did anyone see the angels and the *burāq*? It is obvious that the disbelievers did not see the Holy Prophet (peace and blessings of Allah be upon him) being carried to heaven by the angels nor did they see him descending therefrom. That is why they asserted that the spiritual ascent of the Holy Prophet[sa] was not a fact. How misguided, therefore, are those who are waiting to see Jesus descend from heaven in the company of angels. If the Chief of the Prophets was not seen ascending to or descending from heaven, then will they see Jesus descending therefrom?

لعنة اللّٰهِ على الكٰذبين [155]

Did Abū Bakr Ṣiddīq observe the Holy Prophet (peace and blessings of Allah be upon him) ascend or descend from heaven in the company of angels on the night of *Me'rāj*? Did 'Umar Fārūq enjoy the privilege of such observation? Did 'Alī Murtaḍā partake of such spectacle? Then who are you and what is your standing that you would see the Promised Messiah descending from heaven in the company of angels? The Holy Qur'ān rejects the very idea of such a spectacle.

[Majmū'ah Ishtihārāt, vol. 3, pp. 326-327]

Muslims should beware of the dangerous situation in which the Jews placed themselves by insisting on the literal fulfilment of the prophecy concerning the second coming of Elijah. It is sheer folly to insist upon something of which there has been no instance before and the falsity of which has been repeatedly demonstrated. God Almighty has said:

---

[155] 'May Allah's curse be upon the liars.' **[Publisher]**

فَسْـَٔلُوْٓا اَهْلَ الذِّكْرِ اِنْ كُنْتُمْ لَا تَعْلَمُوْنَ [156]

'Ask the Jews and the Christians for an example of the ways of Allah, if you do not know.'

[Kitāb-ul-Bariyyah, Rūḥānī Khazā'in, vol. 13, p. 43]

The Ḥadīth of *Ṣaḥīḥ Muslim* which says that the Messiah would descend near the white eastern minaret of Damascus has throughout puzzled the scholars, for it is not clear what relationship Messiah has with Damascus....

A little attention resolved this difficulty in my mind and it was disclosed to me, in a clear vision, that the intimation in the compilation of Abū Dāwūd that a person designated *Ḥārith* or *Ḥarrāth* [a cultivator] ill appear is correct and is identical with the prophecy of the second advent of the Messiah and that both have reference to me.

It has been disclosed to me that the word Damascus in the prophecy means a town which is home to a people who resemble Yazīd and think and act like him. Their hearts feel no love for Allah or His Messenger and they do not esteem Divine commandments. They worship their selfish desires and are so committed to the dictates of their evil egos, that they esteem the blood of the pure and the holy lightly. They do not believe in the hereafter; and the existence of God Almighty is for them a mystery which they cannot understand. Just as a physician is needed for the sick, it was necessary that the Messiah should appear among such people. It has been disclosed to me that the word Damascus here indicates a place which possesses this important characteristic peculiar to Damascus. The use of this word in connection with the

---

[156] Al-Naḥl, 16:44 **[Publisher]**

place of the appearance of the Messiah is an indication that the Messiah does not mean Jesus who was given the Gospel but he is someone from among the Muslims who, in his spiritual condition, resembles both the Messiah and Imam Ḥussain....

The word Damascus clearly indicates that Jesus in not the Messiah who was to come, but as the Yazīdīs resemble the Jews in the same way the Messiah who is to come resembles Jesus and possesses the temperament of Ḥussain. This is a very subtle point: the word Damascus has been used metaphorically. As the tragedy of Imam Ḥussain was an enormity in the estimation of God Almighty and resembled closely the tragedy of Jesus, as even the Christians would acknowledge, therefore, God Almighty desired that the coming generations may be apprised of its enormity and its resemblance to the tragedy of Jesus. Damascus has been metaphorically mentioned in this context so that the readers might be reminded of the time when the beloved grandson of the Holy Prophet (peace and blessings of Allah be upon him) was, like Jesus, put to the sword most tyrannically by the wretches of Damascus. Thus God Almighty particularly mentioned Damascus, wherefrom such tyrannical directions had issued and which was the home of such hard-hearted and dark-minded people, as an indication that the place which resembled Damascus would now become the headquarter for the propagation of faith and justice.

[Izāla-e-Auhām, Rūḥānī Khazā'in, vol. 3, pp. 134-137, footnote]

I would now like to draw attention to the Ḥadīth narrated by Abū Dāwūd in his compilation. It contains a prophecy that a person designated as *Ḥārith*, or a cultivator, will appear from Transoxiana, that is to say, from the direction of Samarkand, who will lend support to the descendants of the Holy Prophet[sa] and it would be obligatory on every believer to help and support him. It has been revealed to me that this prophecy and the prophecy of the advent of the Promised Messiah, who will be one of the Muslims and will be their Imam, relate to the same event and both have reference to me. The prophecy that relates to the Promised Messiah has two special aspects. One is that through his true teaching he will reform the spiritual condition of the Muslims which will be utterly corrupt at the time of his advent and; he will totally remove their spiritual poverty and inner indigence and present them the jewels of knowledge, verities and comprehension in excess of their need. No seeker after truth from among them will remain spiritually poor and indigent. All those who hunger and thirst for truth will be provided in abundance with the wholesome food of truth and the sweet drink of comprehension. Their pockets will be filled with the pearls of true knowledge and they will be given phialae filled with the perfume of the true meaning of the Holy Qur'ān.

The second special aspect of the prophecy, which relates to the advent of the Promised Messiah, is that he will break the cross, slaughter the swine and kill the one-eyed Antichrist. Every disbeliever who is touched by his breath will die instantly. The spiritual interpretation of this special aspect is that the Promised Messiah will crush under his feet all the glory of the religion of the cross, that he will destroy with the weapon of conclusive arguments those who are afflicted with shamelessness like swine, and who devour filth like pigs, and that he will wipe out with the sword of clear proofs the opposition of those who possess only the eye of the world and are bereft of the eye of the faith in place of which they have only an unsightly taint. Not only such one-eyed ones, but also every disbeliever who views Islām with contempt will suffer spiritual extinction through the glorious breath of Messianic reasoning. In short all these signs are metaphoric, the significance of which has been fully revealed to me. Some may not appreciate it at this time but after waiting for sometime, and despairing altogether of the hopes that they now entertain, all of them will accept it.

[Izāla-e-Auhām, Rūḥānī Khazā'in, vol. 3, pp. 141-143 footnote]

It is an absurdity to interpret literally the Ḥadīth of *Ṣaḥīḥ Muslim* which says that when the Messiah descends from heaven he will be wearing yellow robes. There appears no reason for this peculiarity. If this indication is interpreted according to the principles of the interpretation of dreams, it would mean that when the Promised Messiah announces his claim he would not be in good health.

[Izāla-e-Auhām, Rūḥānī Khazā'in, vol. 3, pp. 142-143]

The account of the *Me'rāj* [spiritual ascent of the Holy Prophet[sa]] set out in *Bukhārī*, which describes his meeting with some of the Prophets, makes no mention that Jesus was there in his physical body. The meeting of the Holy Prophet[sa] with Jesus is described in exactly the same terms as his meeting with Abraham[as] and Moses[as]. His dialogue with Moses[as] is set out in detail. There can, therefore, be no doubt that if on the basis of this Ḥadīth Jesus[as] had been raised bodily to heaven so must Abraham[as] and Moses[as] have been bodily raised, inasmuch as the Holy Prophet (peace and blessings of Allah be upon him) saw all of them in the same condition. He did not observe any particular dress or other sign of a bodily ascent about Jesus, which was not visible with regard to the other Prophets.

[Izāla-e-Auhām, Rūḥānī Khazā'in, vol. 3, pp. 153-154]

Nowhere does the Holy Qur'ān mention the bodily ascent of Jesus to heaven. His death, on the other hand, is specifically mentioned at several different places. One of these contains Jesus' own confession of his death:

وَكُنْتُ عَلَيْهِمْ شَهِيْدًا مَّا دُمْتُ فِيْهِمْ ۚ فَلَمَّا تَوَفَّيْتَنِيْ
كُنْتَ اَنْتَ الرَّقِيْبَ عَلَيْهِمْ ۚ وَاَنْتَ عَلٰى كُلِّ شَيْءٍ شَهِيْدٌ [157]

As his death is established, it follows that his body must have been buried in the earth like the bodies of all dead people. The Holy Qur'ān expressly states that it was his soul that ascended to heaven and not his body. That is why, in the verse just cited, he clearly acknowledged his death. Had he ascended to heaven alive in his physical body, he would not have said that he had departed the earth after his death. And, obviously, if it was only his soul which had ascended to heaven, then how can he possibly descend in his physical body?...

If we were to assume that he had ascended to heaven in his physical body, we would have to acknowledge that, like all human and animal bodies, his body must also be affected by the passage of time and that one day he must die. Thus he may have died in heaven having lived out his normal span of life and may have been interned in a graveyard on some planet which is now supposed to be capable of supporting human life. On the other hand, if we are to assume the impossible—that he is still physi-

---

[157] 'And I was a witness over them as long as I remained among them, but since Thou didst cause me to die, Thou hast been the Watcher over them; and Thou art Witness over all things.'—Al-Mā'idah, 5:118 **[Publisher]**

cally alive, then, after the passage of so many centuries, he must have arrived at extreme old age and will no longer be capable of performing any religious function or service. His descent upon earth in such a condition would serve no useful purpose and would only put him to unnecessary travail.

[Izāla-e-Auhām, Rūḥānī Khazā'in, vol. 3, pp. 125-127]

Evidence regarding the Death of Jesus

We have so many certain and conclusive proofs of the death of Jesus, son of Mary, that they cannot all be set out in this brief publication. Read the Holy Qur'ān carefully and you will find the death of Jesus mentioned so clearly and definitely that it is not possible to interpret it otherwise. For instance, the Holy Qur'ān reports the acknowledgement of Jesus:

فَلَمَّا تَوَفَّيْتَنِيْ كُنْتَ اَنْتَ الرَّقِيْبَ عَلَيْهِمْ [158]

Can we interpret the word *Tawaffi* in this verse as meaning sleep? Would it be right to understand this verse as meaning: Since Thou didst cause me to sleep Thou hast been the One to watch over them? Of course not. The only appropriate interpretation of *Tawaffi* in this context is the straightforward one of death; and the context does not permit us to interpret that death will occur after Jusus' bodily ascent to heaven. This is because the question put to Jesus refers to the going astray of his people, which had happened after his supposed bodily ascent to heaven and had been completed before the advent of the Holy Prophet (peace and blessings of Allah be upon him.)

---

[158] 'Since Thou didst cause me to die, Thou hast been the Watcher over them.'—Al-Mā'idah, 5:118 **[Publisher]**

The Ḥadīth also confirms the death of Jesus[as]. On page 162 of the Commentary *Ma'ālim* it is mentioned on the authority of 'Alī bin Ṭalḥah that Ibn-e-'Abbās[ra] interpreted the verse:

يٰعِيۡسٰۤى اِنِّىۡ مُتَوَفِّيۡكَ وَرَافِعُكَ اِلَىَّ [159]

to mean اِنِّىۡ مُمِيۡتُكَ i.e., 'I will cause you to die.' This is supported by other verses like:

قُلۡ يَتَوَفّٰٮكُمۡ مَّلَكُ الۡمَوۡتِ [160]

اَلَّذِيۡنَ تَتَوَفّٰٮهُمُ الۡمَلٰۤـئِكَةُ طَيِّبِيۡنَ [161]

اَلَّذِيۡنَ تَتَوَفّٰٮهُمُ الۡمَلٰۤـئِكَةُ ظَالِمِىۡۤ اَنۡفُسِهِمۡ [162]

Thus Ibn-e-'Abbās, may Allah be pleased with him, believed that Jesus had died. Our readers must be aware that Ibn-e-'Abbās was among the foremost of those who comprehended the Holy Qur'ān perfectly. The Holy Prophet (peace and blessings of Allah be upon him) had prayed for him that he might be bestowed true knowledge of the Holy Qur'ān.

[Izāla-e-Auhām, Rūḥānī Khazā'in, vol. 3, pp. 224-225]

It is for this purpose that Imam Bukhārī (may Allah have mercy on him), has quoted the verse:

فَلَمَّا تَوَفَّيۡتَنِىۡ كُنۡتَ اَنۡتَ الرَّقِيۡبَ عَلَيۡهِمۡ [163]

---

[159] 'O Jesus, I will cause thee to die *a natural death* and will exalt thee to Myself.'—Āl-e-mrān, 3:56 **[Publisher]**

[160] Say, 'The angel of death…will cause you to die.'—Al-Sajdah, 32:12 **[Publisher]**

[161] 'Those whom the angels cause to die while they are pure.'—Al-Naḥl, 16:33 **[Publisher]**

[162] 'Those whom the angels cause to die while they are wronging their souls.'—Al-Naḥl, 16:29 **[Publisher]**

[163] 'Since Thou didst cause me to die, Thou hast been the Watcher

in *Kitāb-ut-Tafsīr*. In so doing, he intended to convey that the correct interpretation of the word *Tawaffaitanī* is the one which the Holy Prophet (peace and blessings of Allah be upon him) attributed to it, that is to say, 'Thou didst cause me to die'. In the following Ḥadīth:

عَنِ ابْنِ عَبَّاسٍ اَنَّهُ يُجَآءُ بِرِجَالٍ مِن اُمَّتِى فَيُؤْخَذُ بِهِمْ ذَاتَ الشِّمَالِ فَاَقُوْلُ يَا رَبِّ اُصَيْحَابِىْ فَيُقَالُ اِنَّكَ لَا تَدْرِىْ مَا اَحْدَثُوْا بَعْدَكَ فَاَقُوْلُ كَمَا قَالَ الْعَبْدُ الصَّالِحُ وَ كُنْتُ عَلَيْهِمْ شَهِيْدًا مَّا دُمْتُ فِيْهِمْ فَلَمَّا تَوَفَّيْتَنِىْ كُنْتَ اَنْتَ الرَّقِيْبَ عَلَيْهِمْ

the Holy Prophet[sa] says that: "on the Day of Judgement some of my people will be driven to hell, and I will supplicate, 'Lord! these are my companions'. Then it will be said to me, 'You know not what they did after you'. Upon this I will say what a righteous servant of God, i.e., Jesus son of Mary, had said when he was asked: 'Did you teach your people that they should worship you and your mother as gods?' I will say what Jesus had then said: 'I was witness over them while I was amongst them; but since Thou didst cause me to die, Thou hast been the One to watch over them.'" (*Bukhārī*)

The Holy Prophet (peace and blessings of Allah be upon him) meant that he would make the same affirmation as Jesus would make when he would be asked whether he had taught his people to take him and his mother as gods. In this manner the Holy Prophet (peace and blessings of Allah be upon him) interpreted the expression *Tawaffaitanī* as meaning death.

[Izāla-e-Auhām, Rūḥānī Khazā'in, vol. 3, pp. 585-586]

---

over them.'—Al-Mā'idah, 5:118 **[Publisher]**

I put only one question to the clerics who differ with me on the question of the death of Jesus. Had they pondered over it sincerely, it would have been enough to guide them aright, but they did not ponder over it, as none was desirous of being rightly guided. My question is: Twice has Allah the Glorious, applied the expression *Tawaffī* in the Holy Qur'ān with reference to Jesus[as]; and the same has been applied to the Holy Prophet (peace and blessings of Allah be upon him); and it has also been used in the prayer of Joseph (peace be on him.) There are several other places where it has been used in the Holy Qur'ān. Pondering over all these references, a just minded person would be satisfied that in each case *Tawaffī* connotes death and nothing but death. The expression *Tawaffī* has been used in hundreds of places in the Aḥādīth but nobody can show you a single occasion where it has been used to connote anything other than death. If an illiterate Arab were told *Tuwuffiya Zaidun* he would understand by it that Zaid has died. Whenever a companion or a relative of the Holy Prophet[sa] died, he always used the expression *Tawaffī* for the purpose of conveying that the person mentioned had died. When he himself died, the companions used the expression *Tawaffī* to convey that he had died. In the same way, this expression was used to indicate the death of Abū Bakr, 'Umar and all other companions of the Holy Prophet (May Allah be pleased with them.) The use of this word to indicate the death of a Muslim is an honourable way of conveying the news of his death. In view of all this, why is it that this expression, when used with reference to Jesus, should be interpreted in any other way?

[Itmām-ul-Ḥujjah, Rūḥānī Khazā'in, vol. 8, pp. 292-293]

In the idiom of the Holy Qur'ān, the word *Tawaffī* has

always been used in the connotation of death and taking possession of the soul. A minute study of Arabic prose and poetry—both ancient and modern—shows that wherever the expression *Tawaffī* is used for a human being, and the action is attributed to Allah the Glorious, *Tawaffī* invariably means death and taking possession of the soul. In this context, there is not a single instance, where this expression means anything other than taking possession of the soul. Those who are wont to refer to lexicons like *Qāmūs*, *Ṣiḥaḥ*, *Ṣarāḥ*, etc., have not found a single instance where, in the context that we have mentioned, any other connotation has been attributed to the expression *Tawaffī*. There is not the slightest indication of the possibility of any other connotation. Then I studied the books of Ḥadīth to discover whether the Holy Prophet (peace and blessings of Allah be upon him) or his companions had on any occasion applied the expression *Tawaffī* to a human being in any other connotation than that of death and taking possession of the soul. I had to labour hard in this search. What I discovered on checking every page of the compilations of *Ṣaḥīḥ Bukhārī*, *Ṣaḥīḥ Muslim*, *Tirmadhī*, *Ibn-e-Mājah*, *Abū Dāwūd*, *Nasa'ī*, *Dārimī*, *Mu'aṭṭā'* and *Sharḥ-us-Sunnah* etc., was that the expression *Tawaffī* has been used three hundred and forty six times, and in no single instance has it been used, either by the Holy Prophet (peace and blessings of Allah be upon him) or by his companions, to mean anything other than 'death', or 'taking possession of the soul'. I have gone through these books with great care line by line, and I can say that on each and every occasion the expression *Tawaffī* has been used only in the connotation of death or taking possession of the soul. A careful perusal of these books also establishes that, from the moment of the Call and all through his life, the Holy Prophet (peace and blessings of Allah be upon him) never used the expression *Tawaffī* in any connotation other than death and taking possession of the soul....

Imam Muḥammad Ismā‘īl Bukhārī has made a fine point in his compilation which indicates that the Holy Prophet (peace and blessings of Allah be upon him) used the expression *Tawaffī* at least seven thousand times between his Call and his death, and every time he used it in the connotation of death and taking possession of the soul. Seekers after truth should be grateful to Imam Bukhārī for this information.

[Izāla-e-Auhām, Rūḥānī Khazā'in, vol. 3, pp. 583-585]

If anyone can cite a single instance from the Holy Qur'ān or Ḥadīth, or from ancient or modern Arabic poetry and prose, that the word *Tawaffī,* when applied to a human being, God being the subject, has been used in any connotation other than death and taking possession of the soul, for instance, in the connotation of the taking the body, I bind myself on oath that I shall pay that person one thousand rupees in cash by selling some of my property and shall always hold him in high esteem as a great scholar of the Holy Qur'ān and Ḥādīth.

[Izāla-e-Auhām, Rūḥānī Khazā'in, vol. 3, p. 603]

The Holy Qur'ān clearly states that there never was a Prophet who did not pass away:

مَا مُحَمَّدٌ اِلَّا رَسُوْلٌ ۚ قَدْ خَلَتْ مِنْ قَبْلِهِ الرُّسُلُ
اَفَاۡئِنْ مَّاتَ اَوْ قُتِلَ انْقَلَبْتُمْ عَلٰۤى اَعْقَابِكُمْ [164]

---

[164] 'Muḥammad is only a Messenger. Verily, *all* Messengers have passed away before him. If then he die or be slain, will you turn back on your heels?'—Āl-e-Imrān, 3:145 **[Publisher]**

وَمَا جَعَلْنَا لِبَشَرٍ مِّنْ قَبْلِكَ الْخُلْدَ [165]

وَمَا جَعَلْنٰهُمْ جَسَدًا لَّا يَاْكُلُوْنَ الطَّعَامَ وَمَا كَانُوْا خٰلِدِيْنَ [166]

To conceive of Jesus as alive in the face of these verses, and to believe, contrary to the purport of the verse:

وَمَا جَعَلْنٰهُمْ جَسَدًا لَّا يَاْكُلُوْنَ الطَّعَامَ [167]

that Jesus is alive in heaven like the angels, without the need of food, would be to turn away from the Holy Word of God.

I again affirm that if Jesus is alive in heaven in his physical body, then the Divine reasoning set out in one of the above verses—that if the Holy Prophet (peace and blessings of Allah be upon him) were to die it would not be inconsistent with his Prophethood as all Prophets before him have been subject to death—would be accounted as defective and meaningless. Surely God Almighty is far above saying that which is not true and is against the facts.

[Izāla-e-Auhām, Rūḥānī Khazā'in, vol. 3, pp. 277-278]

The Holy Qur'ān says:

وَالَّذِيْنَ يَدْعُوْنَ مِنْ دُوْنِ اللّٰهِ لَا يَخْلُقُوْنَ شَيْـًٔا وَّهُمْ يُخْلَقُوْنَ ۞
اَمْوَاتٌ غَيْرُ اَحْيَآءٍ ۚ وَمَا يَشْعُرُوْنَ ۙ اَيَّانَ يُبْعَثُوْنَ ۞ [168]

(Sūrah Al-Naḥl, Part 14)

This means that: 'Those who are worshipped and called

---

[165] 'We granted not everlasting life to any human being before thee.'—Al-Anbiyā', 21:35 **[Publisher]**

[166] 'And We did not give them bodies that ate no food, nor were they to live forever.'—Al-Anbiyā', 21:9 **[Publisher]**

[167] Ibid.

[168] Al-Naḥl, 16:21-22 **[Publisher]**

upon beside Allah cannot create anything but are themselves created. They are dead, not living. They do not know when they will be resurrected.'

Just see how clearly these verses affirm the death of all those human beings who were worshipped as gods by the Jews and Christians and some of the Arab tribes and to whom they supplicated. If you are still not convinced of the death of Jesus son of Mary, why don't you simply admit that you are not prepared to believe in the Holy Qur'ān?

[Izāla-e-Auhām, Rūḥānī Khazā'in, vol. 3, p. 431]

Question: Though the Holy Qur'ān affirms the death of Jesus, it does not specify when he died. Why not reconcile the Qur'ān and Aḥādīth by adopting the position that Jesus will die after his descent upon earth?

Answer: The Holy Qur'ān clearly says that Jesus died in the period when he was raised to reform the tribes of Israel which had gone astray; as Allah the Glorious, has said:

يٰعِيْسٰۤى اِنِّيْ مُتَوَفِّيْكَ وَرَافِعُكَ اِلَيَّ وَمُطَهِّرُكَ مِنَ الَّذِيْنَ كَفَرُوْا
وَجَاعِلُ الَّذِيْنَ اتَّبَعُوْكَ فَوْقَ الَّذِيْنَ كَفَرُوْۤا اِلٰى يَوْمِ الْقِيٰمَةِ [169]

In this verse, 'I shall cause thee to die' precedes 'I shall exalt thee', which shows that death occurred before exaltation. A further proof is that Allah the Glorious, has said: After thy death I shall place those who follow thee above those who disbelieve (i.e., the Jews), until the Day of Judgement. All Christians and Muslims agree that this

---

[169] 'O Jesus, I will cause thee to die *a natural death* and will exalt thee to Myself, and will clear thee from *the charges of* those who disbelieve, and will place those who follow thee above those who disbelieve, until the Day of Resurrection.'—Āl-e-'Imrān, 3:56 **[Publisher]**

prophecy had been fulfilled before the advent of Islām, inasmuch as God Almighty had subordinated the Jews to Christians and Muslims, and they have continued in that condition of subordination for centuries. The verse cannot be construed to mean that such subordination will take place after Jesus returns from heaven.

Allah the Glorious quotes Jesus in the Holy Qur'ān as saying:

وَأَوْصٰنِيْ بِالصَّلٰوةِ وَالزَّكٰوةِ مَا دُمْتُ حَيًّا ۝ وَّبَرًّا بِوَالِدَتِيْ [170]

That is: 'God has enjoined upon me Prayer and almsgiving throughout my life and has made me dutiful towards my mother as long as I live'.

These commandments can obviously not be carried out in heaven. He who believes that Jesus was raised bodily to heaven will have to accept, according the above verse, that Jesus is still subject to all the commandments of the Torah and the Gospel, whereas this requirement cannot be fulfilled in heaven. It is also strange that, on the one hand, God Almighty should command Jesus to be dutiful to his mother throughout his life, but He should then separate him from her while he was still living; and that He should command him to give alms throughout his life, but should then convey him alive to a place where he cannot give alms himself nor can direct anyone else to do so; and that He should command him to observe Prayer, but should convey him far away from the company of the believers whose companionship was necessary for Prayer services. Did his bodily ascent to heaven have any other result than making him

---

[170] Maryam, 19:32-33 **[Publisher]**

incapable of discharging his obligations towards his fellow beings and from carrying out the duty of enjoining virtue and forbidding vice? Had he continued to live on earth during these 1891 years, how beneficial his person would have been for God's creatures! The only result of his bodily ascent to heaven was that his people went astray and he himself was totally deprived of the opportunity to carry out the functions of Prophethood.

[Izāla-e-Auhām, Rūḥānī Khazā'in, vol. 3, pp. 330-332]

We have established fully that the belief that Jesus had ascended bodily to heaven is not supported by the Holy Qur'ān and true Aḥādīth. It seems to be based upon senseless and contradictory speculation. In this philosophical age, which is accompanied by cultured reason and sharpness of intellect, it would be a great mistake to hope for religious success on the basis of such doctrines. If these meaningless speculations were to be presented to the illiterate Bedouins of Arabia, or the inhabitants of the deserts of Africa, or the wild dwellers of the far off islands in the oceans, they might gain some acceptance; but we cannot hope to propagate among educated people such doctrines as are utterly opposed to reason, experience, laws of nature and philosophy. Moreover, they cannot be attributed to the Holy Prophet (peace and blessings of Allah be upon him); indeed they contradict the Aḥādīth. Nor can we present such doctrines as a gift to the scholars of Europe and America who are discarding the absurdities of their own respective faiths. How can those, whose hearts and minds have been developed by the light of new kinds of knowledge, accept such concepts which are disrespectful to God Almighty, denigrate His Unity, falsify His Law and abrogate the teachings of His Books?

The notion that Jesus will descend bodily from heaven is

only a consequence of the concept that he was raised bodily to heaven. Therefore, we should first consider whether or not the primary factor can be established on the basis of the Holy Qur'ān and Ḥadīth. If the basic factor is established, we will be able to accept that a person whose bodily ascent to heaven is proved could likewise descend bodily from heaven. But if the basic factor is not established on the authority of the Holy Qur'ān and the Ḥadīth and instead contradicts them, we cannot accept the accuracy of the alleged consequence. And if there should be any Aḥādīth whose purport might be indicative of such consequential proposition, we would try to reconcile them to the basic factor.

[Izāla-e-Auhām, Rūḥānī Khazā'in, vol. 3, pp. 235-236]

When the Muslims of our time affirm the death of the Holy Prophet (peace and blessings of Allah be upon him) and his burial on earth, and at the same time affirm that Jesus is still alive, they furnish the Christians with a written acknowledgement that Jesus possessed qualities different from those of the common man and also different from all the Prophets. If it were true that while the Best of Mankind (peace and blessings of Allah be upon him), who appeared six hundred years after Jesus, died after a brief life thirteen hundred years ago, yet Jesus has not yet died, would it not prove that Jesus possesses qualities that are superhuman? Though the Muslim divines of these times formally reject every form of association of partners with God, yet they lend their full support to those who are guilty of such association. It is an outrage that while Allah the Glorious, in His Holy Word, proclaims the death of Jesus, these divines create countless difficulties in the way of Islām by adhering to the notion that he is still alive. They acknowledge Jesus as ever-living and self-subsisting in heaven, and affirm the death and burial upon earth of the Chief of the Prophets (peace and blessings of Allah be upon him)! The Holy Qur'ān records the testimony of Jesus to the effect:

مُبَشِّرًۢا بِرَسُوۡلٍ یَّاۡتِیۡ مِنۡۢ بَعۡدِی اسۡمُہٗۤ اَحۡمَدُ [171]

That is: 'I give glad tidings of a Messenger who will come after me (i.e., after my death,) whose name will be Aḥmad.'

Hence, if Jesus is still bodily alive, it follows that the Holy Prophet (peace and blessings of Allah be upon him) has not yet appeared on earth.

[Ā'īna-e-Kamālāt-e-Islām, Rūḥānī Khazā'in, vol. 5, pp. 41-42].

It is absolutely wrong to say that Jesus (peace be on him) has ascended bodily to heaven. There is no proof of this in the Holy Qur'ān nor in Aḥādīth, nor can reason accept it; indeed the Qur'ān and the Ḥadīth and reason all three reject it. The Holy Qur'ān has clearly said that Jesus (peace be on him) has died, and the Ḥadīth narrating the *Me'rāj* [Spiritual Ascent] of the Holy Prophet[sa] informs us that Jesus[as] has joined the souls of the departed Prophets (peace be on them), and has cut asunder completely from the earth. Reason tells us that it is not the way of Allah that a mortal body should ascend to heaven and, discarding all the characteristics of earthly life like eating and drinking etc., should join the souls who have suffered bodily death and have arrived in the hereafter. Reason can furnish no such instance. Moreover, as the belief that Jesus (peace be on him) ascended bodily to heaven is inconsistent with the Holy Qur'ān, so is the doctrine of his bodily descent inconsistent with the Holy Qur'ān.

---

171 Al-Ṣaff, 61:7 **[Publisher]**

The Holy Qur'ān affirms the death of Jesus in the verses:

فَلَمَّا تَوَفَّيْتَنِي [172]

قَدْ خَلَتْ مِنْ قَبْلِهِ الرُّسُلُ [173]

اَلْيَوْمَ اَكْمَلْتُ لَكُمْ دِيْنَكُمْ [174]

وَلٰكِنْ رَّسُوْلَ اللّٰهِ وَخَاتَمَ النَّبِيّٖنَ [175]

and proclaims the end of normal Prophethood after the Holy Prophet (peace and blessings of Allah be upon him), and clearly affirms that the Holy Prophet (peace and blessings of Allah be upon him) is *Khātam-ul-Anbiyā'* by stating:

وَلٰكِنْ رَّسُوْلَ اللّٰهِ وَخَاتَمَ النَّبِيّٖنَ [176]

But those who insist on bringing Jesus (peace be on him) back to the earth believe that he will return with the status of a Prophet and for forty-five years Gabriel shall continue to convey Prophetic revelation to him. What room does this doctrine leave for the belief that Prophethood ended with the Holy Prophet[sa]? According to them it is Jesus who is the *Khātam-ul-Anbiyā'*.

[Tohfah-e-Golarhviyyah , Rūḥānī Khazā'in, vol. 17, pp. 173-174].

The citation by Ḥaḍrat Abū Bakr (may Allah be pleased with him), on the occasion of the death of the Holy

---

172 'When Thou didst cause me to die.'—Al-Mā'idah, 5:118 **[Publisher]**

173 'Verily, *all* Messengers have passed away before him.'—Āl-e-'Imrān, 3:145 **[Publisher]**

174 'This day have I perfected your religion for you.'—Al-Mā'idah, 5:4 **[Publisher]**

175 'But he is the Messenger of Allah and the Seal of the Prophets.'—Al-Aḥzāb, 33:41 **[Publisher]**

176 Ibid.

Prophet[sa], of the verse:

مَا مُحَمَّدٌ اِلَّا رَسُوْلٌ ۚ قَدْ خَلَتْ مِنْ قَبْلِهِ الرُّسُلُ [177]

shows that he believed Jesus (peace be on him) to be dead. If this verse is to be construed to mean that some Prophets had died before the advent of the Holy Prophet (peace and blessings of Allah be upon him) and some were still living, then it would not support the reasoning of Ḥaḍrat Abū Bakr[ra], as it would not be an authority for the death of all previous Messengers. Yet none of the companions of the Holy Prophet[sa], who were all present on the occasion, took exception to the reasoning of Ḥaḍrat Abū Bakr[ra], which shows that it was supported by the consensus of the companions, which is held as binding and can never err. One of the many favours that Ḥaḍrat Abū Bakr[ra] bestowed upon the Muslims is that during his rightful Khilāfat he opened the door of truth and accuracy to deliver them from the error that was to arise in later times and erected such a strong barrier against the flood of misguidance as cannot be demolished by the divines of this age even if they were assisted by all the Jinns. So we pray that God Almighty may shower thousands of blessings on the soul of Ḥaḍrat Abū Bakr[ra] who conclusively settled, on the basis of pure Divine revelation, that Jesus had died.

[Tiryāq-ul-Qulūb, Rūḥānī Khazā'in, vol. 15, pp. 461-462 footnote]

The Holy Qur'ān has categorically said that Jesus (peace be on him) had died. The verse:

فَلَمَّا تَوَفَّيْتَنِيْ [178]

---

[177] 'Muḥammad is only a Messenger; Verily, *all* Messengers have passed away before him.'—Āl-e-'Imrān, 3:145 **[Publisher]**

[178] When Thou didst cause me to die. —Al-Mā'idah, 5:118 **[Publisher]**

clearly establishes that Jesus (peace be on him) died. *Ṣaḥīḥ Bukhārī* furnishes proof on the authority of Ibn-e-'Abbās (may Allah be pleased with him) that, in this verse, the expression *Tawaffī* connotes death. It is utterly wrong to suggest that the expression *Tawaffaitanī*, which is in the past tense, should be construed to indicate the future, that is to say, that Jesus[as] had not yet died but would die in the latter days. The purport of the verse is that Jesus[as] would submit that his people did not go astray in his lifetime but were led astray after his death. If it is assumed that Jesus (peace be on him) is not dead, it will also have to be acknowledged that the Christians have not yet gone astray, because the verse clearly states that they went astray after the death of Jesus[as]. Only those who are utterly bereft of faith can deny such express authority.

Seeing that the Holy Qur'ān affirms the death of Jesus (peace be on him) and designates the Holy Prophet[sa] as the Seal of Prophets, and Ḥadīth confirms both these verities and also states that the Messiah who is to come will be one of the Muslims, the question arises as to how such a consensus could have reached that Jesus[as] would descend bodily from heaven in the latter days? The answer is that there never was such a consensus, and anyone who claims to the contrary must either be extremely stupid or dishonest. The companions of the Holy Prophet[sa] were in no need of looking into the details of this affair. According to the verse:

فَلَمَّا تَوَفَّيْتَنِي [179]

---

[179] 'But when Thou didst cause me to die.'—Al-Mā'idah, 5:118 **[Publisher]**

they believed that Jesus[as] had died. That is why when Ḥaḍrat Abū Bakr (may Allah be pleased with him), perceived at the time of the death of the Holy Prophet (peace and blessings of Allah be upon him) that some people were in doubt concerning his death, he emphatically affirmed that all Prophets had died and no one of them was alive. He recited the verse:

قَدْ خَلَتْ مِنْ قَبْلِهِ الرُّسُلُ [180]

Not a single person questioned his statement. Then there is Imam Mālik, a great Imam, a reputed scholar of the Qur'ān and Ḥadīth and a righteous one; he believed that Jesus[as] had died. So did Imam Bin Ḥazam whose high status is well known, and so did Imam Bukhārī whose compilation of Aḥādīth is known as the truest book after the Book of God. In the same way, the learned Muḥaddathīn and commentators Ibn-e-Taimiyyah and Ibn-e-Qayyim, who were the Imams of their respective ages, believed that Jesus[as] had died. The Chief of the Sufis, Sheikh Moḥy-ud-Dīn Ibn Al-'Arabī very clearly stated in his commentary that Jesus[as] had died. The same has been the case with leading scholars, Muḥaddathīn and commentators. All the Imams and scholars of the Mu'tazila held the same view. It would, therefore, be a daring invention to say that the bodily ascent of Jesus[as] to heaven and his expected descent has been a matter of consensus. These are the beliefs of the people of the time when thousands of innovations had found their way into Islām. These were the middle ages which are described by the Holy Prophet (peace and blessings of Allah be upon him)

---

[180] 'Verily, *all* Messengers have passed away before him.'—Āl-e-'Imrān, 3:145 **[Publisher]**

as *Faij-e-A'waj*[181]. It is concerning these people that he said:

لَيْسُوْا مِنِّى وَ لَسْتُ مِنْهُمْ

'They are not of me and I am not of them.'

In adopting such a belief, they transgressed from the Holy Qur'ān in four ways. They cannot cite any verse or any Ḥadīth in support of the fiction that Jesus[as] had ascended bodily to heaven. They deceive the common people by adding the word heaven to the word *Nuzūl*, whereas it does not occur in any Ḥadīth whose accuracy is beyond doubt. In Arabic, the word *Nuzūl* merely means 'arrival', like the arrival of a traveller. In our own country, the equivalent of *Nuzūl* is used for the arrival of a stranger and no one has the slightest notion that such a one descends from heaven. A thorough search of the books of Ḥadīth of all Muslim sects would not produce a single Ḥadīth of any kind stating that Jesus[as] had ascended bodily to heaven and would return to earth in some later age. If anyone should set forth such a Ḥadīth, we are prepared to pay him as much as twenty thousand rupees as penalty; we shall also publish a confession of our mistake and burn all our books. Let anyone who wishes come forward to satisfy himself.

[Kitāb-ul-Bariyyah, Rūḥānī Khazā'in, vol. 13, pp. 219-226 footnote]

That Jesus, son of Mary, will appear in the world by way of transmigration of souls is the worst and most shameful of notions. Those who believe in the transmigration of souls, believe that only an impure person would return to this life, but that those who leave the world, having

---

[181] The time of great distortions.— **[Publisher]**

completed all stages of spiritual perfection, would stay in the house of salvation for a long time. Moreover, according to our belief, God Almighty has promised that those who are admitted to heaven would never be expelled therefrom. It surprises us as to why our divines would want to bring Jesus out of paradise. They relate the tale that Enoch, with the permission of the angel of death, stepped into paradise, and when the angel asked him to come out he refused to do so and recited the verse:

وَمَا هُمْ مِّنْهَا بِمُخْرَجِيْنَ [182]

still they assert that Jesus will return to earth from heaven. Would he not be entitled to benefit from this verse? Is this verse to be considered abrogated in reference to him?

[Izāla-e-Auhām, Rūḥānī Khazā'in, vol. 3, pp. 147-148]

True Status of Jesus

I do not deny the high status of Jesus[as], despite the fact that I have been informed by God that the Muḥammadī Messiah occupies a higher status than the Mosaic Messiah. I hold Jesus son of Mary, in high esteem inasmuch as I am spiritually the *Khātam-ul-Khulafā'* in the Islamic dispensation, just as Jesus was *Khātam-ul-Khulafā'* in the Israeli dispensation. In Mosaic dispensation the son of Mary was the Promised Messiah and in the Islamic dispensation I am the Promised Messiah; so I honour greatly the one whose name I bear. Anyone who asserts that I do not hold Jesus son of Mary in high esteem is a mischief-maker and a liar. I honour not only Jesus son of

---

[182] '...Nor shall they *ever* be ejected therefrom.'—Al-Ḥijr, 15:49 **[Publisher]**

Mary but also his four brothers as they were all sons of the same mother. I also regard his two real sisters as holy, for they are all the children of the holy Mary.

[Kashtī-e-Nūḥ, Rūḥānī Khazā'in, vol. 19, pp. 17-18]

Our readers should remember that in dealing with the Christian religion we have to adopt the same form of exposition as they adopt against us. The Christians do not believe in the Prophet 'Īsā (peace be upon him), who called himself a servant of God and believed in the righteousness of previous Prophets and had faith in the advent of the Holy Prophet Muḥammad (peace and blessings of Allah be upon him) and had even made a prophecy concerning him. They believe in someone called Jesus, who is not mentioned in the Qur'ān, and assert that he claimed to be God and designated previous Prophets as robbers etc. They also assert that he vigorously denied the truth of our Holy Prophet (peace and blessings of Allah be upon him) and prophesied that only false Prophets would appear after him. The Holy Qur'ān has not directed us to believe in any such person, but has clearly affirmed that anyone who claims to be God shall be consigned to hell. That is why, when speaking of the Jesus of the Christians, we have not spoken with such respect as is due to a righteous person. Had he not been blind, he would not have said that only impostors would follow him; and had he been good and faithful, he would not have claimed to be God. Our readers should not be misled into thinking that some of the harsh words that we have employed concerning him were intended for Ḥaḍrat 'Īsā (peace be on him.) They have been written concerning the Jesus of whom there is no mention in the Qur'ān or the Ḥadīth.

[Majmū'ah Ishtihārāt, vol. 2, pp. 295-296]

I regret to say that I have had to publish this issue of *Nūr-ul-Qur'ān* in response to a person who instead of referring to our lord and master, the Holy Prophet (peace and blessings of Allah be upon him) with respect, has vituperated him and has, out of his personal vileness, uttered so many calumnies against the Leader of the Righteous and the Chief of the Purified that a pure hearted person trembles at hearing them. In dealing with such a person, we had to adopt a severe tone.

I declare that my belief concerning the Messiah (peace be upon him) is an excellent belief. I hold sincerely that he was a true Prophet of God Almighty and was a loved one of His. I also believe, as the Holy Qur'ān tells us, that he believed sincerely in our lord and master Muḥammad (peace and blessings of Allah be upon him) as the means of his salvation. He was a sincere follower, out of many hundred such followers, of the Law of Moses (peace be on him.) I, therefore, give him all the respect due to his to his exalted status. But the Jesus presented by the Christians—who claimed to be God and considered everyone but himself to be accursed, i.e., he considered them guilty of such vices the punishment of which is a curse—is, in my view not entitled to the mercy of God. The Holy Qur'ān has not made any reference to such an impertinent and vile tongued Jesus. I am shocked by the conduct of one who believed that God could be subject to death and claimed godhead for himself and vilified such righteous ones as were a thousand times better than him. In dealing with Christians I have throughout had that fictitious Jesus in mind. The humble servant of God, 'Īsā, son of Mary, who was a Prophet and who is mentioned in the Holy Qur'ān is not the one against whom my harsh words are directed. I have adopted this method after enduring, for forty years, the abuse which Christian missionaries have hurled against the Holy Prophet (peace and blessings of Allah be upon him.) Some foolish Maulavīs, who should rather be called blind, think that Christians have never reviled the Holy Prophet (peace and blessings of Allah be upon him.) But the truth is that the Christian missionaries are in the forefront of those who refer to the Holy Prophet[sa] with contempt and defame and abuse him. I have a stock of books by Christian missionaries which are full of abuse of the Holy Prophet[sa]. And whoso desires can come and inspect them. I declare that I shall henceforth deal respectfully with any Christian missionary who, discarding the method of abuse, adopts a respectful style of exposition. By having recourse to abuse, they themselves make their fictitious Jesus a subject of criticism. We have become weary of their abuse. If someone abuses another's father, would the wronged one not be justified in abusing the offender's father? What I have said is not abuse but a fact.

إِنَّمَا الْأَعْمَالُ بِالنِّيَّاتِ [183]

[Nūr-ul-Qur'ān, No. II, Rūḥānī Khazā'in, vol. 9, pp. 374-375]

Objections against Jesus

The wretched Jews of the time of Jesus (peace be upon him) planned his ruin and conspired to impose upon his righteous soul the curse of death upon the cross, as the Torah has declared that he who dies upon the rood would be accursed, which means that his heart would become vile and estranged from God and he would be rejected by God like Satan. That is why Satan is called the accursed one. This was an evil scheme which had been thought out

---

[183] 'Actions are judged by their intentions.' **[Publisher]**

with reference to the Messiah (peace be upon him) so that the people should conclude that he was not pure hearted and a true Prophet and a loved one of God but was accursed whose heart was vile, and that he was disgusted with God and God was disgusted with him. But God Almighty frustrated the wicked design of the Jews and not only rescued his righteous Prophet from death on the cross, but bestowed a long life of one hundred and twenty years upon him, during which all his Jewish enemies were destroyed. According to the eternal ways of God Almighty, every Prophet with a high resolve has to migrate on account of the persecution by his people. Therefore, Jesus (peace be upon him) also, after a ministry of three years, and having been rescued from death on the cross, migrated towards India. Having conveyed the Divine message to the other tribes of Israel, who, after the Babylonian dispersal, had settled in India, Kashmir and Tibet, he finally died in Kashmir and was honourably buried in Moḥallā Khānyār of Srinagar. His tomb is quite famous.

[Rāz-e-Ḥaqīqat, Rūḥānī Khazā'in, vol. 14, pp. 154-155]

The Jews raise such strong objections concerning Jesus and his prophecies, that it is difficult for us to refute them. All we can say is that Jesus was undoubtedly a true Prophet, because this is what the Holy Qur'ān says. We have no other proof of his Prophethood. On the contrary, there can be several arguments in refutation of his Prophethood. It is the beneficence of the Qur'ān that he is included among true Prophets. That is why we believe that he was a Prophet, a chosen one of God and free from the calumnies which the Jews had uttered against him and his mother. It appears from the Holy Qur'ān that there were two principal charges against him:

1. He was accursed because his birth was illegitimate.
2. He death was accursed as he died upon the cross.

The Torah declares that a person of illegitimate birth is accursed and will not be admitted to heaven nor will he be spiritually exalted. It was also written that he who dies on the cross will be accursed and will not be spiritually exalted. These are grave charges indeed! The Holy Qur'ān has refuted them together in the same place:

وَبِكُفْرِهِمْ وَقَوْلِهِمْ عَلٰى مَرْيَمَ بُهْتَانًا عَظِيْمًاۙ وَّقَوْلِهِمْ اِنَّا قَتَلْنَا الْمَسِيْحَ عِيْسَى ابْنَ مَرْيَمَ رَسُوْلَ اللّٰهِۚ وَمَا قَتَلُوْهُ وَمَا صَلَبُوْهُ وَلٰكِنْ شُبِّهَ لَهُمْ [184]

(Part Number 6, Sūrah Al-Nisā')

Here the response is given to both the allegations.

The meaning of these verses, in brief, is that: 'Jesus was neither of illegitimate birth nor did he die on the cross. It was mistakenly believed that he had so died. Hence he was accepted of God and was spiritually exalted like the other Prophets.'

There is no mention of his bodily ascent to heaven, as the Maulavīs would allege. The whole controversy was simply about his spiritual exaltation.

The Holy Qur'ān affirms his righteousness, but it is a pity that his prophecies are strongly criticized by the Jews and we have no answer to their criticism. We accept him sincerely as a true Prophet because the Holy Qur'ān so affirms; we have no other proof of his Prophethood. The Christians exalt him to godhood while there is little proof even of his Prophethood.

[I'jāz-e-Aḥmadī, Rūḥānī Khazā'in, vol. 19, pp. 120-121]

---

[184] Al-Nisā', 4:157-158 [Publisher]

If we were to rely solely upon the available record, it would not be possible to establish the Prophethood of Jesus. On the contrary, he would be charged with falsehood and imposture. For instance, he whom he represented as the Prophet Elias denied that he was Elias. But as the Holy Qur'ān affirms the Prophethood of Jesus[as], we believe in him as such and regard his rejection as patent disbelief.

[Ḍiā-ul-Ḥaq, Rūḥānī Khazā'in, vol. 9, pp. 303-304]

Jesus (peace be upon him) has been a victim of the misguided in a strange manner. During his lifetime the disbelieving Jews called him an infidel, liar, deceiver and impostor and denied his spiritual exaltation. When he died, those who were inclined towards the worship of man deified him. The Jews denied his spiritual exaltation and were countered with the doctrine of his physical ascent to heaven. Previous Prophets were exalted to heaven spiritually after they had died, but Jesus was declared to be seated in heaven bodily in his clothes and with all human qualities while he was still alive. This was a reply to his persistent rejection by the Jews and their denial of his spiritual exaltation, but it was an altogether absurd reply.

[Brāhīn-e-Aḥmadiyyah, part V, Rūḥānī Khazā'in, vol. 21, p. 57].

A certain person named Ḥidāyatullāh has published a pamphlet in which he has accused me of denying the miracles of Jesus[as]. In doing so, he has sought support from some paragraphs of my book *Izāla-e-Auhām*. Remember, such people are the victims of their own short sightedness and lack of intelligence. I do not deny the miracles of Jesus (peace be on him); there is no doubt that he did work some miracles. The Gospel accounts of those miracles raise certain doubts about them, for instance, the reference to a certain pool, whose water possessed healing qualities, and the repeated affirmation of Jesus[as] himself that he was not a worker of miracles. Yet we are not concerned with the Gospel; the Holy Qur'ān shows that he had been vouchsafed some signs. It is, however, a mistake on the part of our careless divines that they attribute certain qualities to Jesus wherby he used to fashion, like the Creator of the universe, the frame of a bird and made it alive by breathing into it so that it flew away, and he revived the dead with the touch of his hand, and he had knowledge of the unseen, and he did not suffer death and he is present in heaven in his physical body. If all that is attributed to him were true, then there would be no doubt about his being the knower of the unseen and reviver of the dead. If, on these premises, a Christian were to argue that Jesus was God on the basis of the proposition that the existence of the qualities of a thing is proof of the existence of the thing itself, then what answer would the Muslims give to such a claim? It would be a misinterpretation of the Holy Qur'ān to affirm that these miracles occurred as a result of prayer. The Holy Qur'ān does not mention any prayer in connection with the flight of something that was fashioned in the shape of a bird and was breathed into, nor does it state that such a shape became alive. It is not permissible to add something to the Divine Word from oneself. This was the kind of perversion on account of which the Jews were cursed. *Ma'ālim-ut-Tanzīl* and several other commentaries only state that those shapes flew for a short while and then fell to earth. As there is no proof that they possessed life, we can only assume that they were figures made out of clay which flew about like toys by some human contrivance and under the spiritual influence of a Prophet; for, an affirmation of true creation on the part of Jesus would amount to a grave mischief and an association of partners with God. If all that is desired is proof of a miracle it is enough of a miracle for a lifeless thing to fly about for a short while. If it is alleged that any verse of the Holy Qur'ān affirms that the shape of clay was invested with life or that there is historical proof that those shapes became alive and laid eggs and hatched birds and many of their race are in existence today, then a proof must be produced of such assertions. The Holy Qur'ān affirms that even if the whole world joined together to create a fly it would not be able to do so, because in such a case it would become God's partner in creation. It would be equally absurd to affirm that God Almighty had permitted him to create birds. This would be preposterous, as there is no contradiction in the Word of God, and He does not bestow such permission upon anyone. God Almighty did not bestow upon the Holy Prophet (peace and blessing of Allah be upon him) permission to create even a fly. Then how could the son of Mary obtain such permission? Fear God, and do not seek to convert allegory into physical reality.

[Shahādat-ul-Qur'ān, Rūḥānī Khazā'in, vol. 6, pp. 372-374, footnote]

Miracles of Jesus

Certain Muslim sects believe that Jesus used to fashion different types of birds and used to invest them with life by breathing into them. On this basis I have been asked that as I claim to be the like of Jesus I should also fashion a bird and make it come alive by breathing into it. It is alleged that millions of birds created by Jesus fly about everywhere and that the like of Jesus should also create some birds.

The answer to all these superstitions is that the verses on which they are based are allegorical and it is the height of faithlessness and patent repudiation of the basic values of Islām to construe them as meaning that God Almighty had deliberately associated Jesus in His attribute of creation; inasmuch as it would be a negation of the Godhead to believe that God Almighty should invest someone else with His special attributes and His Divinity. One of these people was asked if he could distinguish those birds that had been created by God from those that were created by Jesus, but he confessed by remaining silent that he was unable to do so.

The doctrine that some birds are the creation of God Almighty and some are the creation of Jesus is altogether vicious and amounts to polytheism. Anyone holding such a belief cannot be a Muslim....

The miracles of Prophets are of two types. One are heavenly manifestations, in which human design and reason have no part, such as the splitting of the moon, which was a miracle of our lord and master, the Holy Prophet (peace and blessings of Allah be upon him) and was manifested by the limitless power of God Almighty as a sign of the greatness of a righteous and perfect Prophet. Secondly, intellectual miracles, which are manifested through the extraordinary intelligence of a Prophet and which resemble Divine revelation. For instance, the miracle of Solomon[as], which was manifested in the shape of:

صَرۡحٌ مُّمَرَّدٌ مِّنۡ قَوَارِيۡرَ [185]

---

[185] 'A palace paved smooth with slabs of glass.'—Al-Naml, 27:45 **[Publisher]**

whereby the Queen of Sheba was blessed with faith.

It appears that this miracle of Jesus was purely intellectual like the miracle of Solomon. History reveals that in those days people were inclined towards the useless pursuit of sleight of hand, which astonished the common people. People like those who, in the time of the Pharaoh, used to manipulate the forms of serpents and other animals and made them move like living animals, had by the time of Jesus spread into the land of the Jews who had learnt magical tricks from them as is also indicated in the Holy Qur'ān. It is, therefore, not a matter of surprise that God Almighty may have instructed Jesus in some method whereby a toy fashioned out of clay could be manipulated by pressing a spring or breathing upon it so as to fly like a bird or to move on its feet. Jesus had worked with his father Joseph for twenty-two years as a carpenter, and carpentry stimulates a man's mind towards inventing different kinds of machines and mechanical instruments.

Miracles are granted to a person in accord with the faculties that he possesses. As the spiritual faculties of our lord and master, the Holy Prophet (peace and blessings of Allah be upon him) were well developed in the appreciation of spiritual verities, he was accordingly bestowed the miracle of the Holy Qur'ān, which is comprehensive of all verities and understandings of the Divine. It should, therefore, not be a matter of surprise if Jesus displayed an intellectual miracle to his opponents, like the one displayed by his ancestor, Solomon[as]. Such a miracle is not beyond the reach of the intellect inasmuch as in our own time many mechanical experts are able to fashion birds that speak and move and wag their tails. I have also heard that some mechanical birds can even fly. Many such toys are manufactured in Bombay, Calcutta, Europe, America and every year new one are introduced into the market.

As the Holy Qur'ān often employs metaphors, these verses can be construed to mean that birds signify the illiterate and simple people whom Jesus chose as his companions, who were like birds under his care, and into whom he breathed spiritual guidance whereby they began to fly.

Moreover, it is possible that such wonders might be performed like a pastime through hypnosis. Those who are experts in *'amal-ut-tirb* [psychokinetic exercises] can, by directing the warmth of their spirits towards certain objects, make them appear as if they were alive. The human soul possesses the capacity of directing its warmth upon a lifeless object so as to make it move as if it was alive. I have seen some practitioners of this phenomenon, who so warmed a wooden tripod by the touch of their hands through the exercise of their animal spirit that it began to move, and though several people mounted on it, it could not be stopped....It should be remembered that such an object which is fashioned out of clay or wood and is warmed by a spirit through *'amal-ut-tirb* does not become alive. It remains solid and lifeless; it is only made to move by the warmth of the spirit of the mesmerist.

It should also be remembered that the Holy Qur'ān does not affirm the movement or flight of such birds, nor their coming to life. It should also be kept in mind that curing diseases and influencing objects with the warmth of the spirit are all branches of mesmerism and there have always been people who healed the paralytics, the lepers and those suffering from tuberculosis through spiritual exercises....It has been conclusively established that, under Divine direction, Messiah, son of Mary, was an expert in mesmerism, like the Prophet Isaiah, though he was not as great an expert as the latter, because even the bones of Isaiah performed the miracle that when they were brought into contact with a corpse, it came back to life; but the corpses of the two thieves who were nailed to the cross at the same time with Jesus were not revived through contact with his body. In any case, these mesmeric activities of Jesus were in accord with the thinking of his age for a special purpose. It should, however, be kept in mind that mesmerism is not worthy of such appreciation as the common people imagine. Had I not looked upon it with contempt and disgust, I could, by the grace of God Almighty and with His support, have performed the same wonders as were performed by Jesus. But I prefer the spiritual method that was followed by the Holy Prophet (peace and blessings of Allah be upon him.) Jesus had adopted this method under Divine direction in view of the earthy and low thinking of the Jews, which had become their second nature. In truth he was not fond of this method.

One evil characteristic of this physical practice is that a person who continues to employ his emotional and intellectual faculties to heal physical maladies suffers a serious decline of the spiritual capacities, which heal spiritual ills through their influence, and is not able to achieve any remarkable success in illumining and purifying souls. That is why Jesus, who healed those afflicted with physical ailments with this method, was not able to achieve any noticeable success in impressing hearts with guidance and the Unity of God and steadfastness of faith. But the Holy Prophet (peace and blessings of Allah be upon him), who did not pay any attention to physical matters, and concentrated on stimulating spiritual guidance in the hearts of his people, was most successful in purifying the souls and helped thousands of God's creatures to achieve it to the highest degree. He achieved matchless success in the spiritual reform of mankind and in bringing about inner change. The dead, whom Jesus revived by the practice *'amal-ut-tirb*, died within a few minutes, as the warmth of the spirit and its life was only temporarily stimulated in them, but those who were spiritually revived by our Holy Prophet (peace and blessings of Allah be upon him) shall live forever.

My designation of mesmerism as *'amal-ut-tirb*, in which Jesus had acquired some proficiency, is under Divine direction. God Almighty disclosed to me that this art is *'amal-ut-tirb*, and it is concerning this that I received the revelation:

هٰذَا هُوَ التِّرْبُ الَّذِىْ لَا يَعْلَمُوْنَ

'This is the *tirb* of whose reality people are unaware.'

It must be realized that God Almighty is Unique in respect of every one of His attributes and does not associate anyone in them. The emphasis which the clear and unambiguous verses of the Holy Qur'ān give to this subject is well known. As Allah, hallowed be His name, says:

اَلَّذِيْ لَهٗ مُلْكُ السَّمٰوٰتِ وَالْاَرْضِ وَلَمْ يَتَّخِذْ وَلَدًا وَّلَمْ يَكُنْ لَّهٗ شَرِيْكٌ
فِي الْمُلْكِ وَخَلَقَ كُلَّ شَيْءٍ فَقَدَّرَهٗ تَقْدِيْرًا ۝ وَاتَّخَذُوْا مِنْ دُوْنِهٖٓ اٰلِهَةً لَّا
يَخْلُقُوْنَ شَيْئًا وَّهُمْ يُخْلَقُوْنَ وَلَا يَمْلِكُوْنَ لِاَنْفُسِهِمْ ضَرًّا وَّلَا نَفْعًا وَّلَا
يَمْلِكُوْنَ مَوْتًا وَّلَا حَيٰوةً وَّلَا نُشُوْرًا ۝ [186]

(Part Number 18)

---

[186] Al-Furqān, 25:3-4 **[Publisher]**

That is: 'God is He Who alone owns the kingdom of the heavens and the earth. He has no partner. He has no son nor has he any partner in His kingdom. He has created everything and has placed limits on their bodies, their power, and their life. The pagans have taken gods—beside that True God—who have not created anything and are themselves created. They do not determine any harm or benefit for themselves and do not control life nor death nor resurrection.'

God Almighty has here clearly affirmed that there is no Creator besides Him. In another verse, it is stated that the whole world together cannot create even a fly. Then it is stated that no one beside Him has control over death and life and resurrection. Had it been His way to associate any one of His creatures in these attributes, He would have made an exception of them and would not have taught His absolute Unity.

It may be asked why then has Allah the Glorious, employed the expression, '*You will create*' with reference to Jesus. The answer would be that this is a metaphoric use of the expression as in the verse:

فَتَبٰرَكَ اللّٰهُ اَحْسَنُ الْخٰلِقِيْنَ [187]

Without a doubt God Almighty is the true Creator and those who fashion toys of clay or wood are also creators but only metaphorically so, because their works are mere show and have no reality.

If it is asked why it is not permissible for Jesus[as] to have fashioned birds under Divine direction which could fly by his breathing into them, by way of a miracle, the an-

---

[187] 'So blessed be Allah, the Best of creators.'—Al-Mu'minūn, 23:15 **[Publisher]**

swer is that God does not make anyone the master of death and life or harm and benefit. Prophets seek miracles through prayer and supplication and do not possess the power to work miracles like a man has the power to use his hands and feet. Thus the power of creation is one of those Divine attributes that are never bestowed upon man and is distinct from a miracle. The essence of a miracle is that God Almighty, in order to demonstrate the truth and honour of a Prophet and the powerlessness and helplessness of his opponents, manifests something that is extraordinary or beyond imagination by His special design or in response to the prayer or supplication of the Prophet. But it is done in a manner which is not inconsistent with His attributes of Unity, Holiness and Perfection and which does not permit of anyone else's power or design.

It is not a miracle that God Almighty should invest a human being with the power of fashioning birds of clay, which would become real birds with flesh and bones and blood and all the limbs of animals when he breathes into them. If God Almighty can make someone the agent of His attribute of creation in the case of birds, He can also bestow the full agency of His attribute of creation. In this event, partnership in Divine attributes would become permissible, though only under His direction and permission, and the comprehension of the true Creator would become doubtful in the presence of such creators whose creations would become indistinguishable from God's. This would not be a form of miracle; it would be partnership in Godhead.

Some wise people try to solve the dilemma of polytheism by asserting that the birds which Jesus created did not live for any length of time but fell down and died after a short flight. But this explanation would help only if it is held that those birds were not invested with true life but only appeared to be alive for a short time as a result of mesmeric influence….

The Holy Qur'ān affirms that Jesus had been given the power to do these things as an exercise of his natural capacity, which is inherent in every human being. Jesus was not unique in this respect. Such capacity is being demonstrated in our own age. The miracles of Jesus were rendered bizarre and doubtful by the pool which had existed even before the birth of Jesus, and which also displayed wonders and a single dip into which bestowed healing upon all those afflicted with diseases such as paralysis, leukoderma, leprosy etc. And there were others who manifested similar extraordinary signs later on, and there was no such pool to cast doubt on their manifestations.

The belief that Jesus fashioned birds of clay and made them come alive as real birds by breathing into them, is entirely false and polytheistic. It was only an exercise of mesmeric capacity that had been developed to some degree by his spiritual propensity. It is also possible that he made use of clay from the pool that had been activated by the Holy Spirit. His miracle was only a kind of sleight of hand and the clay remained only clay like the Samaritan's calf. *Ponder over it, because this is a magnificent point; no one comprehends it except those who have been granted great wisdom.*

[Izāla-e-Auhām, Rūḥānī Khazā'in, vol. 3, pp. 251-263, footnote].

No other Prophet has had so many fictitious miracles attributed to him, as have been attributed to Jesus[as]; some ignorant ones even imagine that he had revived thousands upon thousands of the dead. The Gospels narrate a highly exaggerated statement of an occasion when all the dead buried in a graveyard, which had existed for thousands of years, were revived and all of them walked into the city alive.

Anyone with wisdom can easily understand that despite the fact that millions of the dead who had been revived walked into the city and told their tales to their descendants and confirmed the truth of Jesus[as], the Jews still did not believe in him. Who would credit such hard-heartedness? Indeed, if Jesus occupied himself with reviving thousands of the dead it must be recognized that the revived ones could not all have been deaf and dumb. Some of them must have been the brothers, fathers, sons, mothers, grandmothers, grandfathers and other near relatives of those who witnessed these miracles. Thus Jesus[as] had open to him a vast scheme for converting the disbelievers. Many of the revived dead who were related to the contemporary Jews, must have accompanied Jesus[as], and he must have arranged for them to deliver public addresses in a number of cities that must have been heard with great interest and eagerness. For instance, when a revived one told his audience, 'Many of you who are present here know me as I was buried by your hands. Now I have come to you after having heard from God's own tongue that Jesus is true and he has revived me'. … This would have had a deep affect on the Jews and thousands upon thousands of them would have believed in him. But the Holy Qur'ān and the Gospels affirm that the Jews had totally rejected Jesus[as] and that he was the least successful of the Prophets in his work of reform, and almost all the Jews considered him an impostor and a liar.

It is worth reflecting: should this have been the result of such a great supernatural miracle? When thousands of the revived dead testified to the truth of Jesus[as] and affirmed that they had seen heaven which contained only the Christians who believed in Jesus, and that they had seen hell which contained Jews who had denied Jesus, how could the slightest doubt remain about the truth of Jesus? If anyone was still in doubt, his ancestors who had been revived would have punished them to death proclaiming, 'O Ye wretches! Are you still in doubt after our testimony.' There is no doubt, therefore, that all such alleged miracles are pure fiction.

[Brāhīn-e-Aḥmadiyyah, part V, Rūḥānī Khazā'in, vol. 21, pp. 47-48]

The True Claim of Jesus

Out of the wonders that God has bestowed on me, one is that I have on several occasions met Jesus in visions—in state of complete wakefulness—and have talked to him and have inquired from him about his true claim and his teaching. It is a great thing worthy of attention, that Jesus is utterly disgusted with the doctrines of atonement, Trinity and sonship, as if these are the greatest lies that are attributed to him. This testimony of my visions is not a mere unsupported assertion on my part. Indeed, I am certain that if a seeker after truth should stay with me for a time with complete goodwill and should desire to behold Jesus in a state of vision, he can do so with the blessing of my attention and prayers and can speak to him and can procure his testimony concerning his doctrine and teachings, because I am the one in whose soul dwells the soul of Jesus by way of *burūz* [second coming.]

[Toḥfah-e-Qaiṣariyyah, Rūḥānī Khazā'in, vol. 12, p. 273]

I have beheld Jesus[as] several times in my dreams and have met him in visions. He ate with me from the same dish. On one occasion, I asked him about the misguidance in which his people have become involved. He was completely over-awed and glorified God Almighty and proclaimed His Holiness. He pointed to the earth and said that he was nothing more than a man made out of clay, and was completely innocent of that which was attributed to him. I found him to be a courteous and humble person.

[Nūr-ul-Ḥaq, part I, Rūḥānī Khazā'in, vol. 8, pp. 56-57]

Review of the Christian Faith

When I find that the Christian faith lacks altogether all three methods of the comprehension of God, I wonder on what basis Christians support their worship of Jesus. How unfortunate is it for them that the gates of heaven are closed to them, reason rejects them and they have not available to them documentary proof from the continuous teachings of the previous Prophets, and yet they have no fear of God. A wise person should adopt a religion whose teachings on the principles of comprehension of the Divine should be acceptable to all, and which should be supported by reason and against which the gates of heaven should not be closed. Reflection shows that the Christian faith is bereft of all these three qualities. Its method of comprehension of the Divine is so strange that neither the scriptures of the Jews nor any other heavenly book has taught it. As for the testimony of reason it is enough to point out that the more the Europeans become acquainted with dialectical methods, the greater becomes their mockery of Christian doctrines.

Logical propositions are of universal application as they are determined on the basis of universally accepted principles. Therefore, if a philosopher is convinced that Jesus is God, he must then hold that millions of gods have appeared in the past and can appear in the future, which is absurd.

As regards the heavenly signs, if all Christian clerics

were to beseech Jesus for a heavenly sign throughout their lives, they would not be given any, as Jesus is not God. He is a humble human being and would be unaware of their supplication. Even if he were aware of it, what could he do?....

If on the Day of Judgement, Jesus was to confess that he was not God and inquire from them why they had attributed Godhead to him, what will they do and to whom will they turn? God Almighty has established four witnesses to confound the Christians:

1. The Jews who have borne witness for more than three thousand five hundred years that they were never instructed in the doctrine of Trinity, nor had any of their Prophets predicted that God or a son of God in the true sense would appear on earth.
2. The followers of John the Baptist who are still found in Syria and who have throughout believed that Jesus was a human being, a Prophet and disciple of John the Baptist.
3. The Unitarian sect of the Christians which has been repeatedly mentioned in the Holy Qur'ān and whose members held a discussion with the Trinitarian sect of Christianity in the third century under the direction of the Roman Emperor, and who were held to be in the right and the Emperor had sided with them.
4. The Holy Prophet of Islām (peace and blessings of Allah be upon him) and the Holy Qur'ān both of whom have affirmed that Jesus, son f Mary, certainly was not God or the son of God, but was only a Prophet.

Moreover, thousands of the righteous have testified under Divine guidance that Jesus, son of Mary, was a humble creature of God and His Prophet. God Almighty has raised me as a witness against the Christians and has commanded me to proclaim that the deification of the son of Mary is a false doctrine that amounts to infidelity. He has also honoured me with His converse….

O Christians! be sure that Jesus, son of Mary, is not God. Do not wrong your souls by attributing the greatness of God to one of His creatures. Our hearts tremble at hearing that you call on a weak and helpless creature as if he were God. Turn to the True God so that you may achieve good and may receive salvation.

[Kitāb-ul-Bariyyah, Rūḥānī Khazā'in, vol. 13, pp. 53-55]

Jesus did not Claim to be God

The deification of the son of Mary is a terrible wrong. He is only a man and a Prophet in the Mosaic dispensation. You have not seen him but I have seen him many times. None of you knows him but I know him. He is a honourable man who acknowledges the greatness of Moses[as] and believes sincerely in the greatness of our lord and master Muḥammad (peace and blessings of Allah be upon him) and is, like us, devoted to him. Were he to appear in the world at this time and find that he has been deified and is believed to have atoned for the sins of mankind, he would be so ashamed of this false glorification that he would be ready to suffer death and would supplicate God for forgiveness. What proof have you of his godhead? Do his words or the words of his disciples indicate his godhead? Even if they did, this would be an empty claim unsupported by any proof. This claim cannot be supported even from the Gospels. Nowhere do the Gospels state that the son of Mary ever claimed to be God. Indeed, when the Jews confronted him on one occasion with such a claim on his part, he repudiated it.

[Majmū'ah Ishtihārāt, vol. 2, p. 307]

In John, chapter 10 verses 30-37, Jesus is reported to have said that he was no different from other righteous ones who had been called gods or sons of God in the scriptures. The Jews having heard that Jesus called himself the son of God, charged him with blasphemy, started throwing stones at him, and were much infuriated. What should have been the attitude of Jesus when the Jews attempted to stone him because he called himself the son of God, which in their estimation amounted to blasphemy? How could he have either disclaimed or established his claim? He could have adopted one of two attitudes. If he was truly the son of God, he should have answered, 'My claim is true. I am indeed the son of God and I have two proofs in support of my claim. One is that in your books it is written that the Messiah is the son of God, rather he is God Himself, and he is All-Powerful, knows the unseen and does whatever he wishes. If you doubt this, bring your books, and I will show you the proof of my Godhead from these books. You charge me with blasphemy because of your misunderstanding and lack of knowledge of the Scripture. Your books proclaim me God and All-Powerful then why do you say that I blaspheme? You should instead worship me because I am God.'

His second proof should have been, 'Come and behold the signs of Godhead in me. As God Almighty has created the sun and the moon and the planets and the earth, I too have created a portion of the earth or a planet or some other part of the universe. I can even now create something of that kind and demonstrate my Godhead. I have more power and strength than is manifested in the miracles of the Prophets.' It would also have been appropriate for him to furnish his opponents with a detailed list of his works as God and to challenge them whether Moses[as] or any other Prophet of Israel had performed such works. Had he furnished such proof the Jews would have been confounded and the Scribes and Pharisees would have fallen prostrate before him and would have confessed, 'Surely, you are God and we were in error. You have created a sun in contrast with the sun which has been shining from the beginning and which illumines the day, and you have created a moon which appears at night and illumines it with a beautiful light. This we have witnessed. You have also placed before us the proof of your Godhead from our recognized books. How can we then dare to deny that you are God?' But Jesus set forth none of these proofs. All he did was to offer these statements. Please ponder over them:

> Then the Jews took up stones again to stone him. Jesus answered them, Many good works have I shown you from my Father; for which of those works do ye stone me? The Jews answered him, saying, 'For a good work we stone thee not; but for blasphemy and because that thou being a man makest thyself God.' Jesus answered them, 'Is it not written in your law, I said, ye are gods?' If he called them gods unto whom the word of God came, and the scripture cannot be broken; say ye of him, whom the Father hath sanctified and sent into the world, Thou blasphemest; because I said, I am the Son of God?[188]

Now, it is worthy of reflection whether for repelling the charge of blasphemy and for establishing that he was

---

[188] John, 10:31-36 in the New King James Version. **[Publisher]**

truly the son of God the only appropriate answer was, ‘If I have called myself the son of God, how have I offended you considering that some of those who appeared before me were called gods.’

Deputy ‘Abdullāh Āthām says, that Jesus was frightened by their mob and concealed the true answer and took refuge in subterfuge. But I ask: ‘Is such an attitude worthy of the Prophets who are always ready to lay down their lives in the cause of Allah the Glorious?’ It is said in the Holy Qur’ān concerning them:

الَّذِينَ يُبَلِّغُونَ رِسٰلٰتِ اللّٰهِ وَيَخْشَوْنَهٗ وَلَا يَخْشَوْنَ أَحَدًا إِلَّا اللّٰهَ [189]

This means that: ‘The true Messengers of Allah, who convey His message, do not fear anyone in conveying the messages of Allah.’ Then how is it that Jesus who called himself God Almighty was afraid of the helpless Jews?

It is thus clear that Jesus[as] never claimed to be God or son of God in the true sense. He claimed to be in the same category as those who had been given such titles metaphorically and confessed that his claim was of the same kind….

Confession of Human Weaknesses by Jesus

This is not all. On several occasions he confessed his human deficiencies. When he was asked to indicate when the Judgement would take place, he confessed his ignorance and declared that no one knew of that hour except God Himself.

It is obvious that knowledge is a characteristic of the soul and not of the body. If the soul of Jesus was Divine and

---

[189] Al-Aḥzāb, 33:40 **[Publisher]**

he was God Himself, then how is it that he confessed his lack of knowledge of that Hour? Does God Almighty forget His knowledge? It is written in Matthew 19:16:

> And, behold, one came and said unto him, Good Master, what good thing shall I do that I may have eternal life? And he said unto him, Why callest thou me good? there is none good but one, that is, God.

Matthew 20:20 says:

> Then came to him the mother of Zebedee's children with her sons … She saith unto him, Grant that these my true sons may sit, the one on thy right hand, and the other on the left … But Jesus answered and said … to sit on my right hand, and on my left is not mine to give.

Then how was it that he was All-Powerful? Does the All-Powerful ever lose His power? When there is so much inconsistency in respect of his attributes, that his disciples considered him All-Powerful and he denied it, then what credence can be given to the prophecies when he in whose support they are cited denies being All-Powerful? Matthew 26:38[190] records that Jesus prayed throughout the night for his deliverance and supplicated God in great sorrow and agony that if possible the cup may be taken away from him and also asked his disciples to supplicate on his behalf....Yet his prayer was not accepted and that which was written came to pass. Had he been All-Powerful his power and authority would first have benefited himself. Otherwise it was useless for others to expect anything from him.

[Jang-e-Muqaddas, Rūḥānī Khazā'in, vol. 6, pp. 133-136]

---

[190] Mathews 26:39 in the King James version. **[Publisher]**

True Meaning of 'Son of God'

Those who were perfectly righteous have been called sons of God in the previous scriptures. This does not mean that they were actually the sons of God; such a things would be blasphemous, as God has no sons or daughters. Such expressions only mean that the reflection of God had been displayed in the clear mirrors of those righteous personages. The reflection of a person in a mirror is, metaphorically speaking, his son; for as a son is born of the father, a reflection is born of the original. When a reflection of Divine manifestations appears in a heart that is absolutely pure without any kind of stain, the reflection is metaphorically like a son of the original. That is why Israel was called the first begotten of God in the Torah.

If Christians had confined themselves to describing Jesus, son of Mary, as the son of God just as Abraham[as], Isaac[as], Ishmael[as], Jacob[as], Joseph[as], Moses[as], David[as], Solomon[as] and others were metaphorically called sons of God in the Scripture, there would have been no objection to it. Just as these Prophets were called sons of God, so is the Holy Prophet (peace and blessings of Allah be upon him) metaphorically called God in some prophecies. The truth is that all these descriptions are metaphorical; none of those Prophets were sons of God, nor was the Holy Prophet (peace and blessings of Allah be upon him) God. Such expressions abound in scriptures as indications of God's love.

When a person becomes so devoted in his love for God Almighty that his self disappears altogether, such expressions are applied to him since his ego ceases to exist altogether; as God says in the Holy Qur'ān:

قُلْ يٰعِبَادِيَ الَّذِيْنَ اَسْرَفُوْا عَلٰٓى اَنْفُسِهِمْ لَا تَقْنَطُوْا
مِنْ رَّحْمَةِ اللّٰهِ ۭ اِنَّ اللّٰهَ يَغْفِرُ الذُّنُوْبَ جَمِيْعًا [191]

That is: 'Tell them, O my servants! Despair not of the mercy of Allah; surely Allah will forgive all sins.'

In this verse, 'O my servants' has been used in place of 'O servants of Allah' while mankind are the servants of God and not the servants of the Holy Prophet (peace and blessings of Allah be upon him.) The expression has been used here in the metaphorical sense.

[Ḥaqīqat-ul-Waḥī, Rūḥānī Khazā'in, vol. 22, pp. 65-66]

Christian Doctrine about the Son of Mary

The Christian description of their god is that he was an Israeli male, son of Mary daughter of Jacob. He passed out of this life at the age of thirty-two. When we consider how before his arrest he supplicated throughout the night for deliverance and failed to achieve it, was ignominiously apprehended and was nailed to the cross and died bewailing, 'Eli, Eli', we tremble to think that a person whose supplications were rejected by God and who died in extreme humiliation should be held up as Almighty God. Imagine how Pilate sent Jesus into the custody of Herod after he was arrested. How is it compatible with his divinity that, with his hands and feet in chains, he was taken as a prisoner to Galilee in the custody of a few soldiers; and in this wretched condition, he was transferred from one jurisdiction to another. Pilate wanted to release him on seeing some wonder of his, but he was not able to show any such thing. Ultimately he was handed over in custody to the Jews who despatched him speedily.

---

[191] Al-Zumar, 39:54 **[Publisher]**

Our readers should reflect whether these are the signs of the real and true God! Can any clear conscience reconcile itself to the situation that the Creator of heaven and earth Who possesses unlimited power and authority should become so weak and unfortunate and contemptible that wicked people may rule Him out of existence with their hands? If anyone should worship such a god and should put his trust in him, he is free to do so, but the truth is that if the power and authority of the god of the Christians is compared to that of the permeshwar of Āryās, it would amount to nothing at all. The fictitious permeshwar of the Āryās, though he has no power to create anything, is said to be able at least to put things together, but the god of the Christians was not proved to have even that ability. The Jews having nailed him to the cross told him that if he could save himself they would believe in him. This was not a great task but he was not able to do even this; all he had to do was to join his soul to his body. Afterwards it was declared that he had revived in the tomb. But those who made this affirmation forgot that the Jews had demanded that he should revive himself before their eyes. As he did not come back to life before their eyes, nor did he meet them after his revival in the tomb, what proof is there for the Jews, and indeed for any researcher, that he had truly come back to life?

[Me'yār-ul-Madhāhib, Rūḥānī Khazā'in, vol. 9, pp. 468-470]

The sum and substance of the circumstances of the son of May, shorn of vain and senseless praise, is that he was a humble creature and was one of the Prophets who were subject to the law of Moses[as] and was a follower of that great Prophet but had not himself the same status. That is to say, his teaching was subsidiary to that of Moses[as] and he did not have an independent status. According to the

Gospels, he confessed that he was neither good, nor a knower of the unseen, nor powerful, but only a humble creature. The Gospels also show that before his arrest he supplicated throughout the night for deliverance and beseeched that his prayer may be heard. He was tempted by Satan like any other humble creature. It is thus obvious that having been born through the normal channel of birth, which signifies filth and excrement, he endured hunger, thirst, pain and illness over a period. On one occasion, when suffering from hunger, he approached a fig tree which proved to be fruitless and was frustrated without being able to create a few figs for his sustenance. In short, having spent his days in such conditions and having endured such afflictions, he died, according to the Christians, and was removed from this world. So we enquire whether God Almighty should possess such defective qualities and should be called Holy and Glorious while suffering from such faults and deficiencies? Also, how is it possible that of the five children born to Mary, only one became the son of God and even God Himself, and the remaining four were not bestowed any part of Godhead?

One would have thought that, contrary to the normal rule that a human being is born of a human being and a donkey is born of a donkey, if God can be born of a human creature, then no creature should be born from the same womb; all the children born from it should be gods so that the holy womb should be safeguarded against giving birth to creatures and should be solely a mine for the birth of gods. According to this speculation it was necessary that the brothers and sisters of Jesus should have partaken somewhat of Godhead and the mother of the five should have been honoured as the God of Gods because all five of them derived all their spiritual and physical faculties from her. The Christians have invented all sorts of undue praise for the son of Mary and yet they could not conceal his defects and deficiencies, and so brazenly pronounced him the son of God.

Although the Jews and the Christians, according to their strange scriptures, are all the sons of God, indeed, according to one verse, they are themselves God, yet we observe that the Buddhists have done better than them in their inventions and their impostures. Having acclaimed Buddha as God, they did not ascribe to him a birth through the normal filthy channel or that he had been reared on any impure nourishment. They believe that Buddha was born through the mouth of his mother. Alas for the Christians that though they forged many lies it did not occur to them to ascribe his birth also to the mouth so that they could have safeguarded their god from being mixed with urine and other impurities. Nor did it occur to them to safeguard him against death, which is the utter negation of Godhead. Nor did they think of excising from the Gospels all references to the confessions of Jesus that he was neither good nor wise nor knower of the unseen, nor had he come of his own will, nor did he possess absolute power, nor could he ensure acceptance of his prayers and that he was a humble human being who had been sent by the Master and Lord of the universe. All such references, therefore, should be expunged from the Gospels.

[Brāhīn-e-Aḥmadiyyah, Rūḥānī Khazā'in, vol. 1, pp. 441-443, footnote 11]

We have repeatedly admonished you O' Christians that worship of Jesus is no less than idol worship or the worship of Rama, and that the son of Mary has no superiority over the son of Kaushallia; but have you ever paid attention to our admonitions? You attack all other religions but have you ever reflected over your triune God? Have you ever considered how one who possessed all greatness was afflicted like an ordinary human being, and how the creator was beaten and maltreated by his own creatures? Can it be contemplated that humble creatures should flog their creator, should spit in his face, should seize him and nail him to the cross and he should be helpless in their hands; and that, being God, he should be subject to death? Can it be imagined that there should be three physical gods, one whose physical image was Adam, another Jesus, and the third a pigeon, and that of the three one should have a son and two should be without issue? Can it be contemplated that God should walk behind Satan who should require him to prostrate himself before him and tempt him by offering to bestow the world upon him? Can it be understood that a person with God dwelling in his bones, supplicated throughout the night and yet his supplication was rejected? Is it not surprising that the Jewish scriptures are cited in support of the godhead of Jesus while such a doctrine is an anathema to the Jews, which they repudiate emphatically, and none of their sects subscribes to the doctrine of Trinity? Had the Jews been taught this doctrine by Moses[as] and all the Prophets after him, how was it possible that all of them, divided into so many sects, should have forgotten this teaching?

Is it not worth considering that from the earliest times there existed a Christian Unitarian sect, which was in existence at the time of the Holy Prophet[sa]. It testifies that the unholy doctrine of Trinity emerged only in the third century? Even today there are hundreds of thousands of Unitarians in Europe and America who continue to publish books in support of their doctrine. In view of all this, and as the Christian missionaries still persist in their vile affirmation, is there not the need for Divine Judgement so that those who base themselves on falsehood may be ruined? Those who adhere to falsehood will now take to their heels and will seek refuge in false pretences.

[Anjām-e-Ātham, Rūḥānī Khazā'in, vol. 11, pp. 41-42]

Jesus as a Prophet

One strong argument in support of the truth of a Prophet is that he should bring about spiritual reform on a large scale. We find very little of this in the life of Jesus. He had twelve disciples and their example is most discouraging. They professed great devotion towards Jesus but their example was unmatched in treachery and cowardice. Did it behove a disciple to betray his Prophet and beloved leader to his enemies in return for thirty pieces of silver? What was it that compelled his principal disciple Peter to abuse and curse him to his face? Was it appropriate for his disciples to desert him and disappear as soon as he was arrested? Should this be the attitude of those whose beloved Prophet is apprehended on a capital charge? Afterwards creature worshippers invented all sorts of stories and elevated Jesus to heaven; but the record of their lack of faith is still preserved in the Gospels.

Thus the proof of the truth of a righteous Prophet is not to be found in the case of Jesus. Had the Holy Qur'ān not confirmed his Prophethood, we could not have counted him as a true Prophet. Can one who taught that he was the son of God, and even God Himself, and that he didn't have to worship anyone and his intelligence was so defective as to make him imagine that people would be delivered from sin by his suicide, be considered for one moment as a wise person who follows the straight path? But praise be to Allah that the Holy Qur'ān has revealed to us that all these are calumnies against the son of Mary. There is no trace at all of the Trinity in the Gospels. The expression 'son of God', which had been applied to thousands of people from Adam[as] downwards in the scriptures, was applied to Jesus as well. Later, it was exaggerated and was seized upon for the deification of Jesus. He never claimed that he was God nor did he ever express a desire for suicide. If he had done so, his name would have been erased from the list of the righteous in accordance with the Word of God. It is also difficult to believe that these shameful lies had their root in the erroneous thinking of the disciples. Though, according to the Gospel, they were men of average intelligence and could easily fall into error, yet we cannot reconcile ourselves to the notion that having kept company with a Prophet they were capable of propagating such nonsense.

The truth appears to be—and this can be gathered from a study of the writings that are complementary to the Gospels—that all this was a device of Paul who had recourse to deep cunning like political adventurers.

The son of Mary, who is mentioned in the Holy Qur'ān, was bound by the eternal guidance that had been prescribed for mankind from the beginning. Whatever doubts and suspicions the Gospels may raise concerning his Prophethood, the testimony of the Holy Qur'ān is enough to establish its truth. *Peace be on him who follows the true guidance.*

[Nūr-ul-Qur'ān, part 1, Rūḥānī Khazā'in, vol. 9, pp. 370-372]

Absurdity of the Doctrine of Trinity

The doctrine of Trinity is a strange doctrine indeed. Has anyone ever heard of three perfect entities which are at the same time one: three separate and perfect gods combined as one perfect God? The Christian faith is a strange compound of error and misguidance, and despite all these darknesses all possibility of guidance through revelation and inspiration is excluded for the future. Therefore, the errors of the Gospels cannot, according to the Christians, be corrected through new revelations, inasmuch as they believe that there can be no revelation in future. Now their whole reliance is upon individual speculation, which is not free from darkness and ignorance.

The Gospels are a collection of countless absurdities: like the deification of a humble creature, his crucifixion as atonement for the sins of others and his condemnation to hell for three days. They deify Jesus and yet attribute weakness and falsehood to him. There are several statements in the Gospels, which prove Jesus to be a liar. For instance, he promised a thief that he would sup with him that day in heaven and then, contrary to his promise, he chose to go to hell and to abide therein for three days. It is also recorded in the Gospels that Satan led Jesus to various spots to try him. Strange it is that though Jesus became God, he could not escape being tried by Satan and that Satan had the daring to try God. This philosophy of the Gospels is beyond comprehension. If Satan had in truth come to Jesus, he was afforded a good opportunity of exhibiting Satan to the Jews as the Jews were persistently denying his Prophethood.

[Chashma-e-Masīḥī, Rūḥānī Khazā'in, vol. 20, pp. 348-349]

Be sure that the True God is the One to Whom the Holy Qur'ān calls us. Beside Him there is nothing but worship of man or the worship of stones. Without a doubt Jesus, son of Mary, has also drunk of the fountain of which we drink and has eaten of the fruit of which we eat, but these things have nothing to do with Godhead or sonship of God. The Christians have invented a device for making Jesus a limited God, which is that they have made him accursed. If he did not become accursed, his Godhead would be useless and his being the son of God was in vain. Yet according to all the lexicographers the meaning of being accursed is that the heart should be disgusted with God, should lose all faith, should turn away from truth, should become an enemy of God, should become wholly bleak and worse than dogs and swine and apes, as is testified to by the Torah. Can it be imagined that even for a second Jesus ceased to be a loved one of God? Did his heart ever become disgusted with God? Did he ever think of discarding his faith? Did he ever become the enemy of God and God became his enemy? If nothing of this sort happened, then what portion did he suffer of the curse upon which the whole doctrine of salvation has been constructed? Does not the Torah affirm that he who dies on the cross is accursed? If he who is crucified is accursed then no doubt that curse would have fallen on Jesus as well. But it is the unanimous view that curse connotes distance from God and disgust with Him. To be afflicted with misfortune does not mean that one is accursed. Curse means turning away from God, hating God and even becoming His enemy. The accursed one is the title of Satan. Then reflect whether it is permissible for a righteous one to be considered an enemy of God and disgusted with God, should be designated as Satan and one of whom God is an enemy? It would have been better for the Christians if they had accepted hell for themselves and had not condemned a chosen one of God as accursed and Satan. Cursed is the salvation that can only be achieved by declaring righteous ones to be faithless and Satans.

Jesus not Accursed

The Holy Qur'ān has proclaimed the truth that Jesus did not die on the cross and did not become accursed. This is also borne out by the Gospels inasmuch as Jesus described his own case as resembling that of the Prophet Jonas; and every Christian knows that Jonas did not die in the belly of the whale. If Jesus lay dead in the sepulchre, what resemblance would he have with Jonas who was kept alive in the belly of the whale? It is also known that after deliverance from the cross Jesus exhibited his wounds to the disciples. If he had been bestowed a glorious body after death, how was it that he still retained the wounds received by his previous body? Had there been some deficiency left in the glory and, if so, how can it be expected that those injuries would be healed till the Judgement Day?

All these are senseless tales on which the beam of Godhead has been rested; but the time approaches fast, rather it has already come, when God Almighty will blow away all these tales like the carding of wool.

[Sirāj-e-Munīr, Rūḥānī Khazā'in, vol. 12, pp. 64-65]

It is the agreed doctrine of all Christians that Jesus, having been crucified, became accursed for three days, and this curse is what their salvation is based on. This doctrine is open to so serious an objection whereby the whole doctrinal structure of the Trinity, atonement and forgiveness of sins is utterly falsified and disappears. If anyone is interested in maintaining the justification of these doctrines, let him come forth and answer this objection, otherwise this entire structure will fall and the whole bundle of Christian doctrines will be crushed. Then neither Trinity nor atonement nor the forgiveness of sins will survive. The entire doctrine of the cross will be demolished by the power of God.

In order to facilitate appreciation of this objection, we proceed to set forth the meaning of *la'nat* [curse.] In *Lisān-ul-'Arab*, which is an old Arabic lexicon and is an Islamic publication, in *Qaṭr-ul-Muḥīṭ*, *Muḥīṭ* and *Aqrab-ul-Mavārid* which have been compiled by two Christian lexicographers and have been recently published in Beirut, and in all other lexicons, the meaning of *la'nat* is set out as follows:

اللّعنُ: الابعادُ والطردُ من الخيرِ و من اللّٰهِ و من الخلقِ و من
اَبعده اللّٰهُ لم تلحقهُ رحمتهُ و خلّد فى العذابِ ـ واللّعينُ
الشّيطانُ الممسوخُ ـ و قال الشمّاخُ مقام الذئبِ كالرّجل اللّعينِ[192]

> An accursed one is he who is deprived of all good and of the mercy of God and the comprehension of God and is condemned to everlasting torment, that is to say, his heart is wholly deprived of all good and becomes Satan and acquires the qualities of swine and apes. The poet Shammākh calls an accursed one a wolf because his inner self has become corrupted.

When it is said that a person is under God's curse everyone understands that he has become truly vicious and faithless and a Satan in the estimation of God and that God is disgusted with him and he has turned away from God....We wish to inquire most respectfully from Christian clerics if it is true that such a curse, with all its characteristics, had been imposed by God Almighty on Jesus and that under this curse he had fallen under the wrath of God and become black-hearted and had turned away from God? In my estimation such a person who designates a chosen one of God

---

[192] The word *la'n* is common in Arabic and Hebrew. **[Author]**

as accursed, that is to say, as black-hearted, disgusted with God and of satanic character, is himself accursed. Can it be said that a loved one of God had truly become accursed which means bitter enmity towards God....

To designate a dear one of God as Satan is a satanic act. I cannot conceive that any decent person would for a second apply all these designations to Jesus. If this is not permissible then the whole structure of atonement falls to the ground and the doctrine of Trinity is demolished and the cross is broken. Is there anyone in the world who can challenge this objection?

[Majmū'ah Ishtihārāt, vol. 2, pp. 333-335]

The Christians believe that Jesus (peace be upon him), having been apprehended in consequence of the treachery of Judas Iscariot, was crucified and, having been resurrected, ascended bodily to heaven. But a careful study of the Gospels discloses that this doctrine is altogether false. In Matthew 12:40, it is written:

> For as Jonas was three days and three nights in the whale's belly; so shall the son of man be three days and three nights in the heart of the earth.

We know that Jonas did not die in the belly of the whale; at the most he suffered unconsciousness. The scripture shows that by Divine grace Jonas remained alive in the belly of the whale and emerged therefrom alive and was in the end accepted by his people. If Jesus (peace be upon him) died in the belly of the whale[193], what resemblance would there be between him and Jonas?

The truth is that as Jesus was a true Prophet and believed

---

[193] This is a misprint in the first edition, the word 'whale' should be read 'earth'. **[Publisher]**

that God, to whom he was dear, would safeguard him against an accursed death, he had, under Divine revelation, prophesied in this manner in order to convey that he would not die on the cross but would become unconscious like the Prophet Jonas. In this prophecy Jesus had also indicated that after emerging from the belly of the earth he would meet his people and would be honoured by them as Jonas had been honoured by his people. This prophecy was also fulfilled, inasmuch as after emerging from the belly of the earth, Jesus travelled to his people who were settled in Kashmir, Tibet and other Eastern countries. These were the ten lost tribes of Israel which had been captured from Samaria by Salamendor, King of Assyria, seven hundred and twenty-one years earlier, and who had migrated towards India and had settled in various countries.

It was necessary that Jesus should have undertaken this journey because the ultimate purpose of his Prophethood was to meet the lost tribes who were settled in India and other countries. They were indeed the lost tribes of Israel because after they had settled in these countries they had given up the religion of their ancestors and most of them had become Buddhists, and, in course of time, they had become idol worshippers….

Moreover deliverance from the cross was also necessary for Jesus because scripture says that he who dies upon the rood is accursed. The meaning of curse is such that its application to Jesus for even a moment would be the height of cruelty and injustice. Curse is related to the heart. A person is called accursed when his heart, being alienated from God, becomes black and is bereft of His mercy, becomes a stranger to His love, is emptied completely of His comprehension, becomes blind and is filled with the poison of misguidance like Satan; and not a ray of the love and understanding of God survives in it. It is cut asunder from all faith and loyalty. Rancour, hatred, aversion and enmity are generated between it and God, so much so that God becomes its enemy and it becomes the enemy of God; and it becomes averse to God and God becomes averse to it. In short, curse means to become the heir of Satan in all his qualities. That is why Satan is designated the accursed….Can we say that the heart of Jesus had ever turned away from God and had denied God and had become disgusted with God and God had become his enemy? Can we imagine that the heart of Jesus at any time felt that it had become disgusted with God and had become His enemy and was sunk in the darkness of disbelief and denial? If the heart of Jesus never felt so and was ever filled with the light of love and comprehension, then ponder, O wise ones, how can we say that it had become subject not to one but to a thousand curses, with all that they entail. God forbid, certainly not. Then how can we say that Jesus became accursed?...

Such a notion is not only inconsistent with the status of Jesus[as] as a Prophet and a Messenger but is also inconsistent with his claim of perfection and purity and love and comprehension of God, which is mentioned time and again in the Gospels. A perusal of the Gospels shows that Jesus[as] affirmed, 'I am the light of the world'; 'I am the guide'; 'I have a relationship of deep love with God'; 'I have been bestowed a holy birth by Him'; 'I am the beloved son of God'. Then, despite these inalienable and holy relationships with God, how can the concept of curse be attributed to his heart? Jesus certainly did not die on the cross and his heart was safeguarded against the unholy condition of being accursed. If he did not die on the cross, he also did not ascend bodily to heaven, for such ascension was a part of the whole project of his crucifixion. If he did not become accursed nor was committed to hell for three days, his bodily ascension to heaven, which was part of this whole drama, also falls to the ground. The Gospels furnish other evidence to the same effect, which is as follows: Jesus is reported to have said:

> But after I am risen again, I will go before you into Galilee. (Matthew, 26:32)

This shows that after emerging from the sepulchre Jesus went to Galilee and not to heaven. The expression 'after rising again' cannot be construed to mean resurrection after death. Jesus employed this expression in anticipation of the notions of the Jews and the common people concerning his end on the cross. Also such an expression would not be inept with reference to a person who was nailed to the cross and appeared to be dead while he was unconscious. If a person, on being delivered from such a situation, claims to have risen from the dead, it would be no exaggeration on his part….

This shows that on emerging from the sepulchre Jesus proceeded towards Galilee. It is written in the Gospel of Mark, that he was seen walking towards Galilee and met the eleven disciples when they were at supper and showed them his hands and feet, which bore marks of wounds. They had imagined that he was a spirit, whereupon he asked them to touch him and see that a spirit could not have flesh and bones as he had. He took from them a piece of broiled fish and honeycomb and ate before them. See Mark, 16:14 and Luke, 24:39-42. These verses show clearly that Jesus did not ascend to heaven but on emerging from the sepulchre went to Galilee in his normal body and clothes. Had he risen from the dead, his glorious body would not have borne the marks of the injuries inflicted upon him on the cross, nor would he have been in need of nourishment. If despite his having risen from the dead he was still in need of food, he must need food in heaven also.

The cross was not like the modern gallows deliverance from which is almost impossible. In crucifixion no rope was put round the neck of the offender, nor was he suspended after being pushed from a platform. He was only nailed to the cross through his hands and feet and, in case it was not the intention to kill him, he was taken down after one or two days and his bones were not broken. If death was intended, he was left on the cross for two or three days without food or drink and was exposed to the heat of the sun. Thereafter his bones were broken and he died as a result of all this torment.

In the case of Jesus[as], the grace and mercy of God safeguarded him against all such torment as might have ended his life. The Gospels show that Jesus[as] did not remain on the cross for three days exposed to the sun without food or drink, nor were his bones broken. He remained on the cross for just about two hours. The grace and mercy of God so ordained that he was put upon the cross late on Friday when only a brief part of the day was left. The next day was the Sabbath and it was also the day of Passover and it was forbidden in the Jewish law to leave anyone on the cross on the night of the Sabbath, which began with sunset on Friday. This was the natural juxtaposition of the events. Then God Almighty caused a storm to arise at the sixth hour after midday, which darkened the earth and lasted for three hours. (Mark, 15:33.) The Jews were afraid lest in the darkness the sun might set and the Sabbath begin and they might be held guilty of breach of the Sabbath and become liable to punishment. So they took down the body of Jesus from the cross and also the bodies of the two thieves.

Another heavenly intervention that occurred was that when Pilate sat in the Judgement seat his wife sent him word:

> Have you nothing to do with that just man; for I have suffered many things this day in a dream because of him. (Matthew, 27:19)

The appearance of the angel to the wife of Pilate in her dream was a sure sign that it was God's design not to let Jesus suffer death on the cross….

Another piece of evidence furnished by the Gospels in support of the deliverance of Jesus from death on the cross is his long journey to Galilee, which he undertook after emerging from the sepulchre. On Sunday morning he first met Mary Magdalene who immediately notified the disciples that Jesus was alive, but they did not believe her. Then he was seen by two of the disciples who were going into the country. Then he appeared to the eleven when they were at supper and rebuked them over their lack of faith and their hard-heartedness. See Mark 16:9-14. When Jesus met the two disciples near Emmaus, which is at a distance of three or four miles from Jerusalem, he desired to go forward but they stopped him to spend the night with them and he supped with them. See Luke, 24:13-31. It is thus obvious that all these incidents like eating and drinking and sleeping and going on a long journey to Galilee, a distance of seventy miles from Jerusalem, all of which are relevant to a mortal body, were utterly inconsistent with a glorious body with which Jesus is imagined to have been invested after death. Despite the many changes that have found their way in the different accounts of the Gospels due to prejudiced thinking, it appears clearly that Jesus did meet his disciples in his corporeal and mortal body and undertook a long journey on foot all the way to Galilee, showed his wounds to the disciples, supped with them and spent the night in their company. We shall prove later that he also treated his wounds with an ointment.

Here one must pause and consider as to how it was that Jesus, after being invested with a glorious and eternal body with which he was to sit eternally on the right hand of God Almighty, and which should have been exempt from the need of food and drink and should have been free from every stain and pain and deficiency and should have reflected the glory of God the Eternal, he was still bearing the marks of the wounds suffered on the cross, which were bleeding and hurting him, and for which an ointment had been prepared. This glorious and immortal body, which should have endured through eternity secure, faultless, perfect and unchangeable, was so full of defects. Indeed, Jesus himself showed his flesh and bones to his disciples....

Thus without a doubt the truth is that Jesus did not die on the cross, nor was he invested with a new glorious body. He had become unconscious and appeared to have died, but Divine grace so ordained that the sepulchre, in which he was placed, was not like the graves in this country. It was a commodious, ventilated chamber with a window. It was customary with the Jews at that time to build such chambers beforehand and place corpses in them when the need arose….

Of the testimonies contained in the Gospel is the one concerning the statement of Pilate recorded in Mark, which reads as follows:

> And now when the even was come, because it was the preparation ... Joseph of Arimathea, an honourable counsellor, which also waited for the kingdom of God, came, and went in boldly unto Pilate, and craved the body of Jesus. And Pilate marvelled if he were already dead. (Mark, 15:42-44)

From this, we are led to conclude that, soon after Jesus was put on the cross, doubt was expressed about his death by one who knew from experience how long it took for a man to die on the cross.

Of the testimonies contained in the Gospel, is the one which we reproduce below:

> … because it was the preparation, that the bodies should not remain upon the cross on the Sabbath day, (for that Sabbath day was an high day,) besought Pilate that their legs might be broken, and *that* they might be taken away. Then came the soldiers and break the legs of the first and of the other which was crucified with him. But when they came to Jesus and saw that he was dead already, they break not his legs: but one of the soldiers with a spear pierced his side, and forthwith came there out blood and water. (John, 19:31-34)

These verses clearly show that, in order to put an end to the life of a crucified person, it was the practice in those days to keep him on the cross for several days and then to break his bones. But in the case of Jesus, his bones were purposely not broken and he must have been taken down from the cross alive, unlike the two thieves. That is why blood flowed out from his side when it was pierced, while the blood of a dead man is congealed.

This also shows very clearly that all this was a covert design. Pilate was a God-fearing and good-hearted man. He was afraid to show overt favour to Jesus, as the Jews had threatened to inform Caesar against him. All the same, Pilate was lucky to have beheld Jesus, but Caesar was not so fortunate. Pilate not only saw him but also treated him with favour and did not at all wish that Jesus should die on the cross. It is clear from the Gospels that Pilate sought several times to release him, but the Jews cried out that if he let Jesus go he would be no friend of Caesar….

Among the testimonies which bear out that Jesus[as] was indeed saved from the cross is the one narrated in Matthew 26:36-46. It relates that, having been informed by revelation of his impending arrest, Jesus[as] prayed to God all night, crying and prostrating. These prayers, which Jesus[as] offered in such humility, and for which he was given ample time, could not have gone unaccepted. God never turns down the prayer of a chosen one when he prays in distress. How could Jesus[as]' prayer have been turned down, which he offered all night in a state of anguish and distress, particularly when he had himself claimed that his Father in heaven listened to his prayers. How could one believe that God heard his prayers, if this prayer, which was offered in such anguish, was not accepted?

The Gospels also show that Jesus[as] was sure that his prayer had been heard and he had great faith in his prayer. That is why when he was arrested and nailed to the cross, he found things contrary to his expectation and involuntarily cried out: '*Eli, Eli, Lima sabachtani'*—My Lord, My Lord, why has Thou forsaken me? That is, 'I never expected things to come to this pass, and that I would have to die on the cross. I expected You to hear my supplications.'

God Almighty does indeed accept prayers, especially

when the oppressed fall at His threshold with implicit faith in Him. He responds to their cries and helps them in strange ways. To this I myself am a witness. How could it be that the prayer of Jesus offered in such anguish was not heard? Indeed it was heard and God did save him, and for this purpose He caused things to happen on earth, and in heaven. John, or the Prophet Yaḥyā, was granted no time to pray for his time had come, but Jesus was granted a whole night for prayer and he spent it in supplication, standing and prostrating before God. This was so because God had so willed that Jesus should give expression to his distress and pray for deliverance to Him for Whom nothing is impossible. God, in keeping with His eternal practice, heard his prayer. The Jews were false when they taunted him at the time of the crucifixion as to why God had not saved him despite his trust in Him. God frustrated all the designs of the Jews and saved his beloved Messiah from the cross and the attending curse. The Jews indeed failed.

Among the testimonies of the Gospels which have reached us, are the following verses from Matthew:

> That upon you may come all the righteous blood shed upon the earth, from the blood of righteous Abel unto the blood of Zacharias son of Barachias, whom ye slew between the temple and the altar. Verily, I say unto you, all these things shall come upon this generation. (Matthew, 23:35-36)

In these verses, Jesus (peace be on him) clearly says that the chain of the slaying of the Prophets by the Jews had come to an end with the assassination of the Prophet Zechariah, and that thereafter they would not have the power to kill any Prophet. This is a great prophecy and it clearly spells out that Jesus[as] did not die on the cross. He was, on the contrary, delivered from the cross and ultimately died a natural death. Had it been that Jesus[as], like Zechariah, was also to be killed by the Jews, he would certainly have hinted at it in these verses.

[Masīḥ Hindustān Meiń, Rūḥānī Khazā'in, vol. 15, pp. 16-34]

The Jews have always been at a loss to explain how Jesus[as] died within two or three hours of being nailed to the cross, when even his bones had not yet been broken. This has led some of them to invent another plea that, in fact, they had killed Jesus with the sword. But the history of the Jews does not support this claim.

In order to save Jesus, Divine might and majesty intervened and caused darkness to prevail, which was followed by an earthquake. Pilate's wife's dream, the approach of the night of Sabbath when it was not permissible to leave anyone on the cross, and Pilate's inclination to save Jesus because of the nightmare, all these coincided to save Jesus. Jesus was also made to lose consciousness so that he would appear dead.

The Jews became frightened of Divine chastisement, because of the terrible signs like the darkness and earthquake. They were also afraid lest the bodies should remain on the cross during the night of Sabbath. And when they saw Jesus in a swoon, they thought him dead. It was dark and there was an earthquake and great panic. They were also anxious about their homes and what their children must be going through in the darkness and earthquake. They were also perplexed that if Jesus was a liar and an apostate, which they thought he was, then why had such terrifying and unprecedented signs coincided with the torture to which he was subjected. They were so upset that they were unable to find out for themselves whether Jesus had really died or what exactly his condition was. All this was part of God's design to save Jesus, and to which this verse refers:

وَلٰكِنْ شُبِّهَ لَهُمْ [194]

This means that the Jews did not kill Jesus, but it was God Who made them believe that they had killed him. It is these circumstances which encourage the righteous to place great trust in God and to believe that He can save His servants as He pleases.

[Masīḥ Hindustān Meiń, Rūḥānī Khazā'in, vol. 15, pp. 51-52]

Some people may be troubled by the notion that the Gospels repeatedly mention that Jesus (peace be on him) died on the cross and that after resurrection he ascended to heaven. I have already answered such objections briefly, but I find it appropriate to repeat that Jesus (peace be on him) met his disciples after the crucifixion, journeyed to Galilee, ate bread and broiled meat, showed them his wounds, spent the night with his disciples at Emmaus, escaped secretly from Pilate's territory, and, like Prophets before him, migrated from the country and travelled under the shadow of fear. All these facts indicate that he did not die on the cross, that he retained the functions of his mortal body and underwent no visible change.

The Gospels do not contain any eyewitness account of ascension to heaven. Even if there had been such evidence, it would have lacked credibility, for the evangelists seemed to be in the habit of making mountains out of a molehill. To illustrate, one of them may have said that Jesus was the son of God, whereupon another became anxious to make him God and a third invested him with

---

[194] Al-Nisā', 4:158 **[Publisher]**

authority over heaven and earth and a fourth had no hesitation in asserting that there is no God beside him. In short, the tendency to exaggerate carries them too far. A vision in which someone saw that the dead had emerged from their graves and had walked into the town was changed into an actual event that the dead had truly emerged from their graves and had arrived in Jerusalem and met other people. Just imagine how a feather was turned into a crow, and a crow into millions of crows. With such exaggeration, how is it possible to get to the truth?

It is also worth considering that the Gospels, the so-called books of God, contain inflated statements such as that if all the works of Jesus had been committed to writing, there wouldn't be room enough in the whole world to accommodate them. Can such exaggeration be the way of honesty and truth? If the works of Jesus were so unlimited and beyond count, how were they confined within the brief space of three years?...

Then, in the same Gospel of Matthew, we read:

> And when they were assembled with the elders, and had taken counsel, they gave large money unto the soldiers, saying, Say ye, His disciples came by night, and stole him *away* while we slept. (Matthew, 28:12-13)

Look, just how childish and absurd such statements are. If it means that the Jews wanted to cover up the fact that Jesus had risen from the dead and had bribed the watchmen so that this great miracle should not become known to the people, then why did Jesus, whose primary duty it was to proclaim this miracle among the Jews, keep it a secret and forbid others from disclosing it? And if it is said that he was afraid of being apprehended, then I would say that when the decree of God had been carried out once and for all and he was resurrected after death and blessed with a glorious body, what fear did he have of the Jews? Surely, they had no power over him as he was now beyond mortal existence. On the one side it is said that he had been blessed with a glorious body upon his resurrection and met the disciples and journeyed to Galilee and then ascended to heaven, while on the other hand, he was afraid of the Jews at every step, and, in spite of his glorious body, fled secretly from the country lest the Jews should recognize him and, to save his life, undertook a 70 *kose* journey to Galilee and more than once told his disciples not to mention this incident to anyone. Are these the ways and signs of a glorious body? Indeed no.

The truth is that his body was neither new nor glorious; it was the same wounded body which had been saved from death; and as he still faced the threat from the Jews, he took all the necessary precautions and left the country. All statements to the contrary are simply absurd.

[Masīḥ Hindustān Meiń, Rūḥānī Khazā'in, vol. 15, pp. 46-49]

Ointment of Jesus

I have discovered a piece of highly valuable evidence concerning the escape of Jesus from the cross, whose authenticity cannot be doubted. It is a medical preparation called *Marham-e-'Īsā*, or Ointment of Jesus. It is recorded in hundreds of books on medicine. Some of these are written by Christians, some by Magians and Jews, and some by Muslims. Most of them are very old. Research has disclosed that at first this prescription became known to thousands of people by word of mouth and it was later duly recorded. In the days of Jesus[as], shortly after the crucifixion, a pharmacopoeia was compiled in Latin, which contained this prescription and testified that it had been prepared for Jesus[as]' wounds. This work was later translated into several languages and, in the time of the Abbasid Caliph Māmūn Rashīd, it was also translated into Arabic. Strange are the ways of Divine providence that eminent physicians of all religions, Christians, Jews, Magians and Muslims, have recorded this prescription in their books and have admitted that it was prepared for Jesus (peace be on him) by his disciples. It appears from the study of different pharmacopoeias that this ointment is most useful in injuries sustained by blows or a fall; it immediately stops bleeding as it contains myrrh. It is useful as an antiseptic and is also helpful in cases of the plague and is useful for all kinds of boils, etc. It is not clear whether the prescription was revealed to Jesus[as] after he suffered injuries on the cross or whether the ointment was prepared under the directions of a physician. Some of its components work like an elixir, particularly myrrh which is mentioned in the Torah.

Anyway, with the use of this ointment, injuries of Jesus[as] were healed in a matter of days and he recovered enough strength to travel on foot from Jerusalem to Galilee, a distance of seventy *kose*, in three days. It is enough praise for this ointment that it healed the injuries of Jesus who used to heal the others. The number of books of medicine which contain this prescription is more than a thousand....

In short the ointment of Jesus is a grand testimony for seekers after truth. If this testimony were not accepted, all historical evidences in the world would lose their credibility.

[Masīḥ Hindustān Meiń, Rūḥānī Khazā'in, vol. 15, pp. 56-61]

Jesus in Search of the Lost Sheep

It was extremely important for Jesus (peace be on him) to travel to the Punjab and its neighbouring lands in order to discharge his Prophetic functions. This was because ten tribes of Israel, who have been designated in the Bible as 'the lost sheep of the house of Israel', had settled there—a fact which no historian can deny. It was, therefore, necessary for Jesus[as] to travel to these lands, seek out the lost sheep and convey God's message to them. Unless he did that, the purpose he had been sent for would have remained unfulfilled. His mission was to preach to the lost sheep of Israel, if he had died without seeking them, or, having found them, failing to teach them the way to salvation, he would have been like the man who was appointed by a king to go to a certain tribe in the desert and dig a well to provide them water, but he spent three or four years roaming in other places and returned without doing anything to find the people to whom he had been sent. Could it be said of him that he carried out the command of his master? Certainly not. In fact he cared too much for his own comfort to do anything for the people.

[Masīḥ Hindustān Meiń, Rūḥānī Khazā'in, vol. 15, pp. 93-94]

Jesus in Kashmir

One of the verses of the Holy Qur'ān clearly indicates that Jesus and his mother travelled to Kashmir after the incident of crucifixion. It is said

وَآوَيْنٰهُمَآ إِلٰى رَبْوَةٍ ذَاتِ قَرَارٍ وَّمَعِيْنٍ [195]

---

[195] Al-Mu'minūn, 23:51 **[Publisher]**

'We gave Jesus and his mother shelter at a plateau which was an abode of peace and was provided with springs of clear water.'

In this verse God Almighty has drawn an accurate picture of Kashmir. The expression *Āwa* in Arabic is used for providing shelter against calamity of misfortune; and before the crucifixion Jesus and his mother underwent no period of hardship as would require shelter. It is thus established that it was only after the incident of the crucifixion that God Almighty led Jesus and his mother to this plateau.

[Kashtī-e-Nūḥ, Rūḥānī Khazā'in, vol. 19, p.17, footnote]

I am the humble one who has been sent to sow the seed of true purity in the hearts of men, like the holy servant of God in the time of the Roman Empire nearly nineteen hundred years ago, who was sent to preach true salvation to the people of Galilee. Having endured great suffering at the hands of the Jews at the time of Pilate, he had to migrate from Judea, according to the eternal way of God Almighty. He came to India to convey the message of God to the Jews, who after the dispersal of Babylone, had come to these countries. At the age of 120, he departed from this mortal world and returned to his True Beloved, and Kashmir had the great honour of being his burial place. How fortunate are Srinagar, Anmoza and the Moḥalla of Khānyār, unto whose blessed dust that eternal prince and righteous Prophet of God committed his holy body, and enabled many a dweller of Kashmir to partake of true salvation and eternal life. May the glory of God be with him forever, Āmīn.

[Kashf-ul-Ghiṭā', Rūḥānī Khazā'in, vol. 14, pp. 191-192].

The truth is that when Jesus (peace be upon him), after

his deliverance from the hands of the unfortunate Jews, honoured the Punjab with his presence, God Almighty invested him with great honour and prestige in this country and he found himself amongst the ten lost tribes of Israel. It appears that after settling in these countries most of them had become Buddhists and some had taken to a low form of idol worship. With the coming of Jesus, a large majority of them reverted to the straight path. As Jesus had prepared them to accept the Prophet who was to come, the ten tribes, who came to be known as Afghans and Kashmiris, all became Muslims in the end. Thus Jesus was greatly honoured in this land.

Recently a coin has been found in the Punjab on which the name of Jesus (peace be on him) is inscribed in Pali characters. The coin is of the time of Jesus. This confirms that Jesus[as] was bestowed royal honour in this country. This coin was probably struck in the reign of a monarch who believed in Jesus. Yet another coin has been found which bears the fac-simile of an Israeli male. This is most probably the fac-simile of Jesus. The Holy Qur'ān also contains a verse to the effect that God had blessed Jesus wherever he went.[196] These coins also show that he was greatly blessed and did not die till he was bestowed royal honours.

[Masīḥ Hindustān Meiń, Rūḥānī Khazā'in, vol. 15, pp. 53-54]

Jesus (peace be on him) came to the Punjab via Afghanistan with the ultimate intention of going to Kashmir. The fact is that Chitral and a part of the Punjab separate Kashmir from Afghanistan. If we travel from

---

[196] The reference is to the verse: 'And He has made me blessed wheresoever I may be.'—Maryam, 19:32 **[Publisher]**

Afghanistan to Kashmir through the Punjab, it is a distance of about 80 *kose*, which is equal to 130 miles, and if we go through Chitral, it is about 100 *kose*. Jesus wisely chose the Afghanistan route so that the lost tribes of Israel known as the Afghans may also benefit from his presence. The eastern boundary of Kashmir touches Tibet. From Kashmir he could easily go there. By travelling through the Punjab, Jesus could easily visit other parts of India before proceeding to Kashmir and Tibet. As some ancient records indicate, it is even probable that Jesus visited Nepal, Benares and other places, and later travelled to Kashmir via Jammu or Rawalpindi. Since he belonged to a cold region, he must have stayed in these parts through the winter and left for Kashmir at the end of March or beginning of April. As Kashmir resembles Shām,[197] he must have settled down there permanently. It is also possible that he may have spent some time in Afghanistan and it is not unlikely that he married there. One of the Afghan tribes is known as 'Īsā-Khel. It would not be surprising if they are the descendants of Jesus. It is a great pity that the history of the Afghans is very ambiguous and it is very difficult to arrive at anything definitive by studying their tribal chronicles. There is no doubt however that the Afghans too are Israelites like the Kashmiris.

[Masīḥ Hindustān Meiń, Rūḥānī Khazā'in, vol. 15, pp. 69-70].

Research has disclosed that after his deliverance from the cross Jesus (peace be on him) travelled to India and Nepal and continued on to Tibet, from where he eventually came to Kashmir, where he stayed for quite some time,

---

[197] Syria and its neighbouring territory. **[Publisher]**

and preached to the Children of Israel who had settled in Kashmir after the Babylonian dispersal. He died in Srinagar at the age of 120 years and was buried in the quarter of Khānyār. He came to be known as Prophet Yūz Āsaph, through some confusion of names.

[Rāz-e-Ḥaqīqat, Rūḥānī Khazā'in, vol. 14, p. 161, footnote]

The tomb of Jesus[as] in Kashmir, which is said to be about 1900 years old, constitutes evidence of the highest quality to prove this point. It is probable that there may have been some tombstones with this grave which now lie hidden.

[Rāz-e-Ḥaqīqat, Rūḥānī Khazā'in, vol. 14, p. 163, footnote]

Evidence from Buddhist Scriptures

I have discovered various kinds of evidence from Buddhist scriptures, the collective appraisal of which definitely and conclusively establishes that Jesus (peace be on him) travelled to the areas like Punjab and Kashmir. These are as follows….

First, the titles bestowed on the Buddha bear a strong resemblance to the titles given to Jesus, and some events in Buddha's life closely resemble the events in the life of Jesus. Here I mean the Buddhism which prevails in areas around Tibet, like Leh, Lhasa, Gilgit and Hims, which are proved to have been visited by Jesus. As regards titles, Jesus (peace be on him) in his teachings called himself 'the Light', similarly Gautama was called Buddha, which in Sanskrit means 'Light'. Jesus is also called 'Teacher' in the Gospels, similarly the Buddha is called Sāsta, which means 'Teacher'. Jesus is called 'Blessed' in the Gospels, and in the same way one of the names of Buddha is Sagpat, which means 'Blessed'. Jesus is called 'Prince' and so is the Buddha. One of the names of Jesus in the Gospels connotes that he would fulfil the purpose of his advent, and the Buddha has been called Sadhartah, which means one who fulfils the purpose of his advent. One of the titles of Jesus is the Refuge of the weary, and one of the names of Buddha is Asran Sam, which means the Shelter for the shelterless. Jesus has been called 'King' in the Gospels though what he meant was the kingdom of heaven; likewise the Buddha has also been called 'King'.

The similarity of events in the lives of the Buddha and Jesus appears from the following. It is stated in the Gospels that Jesus (peace be on him) was tempted by the devil, who said to him, 'If you will worship me, you will have all the riches and kingdoms of the world.' The Buddha was tempted in the same way and the devil said to him, 'If you obey me and return home renouncing your ascetic ways, I shall confer the glory of kingdom on you.' Just as Jesus did not obey the devil, neither did the Buddha....

Another resemblance between the Buddha and Jesus is that, according the Buddhist chronicles, the Buddha fasted for forty days when he was tempted by the devil. Readers of the Gospels know that Jesus also observed a forty-day fast.

Anyone who is acquainted with the teachings of both the Buddha and Jesus will also marvel at the close similarity between the moral teachings of the two....

Just as Jesus sent his disciples to different countries and himself travelled to another country, the same is recorded of the Buddha. It is recorded in *Buddhism* by Sir Monier Williams that the Buddha sent his disciples to different parts of the world to convey his message, and addressed them as follows: "Go forth and wander everywhere, out of compassion for the world and for the welfare of gods and men. Go forth, one by one, in different directions. Proclaim a life of perfect restraint, chastity and celibacy." He added: "I will go also to preach this doctrine." He went to Benares and there he performed many miracles. He delivered a very moving sermon on a hill just as Jesus did on the mount. It is also recorded in the same book that the Buddha often taught in parables and used to discuss spiritual matters in terms of physical phenomena….

The exact adoption by Buddha of this method of preaching through parables, especially those recorded in the Gospels, is indeed most surprising….

Buddhist records also show that Gautama Buddha had prophesied the coming of a second Buddha whom he named Metteyya. This prophecy is contained in *Lagavati Satta,*[198] a Buddhist record to which reference is made on page 142 of Oldenberg's book. It reads as follows:

> He will be the leader of a band of disciples numbering hundreds of thousands, as I am now the leader of bands of disciples, numbering hundreds.

It should be remembered that the Pali name 'Metteyya' is the same as 'Mashiha' in Hebrew …. The future Metteyya prophesied by Buddha is none other than the Messiah himself. One strong evidence in support of this is that the Buddha himself prophesied that the faith he had founded would not endure on earth for more than five hundred years, and that at the time of the decline of the

---

[198] This seems to be a misprint in the original Urdu text. The correct name should be *Cakkavatti Suttanta*. **[Publisher]**

faith and its teachings, the Metteyya would appear in this country and re-establish these moral teachings in the world. We find that Jesus appeared 500 years after the Buddha and, just as the Buddha had foretold the time for the decline of his faith, Buddhism suffered deterioration and decadence. It was then that Jesus, having escaped from the cross, travelled to these areas where the Buddhists recognized him and treated him with great reverence….

It must be noted that the name Metteyya in Buddhist literature undoubtedly refers to the Messiah. On page 14 of the book *Tibet, Tartary, Mongolia* by H.T. Prinsep, it is written about the Metteyya Buddha, who in reality is the Messiah, that the first Christian missionaries, having heard and seen at first conditions obtaining in Tibet, came to the conclusion that in the ancient books of the Lamas there were to be found traces of the Christian religion. On the same page it is stated that there is no doubt about it that these earlier writers believed that some disciples of Jesus were still alive when the Christian faith reached there. On page 171 it is stated that there is not the slightest doubt that at that time everybody was eagerly waiting for the great Saviour to appear. Tacitus says that the Jews were not the lone holders of this belief, Buddhism too was responsible for laying the foundations of this expectation, inasmuch as it prophesied the coming of Metteyya. The author of the English work has moreover added a note to the effect that the books *Pitakattayan* and *Attha-katha* contain a clear prophecy about the advent of another Buddha who would appear a thousand years after Gautama or Sakhiya Muni. Gautama states that he is the twenty-fifth Buddha and that the Bagwa Metteyya is still to come, that is why after he has gone,

one whose name will be Metteyya and who will be fair-skinned will come.…This is why the followers of Buddhism had all along been waiting for the Messiah to appear in their country.

The Buddha, in his prophesy about the future Buddha, called him Bagwa Metteyya. Bagwa in Sanskrit means 'white'. Jesus, being of Syrian origin, was Bagwa—of white of complexion. The people of the land where this prophecy was made, i.e., Magadh, where Raja Griha was located, were dark-skinned and Gautama Buddha himself was dark. Therefore, the Buddha related to his followers two distinct signs of the future Buddha: first that he would be Bagwa—of white complexion, and secondly, he would be Metteyya—a traveller who would arrive from a foreign land.…

We can never approve of the method adopted by European scholars who are so eager to prove one way or the other that the teachings of Buddhism had already reached Palestine by the time of the Messiah. It is most unfortunate that while the very name of Jesus is to be found in the ancient books of Buddhism, these researchers adopt the devious course of trying to find traces of Buddhism in Palestine. Why do they not rather try to find the blessed footprints of Jesus[as] on the mountains of Nepal, Tibet and Kashmir? I know that it was not for the likes of them to uncover by themselves such a great truth which lay hidden behind thousands of veils of darkness. It was for God Himself to do so, for He watched from on high that creature worship was running rampant in the earth and that worship of the cross and the supposed sacrifice of a human being had alienated the hearts of millions from the True God. Then, in His indignation, he sent to the world His servant in the spirit of Jesus of Nazareth in order to demolish the creed of the cross.

Breaking of the Cross by the Promised Messiah

And he came in accordance with the time honoured Divine promise. Then, at long last, came the time for the breaking of the cross: the time when the error of the creed of the cross was to be exposed with such clarity as the splitting a piece of wood into two. Heaven has thrown open the door to the breaking of the cross, so that whoever seeks the truth may seek and learn.

True, the notion of the bodily ascent of Jesus to heaven was false, yet it had a significance of its own. The truth about the life of Jesus which had become extinct, like a dead body swallowed by the earth, was preserved in heaven like a physical person and it was decreed that it should descend again in the latter days. Thus that Messianic reality has now descended like a physical person and has broken the cross. The evil qualities of falsehood and worship of falsehood, which the Holy Prophet[sa] has described in the Ḥadīth concerning the cross as swine, have been broken with the breaking of the cross, just as swine is cut by the sword.

This Ḥadīth does not mean that the Promised Messiah would slaughter the disbelievers or would go about breaking crosses. What the breaking of the cross means is that in this age the God of heaven and earth will disclose a hidden reality, whereby the whole structure of the cross will collapse at one stroke. And the slaughter of swine does not mean the slaughter of people or of swine, but it means the swinish habits like lying persistently, which is tantamount to swallowing of filth. Just as a dead pig can not swallow filth, in the same way, a time comes—indeed it has come—when dispositions will be stopped from swallowing such filth....

Do not think that I have come to wield the sword. No. What I have come to do is to put the swords back into their scabbards. Too long has the world been groping in the dark. Many have conspired against their well-wishers, wounded the hearts of their true friends and hurt their dear ones; but now darkness will be no more. The night is gone and the day has dawned. Blessed is he who does not remain deprived any more.

[Masīḥ Hindustān Meiń, Rūḥānī Khazā'in, vol. 15, pp. 72-88]

Divine Mystery of Jesus' Second Coming

It is one of the Divine mysteries that when the law which is brought by a Prophet or by a Messenger is corrupted after his death, his true teaching and guidance are perverted and absurdities are attributed to him, and all this misguidance is attributed to the Prophet himself, the soul of that Prophet is greatly moved for the removal of all the corruption and calumnies that are attributed to him, and then his soul demands that a substitute of his should appear on earth.

Now listen attentively to this subtle spiritual verity, that the soul of Jesus (peace be upon him) had two occasions to demand a substitute. The first was six hundred years after his death. This was when the Jews insisted more than ever that he was an impostor and a liar and that his birth was illegitimate and that is why he died on the cross. While the Christians on the other hand proclaimed that he was the son of God and even God himself, and that he had laid down his life on the cross for the salvation of mankind. Thus the wretched Jews accosted so insolently the blessed person of Jesus[as], and on the basis of the verse in Deuteronomy[199] which says that he who dies on the rood is accursed, called him accursed, and labelled him a mischief maker, liar and of illegitimate birth. The Christians, on the other hand, raised him to the status of Godhead and uttered the calumny that this was his teaching. It was then that the soul of Jesus was moved and demanded to be exonerated from all these charges and beseeched God for a substitute. Thereupon the Holy Prophet (peace and blessings of Allah be upon him) was raised, one of the many purposes of whose advent was to clear Jesus of all the false charges made against him and to bear witness on his behalf. This is why Jesus is reported to have said in John chapter 16:

> Nevertheless I tell you the truth; It is expedient for you that I go away: for if I go not away, the Comforter (i.e., Muhammad *salallāho alaihi wasallam*)[200] will not come unto you; but if I depart, I will send him unto you. And when he is come, he will reprove the world of sin, and of righteousness, and of judgment: Of sin, because they believe not on me; Of righteousness, because I go to my Father, and ye see me no more; Of judgment, because the prince of this world is judged....Howbeit when he, the Spirit of truth, is come, he will guide you into all truth....He shall glorify me: for he shall receive of mine, and shall show it unto you....

In Luke chapter 14 (he is reported to have said:)

> Verily I say unto you, Ye shall not see me, until the

---

[199] Deuteronomy, 21:23 **[Publisher]**

[200] The brackets in these quotations give the author's explanation of the words like 'Comforter' and 'Lord'.**[Publisher]**

> time come when ye shall say, Blessed is he that cometh in the name of the Lord (i.e., in the name of the Messiah—peace be on him.)[201]

In these verses the sentence: 'I shall send him to you', clearly indicate that the soul of Jesus will be moved for his advent; and the phrase 'The Father will send him in my name', indicates that he who would come would comprehend the whole spirituality of Jesus and, by virtue of one branch of his qualities, would be the Messiah, just as by virtue of another branch he would be Moses[as]....

The Holy Prophet (peace and blessings of Allah be upon him) has said: 'I have a strong resemblance to Jesus; my being is joined to his being.' This Ḥadīth confirms the statement of Jesus that the Prophet whose advent he prophesied would come in his name. So it happened that when our Messiah (peace and blessings of Allah be upon him) came, he completed all the incomplete works of Jesus of Nazareth, and bore witness to his truth and cleared him of the calumnies which the Jews and the Christians had heaped upon him, and thus provided comfort for the soul of Jesus. This was the first agitation of the soul of Jesus of Nazareth which achieved its purpose in the advent of our lord and master, our Messiah, the Seal of Prophets (peace and blessings of Allah be upon him.) *All praise belongs to Allah.*

The second time when the soul of Jesus was agitated was when the Christians completely assumed the qualities of Antichrist, and, as predicted, the Antichrist was to lay claim to both Prophethood and Godhood, this is exactly what these people did. They claimed Prophethood by

---

[201] The reference seems to be from Luke, 13:35 **[Publisher]**

interfering with the Divine word and framing regulations and carrying out changes that were the functions of a Prophet. They established what they wished, and invented doctrines and modes of worship and intervened so freely as if they had been commanded to do so by Divine revelation. Such unwarranted interference with Divine scriptures amount to claiming Prophethood.

And they claimed Godhead in the sense that their philosophers and thinkers designed to assume all the functions of Godhead. Their plans testify to their intents. For instance they are planning night and day to bring down the rain on their own, and control births by conveying the male sperm by means of some instrument to the womb of a woman. They believe that Divine decree has no meaning, and assert that it is only the failure of a project by some mistake which is taken to as Divine decree. They think that whatever is attributed to God Almighty is because previously the natural causation of everything had not been discovered and man's extreme frustration was named God or God's decree. According to them, when the system of physical causation is completely understood these 'false' notions would automatically disappear....

Thus in this age the soul of Jesus was agitated a second time and longed for his substitute to appear in the world. When this desire reached its climax, God Almighty raised one who was his spiritual reflection to defeat the Antichrist of this age. That substitute is called the Promised Messiah, inasmuch as the reality of the Messiah is incarnated in him, i.e., the reality of the Messiah was united with him and he appeared in consequence of the demand of the soul of Jesus[as]. That reality is reflected in him like a reflection in a mirror. As he has appeared in consequence of the agitation of the soul of Jesus, he has been named after him. The souls of Jesus desired from the All-Powerful God someone in his own image to come down on earth, who should be invested with the reality of the Messiah; this is exactly what happened.

This also explains why the Messiah was chosen for this purpose instead of Moses[as], Abraham[as] or David[as]. On account of the current troubles, it was only the advent of the Messiah that was called for. It was his people who had been corrupted and among whom the qualities of the Antichrist had spread. Therefore, it was only proper that the soul of Jesus should have been agitated. This is the subtle spiritual comprehension that has been bestowed upon me through a vision. It has also been disclosed to me that, after a time of piety and purity and the supremacy of Divine unity, the world will again return to polytheism and transgression. Some will devour others like insects, ignorance will prevail, Jesus will be worshipped once again, and the error of creature-worship will be widespread. All this mischief will proceed out of Christianity in the last part of these latter days. Then again the soul of Jesus will be greatly troubled and will seek its descent in a majestic form. Then, with the advent of a awe- striking semblance of his, this age will come to an end. That will be the end and the expanse of the world will be rolled up.

This shows that on account of the unworthy behaviour of the followers of Jesus, it had been decreed that the spirituality of Jesus should descend into the world three times.

[Ā'īna-e-Kamālāt-e-Islām, Rūḥānī Khazā'in, vol. 5, pp. 341-346]

7

DAJJĀL OR THE ANTICHRIST

The word Dajjāl has two connotations: First, it signifies a group which supports falsehood and works with cunning and deceit. Secondly, it is the name of the Satan who is the father of all falsehood and corruption.

[Ḥaqīqat-ul-Waḥī, Rūḥānī Khazā'in, vol. 22, p. 326]

Dajjāl and Satan

The Dajjāl mentioned in the Aḥādīth is described by the Holy Qur'ān as the Satan, whom it quotes as saying:

قَالَ اَنْظِرْنِيْٓ اِلٰى يَوْمِ يُبْعَثُوْنَ ۝ قَالَ اِنَّكَ مِنَ الْمُنْظَرِيْنَ ۝ [202]

'He (Satan) pleaded in the presence of God to be granted respite until those who are dead of heart are revived. God said: You are given respite till that time.'

Thus the Dajjāl who is mentioned in the Aḥādīth is none other than the Satan who will be slain in the latter days. This is recorded in the book of Daniel as well as in some Aḥādīth. As Christianity is the perfect manifestation of Satan, *Sūrah Al-Fātiḥah* makes no mention of Dajjāl, but prescribes supplication for refuge against the evil of the Christians. If the Dajjāl had been some other mischief-maker, the Holy Qur'ān would not have enjoined us to seek refuge against the mischief of *Ḍāllīn* [those who have gone astray] but for security against the Dajjāl.

The verse اِلٰى يَوْمِ يُبْعَثُوْنَ mentioned above does not mean the

---

[202] Al-A'rāf 7:15-16 **[Publisher]**

day of resurrection, because Satan will remain alive only so long as men are alive. Satan does not operate on his own, but through his agents, who are the people who deify a human being. Being a group of people, they are called Dajjāl as in Arabic Dajjāl also connotes a group.

If Dajjāl is taken to mean someone other than the misguided preachers of Christianity, this would entail a contradiction, because the very Aḥādīth which indicate that the Dajjāl will prevail over the earth in the latter days, also indicate that in those days the power of the church will overwhelm all religions. This contradiction can only be solved by affirming that the two are one and the same.

[Ḥaqīqat-ul-Waḥī, Rūḥānī Khazā'in, vol. 22, p. 41]

The Word Dajjāl Signifies a Group

Dajjāl is not the name of one man. According to the Arabic lexicon, Dajjāl signifies a group of people who present themselves as trustworthy and pious, but are neither trustworthy nor pious. Rather, everything they say is full of dishonesty and deceit. This characteristic is to be found in the class of Christians known as the clergy. Another group is that of the philosophers and thinkers who are busy trying to assume control of machines, industries and the Divine scheme of things.

They are the Dajjāl because they deceive God's creatures by their actions and tall claims as if they are partners in God's dominion. The clergy are arrogating to themselves the status of Prophethood because they ignore the true heavenly Gospel and spread a perverted and corrupted version as the supposed translation of the Gospel.

[Kitāb-ul-Bariyyah, Rūḥānī Khazā'in, vol. 13, pp. 243-244, footnote]

Christian Priests as Dajjāl

Dajjāl in fact is none other than the people known as Christian missionaries and European philosophers. They act like the two jaws of the Promised Dajjāl with which he devours people's faith like a python. First it is the common and ignorant people who get caught in the wiles of the missionaries; and then, those who happen to escape their clutches being disgusted with the disgraceful and false beliefs, are caught in the net of the European philosophers. I see that the common people are more vulnerable to the lies of the clergy, whereas the intellectual ones are more susceptible to the falsehood spread by the philosophers.

[Kitāb-ul-Bariyyah, Rūḥānī Khazā'in, vol. 13, pp. 252-253, footnote]

There have been many Dajjāls and there may be more to come. But the greatest Dajjāl, whose deceit is so vile in God's estimation that heaven might well be rent asunder by it, is the group which deifies a mere human being. God Almighty has set forth in the Holy Qur'ān various kinds of deceit practised by the Jews, the Polytheists and others, but does not single out any which might cause heaven to be rent asunder. Therefore, we should not designate any group as the greatest Dajjāl but the one so designated by God in His Holy Word. It would be most unfair and cruel to try to find someone else as the greatest Dajjāl.

On no account can we justify the existence of a greater Dajjāl than the present day Christian clergy. Whereas God has designated them in His Holy Word as the greatest Dajjāl, it would be the height of faithlessness to consider anyone else to be the greatest Dajjāl in contrast to the Word of God. Had there been any possibility at any other time of the existence of such a Dajjāl, God Almighty, Whose knowledge transcends the past, the present and the future, would have designated him and not these people as the great Dajjāl. The sign of the great Dajjāl, which we can clearly deduce from the Ḥadīth of Bukhārī [203]يَكْسِرُ الصَّلِيْبَ is that the great Dajjāl would deify Jesus and would attribute salvation to the cross.

It is a matter of great delight for the knowledgeable that on this point the definitive verses of the Holy Qur'ān and authentic Aḥādīth are both in agreement. Thus, the truth about this controversial issue has come to the open. The Holy Qur'ān unambiguously designates the Christian clergy as the greatest Dajjāl and terms their lies to be so great as could destroy heaven and earth. And the Ḥadīth also specifies that the true sign of the Promised Messiah would be that he would break the cross and slay the great Dajjāl. Our stupid Maulavīs do not seem to reflect that the main objective of the Promised Messiah is the breaking of the cross and slaying of the great Dajjāl. The Holy Qur'ān has foretold that the great deception and mischief whereby the order of the entire universe might be upset and the world brought to an end is the mischief of the Christian missionaries. From this it clearly follows that there is no greater Dajjāl than the clergy and that he who, having witnessed the revelation of this great mischief, waits for some other, denies the truthfulness of the Holy Qur'ān.

Moreover, as the literal meaning of the word Dajjāl is a group that pollutes the earth with its deceit, and, according to the Aḥādīth, the singular sign of the great Dajjāl

---

[203] 'He (the Promised Messiah) will break the Cross.' **[Publisher]**

would be his advocacy of the cross, if someone still fails to consider the Christian clergy as the great Dajjāl, he is indeed spiritually blind.

[Anjām-e-Ātham, Rūḥānī Khazā'in, vol. 11, pp. 46-48]

The Holy Qur'ān then specifies that in the latter days the Christians will dominate the earth, and they shall be the cause of all kinds of mischief running rampant. Waves of calamities will rise on all sides and will race down from every height....They will possess great material strength and dominion, against which all other powers and states will seem powerless. They will also enjoy supremacy in all kinds of knowledge and sciences and establish new and wonderful industries. They will also be dominant in their policies, projects, and good administration, and will show great resolve in their worldly enterprises and will also excel in their endeavour to spread their faith. They will leave behind all other nations in their social, agricultural and commercial policies, as indeed in everything else. This is the meaning of:

مِّنْ كُلِّ حَدَبٍ يَّنْسِلُوْنَ [204]

Ḥadab means high ground and *Nasal* means to run ahead and to excel. In other words, they will leave behind every other nation in whatever is great and prestigious. This is the major sign of the people of the latter days who were designated as Gog and Magog and this is also the sign of the mischievous group of Christian clerics who are called the Promised Dajjāl. Since *Ḥadab* means an elevated part of the earth, this indicates that they will achieve all earthly heights but will be deprived of the spiritual

---

[204] 'They shall hasten forth from every height.'—Ṭā Hā, 21:97 **[Publisher]**

heights. This proves that these people are called Gog and Magog in view of their national dominance. Among them are the people who have left no stone unturned in spreading misguidance and consequently came to be known as the Great Dajjāl. And God Almighty has said that at the height of misguidance, the trumpet will be blown and people of all faiths will be assembled at one place.

[Shahādat-ul-Qur'ān, Rūḥānī Khazā'in, vol. 6, pp. 361-362]

Dajjāl and the Misguided Maulavīs

Remember, the sum total of the evils which the Holy Prophet (peace and blessings of Allah be upon him) prophesied would spread in the latter days, is Dajjāliyyat, of which the Holy Prophet (peace and blessings of Allah be upon him) has said there are hundreds of branches. Hence, those Maulavīs are also branches of the tree of Dajjāliyat who blindly follow the beaten path and have abandoned the Holy Qur'ān, so that though they recite it, it doesn't get past their tongues. Today Dajjāliyat is spreading its web like a spider. The disbeliever with his disbelief, the hypocrite with hypocrisy, the alcoholic with his drinking, and the Maulavī with his preaching without practice and with his black heart, are all weaving the net of Dajjāliyat. Nothing can break up this web but the heavenly weapon, and no one can wield this weapon but 'Īsā who should descend from that very heaven. So 'Īsā has descended *and the promise of God was bound to be fulfilled.*

[Nishān-e-Āsmānī, Rūḥānī Khazā'in, vol. 4, p.369]

The word 'Messiah' refers to the truthful one whose *Masaḥ* (i.e. touch) as been blessed by God, and whose breath, word and speech have been given the power to give life. This word particularly applies to the Prophet who does not wage war and reforms mankind through his spiritual power alone. As against this, the word 'Messiah' also applies to the Promised Dajjāl whose evil power and influence produce calamities, atheism and faithlessness. Even without employing coercive means to destroy the truth, he can make righteousness and love for God grow cold merely by concentration, speech, writing, association and by the influence of his satanic spirit. On the other hand, misconduct, drunkenness, lying, promiscuity, materialism, fraud, tyranny, oppression, famine and epidemics become the order of the day. These are the meanings which emerge from a collective study of standard Arabic lexicons like *Lisān-ul-'Arab*; and these are the meanings which God has disclosed to me.

[Ayyām-uṣ-Ṣulḥ, Rūḥānī Khazā'in, vol. 14, p. 294]

Remember, it is also written about the Messiah—the bearer of spiritual blessings, whose advent in the latter days has been promised to the Muslims—that he would slay the Promised Dajjāl. But it does not mean he will actually kill him with a gun or a sword. What it means is that he will do away with all deceitful innovations in religion.

A study of Aḥādīth reveals that Dajjāl is actually the name of Satan. And the people whom Satan will employ to serve his purpose are also metaphorically called Dajjāl, because they are like his limbs. The following verse of the Holy Qur'ān means that the creation of God is far greater than that of men:

لَخَلْقُ السَّمٰوٰتِ وَالْاَرْضِ اَكْبَرُ مِنْ خَلْقِ النَّاسِ [205]

It refers the people concerning whom it is written that

---

[205] Al-Mu'min, 40:58 **[Publisher]**

they would make great inventions in the latter days and will try to interfere with God's creation. According to the commentators [of the Holy Qur'ān], the people mentioned here are actually the Dajjāl. This indicates that Dajjāl does not mean one single person, or else the expression *Nās* [people] would not have been applied to him. The word undoubtedly refers to a group of people. The group that acts under the command of Satan is called Dajjāl. This is also indicated by the sequence of the Holy Qur'ān which begins with the verse:

اَلْحَمْدُ لِلّٰهِ رَبِّ الْعٰلَمِيْنَ [206]

and concludes with:

اَلَّذِيْ يُوَسْوِسُ فِيْ صُدُوْرِ النَّاسِ ۝ مِنَ الْجِنَّةِ وَالنَّاسِ ۝ [207]

In this verse too the word *Nās* refers to the Dajjāl.... Mentioning these people at the end also indicates that this group of people will be supreme in the latter days, and they will be accompanied by:

نَفّٰثٰتِ فِي الْعُقَدِ [208]

i.e., Christian women who will go from house to house seeking to separate wives from their husbands, and to break the bond of marriage.

It should never be forgotten that the last three chapters of the Holy Qur'ān contain a warning about the age of Dajjāl and we have been enjoined to seek refuge with God against the mischief of that time. This is an indication that the mischief of those days will only be dispelled

---

[206] 'All praise belongs to Allah.'—Al-Fātiḥah, 1:2 **[Publisher]**

[207] 'Who whispers into the hearts of men, from among the Jinn and mankind.'— Al-Nās, 114: 6-7 **[Publisher]**

[208] Al-Falaq, 113:5 **[Publisher]**

through the heavenly light and blessings which the heavenly Messiah will bring with him.

[Ayyām-uṣ-Ṣulḥ, Rūḥānī Khazā'in, vol. 14, pp. 296-297]

The Meaning of Dajjāl Circuiting the Ka'bah

Our Holy Prophet (peace and blessings of Allah be upon him) saw in a vision that the Dajjāl was performing the circuit of the Ka'bah, and was doing it stealthily, like a thief, so that he could destroy the Ka'bah whenever the opportunity offered.... Obviously, no one can say that the Dajjāl would actually become a Muslim and perform the circuit of the Ka'bah. Every intelligent person will interpret this revelation as a vision through which the spiritual condition of the Dajjāl was revealed to the Holy Prophet (peace and blessings of Allah be upon him), and that this allegory presented itself to him in a vision in which he saw the Dajjāl was circuiting the Ka'bah like an actual person. What it meant was that the Dajjāl would be a bitter enemy of Islām and would hover around the Ka'bah with evil intentions. We know that just as the watchman goes around the houses at night, so does a thief. But while the watchman seeks to protect the houses and to catch the thief, the thief's motive is to steal and plunder. Thus the interpretation of this vision of the Holy Prophet (peace and blessings of Allah be upon him) is that the Dajjāl will be preoccupied with trying to violate the sanctity of the Ka'bah, while the Promised Messiah, who was also seen performing circuit of the Ka'bah, would be busy protecting the House of Allah and trying to apprehend the Dajjāl.

[Ayyām-uṣ-Ṣulḥ, Rūḥānī Khazā'in, vol. 14, pp. 274-275]

The fact that both the Promised Messiah and the Dajjāl will perform circuits of the Ka'bah proves that this does not mean that they will physically perform circuits of the Ka'bah, for in that case we would have to concede that the Dajjāl will succeed in entering the Ka'bah or that he will become a Muslim; both of which assertions go against the clear purport of Aḥādīth. This Ḥadīth has to be interpreted, and the interpretation which God has made manifest to me is that, in the latter days, a group of people will emerge who will be called Dajjāl. This group will be a bitter enemy of Islām, and, in order to completely bring down the structure of Islām, it will go circuiting round the Ka'bah, which is the centre of Islām, like a thief. As against this, the Promised Messiah will also perform the circuit of the centre of Islām, which the Ka'bah symbolises. The purpose of the Promised Messiah in performing the circuit of the Ka'bah would be to apprehend the thief named Dajjāl, and to safeguard the centre of Islām from his designs. We know that the thief goes around the houses at night and so does a watchman, but while the purpose of the thief is to rob and plunder a household, the purpose of the watchman is to apprehend the thief and to have him locked behind bars so that people are safeguarded from his mischief.

Thus this Ḥadīth indicates that in the latter days the thief, who is designated Dajjāl, will try his utmost to demolish the structure of Islām, and that the Promised Messiah, out of his devotion to Islām, will raise his supplications to heaven, and that all angels will lend him their support so that he should be victorious in this last final battle. He will neither get tired, nor dejected, nor will he slacken his efforts, but will try his utmost to catch the thief. When his supplications reach their climax, God will see how his heart has melted in his love for Islām. Heaven will do what the earth cannot. And the victory that cannot be achieved by man will be won at the hands of angels.

[Ḥaqīqat-ul-Waḥī, Rūḥānī Khazā'in, vol. 22, pp. 323-324]

If—God forbid—it had truly been written in the Holy Qur'ān that, contrary to the Divine law which binds all of mankind, Jesus was raised bodily to heaven and will survive till the Day of Judgement, the Christians would have been furnished with tremendous means to mislead mankind. **Excellent, therefore, it is that the god of the Christians suffered death. This assault that has been mounted by this humble one, on behalf of God Almighty, in his character as messiah son of Mary, against the people of Dajjāl-like character who were bestowed holy things but mixed them with pollution and who performed that which should have been performed by Dajjāl, is not in any respect less than an assault with a sharp sword.**

It may be asked: Jesus, son of Mary, was to come to vanquish the Dajjāl, and if it is you who have come in the spirit of Jesus, son of Mary, who then is the Dajjāl against you? My answer is that, though I admit the possibility of another Messiah son of Mary coming after me, and he may even be the promised one in the context of some Aḥādīth, and a Dajjāl may also come to mislead the Muslims, yet my belief is that so far there has not been any Dajjāl like the Christian clergy of these days, nor shall there ever be till the Day of Judgement. A Ḥadīth of *Muslim* reads:

و عن عمران بن حصين قال سمعت رسول اللّٰه صلى اللّٰه عليه و سلم يقول ما بين خلق آدم الٰى قيام الساعة امر اكبر من الدجّال

> 'Imrān son of Ḥusain reports: I heard the Holy Prophet (peace and blessings of Allah be upon him) say: From the creation of Adam^as to the Judgement Day there will be no greater catastrophe than that of the Dajjāl....

Considering the import of this Ḥadīth of *Muslim*, I say that if we were to examine all documentary evidence available to us from the creation of Adam[as] to this day, and examine the activities of all those who have ever taken upon themselves to do the work of Dajjāl, we shall not find anything matching the Dajjāl-like activity of the Christian clergy of this day. They have in mind an imaginary Messiah who, according to them, is alive and claims to be God. Jesus son of Mary never made any such claim, rather it is these self-appointed advocates of his who claim that he is God. They have had recourse to every kind of distortion and deception in support of their claim, and there is hardly a place, with the exception of Mecca and Medina, where they have not gone in pursuit of their objective. There is no form of deception, conspiracy or design to mislead, which they have not adopted. Is it not true that in pursuit of their Dajjāl-like designs they have encircled the whole world? Wherever they go and establish a mission they turn everything upside down. They are so wealthy that all the treasures of the world seem to lie at their feet. Although the British Government is concerned only with administration and has no concern with religion, the missionaries have a government of their own which possesses unlimited wealth and is spreading its tentacles all over the world. They carry with them all kinds of heaven and hell. One who is inclined to follow them is shown the heaven, and the one who chooses to oppose them is threatened with hell. They are accompanied by mountains of bread wherever they go, and many, who are the slaves of their stomachs, are carried away by the sight of white loaves of bread, and start proclaiming: '*The Messiah is our Lord.*' There is no quality of the Messianic Dajjāl that is not to be found in them. In a manner, they even revive the dead and kill the living. (Let him who possesses understating understand.) And there is no doubt that these people possess only one eye, which is the left one. If they possessed the right eye as well, they would have feared God Almighty and refrained from deifying Jesus. All previous scriptures mention this Dajjāl, as do the Gospels on the authority of Jesus son of Mary. It was only proper that every Prophet should have warned against this Dajjāl, and each of them has done so, whether expressly or implicitly, directly or indirectly. From the time of Noah down to the time of our lord and master, Seal of the Prophets (peace and blessings of Allah be upon him), we find warnings about this Dajjāl, and this is something I can readily prove.

No one can even imagine the extent of the damage that Islām has suffered at their hands and how truth and justice have suffered. Prior to the thirteenth century of the blessed Ḥijra, there was no trace of such mischief. But around the middle of the thirteenth century this Dajjāl-like group suddenly emerged and started to expand progressively, until at the end of this century, according to Reverend Mr. Baker, half a million people had been converted to Christianity in India alone, and it is estimated that every twelve years one hundred thousands new converts enter the fold of Christianity and start to believe in a humble man as God.

No sensible person can be unaware of the fact that Christian missionaries have brought under their sway a large number of poor and needy Muslims by giving them bread and clothes; those who could not be lured by these means were seduced through women; and those who could not be so trapped were exposed to all kinds of atheistic philosophy which now holds captive hundreds of thousands of young Muslims, who make fun of the Islamic prayer and fasting and consider revelation to be a kind of hallucination. For those who are not able to learn European philosophy, a large stock of fictitious tales was cooked up—too easy a job for the clerics' sleight of hand—which derided Islām in the guise of stories and historical events and was very widely published. In addition, they compiled countless books in refutation of Islām, blaspheming our lord and master the Holy Prophet (peace and blessings of Allah be upon him) and widely distributed them free of cost. Most of these have been translated into other languages....

Allah is Great. If our people still do not consider these missionaries to be Dajjāl of the highest order, for whose refutation a Messiah is needed, then the plight of our people is pitiable indeed!

Look, ye heedless ones, just look how hard these people are trying to demolish the edifice of Islām and what large resources they have employed for this purpose. In their endeavours they have exposed their lives to danger, spent their wealth like water, and indeed they have carried their human abilities to the limit. They have adopted shameful means and implemented them to undermine righteousness, and they have laid down mines to destroy the truth and honesty. All the finely fabricated details of falsehood and pretence have been strenuously invented to bring ruin to Islām. If people's minds could not be corrupted by other means, they invented thousands of supposed stories and dialogues to do this. Is there any method of the ruin of truth that they have not invented? Is there any way of misguidance that they have not adopted? Thus it becomes obvious that all these tricks and charms which the Christians and advocates of Trinity have resorted to, could not proceed from anyone but the great Dajjāl and we have no choice but to identify this group of Christian missionaries with him. When we observe to the past history of the greater part of the world, we gain the impression that, as far as it can be ascertained, there has been no precedent of such successful deception and misguidance as undertaken by these people. And as the Aḥādīth say, the Dajjāl will cause such mischief as would be unmatched since the beginning of the world. It follows, therefore, that these people are the great Dajjāl who was to come from the church, and to counter whose magic a miracle was needed. He who disputes this should produce a matching instance from the Dajjāls of the past.

[Izāla-e-Auhām, Rūḥānī Khazā'in, vol. 3, pp. 361-366]

8

DHULQARNAIN

I will now set out the meanings of the verses in *Sūrah Al-Kahf* which relate the story of Dhulqarnain, and the prophecy they contain about me, of which I have been informed by God Almighty. I do not deny the meaning of these verses which relates to the past, but what has been revealed to me is about the future.

Prophecy about the Promised Messiah in Sūrah Al-Kahf

The Holy Qur'ān is not a book of old stories. Every event mentioned in it is a prophecy, and the story of Dhulqarnain contains the prophecy about the time of the Promised Messiah. The Holy Qur'ān says:

وَيَسْـَٔلُوْنَكَ عَنْ ذِى الْقَرْنَيْنِ ۖ قُلْ سَاَتْلُوْا عَلَيْكُمْ مِّنْهُ ذِكْرًا [209]

'They enquire from thee about Dhulqarnain. Tell them that for the moment I shall relate to only you a little about him.' Then it says:

اِنَّا مَكَّنَّا لَهٗ فِى الْاَرْضِ وَاٰتَيْنٰهُ مِنْ كُلِّ شَىْءٍ سَبَبًا [210]

'We shall establish him on earth, i.e., the Promised Messiah, who will also be known as Dhulqarnain, in such a way that no one will be able to harm him; and We shall provide him with all the means for achieving his purpose and shall make everything easy and plain for him.'

---

[209] Al-Kahf, 18:84 [Publisher]

[210] Al-Kahf, 18:85 [Publisher]

Remember, the same revelation concerning me was published in the previous volumes of *Brāhīn-e-Aḥmadiyyah*, in which God Almighty said:

أَلَمْ نَجْعَلْ لَكَ سُهُوْلَةً فِيْ كُلِّ أَمْرٍ

'Have We not facilitated everything for you?' Have We not provided you with all the means for the communication and propagation of the truth? Of course, I have been provided with all the means for the propagation of the truth which were not even available at the time of any other prophet. Means of communication have opened between nations; travel has become so easy that a journey of years now takes only a few days; transmission of news is such that within minutes messages can be sent over thousands of miles; ancient texts of nations which were out of sight have begun to be published; means have become available for the delivery of everything where it is needed; difficulties in the publication of books have been removed with the introduction of the printing press, so much so that more copies of a book can be printed in ten days than was previously possible in ten years! A piece of writing can now be published throughout the world within forty days, whereas previously a man could not achieve this even in a hundred years.

Then Allah says in the Holy Qur'ān:

فَأَتْبَعَ سَبَبًا ۝ حَتّٰٓى إِذَا بَلَغَ مَغْرِبَ الشَّمْسِ وَجَدَهَا تَغْرُبُ فِيْ عَيْنٍ
حَمِئَةٍ وَّوَجَدَ عِنْدَهَا قَوْمًا ۬ قُلْنَا يٰذَا الْقَرْنَيْنِ إِمَّآ أَنْ تُعَذِّبَ وَإِمَّآ أَنْ
تَتَّخِذَ فِيْهِمْ حُسْنًا ۝ قَالَ أَمَّا مَنْ ظَلَمَ فَسَوْفَ نُعَذِّبُهٗ ثُمَّ يُرَدُّ إِلٰى
رَبِّهٖ فَيُعَذِّبُهٗ عَذَابًا نُّكْرًا ۝ وَأَمَّا مَنْ اٰمَنَ وَعَمِلَ صَالِحًا فَلَهٗ
جَزَآءَ ۨالْحُسْنٰى ۚ وَسَنَقُوْلُ لَهٗ مِنْ أَمْرِنَا يُسْرًا ۝ [211]

---

[211] Al-Kahf, 18: 86-89 **[Publisher]**

'When Dhulqarnain (who is the Promised Messiah), is furnished with all the means, he will follow a certain path, (i.e., he will resolve to reform the people of the West). He will find that the sun of truth and righteousness has set in a muddy pool, near which he will find a people in the darkness. (These are the Christians of the West who will be steeped in darkness; they will have no sun to get light from, nor will they have clean water to drink, i.e., both in practice and doctrine they will be in a terrible state; they will be bereft of spiritual light and spiritual water.) Then We shall say to Dhulqarnain (the Promised Messiah): It is up to you either to punish them or to treat them with kindness. Dhulqarnain (the Promised Messiah) will say: We only desire the wrongdoers to be punished. They will be punished in this life (through our supplications), and will suffer severe torment in the hereafter. But he who does not deny the truth and does good deeds will have his reward. He will be required only to do what can be done with facility and ease.'

In short, these verses contain a prophecy that the Promised Messiah will appear at a time when the people of the West will be steeped in darkness. The sun of truth will completely disappear from their eyes and will set in a dirty, stinking pool, (i.e., instead of truth, they will be infested with foul beliefs and deeds). That will be the water they will drink. They will have no light whatsoever and will wallow in darkness. This exactly is the condition of the Christian faith today, as described by the Holy Qur'ān, and the great centre of Christianity is also in the Western countries. Then God Almighty says:

ثُمَّ اَتْبَعَ سَبَبًا ۝ حَتّٰۤى اِذَا بَلَغَ مَطْلِعَ الشَّمْسِ وَجَدَهَا تَطْلُعُ عَلٰى
قَوْمٍ لَّمْ نَجْعَلْ لَّهُمْ مِّنْ دُوْنِهَا سِتْرًا ۝ كَذٰلِكَ ؕ وَ قَدْ اَحَطْنَا

بِمَا لَدَيْهِ خُبْرًا ۝[212]

That is, 'Dhulqarnain (the Promised Messiah who will be equipped with every means) shall follow another path, (i.e., he will observe the state of the people of the East) and will discover a people at the place of the rising of the sun of truth who will be so ignorant that they will have no means of protecting themselves from the glare of the sun (i.e., they will be scorched by the heat generated by their adherence to the letter and their extremism), and they will be unaware of the truth. Dhulqarnain (the Promised Messiah) will have all the means of true peace and happiness of which We are aware, but the people will not accept them. They will have no shelter against the glare of their extremism—neither houses, nor shady trees nor suitable clothes to protect them from the heat. In this way the rising sun of truth will bring about their ruin.'

This is an instance of people who have the light of the sun of guidance available to them, and who are not like those whose sun has set, but they derive no benefit from the sun of guidance; only their skins are scorched, their complexion is darkened and they lose their eyesight.

This division indicates that the Promised Messiah will encounter three kinds of people in the course of his mission. (1) First, he will encounter a people who have lost the sun of guidance and are wallowing in a muddy and dark pool. (2) His second encounter will be with a people who are sitting in the sun stark naked, i.e., they do not behave with respect, humility, courtesy and goodwill. They are worshippers of the letter, as if they want to fight

---

[212] Al-Kahf, 18:90-92 **[Publisher]**

the sun. Thus they too are deprived of the benefit of the sun, and all they get is their skins burnt. This refers to the Muslims among whom the Promised Messiah appeared, but they denied him and opposed him and did not behave with modesty and fairness, and consequently deprive themselves of good fortune.

Then Allah Almighty further says:

ثُمَّ اَتْبَعَ سَبَبًا ○ حَتّٰۤى اِذَا بَلَغَ بَيْنَ السَّدَّيْنِ وَجَدَ مِنْ دُوْنِهِمَا قَوْمًا لَّا يَكَادُوْنَ
يَفْقَهُوْنَ قَوْلًا ○ قَالُوْا يٰذَا الْقَرْنَيْنِ اِنَّ يَاْجُوْجَ وَمَاْجُوْجَ مُفْسِدُوْنَ فِى الْاَرْضِ فَهَلْ
نَجْعَلُ لَكَ خَرْجًا عَلٰۤى اَنْ تَجْعَلَ بَيْنَنَا وَبَيْنَهُمْ سَدًّا ○ قَالَ مَا مَكَّنِّىْ فِيْهِ رَبِّىْ
خَيْرٌ فَاَعِيْنُوْنِىْ بِقُوَّةٍ اَجْعَلْ بَيْنَكُمْ وَبَيْنَهُمْ رَدْمًا ○ اٰتُوْنِىْ زُبَرَ الْحَدِيْدِ ؕ حَتّٰۤى
اِذَا سَاوٰى بَيْنَ الصَّدَفَيْنِ قَالَ انْفُخُوْا ؕ حَتّٰۤى اِذَا جَعَلَهٗ نَارًا ۙ قَالَ اٰتُوْنِىْۤ اُفْرِغْ
عَلَيْهِ قِطْرًا ○ فَمَا اسْطَاعُوْۤا اَنْ يَّظْهَرُوْهُ وَمَا اسْتَطَاعُوْا لَهٗ نَقْبًا ○ قَالَ هٰذَا
رَحْمَةٌ مِّنْ رَّبِّىْ ۚ فَاِذَا جَآءَ وَعْدُ رَبِّىْ جَعَلَهٗ دَكَّآءَ ۚ وَكَانَ وَعْدُ رَبِّىْ حَقًّا ○ وَتَرَكْنَا
بَعْضَهُمْ يَوْمَئِذٍ يَّمُوْجُ فِىْ بَعْضٍ وَّنُفِخَ فِى الصُّوْرِ فَجَمَعْنٰهُمْ جَمْعًا ○ وَّعَرَضْنَا
جَهَنَّمَ يَوْمَئِذٍ لِّلْكٰفِرِيْنَ عَرْضَا ○ اِۨلَّذِيْنَ كَانَتْ اَعْيُنُهُمْ فِىْ غِطَآءٍ عَنْ ذِكْرِىْ
وَكَانُوْا لَا يَسْتَطِيْعُوْنَ سَمْعًا ○ اَفَحَسِبَ الَّذِيْنَ كَفَرُوْۤا اَنْ يَّتَّخِذُوْا عِبَادِىْ مِنْ
دُوْنِىْۤ اَوْلِيَآءَ ؕ اِنَّاۤ اَعْتَدْنَا جَهَنَّمَ لِلْكٰفِرِيْنَ نُزُلًا ○ [213]

Dhulqarnain (the Promised Messiah) will then follow another course and will find himself at a very critical time, which can be described as between two barriers or mountains. This means that he will find a time when people on either side will be in fear, and the powers of darkness, in collaboration with the powers of state, will present an awe-striking spectacle. Under both these powers he will find a people who will find it difficult to understand him, i.e., they will be the victims of false beliefs on account of which they will find it difficult to

---

[213] Al-Kahf, 18: 93-103 **[Publisher]**

understand the guidance which he will present to them. But in the end they will understand him. These are the third kind of people who will benefit from the guidance of the Promised Messiah. They will say to him: 'Dhulqarnain, Gog and Magog have filled the land with disorder. If you so please, let us collect a fund for you so that you may erect a barrier between them and us.' He will say in reply: 'The power God has given me is better than your funds, but if you be so inclined, you can help me according to your means so that I may erect a wall between you and your opponents (i.e., he would put forth such conclusive proofs and arguments that their enemies will not be left with any ground for criticism or objection against their religion.) He will say to them: 'Bring me slabs of iron so that their movement can be stopped, (i.e., hold fast to my teachings and my arguments, be steadfast, and block the enemy's onslaught like a wall of iron.) Then blow fire into the iron until it appears to be fire itself (i.e., feed the flames of love for God until you yourselves assume the Divine complexion)....

After these verses, God Almighty goes on to say: Then Dhulqarnain (the Promised Messiah) will say to the people who are afraid of Gog and Magog: 'Bring me copper so that I may melt it and pour it over the wall. Thereafter, Gog and Magog will not have the power to scale it or to make holes in it.'

Here it should be noted that though iron assumes the qualities of fire when left in it for a long time, it does not melt easily. Copper, on the other hand, melts very quickly; and it is necessary for a seeker to melt in the path of God. This means that the Promised Messiah will need such eager hearts and mild dispositions as would melt under the influence of Divine signs. These signs have no effect on the hard-hearted. A person can only become immune to Satanic attacks when he becomes steadfast like iron and that iron becomes like fire when touched by the fire of Divine love, and then the melted heart should melt and cover the iron to secure it against disintegration and decay. These are the three conditions which, when combined, form a wall which cannot be scaled or bored through by the spirit of Satan. Then God says that all this will come about by His grace. It is His hands which will accomplish everything and human design will have no part in it. When the Day of Judgement approaches, mischief will reign supreme once again. This is the promise of God.

Time of the Promised Messiah

Then He says that at the time of Dhulqarnain (Promised Messiah) all people will rise up in support of their own religion and will attack each other like the waves of the sea. Then the trumpet will be blown in heaven, i.e., God will raise the Promised Messiah and create a third people for whom He will show great signs until all good people gather under the banner of Islām. They will respond to the call of the Promised Messiah and will run towards him; then there will be only one shepherd and one flock. Those days will be hard and God will reveal His countenance with awe-striking signs. Those who persist in disbelief will experience hell in this very world in the shape of calamities. God says: These are the people whose eyes were veiled against My Words, and their ears heeded not My commandments. Did the disbelievers imagine that they could take humble men to be God and that I should stand dismissed? We shall reveal hell in this very world as entertainment for the disbelievers, i.e., great and terrible signs will appear.

All these signs will testify to the truth of the Promised Messiah. See, how the grace of the Beneficent One has bestowed all these favours on this humble one, who is labelled a disbeliever and Dajjāl by his opponents!

[Brāhīn-e-Aḥmadiyyah part V, Rūḥānī Khazā'in, vol. 21, pp 119-126]

One Ḥakīm Mirzā Maḥmūd Īrānī, in his letter dated 2 September 1902, has asked me to explain the meanings of the verse:

وَجَدَهَا تَغْرُبُ فِيْ عَيْنٍ حَمِئَةٍ [214]

First of all, let it be clear that this verse holds many a hidden meaning which it is not possible to encompass, and under its apparent meanings lie hidden meanings. The meaning which God has disclosed to me is that this verse, taken together with the preceding and following verses, comprises a prophecy about the Promised Messiah and specifies the time of his appearance. The explanation is that the Promised Messiah is also Dhulqarnain, as the Arabic word *qarn* connotes a century and the Qur'ānic verse indicates that the birth and advent of the Promised Messiah will cover two centuries. I have lived in two centuries according to every known calendar, be it Islamic, Christian or Bikramjiti. My birth and advent have not been confined to a single century, and in this sense I am Dhulqarnain. In some Aḥādīth too the Promised Messiah has been called Dhulqarnain in the same sense as I have just mentioned.

The interpretation of the rest of the verse in the context of prophecy is that there are two major peoples who have been given the glad tiding of the Coming of the Promised

---

[214] 'He found it setting in a pool of murky water.'—Al-Kahf, 18:87 **[Publisher]**

Messiah, and who are the primary addressees of his mission. In these verses, God Almighty describes metaphorically that the Promised Messiah, who is Dhulqarnain, will encounter two peoples in the course of his journey. He will find a people sitting in the dark by an evil smelling pool of water, which is not fit for drinking, and is so full of stinking mud that it can no longer be described as water. These are the Christians who are in the dark and who, out of their own wrongdoing, have converted the Messianic spring into a pool of stinking mud.

In the course of his second journey, the Promised Messiah, who is Dhulqarnain, came upon a people sitting in the blazing sun without any shelter to protect them. They get no light from the sun, except that their bodies are scorched by its blaze and their skins become dark. These are the Muslims, who, despite being blessed with the sun of Divine Unity, have not derived real benefit from it, but to be scorched by its blaze. In other words, they have lost the true beauty and true moral qualities of faith and have instead partaken of rancour, malice, fiery temper and beastliness.

In this manner, Allah the Almighty has indicated that the Promised Messiah, who is Dhulqarnain, will appear at a time when the Christians will be in darkness, and stinking mud, which is called *Ḥama'* in Arabic, will be their lot. The Muslims for their share will have only a dry belief in the Unity of God and they will suffer from the sunburns of bigotry and beastliness and no spiritual value shall remain unstained.

Then the Promised Messiah, who is Dhulqarnain, will come across a people who will be suffering at the hands of Gog and Magog. These people will be deeply religious and pious by nature, and will seek the help of Dhulqarnain (the Promised Messiah) against the aggression of Gog and Magog. And he will erect a bright rampart for them, in other words, he will teach them such strong arguments in support of Islām as will finally repulse the attacks of Gog and Magog. He will wipe their tears, help them in every way and stand by them. These are the people who accept me.

This is a grand prophecy which tells about my advent, my time and my Jamā'at. Blessed is he who reads these prophecies with care. Such prophecies are typical of the Holy Qur'ān, whereby it tells about someone in the past, but its real purpose is to foretell the future. For instance, *Sūrah Yūsuf*, which on the face of it is only a narrative, contains the hidden prophecy that as Joseph[as] was initially looked down upon by his brothers but was made their chief in the end, the same would happen with the Quraish. They rejected the Holy Prophet (peace and blessings of Allah be upon him) and expelled him from Mecca. But he who was rejected came to be their leader and their chief.

[Lecture Lahore, Rūḥānī Khazā'in, vol. 20, pp. 199-200]

9

GOG AND MAGOG

Yājūj [Gog] and *Mājūj* [Magog] are two peoples who have been mentioned in earlier scriptures. The reason why they are so called is that they make extensive use of *Ajīj* [fire], and would reign supreme on earth and dominate every height. At the same time, a great change will be ordained from heaven and will usher in days of peace and amity.

[Lecture Siālkot, Rūḥānī Khazā'in, vol. 20, p. 211]

I have also proved that it is essential for the Promised Messiah to appear at the time of Gog and Magog. Since *Ajīj*, from which the words Gog and Magog are derived, means 'fire', God Almighty has disclosed to me that Gog and Magog are a people who are greater experts in the use of fire than any other people. Their very names indicate that their ships, trains and machines will be run by fire. They will fight their battles with fire. They will excel all other people in harnessing fire to their service. This is why they will be called Gog and Magog. These are the people of the West, as they are unique in their expertise in the use of fire. In Jewish scriptures too it was the people of Europe who were described as Gog and Magog. Even the name of Moscow, which is the ancient capital of Russia, is mentioned. Thus it was preordained that the Promised Messiah would appear in the time of Gog and Magog.

[Ayyām-uṣ-Ṣulḥ, Rūḥānī Khazā'in, vol. 14, pp. 424-425]

Religious Disputes at the Time of Gog and Magog

There is yet another prophecy in the Holy Qur'ān, which predicts a spiritual union to follow physical union. It is as follows:

وَتَرَكْنَا بَعْضَهُمْ يَوْمَئِذٍ يَّمُوْجُ فِيْ بَعْضٍ وَّنُفِخَ فِي الصُّوْرِ فَجَمَعْنٰهُمْ جَمْعًا [215]

This means that in the latter days, which will be the age of Gog and Magog, people will become involved in religious disputes and fights and nations will attack nations just as one wave of a river surges against another, and there will be many other conflicts as well. In this way, great division will spread in the world and great contentions, rancour and hatred will be generated among the peoples. And when these events reach their climax, God will blow His trumpet, that is to say, He will transmit a voice to the world through the Promised Messiah, who is like His trumpet, and upon hearing this voice all good people will come together under the banner of one religion. All dissension will disappear and the people of the world will become one. In another verse, He says:

وَعَرَضْنَا جَهَنَّمَ يَوْمَئِذٍ لِّلْكٰفِرِيْنَ عَرْضًا [216]

Hell will be presented to those who do not respond to the call of the Promised Messiah on that day. That is to say, God will send down various kinds of calamities which will be a foretaste of hell. Then He says:

اَلَّذِيْنَ كَانَتْ اَعْيُنُهُمْ فِيْ غِطَآءٍ عَنْ ذِكْرِيْ وَكَانُوْا لَا يَسْتَطِيْعُوْنَ سَمْعًا [217]

Meaning that these will be people whose eyes will be veiled against the Call and Message of the Promised

---

[215] Al-Kahf, 18:100 **[Publisher]**

[216] Al-Kahf, 18:101 **[Publisher]**

[217] Al-Kahf, 18:102 **[Publisher]**

Messiah. They will not be prepared even to listen to him and will be full of aversion for him. This is why the punishment will be sent down. Here the word 'Trumpet' refers to the Promised Messiah, inasmuch as the Prophets of God are His trumpets into whose hearts He breathes His voice. This idiom has been employed in earlier scriptures, and Prophets of God have been called His trumpets. Just as the trumpeter blows his tune into the trumpet, so does God breath His Word into the hearts of Prophets. The reference to Gog and Magog also conclusively proves that the trumpet mentioned here is the Promised Messiah, for it is fully established by the authentic Aḥādīth that the Promised Messiah would appear in the age of Gog and Magog.

European Powers are Gog and Magog

On the one hand, it is proved from the Bible that the Christians of Europe are Gog and Magog, and, on the other, the Holy Qur'ān has mentioned specific signs concerning Gog and Magog which can only be applied to European powers, as, for instance, it is written that they will scale every height, i.e., they will overcome all other powers and be supreme in all worldly matters. Similarly, it is also mentioned in the Aḥādīth that no country will be able to stand up to them. Thus it is conclusively established that these powers are Gog and Magog. To deny this is sheer obstinacy and opposition to God's Word. Who can deny that in accordance with the Word of God Almighty and the explanation of the Holy Prophet (peace and blessings of Allah be upon him), these are the people who, in their worldly power, are superior to every other people. They have no equal in the art of war and statecraft. Their inventions and machines have established new patterns, both in war and in worldly comforts and luxuries. They have brought about an amazing revolution in the culture of mankind and have displayed such mastery in statecraft and in providing equipment for war and peace, as has no parallel since the creation of the world.

Thus, centuries after the prophecy of the Holy Prophet (peace and blessings of Allah be upon him), the rise of European powers is the event in accordance with the sign specified in his prophecy. As God has disclosed the meaning of Gog and Magog and events have proven that a certain people fit the signs that have been mentioned, refusal to acknowledge this would be denial of an established verity. No one can stop a person from persisting in his denial, but every just-minded one who is a seeker after truth would, on being informed of all these particulars, testify with full confidence that these people are Gog and Magog.

[Chashma-e-Ma‘rifat, Rūḥānī Khazā’in, vol. 23, pp. 83-88]

There would seem to be a contradiction in the Aḥādīth, for on the one hand it is stated that, at the time of the advent of the Promised Messiah, Gog and Magog will have spread all over the world, and, on the other, it is stated that the Christians will prevail in the world; for instance, it is said that the Promised Messiah will break the cross, which means that the Christians will be dominant at that time. Another Ḥadīth also indicates that the Romans, i.e., the Christians, will be in power. At the time of the Holy Prophet (peace and blessings of Allah be upon him) the Roman Empire was Christian, as Allah says in the Holy Qur’ān:

غُلِبَتِ الرُّوْمُ ۝ فِيْٓ اَدْنَى الْاَرْضِ وَهُمْ مِّنْۢ بَعْدِ غَلَبِهِمْ سَيَغْلِبُوْنَ ۝ [218]

---

[218] ‘The Romans have been defeated, in the land nearby, and they, after their defeat, will be victorious.’—Al-Rūm, 30:3-4 **[Publisher]**

Here the word Romans refers to Christians. Some Aḥādīth also indicate that at the time of the appearance of the Promised Messiah, Dajjāl would be supreme all over the world with the exception of Mecca.

Now will any Maulavī Ṣāḥib tell us how this contradiction can be reconciled? If Dajjāl prevails over the earth, where will the dominion of the Christians lie, and where will Gog and Magog go, whose world empire is foretold by the Holy Qur'ān? These are the errors from which those who reject me and call me a disbeliever suffer. Events bear out that the characteristics of both Gog and Magog and of the Dajjāl are to be found in the European powers. As described by the Aḥādīth concerning Gog and Magog, no power will be able to withstand them in battle, and the Promised Messiah too will only have recourse to prayer against them. These characteristics are unquestionably found in the European powers. The Holy Qur'ān too confirms this, as it says:

وَهُمْ مِّنْ كُلِّ حَدَبٍ يَّنْسِلُوْنَ [219]

About Dajjāl, it is stated in Aḥādīth that he will use deception and create religious mischief and turmoil. According to the Holy Qur'ān, this particular characteristic belongs to the Christian clerics. For instance it says:

يُحَرِّفُوْنَ الْكَلِمَ عَنْ مَّوَاضِعِهٖ [220]

All this shows that all these three groups are actually one. That is why *Sūrah Al-Fātiḥah* teaches definitively that we should seek security against the mischief of Chris-

---

[219] 'And they shall hasten forth from every height.'—Al-Anbiyā', 21:97 **[Publisher]**

[220] 'They pervert the words from their proper places.'—Al-Nisā', 4:47 **[Publisher]**

tians. We have not been taught to pray for security against Dajjāl. **Had there been another Dajjāl, whose mischief was to be greater than that of the Christian clergy, the Word of God would never have ignored the greater mischief and taught us to pray for security against the mischief of the Christians**, nor would we have been warned that the Christian mischief was such that it might rend heaven apart and shatter the mountains into pieces. Instead, we would have been warned that the evil of the Dajjāl is such as might well cause heaven and earth to rent asunder. To ignore a greater mischief and warn against a smaller one would have been totally unreasonable.

[Chashma-e-Ma'rifat, Rūḥānī Khazā'in, vol. 23, pp 85-87, footnote]

10

WOMEN

Issues relating to the treatment of women and children have been grossly misunderstood by most people, and they have consequently deviated from the straight path. It is written in the Holy Qur'ān:

عَاشِرُوْهُنَّ بِالْمَعْرُوْفِ [221]

The current practice, however, is against this injunction.

Extreme Attitudes about Women

In this respect there are two categories of men. There are those who have given women free licence to do whatever they want. Such women pay no heed to religion and conduct themselves in an un-Islamic manner, and there is no one to question them. On the other extreme, there are those who treat women with such severity and harshness that it is hard to distinguish their women from animals. They are treated worse than slaves and beasts. They beat them so mercilessly as if they were lifeless objects. They are treated so cruelly, that it has a become a proverb in the Punjab that a woman is like a pair of shoes which may be thrown away and replaced at will. Such attitude is extremely dangerous and contrary to Islām.

Kind Treatment of Women

The Holy Prophet (peace and blessings of Allah be upon him) is the perfect example for us in every aspect of life.

---

[221] 'Consort with them in kindness.'—Al-Nisā', 4:20 **[Publisher]**

Study his life and see how he conducted himself in relation to women. In my esteem, a man who stands up against a woman is a coward and not a man. If you study the life of the Holy Prophet (peace and blessings of Allah be upon him) you will find that he was so gracious that, despite his station of dignity, he would stop even for an old woman and would not move on until she permitted him to do so.

[Malfūẓāt, vol. 4, p. 44]

Do not ever consider women to be contemptible and insignificant!! Our perfect guide, the Holy Prophet (peace and blessings of Allah be upon him) has said:

خَيْرُكُمْ خَيْرُكُمْ لِأَهْلِهِ

'The best among you is he who is best towards his wife.'

How can one claim to be pious when he does not behave well towards his wife…. It is unacceptable to get furious or hit one's wife on the slightest pretence. There have been instances where an enraged husband hit his wife over some slight matter… and mortally wounded her. This is why God Almighty has said concerning them:

وَعَاشِرُوْهُنَّ بِالْمَعْرُوْفِ [222]

There is no doubt that admonition is necessary if a woman behaves improperly. A husband ought to impress upon his wife that he will not tolerate anything which is contrary to the faith, and yet he is not a tyrant who will not overlook any mistake on her part.

For a woman, her husband is a manifestation of the Divine. According to a Ḥadīth, had God been pleased to en-

---

[222] Ibid.

join prostration before anyone but Himself, He would have enjoined upon a woman to prostrate herself before her husband. Hence a man should be both hard and soft suiting the occasion.

[Malfūẓāt, vol. 3, p. 147]

With the exception of indecency, all weaknesses and petulant behaviour peculiar to women should be tolerated. I find it shameful that a man should fight a woman. God has made us men, which is the consummation of His grace upon us, and we should express our gratitude for this great bounty by treating women with kindness and compassion.

[Malfūẓāt, vol. 1, p. 307]

As for me, I once addressed my wife in a loud voice and I felt that my tone was indicative of displeasure though I had uttered no harsh words. Yet thereafter I sought forgiveness from God for a long time and offered supererogatory prayers with great humility and also gave alms because I felt that my harshness towards my wife might have been occasioned by some unconscious weakness in my obedience to God Almighty.

[Malfūẓāt, vol. 2, p. 2]

[Divine revelation to the Promised Messiah[as]]

'Such behaviour is not appropriate; 'Abdul Karīm, the leader of Muslims, should be dissuaded from it.'

[Promised Messiah's footnote about the above revelation]: ...This revelation contains guidance for the whole Jamā'at, that they should treat their wives with kindness and courtesy. Your wives are not your slaves. In point of fact, marriage is a covenant between man and woman. Try therefore not to break this covenant. God Almighty says in the Holy Qur'ān:

وَعَاشِرُوْهُنَّ بِالْمَعْرُوْفِ [223]

'Lead a life of kindness and equity with your wives.' And it is mentioned in a Ḥadīth:

خَيْرُكُمْ خَيْرُكُمْ لِاَهْلِهٖ

'The best among you is he who is best towards his wife.'

Therefore, be good to your wives both spiritually and physically. Keep praying for them and avoid divorce. A person who is hasty in divorce is sinful in the eyes of God. Do not hasten to break like a dirty vessel that which God has brought together.

[Tohfah-e-Golarhviyyah , Rūḥānī Khazā'in, vol. 17, p. 75]

A Man's Right to Divorce

One of our readers has raised the objection as to why the Holy Qur'ān has left the matter of divorce to the pleasure of the husband. What he seems to be saying is that men and women being equal, it is unfair to leave divorce solely in the hands of the husband. The answer is that men and women are not equal. Universal experience has shown that man is superior to woman in physical and mental powers. There are exceptions, but exceptions don't make the rule. Justice demands that if man and wife want to separate, the right to decide should lie with the husband. But what surprises me is that this objection should have been raised by an Āryā, according to whose beliefs the status of man is far above that of a woman, and even salvation is not possible unless one begets a male issue....Everyone knows that if an Āryā has forty or

---

[223] Ibid.

even a hundred daughters he is still anxious to have a son for his salvation, and, according to his faith, a hundred daughters are not equal to one son.... Moreover, *Manū Shāstar* clearly says that if a wife turns against her husband, tries to poison him, or for some other just cause, the husband has the right to divorce her. This is also the practice of all descent Hindus, that they divorce their wives if they find them unchaste and adulterous. Throughout the world, human nature has approved the authority of the husband to divorce the wife for just cause. But, at the same time, the husband is responsible for providing all the needs and amenities for his wife, as Allah Almighty says in the Holy Qur'ān:

وَعَلَى الْمَوْلُوْدِ لَهٗ رِزْقُهُنَّ وَكِسْوَتُهُنَّ [224]

'The husband is responsible for providing all the needs of the wife in respect of food and clothing.'

This shows that man is his wife's guardian and benefactor and is responsible for her well-being. For her, he is like a master and provider. Man has been blessed with stronger natural powers than a woman, this is why he has ruled woman ever since the world was created. The naturally superior faculties which have been given to man have not been given to the woman in the same degree. The Holy Qur'ān enjoins that if man has given his wife a mountain of gold as a gesture of his affection and kindness, he is not supposed to take it back in case of divorce. This shows the respect and honour Islām gives to a woman; in fact, men are in certain respects like their servants. They have been commanded in the Holy Qur'ān:

عَاشِرُوْهُنَّ بِالْمَعْرُوْفِ [225]

---

[224] Al-Baqarah, 2:234 **[Publisher]**

i.e., consort with your wives in such a manner that every reasonable person can see how kind and gentle you are to your wife.

A Woman's Right to Divorce

This is not all. The law of Islām has not left the matter of divorce entirely in the hands of the husband; women too have been given the right to seek divorce through the relevant authorities. Such divorce is designated in Islamic Shairah as *khulā'*. In case a husband ill treats his wife, beats her unreasonably, or is otherwise unacceptable, or is not capable of discharging his obligations towards her, or if he changes his religion, or it becomes difficult for the wife to live with him on account of some incompatibility; in all these situations, she or her guardian ought to report to the judge. If he finds that the complaint is justified, he would decree dissolution of the marriage. The judge is, however, also bound to summon the husband and ask him why the wife should not be allowed to leave him.

Just as Islām does not approve of a woman marrying without the consent of her guardian, i.e., her father, brother, or other near male relative, likewise it does not approve of a woman to separate from her husband on her own. It orders even greater care in case of divorce, and enjoins recourse to the authorities to protect her from any harm she may do to herself on account of her lack of understanding.

[Chashma-e-Ma'rifat, Rūḥānī Khazā'iṇ, vol. 23, pp. 286-289]

---

[225] Al-Nisā', 4:20 **[Publisher]**

Propagation of the Human Race through Marriage

Again, the critic alleges that, according to the Qur'ān, women are merely a means of sexual satisfaction and are like fields to be tilled. Just look how far this ill-thinking Hindu has gone in his malicious accusations, and how he fabricates words and ascribes them to the Holy Qur'ān! To such a one we can only say: *The curse of Allah be on the liars.* What the Holy Qur'ān has said is only that:

نِسَآؤُكُمْ حَرْثٌ لَّكُمْ فَأْتُوا حَرْثَكُمْ أَنّٰى شِئْتُمْ [226]

Your wives are your tilth for the purpose of procreation, so approach your tilth as you may desire, but keep in mind the requirements of tilth, that is, do not have union in any manner that might obstruct the birth of children....

Of course, if the wife is ill, and it is certain that pregnancy would put her life in danger, or if there is some other valid reason, these will count as exceptions. Otherwise, it is strictly forbidden in the Shariah to obstruct the birth of children.

Every sensible person can appreciate that a woman is described as tilth because children are born of her. One of the purposes of matrimony is that righteous servants of God may be born who remember Him. Another Divine purpose is that husband and wife may safeguard themselves against illicit looks and conduct. There is a third purpose, which is that, because of their mutual attachment, they should spare themselves the pangs of loneliness. All these injunctions are present in the Holy Qur'ān, we need not elaborate any further.

[Chashma-e-Ma'rifat, Rūḥānī Khazā'in, vol. 23, pp. 292-293]

---

[226] Al-Baqarah, 2:224 **[Publisher]**

Polygamy

Critics often object that polygamy involves intemperance and monogamy is the ideal system. I am surprised at their needless interference in other people's affairs. It is well known that Islām permits a man to marry up to four wives at a time; and this is a permission, not a compulsion. Every man and woman is well aware of this doctrine. Women have the right to lay down the condition that the husband will, in no circumstance whatsoever, marry another woman. If this condition is laid down before marriage, the husband will be guilty of breach of contract if he goes on to marry another. But if a woman does not prescribe any such condition, and is content with the law as it is, an outsider has no right to interfere. In such a case, the proverb seems relevant: 'If the husband and wife are happy, the Qāḍī has nothing to do.'

Every sensible person can understand that God has not made polygamy obligatory, He has only declared it lawful. If a husband desires, for some genuine reason, and under Divine law, to avail this permission, and his wife is not happy about it, she has the options to demand divorce, and be rid of this anxiety. And if the other woman, whom he wishes to marry, is not happy, she too has the easy option to decline the offer of such a suitor. No one is under compulsion. But if both women agree to this second marriage, what right then does an Āryā have to interfere? Does this man propose marriage to the two ladies or to this Āryā critic? If a woman agrees to her husband having a second wife, and the latter too is happy with the arrangement, no one has the right to interfere in the matter. This is a matter of human rights. If anyone chooses to have two wives, he doesn't do God any harm. The only loser is the first or the second wife. If the first wife feels that her rights as a wife will be placed in jeopardy by the second marriage of her husband, she can seek a way out of the situation by demanding a divorce; and should the husband be unwilling to comply with her demand, she can enforce separation through the court. If the prospective second wife considers the situation to be unacceptable, she is the better judge of her own rights and interests.

It is unwarranted and idle to object that justice is compromised in this situation. God Almighty has directed that a husband who has more than one wife should deal equitably with each of them, otherwise he should confine himself to only one wife.[227]

It is mere prejudice and sheer ignorance to suggest that polygamy is resorted to out of a desire for sexual indulgence. I have known people who were inclined towards such indulgence, but were able to save themselves by recourse to blessed system of polygamy—a system which helps such people to lead virtuous and pious lives. Failing this, many who are carried away by the fierce storm of carnal passions, end up at the doors of women of ill fame, and contract venereal and other dangerous diseases. They indulge openly and covertly in such evil practices to which those who are happily married to two or three wives never succumb. Such people restrain themselves for a short while and then yield suddenly to the fierce onslaught of their passions like the bursting of a dam, whereby vast areas are flooded and ruined.

The truth is that actions are judged by their intentions. Those who feel that by taking a second wife they will be

---

[227] The reference is to Al-Nisā', 4:4 **[Publisher]**

able to live pious lives, or will be saved from sexual promiscuity, or that they will leave behind righteous offspring, such people should certainly have recourse to this sacred institution. In Divine estimation, fornication and lustful ogling are such great sins as destroy all virtue and lead to physical suffering in this very world. One who chooses to have more than one wife in order to hold himself back from sin, wants to become like angels. I know well that this blind world is a victim of false logic and baseless arrogance. Those who are not constantly engaged in search of virtue, and make no plans for achieving it, and do not even pray for it, are like a boil which shines on the surface but contains only pus. Those who lean towards God, and care the least about the reproaches of the world, seek the way of righteousness as a beggar seeks bread. Those who plunge into the blazing fire of calamities for the sake of God, who are ever anguished, whose souls are melted and whose backs are broken by the effort of achieving great goals in the cause of God, He Himself desires that such people should spend some times of the day and night with their beloved wives and draw comfort for their tired and broken selves, so that they may return to their religious duties with renewed vigour. No one understands these things but those who have the knowledge and experience of this path.

[Chashma-e-Ma'rifat, Rūḥānī Khazā'in, vol. 23, pp. 246-248]

Equal Treatment of Wives

Apart from the degree of love one has for them, a man must treat all his wives equally, for example, in the matter of clothing, food, pocket money and companionship and even in bed. If one were to realize fully all the obligations in this regard, he would prefer to remain celibate rather than to marry. Only a person who spends his life under the constant admonition of God Almighty can hope to fulfil all these obligations. It is a thousand times better to live a life of hardship than to indulge in such pleasures as are likely to invoke Divine chastisement. We permit polygamy only to save a person from falling into sin, and the Islamic law allows it only as a remedy. If a person finds that he is moved and overwhelmed by thoughts about sex and his glances are persistently laden with sexual desire, he had better have a second wife to save himself from adultery. But he must not usurp the rights of the first wife. The Torah also lays down that in such a case the husband should be all the more solicitous and caring about his first wife with whom he has spent the greater part of his youth and established a deep relationship.

A husband should have such regard and respect for the feelings of his first wife, that if he feels the need of a second wife, but is afraid that it would hurt his first wife and break her heart, in such a case, if he can exercise restraint without falling into sin and without sacrificing his lawful needs, it would be preferable for him to forego the advantages of a second marriage for the sake of comforting his first wife....

I set forth whatever God Almighty has given me to understand in this context. The reason why the Holy Qur'ān permits more than one wife is that you earn the pleasure of God by holding fast to *Taqwā* [righteousness] and by other means such as begetting pious offspring, looking after the near of kin and fulfilling the obligations owed to them. For the achievement of this purpose marriage is permitted with as many as four women at one time, but if you feel that you may not be able to maintain equality between them you should confine yourselves to one wife, as in such cases marrying more then one would be disobedience and a cause of punishment rather than a source of merit... It is a great sin to hurt somebody's feelings, and female sentiments are very delicate. Just imagine for a moment all the hopes and expectations of the girl when she leaves her parents and is consigned to the care of another man. We can understand their feelings through the Divine injunction:

عَاشِرُوْهُنَّ بِالْمَعْرُوْفِ [228]

… The law of God Almighty should not be used contrary to its purpose, nor should it be invoked to serve as a shield for self-indulgence. To do so would be a great sin. God Almighty has repeatedly admonished against yielding to carnal passions. Righteousness alone should be your motive for everything.

[Malfūẓāt, vol. 7, pp. 63-65]

Islām and the Rights of Women

No other religion has safeguarded the rights of women as Islām has done. It lays down the injunction so succinctly:

وَلَهُنَّ مِثْلُ الَّذِيْ عَلَيْهِنَّ [229]

'Just as men have rights upon women, so do women have rights upon men.'

It is said of some people that they treat their wives like shoes and require them to perform the lowliest of services. They abuse them and despise them and enforce the injunction regarding the veil with such harshness, as to virtually bury them alive. The relationship between a husband and wife should be like two true and sincere

[228] 'Consort with them in kindness.'—Al-Nisā', 4:20 **[Publisher]**

[229] Al-Baqarah, 2:229 **[Publisher]**

friends. After all, it is the wife who is the primary witness of a man's high moral qualities and his relationship with God Almighty. If his relationship with his wife is not good, how can he be at peace with God? The Holy Prophet (peace and blessings of Allah be upon him) has said:

خَيْرُكُمْ خَيْرُكُمْ لِأَهْلِهِ

'The best among you is he who is best towards his wife.'

[Malfūẓāt, vol. 5, pp. 417-418]

Importance of Inculcating Piety in Ahmadi Women

It is incumbent upon the members of my Jamā'at that they should inculcate piety in their women in order to ensure their own piety, otherwise they will be guilty of a sin. If a wife is in a position to point out the shortcomings of her husband to his face, how can she have fear of God? If the parents are not righteous, their children would not be pure. Piety of children requires a long line of virtues; without it, the children would be bad. Therefore, the men should repent and should set a good example for the women. A woman keeps a watchful eye on her husband, and a man cannot hide his faults from her. Moreover, women are wise without showing it. Do not ever think that they are fools. In a subtle way, they are influenced by everything you do. If the husband is righteous, she will not only be respectful to him but also to God.... The wives of the Prophets and the righteous were pious, because they were the recipients of their husbands' benign influence. The wives of the wicked and vicious are also like their husbands. How can the wife of a thief ever think of getting up to pray *Tahajjud* in the latter part of the night, when she knows that her husband has gone to steal. This is why it is said:

اَلرِّجَالُ قَوّٰامُوْنَ عَلَى النِّسَآءِ [230]

Women are influenced by their husbands. To the extent that a husband excels in piety and righteousness, his wife will also partake of it. Similarly, if the husband is wicked, the wife too will share his evil.

[Malfūẓāt, vol. 5, pp 217-218]

If you desire to reform your own selves, it is essential that you also seek to reform your women. Women are the root of idol worship, for they are naturally devoted to decoration and ornaments. This is why idolatry started with women. They are also less courageous. Under the slightest stress of hardship, they begin to cringe before their fellow creatures. Hence those who are completely under the influence of their women gradually acquire their characteristics. It is, therefore, necessary to constantly try to reform them. God Almighty says:

اَلرِّجَالُ قَوّٰامُوْنَ عَلَى النِّسَآءِ [231]

This is why men have been bestowed greater faculties than women. One marvels at the modern man who insists on the equality of the sexes and asserts that men and women have equal rights. Let these people raise armies of women and send them into battle and see the result for themselves. How would a pregnant woman discharge her duties in the battlefield? In short, women have fewer and weaker faculties than men. Men should, therefore, keep them under their care.

[Malfūẓāt, vol. 7, pp. 133-34]

---

[230] 'Men are guardians over women.'—Al-Nisā', 4:35 **[Publisher]**

[231] Ibid.

Noble Example of the Wives of the Holy Prophet[sa]

No one can claim a higher status than that of the wives of the Holy Prophet (peace and blessings of Allah be upon him.)Yet they performed all domestic chores and swept their chambers. With all that, they were also diligent in worship, so much so that one of them had invented a method to keep her from dozing off during worship. One part of a woman's worship is to discharge her duty to her husband and the other is to offer her gratitude to God.

[Malfūẓāt, vol. 6, p. 53]

11

THE VEIL

Today the veil is under attack, but the critics do not know that the Islamic veil does not mean imprisonment; rather it is a barrier which seeks to restrict the free mixing of men and women. The veil will protect them from stumbling.

Wisdom behind the System of Veil

A fair-minded person will appreciate that the free mixing of men and women and their going about together would expose them to the risk of succumbing to the flare of their emotions. It has been observed that some people see no harm in a man and woman being alone together behind closed doors. This is considered civilized behaviour. To avoid such untoward situations from arising, the Law-Giver of Islām has forbidden all such acts as might prove to be a temptation for anyone.

In a situation of this kind where a man and a woman, whom the law does not allow to meet thus, happen to meet privately, Satan becomes the third member of this party. Imagine the harm that is being done in Europe in consequence of such reckless freedom. In certain parts of Europe a life of shameless promiscuity is being led which is the end product of such thinking. If you want to save a trust, you have to stand guard over it. But if you are not watchful, then remember that despite the people being ostensibly nice, the trust will definitely be violated. Islamic teaching in this behalf safeguards social life against unlawful indulgence by keeping men and women apart. Free mixing leads to the kind of destruction of family life and frequent suicides that have become common in Europe. That some women, who otherwise belong to noble families adopt the ways of prostitutes, is the direct result of the prevailing freedom.

[Malfūẓāt, vol. 5, p. 33]

The Islamic system of the veil does not at all require women to be shut up as in a prison. What the Holy Qur'ān directs is that women should avoid displaying their beauty and should not look at strange men. Those women who have to go out in order to fulfil their responsibilities may do so, but they must guard their glances.

[Malfūẓāt, vol. 1, p. 430]

However much the Āryās may dislike the Muslims and be averse to Islamic teachings, I would earnestly request them not to do away with the veil completely, as the resulting evils will make themselves felt sooner or later. Any intelligent person will appreciate that a large portion of humanity is governed by natural desires and, under the sway of the baser self, pays no heed to Divine chastisement. At the sight of young and beautiful women most men can't help but stare. Women too do not hesitate to stare at strangers. Such unrestricted freedom will result in the kind of situation prevalent in Europe today. When people become truly purified and shed their baser appetites, and get rid of the Satanic spirit and when they have the fear of God in their eyes, and when they become fully conscious of the majesty of God, and they bring about a transformation and adorn the robes of *Taqwā*, only then will they have the right to do what they like; for then they will be like pawns in God's hands and, in a manner of speaking, they will cease to be males, their eyes will become oblivious to the sight of women and to such evil thoughts. But dear ones, may God direct your hearts, time is not right for this. If you usher in freedom today, you will sow a poisonous seed in your culture. These are difficult times. Even if it was not needed before, the veil is essential now, because this is the last era of mankind, and the earth is full of vice, debauchery and drunkenness. Hearts are filled with atheism and are devoid of respect for Divine commandments. Tongues are so loquacious and lectures are loaded with logic and philosophy, but the hearts are empty of spirituality. At such a time it would be a folly to expose your helpless sheep to the mercy of wolves.

[Lecture Lahore, Rūḥānī Khazā'in, vol. 20, pp. 173-174]

Many people urge the adoption of permissiveness like that prevalent in Europe, but this would be most unwise. Such unbridled freedom of sexes is the root of all immorality. Look at the moral situation in countries that have adopted this freedom. If freedom of sexes has helped increase their chastity and virtue, we will readily confess that we were mistaken. But it is crystal clear that when men and women are young, and have the licence to mix freely, their relationship will be most dangerous. It is but human to exchange glances and be overwhelmed by lustful desires. As there is intemperance and vice, despite the observance of the veil, it may be imagined what the situation will be like in case of unrestricted freedom. Look at men, how unbridled their behaviour is! They have neither fear of God nor faith in the hereafter. They only worship mundane pleasures. It is necessary therefore, that before granting such freedom as is being advocated, the moral condition of men should be improved and rectified. After men have developed enough self-temperance to restrain control their passions, you may consider whether the veil is necessary or not. To insist upon unrestricted freedom in the present circumstances would be like putting sheep at the mercy of lions.

What ails our people that they do not reflect upon the consequences of things? Let them at least take counsel with their consciences whether the condition of men is so much improved that women may go about among them unveiled. The Holy Qur'ān, which lays down appropriate directions consistent with the natural desires and weaknesses of men, adopts an excellent position in this regard:

قُلْ لِّلْمُؤْمِنِيْنَ يَغُضُّوْا مِنْ اَبْصَارِهِمْ وَ يَحْفَظُوْا فُرُوْجَهُمْ ذٰلِكَ اَزْكٰى لَهُمْ [232]

'Tell the believing men to restrain their looks and to guard their private parts. This is the act through which they will attain purification….'

The Islamic injunction that men and women should both restrain themselves in certain ways, aims at safeguarding them against slipping and stumbling; for, in the early stages human beings are inclined towards vice, and, at the slightest provocation, fall upon it as a starving person falls on delicious food. It is every one's duty to safeguard himself.

[Malfūẓāt, vol. 7, pp. 134-136]

Remedies for Unchastity

God Almighty has not only set forth excellent teaching for acquiring chastity, but has also furnished man with five remedies to safeguard himself against unchastity. These are to restrain one's eyes from gazing at women

---

[232] Al-Nūr, 24:31 **[Publisher]**

who are outside the prohibited degrees; to avoid listening to their voices, to refrain from hearing stories about them, to avoid occasions which might furnish incitement to vice and to control oneself during celibacy through fasting, etc.

We can confidently claim that this excellent teaching with all its devices that is set forth in the Holy Qur'ān is peculiar to Islām. However, one point should be kept in mind: since the natural condition of man, which is the source of his appetites, and from which he cannot depart without a complete change in himself, is such that his passions are bound to be roused when they are confronted with the occasion and opportunity for indulging in such vice, God Almighty has, therefore, not instructed us that we may freely look at women outside the prohibited category, and we may contemplate their beauty and observe all their movements in dance, etc., but that we should do so with pure looks. Nor have we been instructed to listen to the singing of these women and to lend ear to the tales of their beauty, but with pure intent. Instead we have been positively prohibited from looking at their beauty, whether with pure intent or otherwise, or listening to their musical voices or relating descriptions of their beauty, whether with pure intent or otherwise. We have been directed to eschew all this as we eschew carrion, lest we stumble due to our unlawful glances.

As God Almighty desires that our eyes and hearts and all our limbs and our susceptibilities should remain pure, He has furnished us with this excellent teaching. There can be no doubt that lack of restraint causes missteps. If we place soft bread before a hungry dog, it will be vain to hope that the dog will pay no attention to it. Thus God Almighty desired that human faculties should not be provided with any occasion for secret functioning and should not be confronted with anything that might incite dangerous tendencies.

This indeed is the philosophy that underlies the Islamic injunctions regarding the veil, and this is what the Shariah demands. The Book of God does not aim at keeping women in captivity like prisoners. This is the thinking of the ignorant who are not aware of the Islamic ideals. The purpose of these regulations is to restrain men and women from letting their eyes rove freely and from displaying their beauty and charm, for this is to the benefit of both men and women. Remember, in Arabic *Ghaḍḍ-e-Baṣar* means to restrain oneself from casting even a cursory glance at the wrong place, while at the same time seeing things which are permissible.

It does not behove a pious person, who desires to keep his heart pure, that he should lift his eyes in an unbridled manner like a beast. It is necessary for such a person to cultivate the habit of *Ghaḍḍ-e-Baṣar* in his social life. This is a blessed habit through which a person's natural impulses are transferred into a high moral condition without adversely affecting his social needs. This is the quality which, in Islām, is called *Iḥṣān* or chastity.

[Islāmī Uṣūl kī Philosophy, Rūḥānī Khazā'in, vol. 10, pp. 343-344]

Extreme Attitudes about the Veil

People have adopted extreme attitudes in respect of the veil. Europe has gone to one extreme in abolishing it altogether and now some naturalists too wish to follow suit, whereas it is patent that this licentiousness has flung open the gates of vice in Europe. On the other hand, some Muslims go to the other extreme and do not let their women step out of their homes at all, even though it is often necessary for them to travel or to go out on account of some other need. We believe that both these types are in error.

[Malfūẓāt, vol. 6, p.322]

12

PROPER UPBRINGING OF CHILDREN

I believe that beating children in a manner that the ill-behaved child-beater pretends to be Allah's partner in guiding and training children is a type of polytheism.

Pray for Children instead of Punishing Them

When a hot-tempered person is provoked and punishes a child, he takes on the role of an enemy in the stress of his anger and imposes punishment far in excess of the wrong which has been done. An individual with self-respect and control over himself, who is also forbearing and dignified, has the right to correct a child to a certain extent as the occasion demands or seek to guide the child. But a wrathful and hot-headed person who is easily provoked is not fit to be a guardian of children. I wish that, instead of punishing children, parents would have recourse to prayer, and should make it a habit to supplicate earnestly for their children; for the supplications of parents on behalf of their children meet with special acceptance.

[Malfūẓāt, vol. 2, p. 4]

True guidance and training belongs to God Almighty. To pursue a matter persistently and to insist upon it unduly and to rebuke children upon every matter indicates that such a person imagines himself to be the source of guidance and believes that he will bring the children to order by pursuing his own method. This kind of attitude savours of a hidden assumption of association with the Divine and should be avoided by the members of our community. I pray for my children and require them to follow a broad set of rules of behaviour and no more. Beyond this I put my full trust in Allah Almighty in the confidence that the seed of good fortune inherent in each of them will flower at its proper time.

[Malfūẓāt, vol. 2, p. 5]

13

REPEATED CHALLENGES

NO ONE CAN DIE ON EARTH UNTIL HIS DEATH IS DECREED IN HEAVEN

I believe with certainty that God Almighty will not let me be vanquished by any opponent, because I am from Him and have come by His command to revive the faith.

My Opponents are Doomed to Fail

God Almighty has singularised me with His lights, which He bestows only on His chosen servants, and which cannot be equalled by others. If you have any doubts, come forth in opposition to me. But you will certainly not be able to do so, because you have tongues but no hearts; you have bodies but no life; your eyes have pupils but no capacity for sight. May God Almighty bestow sight upon you so that you may be able to see.

[Fat-ḥe-Islām, Rūḥānī Khazā'in, vol. 3, p.14, footnote]

In this age too, God Almighty manifests great signs in support of Islām, and I say this from my own experience. If all nations of the world should unite against me and a test were made to whom God reveals the unseen, whose prayers does He accept, whom does He help and for whom does He manifest great signs, I affirm, in the name of God, that I would emerge supreme. Is there anyone who will step forth against me for such a trial? God has bestowed thousands of signs upon me to let my opponents know that Islām is indeed the true faith. I seek no honour for myself, but only the honour of that for which I have been sent.

[Ḥaqīqat-ul-Waḥī, Rūḥānī Khazā'in, vol. 22, pp.181-182]

Divine Support for the Righteous

God Almighty has promised in the Holy Qur'ān four types of heavenly support for perfect believers and those who are perfectly righteous, on the basis of which they can be recognized.

1. A perfect believer is frequently given glad tidings by God Almighty of the acceptance of his supplications relating to him or his friends.
2. A perfect believer is often given advance knowledge, not only of events concerning him and his associates, but also of the decrees of God about to unfold in the world at large, or the changes about to affect some of the well known personalities.
3. Most of the prayers of the perfect believer are accepted. He is often given prior knowledge of their acceptance.
4. The perfect believer is the greatest recipient of the deeper meanings, new points of wisdom, subtleties and singular qualities of the Holy Qur'ān.

In respect of these four qualities, the perfect believer will always surpass others. It is not an unchanging rule that a perfect believer will receive glad tidings from God Almighty continuously and all the times, or that every one of his supplications will be granted, or that he will be warned in advance of all great events, or that knowledge of Qur'ānic insights will be continuously bestowed upon him, but, at a time of comparison with an opponent, all these four signs overwhelmingly favour the believer. It is possible that a less perfect believer may also, on occasion, be bestowed a small portion of these bounties, but it is the perfect believer alone who is their true heir.

Unless seen in comparison, the perfect station of the believer cannot be clearly understood by every unclean, dull and short-sighted person. Hence, the most clear and easy method for recognizing a perfect believer is by comparison alone. Though all these signs proceed naturally from a perfect believer, yet there are occasional difficulties in the way of their unilateral manifestation. For instance, it often happens that some persons approach a perfect believer and beseech his supplication in respect of matters that have been absolutely decreed against them.... On account of their frustration, they are not able to witness this sign; rather, they increase in their doubts and are not able to appreciate truly the perfect qualities of the true believer.

A perfect believer occupies a high rank and status in the estimation of God Almighty. Many complicated matters are set right for his sake and in consequence of his earnest prayers. Even some matters which have been decreed, and which appear to be absolute, are changed; nevertheless, a truly absolute decree cannot be modified through the supplications of a perfect believer, even if he should be a Prophet or a Messenger. A perfect believer is clearly distinguishable from others in respect of these four signs, though he cannot be permanently and uniformly successful. Therefore, as it is clear that a true and perfect believer is bestowed a proportionately much larger share of glad tidings, acceptance of prayers, disclosure of the unseen and disclosure of Qur'ānic verities, the best way to distinguish between him and others would be to institute a comparison between the claimants on the basis of these four signs which are the criteria to judge who is perfect and who is not….

Now let the whole world bear witness that purely for the sake of Allah and for the manifestation of truth, I accept this challenge with all my heart and soul. The first among those who should want to take up this challenge is Miāń Nadhīr Ḥussain of Delhi. He has taught the Holy Qur'ān and Ḥadīth for more than half a century, but the example of his learning and practice is that, without any enquiry or study, he proclaimed me a disbeliever and thus incited thousands of ill-natured wild people to revile me. He also let loose Batālvī[233] to spew forth the foam of condemnation from his mouth, and to curse me like a wild beast. And he has arrogated to himself the status of the perfect believer, eminent scholar and leader of the entire Muslim world. First and foremost, he is the one I invite to take up this challenge. He is free to bring with him the Batālvī who now claims to have true dreams. I would also let him, if he so wishes, include 'Abdul Jabbār Ṣāḥib, son of a righteous servant of Allah, the late Maulavī 'Abdullāh Ṣāḥib, and also Maulavī 'Abd-ur-Raḥmān Ṣāḥib of Lakhoke, who made public his revelation about me being eternally misguided, and denounced me as an apostate. He can also bring along Maulavī Muḥammad Bashīr Ṣāḥib of Bhopāl who is one of his followers. If Miāń Nadhīr Ḥussain should evade my challenge, as he has often done earlier, then let these gentlemen, whose names I have mentioned above, come forth to challenge me. Should they fail to do so, then let Maulavī Rashīd Aḥmad Ṣāḥib of Gangohā make a bold move to take up this chal-

---

[233] The reference is to Maulavī Muḥammad Ḥussain of Batālā. **[Publisher]**

lenge, as he is the foremost of the orthodox. Anyone else among the well-known Sufis, Pirzādas or hereditary divines who considers me a disbeliever, an impostor, a liar and a hypocrite, as do these others, may also join him.

If all of them should fail to accept this challenge and try to hide behind false excuses, then let it be known that I have fully discharged my obligation of conveying the message of God Almighty to them. I am the Appointed One. I have been given the tiding of victory and that is why I call these gentlemen to come forth in opposition to me. **Will anyone come forward?**...

These four criteria that I have mentioned are so simple and straightforward that everyone who considers them carefully will acknowledge that there is no clearer and easier spiritual way of deciding the contest between us. I affirm on oath and promise that, if I am defeated in this contest, I shall publicly acknowledge my error, and Miāń Nadhīr Ḥussain Ṣāḥib or Sheikh Batālvī will have no more need to condemn me as a disbeliever or impostor. In this case, I shall deserve every kind of disgrace and humiliation and I shall acknowledge in an open gathering that God Almighty has not sent me and that all my claims are false. I am, however, certain and clearly perceive that God will not permit such a situation to arise and will never let me perish.

[Āsmānī Faiṣlah, Rūḥānī Khazā'in, vol. 4, pp.323-330]

Inviting All to Come and Witness the Signs

There has been a continuous succession of signs with me from the very beginning, and anyone who spends some time in my company, provided he is sincere and steadfast, can see something of them. In future too, God Almighty will not leave this Movement without signs, nor will He withdraw His support from it. Indeed, according to His holy promises, He will continue to manifest His fresh signs at their appropriate times, until he has clearly established the distinction between truth and falsehood. In a revelation He said to me:

> A Warner came to the world but the world accepted him not; God will accept him and will establish his truth with powerful assaults.

I can never believe that these great signs will fail to appear, although their occurrence is not within my power. I assure you that I stand on truth. And, O dear people, be certain that, unless a person has the support of the God of heaven, he cannot have the courage to stand firm against the whole world and claim to do what is beyond his power. Can anyone who stands against the whole world with such strength and hearty steadfastness do so on his own? Certainly not. Such a person has the support of the hidden hand of God, and is under the shelter of the Powerful One Who controls heaven and earth and every body and soul.

Then open your eyes and realize that God, Who honours me with His converse, has granted me this strength and steadfastness. It is under His clear direction that I have ventured forth with great courage and steadfastness against those who claim that they are leaders of the world's religions and enjoy nearness to God, and some of whom claim to be recipients of Divine revelation and have condemned me as a disbeliever who deserves hell. I have come out into the field under Divine direction to challenge them all, so that God Almighty may demonstrate the distinction between the truthful one and the liars, and that His hand may degrade the false to the lowest degree, and that He may help and support the one who is honoured with His grace and beneficence. Brethren! Please observe that the invitation I have extended to Miāń Nadhīr Ḥussain and his colleagues is a method of resolving the difference between him and me. If these clerics believe that I am a disbeliever, dajjāl, impostor, and one stricken by Satan, as they allege, then why would they hesitate in confronting me? Have they not read in the Holy Qur'ān that in a contest Divine help is bestowed on the faithful? Allah the Almighty, says in the Holy Qur'ān:

وَلَا تَهِنُوْا وَلَا تَحْزَنُوْا وَاَنْتُمُ الْاَعْلَوْنَ اِنْ كُنْتُمْ مُّؤْمِنِيْنَ [234]

'O believers, do not be weary of the fight, nor have any apprehension. In the end, victory belongs to you, if you truly are believers.' It further says:

لَنْ يَّجْعَلَ اللّٰهُ لِلْكٰفِرِيْنَ عَلَى الْمُؤْمِنِيْنَ سَبِيْلًا [235]

That is: 'God will never grant the disbelievers a way to prevail against the believers.'

[Āsmānī Faiṣlah, Rūḥānī Khazā'in, vol. 4, pp. 332-334]

The Promised Messiah has been described in Ḥadīth as a *Nabī'ullāh* [Prophet of Allah] which means that he will receive revelation from God Almighty. But here Prophethood does not mean complete and perfect Prophethood, for a seal has been set on such Prophethood forever. The Prophethood I speak of is confined to Muḥaddathiyyat, which obtains light from the Muḥammadī lamp. This is a special bounty which has been bestowed upon this humble one. Although everyone partakes of

[234] Āl-e-'Imrān, 3:140 **[Publisher]**

[235] Al-Nisā', 4:142 **[Publisher]**

true dreams and visions to a certain extent, nevertheless, if my opponents are in doubt, they can test my claim that no other Muslims of this age has been bestowed such plentiful share of true dreams, visions, acceptance of prayers and true revelations that they approximate those of the Prophets, as I have been. This is indeed a great criterion to judge, for there is no method other than heavenly support for testing the truth of a claimant.

For a certainty, God Almighty supports one who comes from Him and guides him in an extraordinary way in the fields of contest. Therefore, I affirm with full confidence and perfect faith that if all the Muslims of the world, be they Punjabis, Indians, Arabs, Turks, Persians, Africans or others, and their clerics, sufis, leaders, and righteous ones, and all their men and women who consider me to be an impostor, should wish to see whether the signs of acceptance by God are found in me or in them, and whether heavenly doors are opened for me or for them, and whether the True Beloved by virtue of His special bounties and the bestowal of His special knowledge and spiritual insights is with me or with them, they would soon discover that the special grace and mercy which descends upon human heart are bestowed on me in much larger measure than on their respective leaders.

This should not be taken for an arrogant boast; it is only a declaration of God's bounty.

وَ ذٰلِكَ فَضْلُ اللّٰهِ يُؤْتِيْهِ مَنْ يَّشَاءُ [236]

This is also indicated by the revelations vouchsafed to me:

---

[236] This is God's grace, which He bestows upon whomsoever He wills. **[Publisher]**

قُلْ اِنِّیْ اُمِرْتُ وَ اَنَا اَوَّلُ الْمُؤْمِنِیْنَ ۔ اَلْحَمْدُ لِلّٰهِ الَّذِیْ
اَذْهَبَ عَنِّی الْحُزْنَ وَ اٰتَانِیْ مَالَمْ یُؤْتَ اَحَداً مِّنَ الْعَالَمِیْنَ۔ [237]

"Anyone else in the world[238]" refers to the people of this age and of the future.

[Izāla-e-Auhām, Rūḥānī Khazā'in, vol. 3, pp. 478-479]

I say with full confidence that no one can match the blessings that God Almighty has manifested for people in consequence of my resolve, attention and supplications, and soon He will manifest many more signs till my opponents will have to accept my claim. I have often said that I have been bestowed two kinds of blessings: those of Jesus[as] and those of Muḥammad[sa]. I know on the basis of knowledge bestowed on me by God Almighty that the degree of acceptance that can be achieved by my supplications on behalf of the problems of the world cannot be achieved by the supplications of others and the religious and Qur'ānic insights, verities, and mysteries which I can set forth at the highest level of composition, cannot be set forth by anyone else.

If the whole world were to combine against me for such a test, I would emerge victorious. If all people were to confront me, I would, by the grace of God Almighty, prevail over them. O Muslims! You have among you commentators of the Holy Qur'ān and Aḥādīth, and those who claim knowledge and understanding of the Holy Qur'ān,

---

[237] Tell them, I have been commissioned and I am the foremost of those who believe. All praise belongs to Allah Who has removed from me all grief and has bestowed upon me that which has not been bestowed upon anyone else in the world. **[Publisher]**

[238] The phrase in quotation marks is the last phrase of the revelation in Arabic quoted above. **[Publisher]**

and boast of their learning and eloquence. There are others who style themselves as mystics of different orders like Chishtī, Qādrī, Naqshbandī, Suharwardī etc. Arise and bring them to confront me! If I am false in my claim that both these kinds of blessing, those of Jesus[as] and those of Muḥammad[sa] are combined in me, and I am not the person in whom they were to be combined and who was to be *Dhul-Burūzain* [a manifestation of both] I will be defeated in this contest. Otherwise I shall emerge supreme. By the grace of God, I have been bestowed the capacity to exhibit signs of worldly blessings, like Jesus, and to exhibit Muḥammadī signs in the shape of setting forth verities, insights, subtle points, and mysteries of the Divine Law. And I have been granted extraordinary eloquence to accomplish these matters. I am certain that, by the grace of God, and by virtue of His design, there is no one on earth today who combines both these capacities in him. It has already been foretold that the one in whom these two capacities are combined would appear in the latter days. One half of his person would reflect Messianic glory and the other half would display the glory of Muḥammad[sa]. **I am that person.** Let him who so desires, look at me, and let him who wishes to test me, do so. Blessed is he who does not hold back, and most unfortunate is he who chooses darkness while there is light.

[Ayyām-uṣ-Ṣulḥ, Rūḥānī Khazā'in, vol. 14, pp. 406-408]

Appeal to Give up Vilification and Abuse

Purely by way of advice, and for the sake of Allah, I tell the opposing clerics and their soul mates, that abuse and vilification is not the way of decency. If this be your disposition, then so be it. But if you consider me false in my claim, you also have the option to come together in your mosques and pray to God for my ruin, or you can do the same individually. If I am false in my claim, your prayers are bound to be heard. Indeed, you have been praying against me already. But remember, even if you continue to pray thus until your tongues are bruised, and you go on bewailing in your prostrations until your noses are rubbed out, and your tears wipe out your eyelashes, and the weeping reduces your vision, and your brains are so affected that you begin to suffer from epilepsy or melancholia, still your prayers will not be heard; for I have come from God, and anyone who curses me will himself be afflicted with such a curse, though he may not be aware of it. He who enters into a prayer duel with me and supplicates that the one among us who is false may die in the lifetime of the other, will come to the same end which overtook Ghulām Dastgīr of Qaṣūr....

No one can die on earth unless his death is decreed in heaven. My soul is inspired with the same truth with which the soul of Abraham[as] was inspired. I have a relationship with God like that of Abraham[as]. My secret is known to God alone. My opponents ruin themselves in vain. I am not the plant that can be uprooted by their hands. If their predecessors and their successors, and their living and their dead, were all to come together and pray for my ruin, my God would convert their prayers into curses and would fling them back upon them. Do you not see that hundreds of wise people from among you continue to join my Jamā'at? There is uproar in heaven and God's angels are pulling pure hearts in our direction. Can man obstruct this Movement that is proceeding in heaven? Try to obstruct it if you think you have the strength. Use all the cunning and deceit that the opponents of the Prophets employed against them in the past, and leave nothing untried. Use your utmost strength. Call down ruin till you arrive at the door of death. Then see what harm you can bring upon us. Heavenly signs are descending like rain, but the unfortunate ones continue to raise objections from afar. What remedy can we provide to the hearts which have been sealed. Lord have mercy on this Ummah, Āmīn.

Announced by:Mirzā Ghulām Aḥmad
From Qādiān, 29 December, 1900.

[Arba'īn No.4, Rūḥānī Khazā'in, vol. 17, pp. 471-473]

Beseeching Allah for a Heavenly Sign and Decree

O my High, Majestic, Powerful, Holy, Everlasting and Self-Subsisting God, Who always helps His righteous servants, Hallowed be Your name unto eternity. Your mighty works can never be obstructed. Your strong hand always manifests wonders. You did raise me at the beginning of the fourteenth century and commanded me:

> Arise, because I have chosen you to satisfy the needs of Islām in this age, and to spread Islamic truths throughout the world, and to revive and strengthen the faith.

And it was You Who said to me:

> You are accepted in My estimation and I praise you upon My throne.

You did also say to me:

> You are the Promised Messiah whose time shall not be wasted.

And it was You Who addressed me saying:

> You are to Me like My Unity and My Uniqueness.

Again You said to me:

> I have chosen you to call the people. Tell them: I have

> been sent to all of you and I am the foremost of the believers.

And You did say to me:

> I have sent you so that I may illuminate Islām in the eyes of all people, so that none of the religions that are current upon the earth should be able to match Islām in blessings, insight, excellence of teachings, support of God and wonderful signs of God.

And it is You Who said to me:

> You are honoured in My presence and I have chosen you for Myself.

But O my All-Powerful God! You know that most people have not accepted me. They consider me an impostor and call me disbeliever, liar and dajjāl. They revile me and torment me with their harsh tongues. It has been said of me that I swallow that which is forbidden, devour the substance of other people, break my promises, usurp people's rights, revile them, break my covenants, collect wealth for myself and that I am wicked and bloodthirsty.

All this is said about me by people who call themselves Muslims and consider themselves to be virtuous, wise and pious. They believe that whatever they say about me is true. They have seen hundreds of heavenly signs manifested by You and yet they do not believe. They look upon my followers with contempt. Everyone of them who indulges in vilification imagines that he thereby acquires great spiritual merit. O my Powerful Master and God, do guide me, and manifest some sign whereby Your good natured servants may believe firmly that I am accepted of You, and their faith may be strengthened and they may recognize You and fear You and carry out a holy change in themselves according to the directions of this servant of Yours. Do make them set a high example of holiness and piety on the earth so that they may draw every seeker after truth to virtue and thus all the peoples of the earth may witness Your power and Your glory and may know that You are with Your servant and Your glory may shine forth in the world. May the light of Your name flash like the lightning, which illumines in one moment the whole expanse between east and west and shines in the north and south. But, My Beloved Master, if You do not approve of my way, then wipe me out from the face of the earth, so that I may not become a cause of innovation and error.

I do not ask for a quick manifestation, lest I be counted among those who try God, but I pray humbly and with all the respect due to Your Providence, that if I have found favour with You, then sometime within three years, a heavenly sign may be manifested in my support and in accordance with my prayer, which should have no connection with human hands and human designs, just as the rising and setting of the sun has no such connection. Lord, it is true that Your signs can also be manifested at human hands, but at this time I desire my truth to be attested by a sign that should be altogether beyond human power, so that no opponent of mine should be able to describe it as a human conspiracy. O my Lord, nothing is impossible for You. You can do all this if You will. You are mine as I am Yours. I supplicate to You earnestly that if it is true that I am from You and it is You Who has sent me, then do manifest in my support some sign that the public can understand and that is beyond human strength and human planning, so that they may know that I am from You.

O My Powerful God, O Mighty One, Master of all

capacities, no hand is equal to Yours, and no jinn or apparition is a partner in Your kingdom. Worldly people have recourse to every form of deceit and devils mislead people with their false suggestions, but no devil has been given the strength to withstand Your signs and Your awe-striking hand, or to manifest such power as is Yours. You are the One beside Whom there is no other God. You are the High, the Great. The light of powerful predictions, which are filled with Divine strength, greatness and terror, does not accompany the inspirations of those who are incited by Satan. It is only through Your strength that all Your Prophets have manifested their miraculous signs challengingly, and have made great prophecies in which their triumph and the helplessness of their opponents was indicated in advance. Your prophecies exhibit the brightness of Your Glory and have the fragrance of Your Godhood, Power, Greatness and Sovereignty. An angel precedes Your Messengers, so that no Satan should stand in their way. I swear by Your Honour and Your Glory that I submit humbly to Your Judgement. If You do not wish to manifest some heavenly sign in my support and in my confirmation within three years, beginning with January, 1900 and ending with December, 1902, and You reject this servant of Yours like those who are wicked, unclean, faithless, liars, dajjāls, betrayers of trusts and disorderly in Your estimation, then I call You to witness that I will no longer consider myself truthful and shall deem myself deserving of all the calumnies and charges and accusations that are levelled against me. See that my soul flies towards You in full trust as a bird flies towards its nest. I request a sign of Your Power, but not for my own sake or for my honour, but so that people may know You and adopt Your holy ways and should not deprive themselves of guidance by rejecting the one whom You have sent. I bear witness that You have sent me and have manifested great signs in my support.

[Tiryāq-ul-Qulūb, Rūḥānī Khazā'in, vol. 15, pp. 507-511]

Persian Poem

O Mighty Lord, Creator of heaven and earth,
O Merciful, Compassionate and Guide;
Who looks into the hearts;
And from Whom nothing is hidden.

If You see that I am wicked and vicious;
If You have determined that I am evil;
Then break this evil one into pieces;
And gladden the hearts of my opponents.
Shower Thy mercy on their hearts;
Grant of Thy grace all their wishes.
Send down a blazing fire on the walls and doors of my dwelling,
Be my enemy and destroy my work.

But if You do count me as one of Your servants;
And my attention is all concentrated on You;
And if You find my heart full of such love for You,
As is entirely unknown to the world;
Then deal with me by way of love;
And make manifest a little of its mystery.

O You Who comes towards every seeker;
And are aware of the yearning of every heart that is aflame with Your love,
For the sake of the relationship that I have with You;

And for the sake of the love that my heart has cultivated for You;
Come forth Yourself to vindicate me;
O You Who are my Refuge and my Shelter and my last Resort.

With that fire which You have lit in my heart;
And with which You have utterly consumed everything beside You;
Light up my countenance with the same fire;
And convert my dark night into bright day.

[Ḥaqīqat-ul-Mahdī, Rūḥānī Khazā'in, vol. 14, p. 434]

Evidence in the Form of Divine Blessings

I have set out in these announcements the lights of the power of faith that have been manifested to me in an extraordinary manner in the shape of support from the unseen. They are proofs of the grace and mercy of God Almighty and of nearness to Him and have been bestowed on this humble one by virtue of my strong faith and adherence to the straight path. This spiritual station cannot be claimed by any of my opponents. If anyone contests this statement, let him stand forth and compare the blessings bestowed upon him on account of his following his own religion, with those that have been bestowed on me. But no one has stood up to confront me, nor is it within the power of a frail human being to stand up merely on the basis of his cunning, wicked designs or bigoted obstinacy, against this Movement which God Almighty has established with His own hand.

I affirm truly that if anyone stands up against this Movement to display blessings enjoyed by him, he will be struck down with great humiliation, as this Movement is not of man but is from that Mighty and Powerful Being

Whose hand fashioned the heavens and all heavenly bodies and spread out the earth for its dwellers. It is a pity that our clerics and divines are always ready to sit down with paper, pen and inkpot to condemn me as a disbeliever, but do not reflect for a moment whether falsehood can ever inspire such awe and dread that no one dares step forth in answer to such a challenge. Can a false one possess such courage and steadfastness as has been manifested before the whole world in this instance? Let those who doubt the truth of my statements approach the leaders, preachers and teachers of all opponents of Islām and persuade them … to stand against me in a contest regarding spiritual matters, and see whether God Almighty supports me or not.

[Izāla-e-Auhām, Rūḥānī Khazā'in, vol. 3, pp. 156-157, footnote]

O Ye who Doubt! Come to the Heavenly Verdict!

O revered ones! O clerics! And O leaders of the people! May God Almighty open your eyes. Do not transgress the limits in your wrath and anger. Study both parts of this book of mine carefully, for therein lies light and guidance. Fear God Almighty and hold back your tongues from denouncing me as a disbeliever. God Almighty knows well that I am a Muslim.

اٰمنت باللّٰه و ملٰئكتهٖ و كتبهٖ و رسلهٖ والبعث بعد
الموت۔ و اشهد ان لّا اله الا اللّٰه وحدهٗ لا شريك لهٗ و
اشهد ان محمدًا عبدهٗ و رسولهٗ ۔ فاتقوا اللّٰه و لا
تقولوا لست مسلمًا واتقوا الملك الذى اليه ترجعون۔ [239]

---

[239] I believe in Allah, His angels, His books, His Messengers and Resurrection after death. I bear witness that there is no God except Allah, the One without associate; and I bear witness that Muḥammad

If, even after studying this book, you still continue to harbour doubts, then come and test him who is supported by God. O ye opposing clerics, sufis and religious leaders, who reject me and denounce me as an impostor, I have been assured that if all of you together, or individually, stand against me and wish to compete with me in respect of the heavenly signs that are manifested in support of the friends of the Gracious One, God Almighty will put you to shame and will unmask you, and you will see that He is with me. Is there anyone among you who is prepared to come into the field for such a trial, and to compete with me, after a public announcement, about the close relationship that God has with me? Remember, God helps the righteous. Lay aside your tricks for He is close to me. Will you then fight Him? Can anyone rise in stature merely by jumping arrogantly? Will you rip the truth apart with your sharp tongues? Fear Him Whose wrath is greater than all wraths!

إِنَّهُ مَنْ يَأْتِ رَبَّهُ مُجْرِمًا فَإِنَّ لَهُ جَهَنَّمَ لَا يَمُوتُ فِيهَا وَلَا يَحْيَى [240]

[Izāla-e-Auhām, Rūḥānī Khazā'in, vol. 3, p. 102]

The Holy Qur'ān comprises wisdom and insight and has nothing in it that is vain or useless. It explains clearly that which it states and provides for all needs. It has a sign in every aspect of it. Should anyone question this, we are prepared to establish and manifest its miraculous qualities from all aspects.

[Malfūẓāt, vol. 1, p. 83]

---

is His servant and Messenger. Fear Allah and say not: You are not a Muslim. Fear the King to Whom you will be brought back. **[Publisher]**

[240] 'Verily, he who comes to his Lord a sinner, for him is hell; he shall neither die therein nor live.'—Ṭā Hā, 20:75, **[Publisher]**

Let a select group of the learned religious scholars of Nadwah come to Qādiān and demand proofs of miracles and definitive arguments based on the Holy Qur'ān and Ḥadīth which support my claim. Then, if I fail to furnish full proof according to the practice of the Prophets (peace be upon them), I will allow all my books to be burnt. Only a godly one would go to such lengths. Why would the Nadwah take so much trouble? They care the least about the hereafter, so why should they fear God? Yet each of the clerics of Nadwah should remember that he will not remain in this world forever. Death is beckoning. God observes from heaven that the sport and play with which they occupy themselves, and which they call religion, has nothing to do with faith. They are content with the shell and are unaware of the kernel. This is not the service of Islām but is its enmity. Alas! If they had been blessed with eyesight they would have realized that the world has been guilty of a grave sin in rejecting God's Messiah; but this realization would only come after death.

[Tuḥfat-un-Nadwah, Rūḥānī Khazā'in, vol. 19, p. 101]

The nature of converse with the Divine is that God Almighty bestows the honour of such a dialogue upon one who is wholly devoted to the Holy Prophet (peace and blessings of Allah be upon him) as He granted to earlier Prophets. In this dialogue, the *Kalīmullāh* [the servant who is blessed with converse with God] talks to Him like one man to another. He puts a question to God, Who responds to him; even though such question and answer may extend to fifty or more exchanges. Through such dialogue, God Almighty bestows three types of bounties upon His perfect servant:

1. Most of his supplications are granted and he is

foretold about their acceptance.

2. God Almighty discloses many matters of the unseen to him.
3. The philosophy of many teachings of the Holy Qur'ān is revealed to him through revelation.

Whoever rejects me and claims that he himself is blessed with Divine converse, I call upon him in the name of God to compete with me in respect of all these three criteria. Both of us should write an exegesis on any seven verses of the Holy Qur'ān to be agreed upon. My opponent should write on the basis of revelation vouchsafed to him and I shall write on the basis of mine. Each of us should set forth, in advance, some revelations received by him intimating acceptance of prayers and relating to matters beyond human capacity. He should also disclose in advance some hidden matter relating to the future and so should I. Both our statements should be published through posters. Thus truth and falsehood of each party will become evident.

But remember, my opponents will never be able to do this. The hearts of liars have been cursed by God. He will neither disclose to them the light of the Holy Qur'ān, nor accept their supplications, nor inform them of such acceptance in advance, nor will He disclose anything of the unseen to them:

لَا يُظْهِرُ عَلٰى غَيْبِهٖٓ اَحَدًا اِلَّا مَنِ ارْتَضٰى مِنْ رَّسُوْلٍ [241]

Now that I have made this announcement, anyone who neither stands forth against me in the manner set out, nor

---

[241] 'He reveals not His secrets to anyone, except to him who He chooses, namely a messenger *of His*.'—Al-Jinn, 72:27-28 **[Publisher]**

restrains himself from denouncing me as an impostor, will be under the curse of God, the angels and all the righteous ones. *And the only duty of a Messenger is to convey the message.*

[Anjām-e-Ātham, Rūḥānī Khazā'in, vol. 11, p.303, footnote]

An Invitation to Pīr Mehr 'Alī Shāh of Golrah

The readers of this announcement will be aware that, having observed the persistent condemnation and vilification of opposing clerics and custodians of shrines, and having noted their demand for a sign, I had made an announcement that was addressed especially to Pīr Mehr 'Alī Shāh Ṣāḥib. The sum and substance of that announcement was that there have so far been many discussions on religious issues from which the opposing Maulavīs have derived no benefit, but as they continue to ask for heavenly signs, it is possible that they might derive some benefit from them. It was published because Pīr Mehr 'Alī Shāh Ṣāḥib, who claims excellence of sainthood, as well as a high intellectual calibre and, on account of his confidence in his learning, has recently renewed his condemnation of me as a disbeliever, and has published a book in order to provoke the common people against me.... And since God Almighty has honoured me with the revelation:

اَلرَّحْمٰنُ عَلَّمَ الْقُرْآنَ

'The Almighty Allah has taught thee the Holy Qur'ān'; I had, therefore, suggested that it would be enough of a sign for testing my truth or falsehood if Pīr Mehr 'Alī Shāh Ṣāḥib and I both were to write a commentary in clear and eloquent Arabic on some Chapters of the Holy Qur'ān. If he is judged better than me, I shall have no hesitation in acknowledging his superiority. With this in view, my announcement was made entirely in good faith … but he has completely evaded my challenge.…

Today, God Almighty has put a plan in my mind which I set forth to conclusively resolve this matter, and I believe that it will fully expose Pīr Mehr 'Alī Shāh Ṣāḥib, for the whole world is not blind; there are some who are fair and just. The plan is that today I give the following answer to the constant barrage of announcements, which are being published in favour of Pīr Mehr 'Alī Shāh Ṣāḥib. If Pīr Mehr 'Alī Shāh Ṣāḥib is truly exceptional in his knowledge of the Qur'ān and Arabic literature, and is well versed in the arts of persuasion and eloquence, I believe he must still be in possession of those qualities since it is not long since he moved to Lahore. I propose here and now to establish the truth by writing a commentary on *Sūrah Al-Fātiḥah* and setting down the verities and truths of this chapter of the Holy Qur'ān. As for Ḥaḍrat Pīr Ṣāhib, he should also base his evidence regarding the Promised Messiah and the bloodthirsty Mahdī on *Sūrah Al-Fātiḥah*. He is at liberty to deduce his conclusive arguments and crucial verities from *Sūrah Al-Fātiḥah*, written in eloquent and brilliant Arabic. The two books should be printed and published within seventy days beginning from the fifteenth of December, 1900. This will allow knowledgeable people to compare and decide for themselves. If three scholars, who possess literary qualities and are proficient in Arabic and have no connection with either of us, state on oath that Pīr Ṣāḥib's book is superior to mine, both in composition and in setting forth the verities of the Holy Qur'ān, I shall immediately pay five hundred rupees to Pīr Ṣāḥib.… He will be at liberty to seek help in this enterprise from Maulavī Muḥammad Ḥussain of Batāla, Maulavī 'Abdul Jabbār of Ghaznī and

Muḥammad Ḥassan of Bhīn. He is even free to employ three or four Arab scholars who posses literary qualifications for this purpose. These commentaries should not be less than four *juz*[242] each.... If any of us fails to publish such a commentary within the appointed term—between 15 December 1900 and 25 February 1901—he will be considered false in his claim, and no further proof of his falsehood will be necessary. *Peace be upon those who follow the guidance.*

Announced by: Mirzā Ghulām Aḥmad

From Qādiān, 15 December, 1900.

[Arba'īn No. 4, Rūḥānī Khazā'in, vol. 17, pp. 479-484]

Knowledge of Arabic and the Holy Qur'ān as Signs of Divine Support

I once received the revelation:

اَلرَّحْمٰنُ عَلَّمَ الْقُرْآنَ۔ یا اَحْمَدُ فاضَتِ الرَّحْمَةُ عَلٰی شَفَتَیْكَ

'The Gracious One has taught thee the Qur'ān. O Aḥmad, grace flows from thy lips.'

From this revelation I understood that God had, as a miraculous sign, bestowed two types of bounties on me with reference to the Holy Qur'ān and its language.

(1) One is that I have been instructed, in an extraordinary manner, in the high insights of the Holy Qur'ān, in respect of which no one can compete with me. (2) Secondly, I have been bestowed such proficiency in the language of the Holy Qur'ān, namely Arabic, that all the opposing divines combined will not be able to compete

242 One *Juz* comprises 16 pages. [Fīrozul-Lughāt, Published by Feroz Sons, Lahore, p. 458]

with me, and they will see that the sweetness, eloquence and mastery of Arabic that characterises my composition cannot be equalled by them, their friends, their teachers or their revered ones. After receiving this revelation, I wrote a commentary on some Sūrahs and passages of the Holy Qur'ān and compiled several books in fluent Arabic, and invited my opponents to compete with me and offered them large sums of money as award in case of their success. The leaders among them, like Miāń Nadhīr Ḥussain of Delhi and Abū Sa'īd Muḥammad Ḥussain of Batāla, who is the editor of *Ishā'at-us-Sunnah*, were repeatedly invited that if they claimed to possess some knowledge of the Holy Qur'ān or had any proficiency in Arabic or if they considered me false in respect of my claim of being the Promised Messiah, they should put forth matching instances of the verities and insights which I have presented fluently in these books claiming that they are beyond human capacity and constitute the signs of God Almighty. But they failed altogether to take up my challenge. Neither of them set forth a matching instance of the verities and insights which I had described in my commentaries on some of the passages and verses of the Holy Qur'ān, nor was any of them able to compose even two lines in Arabic like the books that I had published in eloquent Arabic. Anyone who has read my books *Nūr-ul-Ḥaq*, *Karāmāt-uṣ-Ṣādiqīn*, *Sirr-ul-Khilāfah*, *Itmām-ul-Ḥujjah,* etc, and the Arabic portions of *Anjām-i-Ātham* and *Najm-ul-Hudā*, will have clearly recognized their high literary standard, both in prose and poetry; and will also have observed how forcefully I have challenged all opposing divines that if they laid claim to some knowledge of the Holy Qur'ān and have any degree of proficiency in Arabic, they should produce a match of these books; otherwise, they should acknowledge that this enterprise of mine has been undertaken under Divine direction and should confess that these books of mine are a sign of my truth. Alas, they neither abandoned their opposition nor were able to match my books. In any case, the message of God Almighty was conveyed fully to them and they were proven guilty of having disobeyed a commissioned one of God.

[Tiryāq-ul-Qulūb, Rūḥānī Khazā'in, vol. 15, pp. 230-231]

To disabuse the minds of the common people that Miāń Muḥammad Ḥussain Batālavī, or other like-minded opposing clerics who share his views and mistakenly believe him to possess a high degree of proficiency in Arabic and in the verities of the Word of God, it has been considered proper to publish this monograph in a final effort to expose the myth of Baṭālvī and the divines associated with him, concerning their knowledge of Arabic and their comprehension of Divine verities. This booklet comprises four Arabic odes and a commentary on *Sūrah Al-Fātiḥah*. Though these odes have been completed within one week, in a few hours in fact, but for the sake of carrying the matter to the final conclusion, I hereby solemnly promise that if within one month of the publication of this booklet, they publish their matching booklet exhibiting the same high degree of literary merit and comprising the same number of Arabic verses that are comprised in my booklet, along with a commentary of the *Sūrah Al-Fātiḥah* matching mine in every respect, **I shall pay them one thousand rupees as reward**....

I further promise that, upon publication of the booklet, if their odes and their commentary are found free from grammatical or idiomatic errors and are acknowledged to be superior to my odes and commentary, and, what is more, if they are able to point out any mistakes in my compositions, I shall pay them five rupees for every such mistake. Remember, it is easy to criticize, even an ignorant person can do this much; but it is difficult to establish high merit. In respect of the commentary, it should be remembered that a commentary written by merely copying other commentaries will not be acceptable. It must comprise new verities and insights, provided they are not opposed to the Holy Qur'ān and to whatever the Holy Prophet (peace and blessings of Allah be upon him) has said.

[Karāmāt-uṣ-Ṣādiqīn, Rūḥānī Khazā'in, vol. 7, pp. 47-49]

Some opponents of Islām put forward the objection that, although it seems reasonable that the Word of God should be matchless, yet how can the matchlessness of any book be established by plain reasoning. They demand that if the Holy Qur'ān is matchless, this quality should be established by some convincing arguments, inasmuch as its high literary excellence can be appreciated only by one whose mother tongue is Arabic, and it does not constitute a proof of matchlessness for others, nor can others benefit from it. The answer is that this objection is raised only by people who have never sincerely tried to ascertain the matchlessness of the Holy Qur'ān from someone possessing knowledge of it. Instead, they avoid the light of the Holy Qur'ān, lest they should be affected by it. The matchlessness of the Holy Qur'ān is so patent and obvious in the estimation of seekers after truth, that it spreads its rays in all directions, like the sun, in the comprehension of which one need encounter no doubt or difficulty. If there is no intervening darkness of bigotry and hostility, that perfect light can be appreciated with even a little attention. It is true that some aspects of the matchlessness of the Holy Qur'ān are such as to require some knowledge of Arabic for their comprehension, but it is a mistake resulting from ignorance to imagine that the entire range of the miraculousness of the Qur'ān depends upon the knowledge of Arabic, and that all Qur'ānic wonders and all the great qualities of this discriminating Book can be appreciated only by the Arabs, and that non-Arabs are barred from them. This is utterly wrong. It is clear to every knowledgeable person, that most of the aspects of the matchlessness of the Holy Qur'ān are so simple and easy to understand that no knowledge of Arabic is needed. They are so manifest and clear that minimal intelligence, which should be characteristic of every human being, suffices for their understanding. For instance, one aspect of its matchlessness is that, despite its brevity, to the extent that if it is written out by an average pen it can be comprised within a few pages, it comprehends all religious verities which lay scattered in diverse books and in the scriptures of previous Prophets. Furthermore, it also possesses the distinction that whatever verities a person might discover by diligence, effort and search in religious fields through the exercise of his intelligence and perception, or whatever new verities and insights or proofs and arguments he might set forth by the exercise of his reason, or should offer the subtlest verity which the ancient philosophers may have discovered through great labour for a comparison, or should wish to discover from the Holy Qur'ān the remedy for the inner disorders and the spiritual maladies from which most people suffer, he can test the Qur'ān in whichever aspect and by whatever method he might desire, and he will find that, in setting forth its truth and wisdom, the Holy Qur'ān encompasses everything like a circle and no religious verity is left out by it. Indeed the Holy Qur'ān improves and corrects the statements of philosophers that were defective due to their limited knowledge or defective reasoning. Besides, the Holy Qur'ān sets out accurately and correctly truths that no philosopher or thinker has set out, and to which no intellect has gained access. It sets out in full all the fine points relating to knowledge of the Divine which were scattered in hundreds of collections and comprised of many lengthy volumes, but were still imperfect and incomplete. It leaves no room for any wise person in future to set forth a new point. Despite all this, the whole script of the Holy Qur'ān does not exceed 80 pages of normal handwriting. This is an aspect of matchlessness that a person of average intellect cannot doubt.

Every reasonable person can appreciate that it is not within the power of man or any other creature to set out all religious truth, all insights relating to the subject of divinity, all arguments and proofs in support of true principles resulting from intellectual exercises of all thinkers, ancient and modern, with such completeness in a book of moderate size from which no verity has been left out.

For every person, literate or illiterate, there is a clear and straight way for testing this aspect of the Holy Qur'ān. If anyone should be in doubt about the Holy Qur'ān comprising all Divine verities, we are prepared to undertake that a seeker after truth, after making a written promise that if he is satisfied he would accept Islām, should set forth a certain number of religious verities out of a Hebrew, Greek, Latin, English, Sanskrit or any other book, or should set forth some subtle points relating to any subjects of divinity out of his own intellect. If he does so, we shall produce for him the same out of the Holy Qur'ān.

[Brāhīn-e-Aḥmadiyyah, Rūḥānī Khazā'in, vol. 1, pp. 247 -277]

The truth is that if any cleric of this country should wish to compete with me in respect of Qur'ānic insights, and I should write a commentary on a chapter of the Holy Qur'ān and he should write a commentary on the same chapter, he would certainly be humbled and would not be able to stand against me. That is why, despite my insistence, the Maulavīs do not respond to my challenges. This is a great sign, but only for those who possess faith and a sense of justice.

[Anjām-e-Ātham, Rūḥānī Khazā'in, vol. 11, pp. 292-293]

I desire to demolish the Arabs' claim to literary excellence and eloquence. Let these journalists, who call themselves masters of the language having written a few lines, come forth, if they dare, to challenge this sign. Their pens will be broken. If they have any power or proficiency, they can take up this challenge individually or collectively. They will then realize the truth, and the lie which the ignorant are wont to repeat, that I get my books written by Arabs on payment of thousands of rupees, will also be exposed. Then it will also become clear as to who is the Arab that can write a book of such high literary standard and full of such verities and insights. The books that these claimants of proficiency in literary qualities write are like a pile of hard and soft, white and black pieces of stones. While my books, which contain analysis of Qur'ānic verities and insights, are sweet and delicious. That which is composed with the support of the Holy Spirit and the words that are inspired by it, possess a unique sweetness, splendour and power which others cannot master. This will be a great sign indeed!

[Malfūẓāt, vol. 2, p. 375]

Though I have so far published nearly seventeen matchless books in Arabic, against which my opponents have not published even one during the past ten years, it occurred to me today that as those books not only possess high literary merit but also comprise many Qur'ānic truths and insights, it is possible that my opponents might make the excuse that they are not conversant with truths and insights, and that if it had been an Arabic poem of high merit like the average type of odes, they would certainly have produced its match. It also occurred to me that if Maulavī Thanā'ullāh Ṣāḥib were invited to compose a book matching my book *I'jāz-ul-Masīḥ,* he would be sure to demand proof that the book had been written within seventy days. If he were to claim that I had taken two years in writing this book and that he too should be allowed two years for writing a comparable book, it would be difficult to convince him that I had written my book within seventy days. I, therefore, thought it proper to supplicate to God Almighty that He should enable me to compose, with the help of the Holy Spirit, an ode describing the debates that took place at Mud, so that no one should find it difficult to determine the period during which the ode was composed. My supplication was accepted and I completed the compilation of the ode within five days. If I had not been otherwise engaged, the ode could have been composed in one day, and if no delay had been encountered it could have been published on 9th November, 1902.

This is a great sign, to which Maulavī Thanā'ullāh Ṣāḥib is himself a witness, as the ode itself shows that it was written after the debate to which he was a party. The debate took place on 29th and 30th October 1902, and I started writing the ode on 8th November upon the return of our friends. It was completed on 12th November along with this Urdu writing. As I am certain that this ode is a great sign of Divine support, so that God may put my opponents to shame and silence them, therefore I present this sign to Maulavī Thanā'ullāh Ṣāḥib and his helpers with an offer of a reward of ten thousand rupees. If, within five days, they compose a matching ode together with an Urdu writing of the length of this writing, which is also a sign, I shall immediately pay them ten thousand rupees. In addition, I can allow them one week for printing and two days for its transmission through the mail. Thus if fourteen days after receiving my ode and its accompanying Urdu portion, they publish the same number of verses possessing the same high literary merit, I shall pay them ten thousand rupees as reward. They will be free to seek the help of Maulavī Muḥammad Ḥussain Ṣāḥib or any other gentleman.

Another reason why they should make this effort is that in one of my announcements I have predicted that by the end of December 1902, an extraordinary sign would be manifested in my support. Though such a sign has already been manifested in other forms, if Maulavī Thanā'ullāh and other clerics whom I have addressed, fail to respond to this challenge, this will also be a sign in fulfilment of my prediction. So it is incumbent upon them, if they consider my claim to be the result of my own design, that they should accept my challenge and frustrate this sign. I affirm on oath that if, individually or collectively, they publish within the time prescribed an ode in Arabic supplemented by an Urdu writing corresponding to the ode and the Urdu writing that I have composed, and mail them to me within twelve days, I shall not only pay them ten thousand rupees as an award, but their success will prove my falsehood, and Maulavī

Thanā'ullāh Ṣāḥib and his friends will no longer have to invent lies against me, and they will achieve an easy victory. Failing this, they will no longer have any justification for calling me false or denying my signs.

I call heaven and earth to witness that I place my reliance from today onwards on this sign. If my claim is true, and God Almighty knows that it is true, it will not be possible for Maulavī Thanā'ullāh, or any other Maulavī associated with him, to compose an ode and an Urdu writing like mine within five days, as God Almighty will break their pens and will make their minds dull. Maulavī Thanā'ullāh cannot claim that I composed this ode in advance, since it is about the debate which was held at Mud. If I had composed it in advance, then they must acknowledge that I possess knowledge of the unseen, which would still constitute a sign. So they have no way of escape now. Today the revelation has been fulfilled in which God said:

The affairs decreed by the All-Powerful God have been manifested;
Those who issued declarations of kufr have been apprehended.

[I'jāz-e-Aḥmadī, Rūḥānī Khazā'in, vol. 19, pp. 145-148]

Is it not a Divine sign that the one concerning whom it was said that he was an ignoramus and did not know a single rule of grammar, calls upon all the Maulavīs who denounce him as a disbeliever to compete with him in writing a commentary for which he would award them a thousand rupees, and to write a book matching his book *Nūr-ul-Ḥaq* for which he is prepared to deposit five thousand rupees in advance to be awarded to them; and not one of them has the courage to come forward and accept his challenge....

I have called them repeatedly and most emphatically to come forward but they have paid no attention to my invitations. In order to expose Sheikh Ṣāḥib's lack of knowledge of Arabic, I announced in *Nūr-ul-Ḥaq* that if he publishes within three months a book matching it in every respect, he would be awarded three thousand rupees in cash, and would, in this easy manner, prove my revelations to be false. Otherwise, he would not only be defeated but would be accounted as having acknowledged the truth of my revelations. But Sheikh Ṣāḥib paid no attention to any of this. Why such indifference? The only reason is that it is beyond his capacity to take up my challenge.... God Almighty designed to humiliate this arrogant one and to show him how He helps His servants. These books, therefore, were written through the capacity bestowed by God and His special help and under His direction. I had fixed the end of June 1894 as the last date for the acceptance of my challenge relating to the matching of *Karāmāt-uṣ-Ṣādiqīn* and *Nūr-ul-Ḥaq,* and that date is now past.

[Sirrul-Khilāfah, Rūḥānī Khazā'in vol. 8, pp. 398-400]

If Ḥaḍrat Sayyed Maulavī Muḥammad Nadhīr Ḥussain Ṣāḥib or Maulavī Abū Muḥammad 'Abd-ul-Ḥaq Ṣāḥib consider that I am mistaken in my view on the question of the death of Jesus, and imagine that my viewpoint goes against the Holy Qur'ān and Ḥadīth, it is incumbent upon them that, in order to safeguard the public against being misled by me, they should debate the question with me in this city of Delhi. I propose only three conditions with regard to the holding of the debate.

1. They should assume the responsibility for persuading the authorities to make arrangements for maintaining law and order ... since I am only a visi-

tor in the city and am an object of abuse and vilification at the hands of my Muslim brethren....

2. The debate should be conducted in writing. Each party should draw up and sign its question or answer, as the case may be, in the meeting and deliver it to the other party, as oral statements cannot be preserved accurately....

3. The subject of the debate shall be the life and death of Jesus and neither party shall rely on any authority other than the Holy Qur'ān and the books of Ḥadīth; but *Bukhārī* and *Muslim* shall have priority over other compilations, and *Bukhārī* shall have priority over *Muslim*, since it has been accounted the most accurate book after the Book of God.

I promise that if, through this method, it is proved that Jesus son of Mary is still alive, I shall give up my claim of being a recipient of revelation as I realize that no revelation that is opposed to the Holy Qur'ān can be true.

[Majmū'ah Ishtihārāt, vol. 1, pp. 234-235]

In the Name of Allah the Glorious, a Plea to Maulavī Sayyed Nadhīr Ḥussain, for a Debate on the Life or Death of Jesus son of Mary

ندارد کسے با تو ناگفتہ کار

و لیکن چو گفتی دلیلش بیار [243]

Maulavī Sayyed Muḥammad Nadhīr Ḥussain Ṣāḥib! You and your disciples have raised a clamour that my claim of being the Promised Messiah is against the Holy Qur'ān and Ḥadīth, and that I have invented a new relig-

---

[243] *Nobody will have anything to do with what you have said not;*
Until you produce an argument for what you have said. **[Publisher]**

ion and a new doctrine which are altogether opposed to the teachings of God and the Holy Prophet[sa] and are obviously false, since, according to you, the Holy Qur'ān and the Aḥādīth proclaim that Jesus (peace be upon him) was raised bodily to heaven and will descend on earth some later time, and that the notion that he had died a natural death is opposed to the clear authority of the Holy Qur'ān and Ḥadīth. As you have, in your affirmations, described my claim as opposed to the Holy Qur'ān and the Ḥadīth, as a consequence of which thousands of Muslims have been deeply agitated against me, it is incumbent upon you to settle with me whether in holding such a view I have departed from the authority of the Qur'ān and Ḥadīth, or whether you are guilty of such departure in professing the opposite view....

If, in a meeting held for the purpose, you refute my arguments, which I shall set forth from the Holy Qur'ān and from the true Aḥādīth, and present better arguments from these two sources in support of the doctrine that Jesus son of Mary was raised bodily up to heaven and continues there alive, I shall repent at your hand and burn all my books which deal with this question and which are in my possession. I shall publish my recantation publicly. *May the curse of Allah be upon him who conceals in his heart that which is opposed to what he professes with his tongue.* But keep in mind that if you are vanquished and fail to cite a conclusive verse or authentic Ḥadīth in support of the doctrine that you profess, you will also have to publicly withdraw from your false belief. *Allah loves those who repent.*

Dear Sir! I put you under oath in the name of God, the Holy and Glorious, Who created you and has bestowed countless favours upon you, that if you truly believe that the Holy Qur'ān contains clear and categorical verses which prove conclusively that Jesus son of Mary is still alive, and that the verses are supported by true Aḥādīth, on account of which you have been compelled to emphatically deny my claim of being the recipient of Divine revelation, then out of the fear of God in Whose name I call upon you, come forward and debate the question with me....I invite you again, dear sir, in the name of Allah the Glorious, to this debate. I will present myself for this purpose wherever you may wish.... If you do not come forward and try to evade my challenge by relying upon the mischievous clerics, then remember that you will be humiliated and defamed throughout India and the Punjab and will altogether lose the glory of being called the versatile religious scholar....

I wish to add that if you are not prepared to debate this question with me then, in a meeting, listen to all my arguments in support of the death of Jesus[as] and then proclaim three times on oath in the name of Allah the Glorious, that my arguments are not well-founded and that the true and certain argument is that Jesus son of Mary was raised bodily to heaven and that this indeed is your belief which is supported by clear and conclusive verses of the Holy Qur'ān and true Aḥādīth. Thereupon I shall have recourse to humble and earnest prayer for Divine decree in respect of your daring dishonesty, impertinence and bearing false witness. As God has assured me:

اُدْعُوْنِیْ اَسْتَجِبْ لَكُمْ [244]

I have also been assured that if you abandon the way of righteousness and commit this impertinence and ignore

---

[244] 'Call on Me, I shall respond to you.' **[Publisher]**

the verse:

لَا تَقْفُ مَا لَيْسَ لَكَ بِهٖ عِلْمٌ [245]

then, within one year, you will be so sorely affected by the consequences of this impertinence that it will be a sign for others. I therefore request you, that if you are not inclined to hold a debate, then at least try to seek a decision in the manner I have suggested so that those who go on calling for a sign may be shown a sign by God Almighty. *He has power to do all that He wills. And our last pronouncement is: All praise belongs to Allah, Lord of all the worlds.*

[Majmū'ah Ishtihārāt, vol. 1, pp. 241-249]

I have written to him[246] several times that I do not question any of his beliefs, except that I do not believe, as he does, that Jesus (peace be upon him) is still physically alive. I believe, both as a doctrine and as a fact, that Jesus[as] died a natural death, and why should I not believe so, because in His Mighty Book, the Holy Qur'ān, my Lord and Master has mentioned him among the dead and there is no mention at all of the extraordinary phenomenon of him being physically alive or of his expected return to earth. The Holy Qur'ān concludes merely with the announcement of his death. Therefore if my statement is vain, false and blasphemous, then he should come and debate the matter with me. If he succeeds in establishing the continuation of the physical life of Jesus (peace be on him) from the Holy Qur'ān and the Aḥādīth I shall discard my belief and shall burn all my books that deal with

---

[245] 'Follow not that of which thou hast no knowledge.'—Banī Isrā'īl, 17:37. **[Publisher]**

[246] The reference is to Maulavī Nadhīr Ḥussain of Delhi. **[Publisher]**

this question. I have also suggested that if he is unwilling to debate the question, he should affirm on oath that there is no mention in the Holy Qur'ān of the death of Jesus[as] but only of his continuous physical life; or that there exists some true Ḥadīth in which the expression *Tawaffī* has been differently interpreted in the case of Jesus[as] as connoting his physical life. If within one year God Almighty manifests no clear sign to prove that Maulavī Ṣāḥib had taken a false oath, that is to say, if he is not afflicted with some great calamity, I will repent immediately at his hand. Alas, despite my repeated requests, Miāń Ṣāḥib was prepared neither to debate the question nor to make the required affirmation on oath; nor did he restrain himself from denouncing me as a disbeliever....

It was only for this purpose that I bore all the expense and inconvenience of staying in Delhi for a whole month, and if Miāń Ṣāḥib had been ready for a debate why should I have evaded it? As the saying goes, truth has nothing to fear. I am still as ready for a debate on the subject of the death of Jesus[as] as I was then. If Miāń Ṣāḥib would agree to come to Lahore for this purpose, I would defray the expenses of his journey and can even make payment in advance....If he is not willing to attend the debate in person, the debate can be held in writing and he won't have to take undertake the journey. In short, I am willing to agree to whatever might be convenient to him and I await his reply....But remember my prediction that he will never agree to a debate, and if he does, he will be so humiliated that he will not be able to show his face anywhere.

[Āsmānī Faiṣlah, Rūḥānī Khazā'in, vol. 4 , pp. 315-316]

Let it be understood by all Muslims that it has been established beyond any doubt, according to the Holy

Qur'ān and Ḥadīth, that Jesus son of Mary (peace be upon him) died on earth after fulfilling the span of his life in accordance with the verse:

فِيْهَا تَحْيَوْنَ وَفِيْهَا تَمُوْتُوْنَ [247]

It is further clear on the authority of sixteen verses of the Holy Qur'ān, and a number of Aḥādīth contained in *Bukhārī*, *Muslim* and other authentic compilations, that those who die are never sent back to dwell in this world, nor is anyone subjected to death twice, nor does the Holy Qur'ān lay down any law of inheritance for anyone who might return to earth after death. Yet some of the divines insist that Jesus son of Mary has not died but was raised bodily to heaven, and is alive in his physical body. They dare to suggest that the expression *Tawaffī*, which has been applied to Jesus[as] in the Holy Qur'ān, does not connote death, rather it means taking full possession of both body and soul. But this interpretation is utterly false. In the idiom of the Holy Qur'ān, this expression is consistently employed to connote taking possession of the soul and the death of the body. The same idiom is employed in all the Aḥādīth and sayings of the Holy Prophet (peace and blessings of Allah be upon him.)

Ever since the Arabian peninsula has been populated and the Arabic language has come into use, there is not a single ancient or modern instance of the expression *Tawaffī* being employed taking possession of the body. Whenever this expression has been employed for the description of the action of God Almighty in relation to a human being, it has always connoted death and taking

---

[247] 'Therein shall you live, and therein shall you die.'—Al-A'rāf, 7:26 **[Publisher]**

possession of the soul. No lexicon and no Arabic saying contradicts this. There is not the slightest room for any different interpretation. If anyone should cite a single instance from the Holy Qur'ān or from the Aḥādīth or from ancient or modern poetry, or ode, or prose of the Arabs, wherein the expression *Tawaffī* has been employed when indicating the action of God Almighty concerning a human being, as connoting anything beyond death and taking possession of the soul, that is to say, as connoting the taking possession of the body also, I call God to witness that I shall hand over to such a person one thousand rupees in cash and also acknowledge that he possesses expert knowledge of Ḥadīth and the Holy Qur'ān.

[Izāla-e-Auhām, Rūḥānī Khazā'in, vol. 3, pp. 602-603]

A Misguided Assertion of Ḥāfiẓ Muḥammad Yūsuf Challenged

In Lahore, Ḥāfiẓ Muḥammad Yūsuf Ṣāḥib, Ḍila'dār of Canals, under the false doctrines of ignorant and misguided clerics, … has stated confidently that if anyone falsely claims to be a Prophet or a Messenger or a commissioned one by God, and thus seeks to mislead people, he can survive such imposture for twenty-three years and even more. What he means to say is that the survival of such an impostor for more than twenty-three years cannot be a proof of his truth. He also stated that he can cite the names of many people who made such false claims and continued to assert for more than twenty-three years that they were recipients of God's word....

Through this announcement, I demand from Ḥāfiẓ Muḥammad Yūsuf Ṣāḥib to cite such an instance as promised in his signed document. I know for certain that this principle, which is set out in the Holy Qur'ān by God

Himself, can never be contravened....

It is for this reason that I have made this public announcement together with an offer of five hundred rupees as an award for the citation of a single instance to the contrary, and I am prepared to deposit this amount in any government bank in advance. If Ḥāfiẓ Muḥammad Yūsuf Ṣāḥib and those who think like him, whose names I have mentioned in this announcement, will cite an instance with adequate proof in accordance with the Holy Qur'ān, in which a person who falsely claimed to be a Prophet or a Messenger or a commissioned one of God, continued to publish his alleged revelations for more than twenty-three years, I shall pay such a person the sum of five hundred rupees in cash. They will be at liberty to cite such an instance from anywhere in the world within a fortnight of the publication of this announcement.

[Arba'īn, No. III, Rūḥānī Khazā'in, vol. 17, pp. 387-402]

Submitting the Matter to the Judge of Judges

O Ye revered clerics though the falsity of your notion that that you are the true believers and I am a disbeliever, that you are truthful and I am a liar, that you follow Islām and I go against it, that you are the accepted ones of God and I am rejected by Him, that you are the heirs of Paradise and I am condemned to hell, has been established by the Holy Qur'ān in the estimation of those who are given to reflection, and the readers of this book can well understand who is right and who is wrong, yet there is another way whereby distinction can be made between those who are true and those who are false, and between the accepted ones of God and the rejected ones. It has always been the way of God that if an accepted one and a rejected one both beseech God Almighty for heavenly help,

He certainly helps the accepted one and makes His acceptance of him manifest in a manner that is beyond human power. Since you claim to be in the right, and some of you like Maulavī Moḥy-ud-Dīn and 'Abd-ur-Raḥmān Ṣāḥib of Lakhoke and Miāń 'Abd-ul-Ḥaq Ṣāḥib of Ghaznī have denounced me as a disbeliever and as one condemned to hell, it is incumbent upon you to find out through this heavenly method who is designated as the accepted one in heaven and who is the rejected one. I agree that you should supplicate to the Judge of judges for a period of ten weeks that if you are in the right you should be given a sign of your truth or you should be authorized to make a great prophecy or granted a sign as can proceed only from the righteous. On my side I shall also do the same. God the Beneficent and the Powerful has assured me that, if you accept this challenge, victory will be mine….

Whatever belonged to us, belong now to the Beloved;
Today, we belong to the Beloved, and He belongs to us.
Thanks be to Allah, we found that Priceless Ruby;
It matters not if the nation's hearts have turned to stone.

[Izāla-e-Auhām, Rūḥānī Khazā'in, vol. 3, pp. 457-458]

If those among Muslims who are called hermits, religious elders and sufis continue to persist in their denial of my claim and do not accept the truth that I am the Promised Messiah, then there is an easy way of settling the issue between us. Let a person who does not accept this claim of mine, and considers himself a recipient of revelation, call me to a meeting at Batāla, Amritsar or Lahore, and we should both supplicate the Divine that a grand sign, which is beyond human power and above the manipulation of normal human capacity, may be manifested within the period of one year in support of the one of us who is true in the estimation of God. That sign should be such as to influence people of diverse temperaments through its splendour and power and brilliance, whether by way of prophecy or some miracle resembling the miracles of the Prophets.

Thereafter the one whose extraordinary prophecy is fulfilled or in whose support a grand sign is manifested within the period of one year with such majesty as is not equalled in the case of his opponent, would be accepted as true. For the sake of removing dissension from among the ranks of Muslims the one who is vanquished must give up his opposition to the other, and should pledge spiritual allegiance to him and should fear God Whose wrath is a consuming fire.

[Tiryāq-ul-Qulūb, Rūḥānī Khazā'in, vol. 15, p. 170]

It has been revealed to me that, on account of the knowledge granted to me through visions and revelations, I have supremacy over those among the Muslims who claim to be the recipients of revelation. These people should stand up against me. If they are found superior to me in respect of Divine support, heavenly grace and signs, I would submit to being carved up with whatever dagger they might choose. If they dare not compete with me in this manner, then those of them who have denounced me as a disbeliever and whom I am addressing under Divine direction, should publicly state in writing and announce that if they witness any extraordinary sign they would accept my claim without hesitation. I am ready for such a test and my Beneficent God is with me; but I have been directed that, for this purpose, I should challenge only the leaders from among those who denounce me as a disbeliever and that I should enter into a prayer-duel only with them. It should, however, be remembered that they will not stand forth against me as their hearts stand in awe of the truth, and they are well aware of their wrongdoing and transgression.

[Ā'īna-e-Kamālāt-e-Islām, Rūḥānī Khazā'in, vol. 5, pp. 348-349]

Challenge to Reach a Conclusive Settlement

It is a wonderful manifestation of the Divine that the more the opposing Maulavīs try to reduce our numbers and the more they try to stop people from joining our Movement, the more of them join it, so that we are now well in our thousands. This process goes on daily with increasing speed and God Almighty goes on pulling out good plants from the other side and planting them in our garden. We enjoy Divine support increasingly, on the basis of authority, reason and heavenly testimony. If the opposing clerics still imagine that they are in the right and we are in the wrong, and that God is with them and that we are under the curse and wrath of God, then, besides the fact that we have already furnished them with conclusive proofs, we are willing to provide them with another opportunity of distinguishing between truth and falsehood. If they truly consider themselves in the right and imagine that we are in the wrong, and they desire that the truth may be made manifest and falsehood may disappear, then let them adopt the following method. They should pray:

> Lord, if this person, who claims to be the Promised Messiah, is false and a liar and an impostor in Your estimation, and if we are right in our stand and are truthful and are Your accepted servants, then do manifest within one year some extraordinary sign in our support.

On my side I shall supplicate:

> Lord, if You know that I am from You and am truly the Promised Messiah, then do You manifest another sign by way of prophecy in my support within one year.

Thereafter if a sign is manifested in their support and nothing is manifested in my support I will be considered a liar. But if something is manifested in my support and something of the same type is manifested in their support, in that event also I shall be accounted false. But if within one year a clear sign is manifested in my support and none is manifested in their support, I shall be deemed true.

The condition will be that if the opposing party is found to be true according to the explanation set out above, I shall give up my claims and shall burn all those books of mine in which my claims and revelations are set out, for if God should prove me false I cannot regard those books as pure and holy....If God does not desire to bestow honour on me let there be a curse on me if I act contrary to that which I have just stated. But if, in accord with the explanations set out above, God proves me true, then Muḥammad Ḥussain of Batāla, 'Abd-ul-Ḥaq and 'Abdul Jabbār of Ghaznī, and Rashīd Aḥmad of Gangoha should repent at my hands, confirm the truth of my claims, and join my Jamā'at so that this discussion may be put to an end. Internal feuds have ruined the Muslims. This will be a simple and straightforward verdict of God which will not leave any room for either side to prevaricate.

[Majmū'ah Ishtihārāt, vol. 2, p. 411]

A Sincere Appeal to All Muslims of India

To all the Muslims of India, i.e., to all the different sects of Islām which are to be found in India.

Brethren in faith and followers of the Seal of the Prophets (peace and blessings of Allah be upon him!) Although I have already addressed many writings to the clerics and sufis, and have conveyed my message to them fully, it has occurred to me that I should make a general announcement to convey my message clearly to you so that I may discharge my responsibility fully in this respect. Brethren, I wish to convey to you that I indeed am the Promised Reformer, whose advent was to take place at the beginning of the fourteenth century and about whom a large number of righteous people, who were recipients of Divine revelations, had foretold that he would be the Promised Messiah…

Should you be in doubt in this respect, I would suggest to you an easy way of settling this matter: Every one of you should ask his spiritual guide to stand forth in opposition to me in the matter of the manifestation of signs of righteousness. Be sure, in such a case that spiritual guide would be humiliated even more than Bal‘am was humiliated when he stood against Moses[as]. If he does not wish to stand forth in opposition and seeks the truth, God Almighty will, at his request and on his coming to me, manifest some sign for him provided that, in that case, he is ready to join my Jamā‘at. If, after the publication of this announcement, your spiritual preceptors and religious leaders and jurist do not desist from speaking ill of me and denouncing me as a disbeliever, and do not accept my truth and continue to evade such confrontation as I have suggested, then take note that I call God Almighty to witness that they will be humiliated by Him.

[Majmū‘ah Ishtihārāt, vol. 1, pp. 436-438]

Gentlemen! Listen carefully to what I have to say. I state on oath, in the name of Allah the Glorious, that if Ḥaḍrat Maulavī Muḥammad Ḥussain Ṣāḥib would address himself to God Almighty for forty days in opposition to me, and would manifest such heavenly signs or such realities of the unseen as I might manifest, I would agree that he may slay me with the weapon of his choice and mulct me in such sum as he might determine.

> A Warner came to the world and the world did not accept him; but God will accept him and will establish his truth with powerful assaults.

[Al-Ḥaq, Mubāḥatha Ludhiāna, Rūḥānī Khazā'in, vol. 4, p. 124]

I announce in the name of Him in whose hand lies my life, that if you people clear your minds and wish to see another Divine sign, then the All-Powerful God, without being subject to your demand, has the power to manifest a sign out of His own will and authority. I am certain that if you repent sincerely, and demand a sign from me and promise God that if some extraordinary sign, which is beyond human power, is manifested, you will discard all ill-will and rancour, and, seeking only the pleasure of God, will make the pledge of allegiance to me, surely God Almighty will manifest some sign, for He is Merciful and Beneficent. But I do not have the choice to appoint two or three days for the manifestation of a sign or to follow your desires. It is at the choice of God Almighty to appoint whatever date pleases Him....

For the adoption of this method it will be necessary that at least forty leading Maulavīs like Maulavī Muḥammad Ḥussain Ṣāḥib of Batāla, Maulavī Nadhīr Ḥussain Ṣāḥib of Delhi, Maulavī 'Abdul Jabbār Ṣāḥib of Ghaznī, now of Amritsar, Maulavī Rashīd Aḥmad Ṣāḥib of Ghangoha, and Maulavī Pīr Mehr 'Alī Shāh Ṣāḥib of Golrah should publish an agreement in a newspaper attested by fifty respectable Muslims that if a sign, which is truly extraordinary, is manifested, they will give up their opposition out of the fear of God the Glorious, and will make the pledge of allegiance to me.

Should this method be unacceptable…there is another simpler and easier method….It is that, purely out of fear of God Almighty and out of mercy for the Muslims, you should call a meeting in Batāla, Amritsar or Lahore. This meeting should be attended, as far as may be possible, by a large number of respected divines and men of the world. I shall also attend with a number of my followers. Then all of them should supplicate thus:

> Lord, if You know that this person is an impostor and is not from You, and is neither the Promised Messiah nor the Mahdī, then may You remove this cause of dissension from among the Muslims and safeguard Islām and the Muslims against his mischief, as You did safeguard the Muslims against the mischief of Musailama Kadhdhāb and Aswad 'Ansī by removing them from the world, but if he is from You and our minds and intellects are at fault, then may You Powerful One bestow understanding upon us so that we may not be ruined, and make manifest such matters and signs in his support that we should be satisfied that he is from You.

When this supplication is made, my followers and I will say Āmīn aloud. After that, I shall pray, holding in my hand all those revelations that I have set out….I will pray as follows:

> Lord, if these revelations, which are mentioned in this pamphlet that I hold in my hand, and on the basis of

> which I consider myself the Promised Messiah and Mahdī, and hold Jesus[as] to be dead, are not Your words, and if, in Your estimation, I am a liar and impostor and dajjāl who is the cause of dissension among the Muslims, and if I am under Your wrath, I supplicate You earnestly that within one year from this date You cross out my name from among the living and ruin all my enterprises and wipe out my every sign from the earth. But if I am from You and these revelations which I hold in my hand are from You and I am a recipient of Your grace, then O Mighty Benefactor, cause my Jamā'at to grow in an extraordinary manner in the coming year and bestow extraordinary blessings upon us, and bless my life and send down Your heavenly support.

When this supplication is finished, all opponents should say Āmīn. It would be proper that everyone should come to this meeting for the purpose of prayer with pure and serene hearts and not in a spirit of victory or defeat. This prayer should not be considered a *Mubāhalah* [prayer-duel] because its benefit or harm is limited to me alone….The prayer should be offered with concentration and great earnestness. Sincere prayer finds acceptance with God. If all my enterprise is not in the cause of God and is an imposture and a show, the prayers of representative Muslims will soon be heard. But if my Movement is heavenly and has been initiated by God Himself, my supplication will be accepted. O you men of honour! Respond to this request of mine. There is no need for a large gathering, it would be enough if forty representative divines were to take part in the prayer. But they should not be less than forty, for this number has a blessed connection with the acceptance of prayer.

[Arba'īn, No. II Rūḥānī Khazā'in, vol. 17, pp. 374-378]

Challenge to those who Claim Divine Revelation

...If someone who claims to be the recipient of revelation is not satisfied with any of these signs, he is free to adopt another method. He should, on his side, continue to publish his revelations for a period of one year in two newspapers of his people, and, on my side, I shall publish all that is revealed to me by God Almighty in two newspapers of my Jamā'at. The only condition which is binding on both sides is that each of the revelations published should relate to matters unseen and such as are beyond human power. After one year, the judges will decide whose prophecies have been fulfilled and which side has the larger number of the required type of revelations to its credit. If my opponent is declared supreme in this test, I will be considered false; otherwise it will be incumbent upon my opponents at every step to fear God Almighty, give up denouncing me as false and denying my truth and not to ruin their afterlife by opposing one who has been sent by God.

[Ḥaqīqat-ul-Waḥī, Rūḥānī Khazā'in, vol. 22, pp. 400-401]

Holy Qur'ān — A Sign of the Living God

I once again remind every seeker after truth that I have been given signs and heavenly testimonies of the truth of Islām of which our blind divines are unaware. I have been sent to establish that Islām alone is the living faith. I have been bestowed such miracles as cannot be matched by the followers of other religions and by my Muslim opponents. I can demonstrate to every opponent that the **Holy Qur'ān**, by virtue of its teachings, philosophy, deep insights and perfect composition is a far greater miracle than that of Moses[as] and is hundreds of times superior to the miracles of Jesus.

I say again and again, loud and clear, that true love for the **Holy Qur'ān** and the Holy Prophet (peace and blessings of Allah be on him), and following them with sincerity, enables a man to perform miracles. Such a perfect man is given knowledge of the unseen and no follower of any other religion can match him in spiritual blessings. **I have personal experience of these matters** and I see that, except Islām, all religions, their gods, and their followers, are dead, and it is not possible to establish a living relationship with God Almighty except by accepting Islām.

O ye foolish ones! What do you gain by worshipping the dead, and what pleasure do you derive from eating carrion? **Come to me and I will tell you where and with whom the Living God is. He is with Islām.** In this age, Islām is the Mount Sinai of Moses[as] where God speaks. The God Who used to converse with Prophets and became silent is now revealing His words upon the heart of **a Muslim**. Does none of you wish to test this and accept the truth if he finds it? What are you holding on to: a corpse wrapped up in a shroud? What more do you possess? A handful of dust? Can that corpse be God? Can it answer you? Come forward. Shame on you if you fail to respond and compare this decomposed corpse with my God.

I tell you that before forty days have passed, He will put you to shame through heavenly signs. Polluted are the hearts that do not approach with true intent and yet go on denying, and unclean are the temperaments that lean towards mischief and not towards the pursuit of truth.

O clerics who oppose me! If you be in doubt, come and stay in my company for a few days. If you do not witness

God's signs, then seize me and treat me as a liar. I have furnished you with full proofs, and until you refute these proofs you have no answer. The signs of God are descending like rain. Is there no one among you who would come to me with a true heart? Not even one?

> **A Warner came to the world and the world did not accept him. But God will accept him and will establish his truth with powerful assaults.**

Peace be on him who follows the guidance.

[Anjām-e-Ātham, Rūḥānī Khazā'in, vol. 11, pp. 345-347]

This is to announce that the author of *Brāhīn-e-Aḥmadiyyah* has been commissioned by the All-Powerful One, glory be to Him, to strive for the reform of mankind in perfect humility, meekness and courtesy in the manner of the Israeli Prophet of Nazareth, and to lead those who are unaware of the straight path to the path along which a person attains true salvation and experiences in this very life the qualities of heavenly life, and the lights of acceptance by God and His love. It is for this purpose that the book *Brāhīn-e-Aḥmadiyyah* has been compiled....As the compilation of the book will take a long time, it has been decided that—to bring the argument to a conclusion—at this stage a copy of this letter...be despatched to the revered Christian padres of Punjab, India, Britain and other countries which can be reached by the mail, who are considered outstanding and exalted among their respective peoples, and it will also be despatched to leading Brahmus, Āryās, rationalists and respected Maulavīs (who deny miracles and for this reason consider the author misguided.)

This plan has been adopted not by the author's own thinking and deliberation, but under the Divine permission. I have been given Divine assurance that the addressees of this letter, who do not turn to the truth after receiving it, will be accountable to God and will be deemed to have been vanquished. This printed letter is sent to you because you are well known among your people, and are held in respect and have a following. It is hoped that, because of your learning and the high esteem in which you are held, you will pay attention, for the sake of God, to the contents of this letter and will strive to seek the truth. If you do not pay attention to this letter the author will be deemed to have discharged his duty, and a full account of the despatch of this letter to you by registered post and your indifference to it will be published in part V of the book.

The message of this letter, which I am commissioned to convey to you, is that Islām alone is the true faith that is in accord with Divine will, and that the Holy Qur'ān is the true Divine Book which alone is safeguarded and must be followed. The truth of Islām and of the Holy Qur'ān is supported not only by logical arguments, but also by testimony of heavenly signs and prophecies, which can be witnessed by a seeker after truth who is prepared to spend some time in the company of this humble self, the author of Brāhīn-e-Aḥmadiyyah. Should you doubt the truth of Islām or of these heavenly signs, you are invited, as a sincere seeker after truth, to come to Qādiān and witness the signs by staying in the company of the author for one year, on the condition, which would be a guarantee of search for the truth, that having witnessed heavenly signs you will announce from Qādiān itself your acceptance of Islām or, at least, your testimony of having witnessed these extraordinary signs. If you come with this purpose in mind, you will certainly witness heavenly signs, if God Almighty so wills. This is a Divine promise that is bound to be fulfilled. If you do not come, you will be accountable to God, and after waiting for three months an account of your indifference will be set out in part V of the book. If you come and stay for a year and witness no heavenly sign, you will be paid compensation at the rate of two hundred rupees a month. If you consider this sum inadequate, we shall agree to pay you such amount as you may consider adequate, as a compensation for your wasted time or as a fine for our not keeping our promise, provided that it is within our means. Anyone who requires compensation must first seek our consent by means of a registered letter beforehand. A person who does not seek compensation will not need such permission. If you cannot come in person, you may appoint, as your representative, someone whose observation you can trust and can accept as your own, to come in your place; but on the condition that, after the confirmation of your representative, you will not delay your acceptance of Islām or your confirmation of the extraordinary signs. You can set down your announcement on a simple sheet of paper, and a few respectable followers of different religions should testify it to. It will be published in a number of Urdu and English newspapers. We are willing to register our liability to pay compensation as set out above with a guarantee of a proportionate amount of our property.

[Majmū'ah Ishtihārāt, vol. 1, pp. 20-22]

For Followers of Revealed Books who Deny the Truth of the Holy Qur'ān

I, the author of *Brāhīn-e-Aḥmadiyyah*, announce an award of ten thousand rupees on the following conditions. This announcement is addressed to all the fol-

lowers of such religions as deny the truth of the Holy Qur'ān and the Holy Prophet Muḥammad, the Chosen One (peace and blessings of Allah be upon him.) To win the award, a candidate should set forth from the revealed book in which he believes, all the arguments and proofs which we have entered in this book in support of the truth of the Holy Qur'ān and the Seal of the Prophets (peace and blessings of Allah be upon him), all of which are derived from the Holy Qur'ān itself. If he is unable to set out an equal number of arguments and proofs from the revealed book of his religion, he should set out at least one half or one third or one quarter or one fifth of them. Should he be unable to set out anything at all matching our arguments and proofs he should refute our arguments and proofs one by one. Then on the certification of three just minded persons, agreed to by the parties, that the conditions set out above have been fulfilled, I shall, without hesitation, transfer to the successful candidate my property worth ten thousand rupees. It must, however, be made clear that if any of the opponents is unable to set out the required number of arguments and proofs from the revealed book in which he believes, or is unable to offer at least one fifth of the arguments and proofs, as required in the announcement, he would have to declare in writing that he is unable to do so because of the imperfection or unreasonableness of that book. If he sets out the required arguments and proofs from that revealed book numbering one fifth of our arguments and proofs, he would have to set out one half, one third, one quarter or one fifth of each of type of argument that we have set out and not merely one half, one third, one fourth,

one fifth of the total number set out by us.

[Brāhīn-e-Aḥmadiyyah, Rūḥānī Khazā'in, vol. 1, pp. 24-31]

Evidence in the form of Countless Signs

Up to this day... Friday 22nd September 1893... more than three thousand signs have been manifested through me, which have been witnessed by hundreds of people. Thousands of Hindus, Christians and followers of other religions have witnessed the fulfilment of some of my prophecies....There are about sixteen thousand people in India, Britain, Germany, France, Russia and Italy, who include Pundits, Jewish scribes, leaders of Zoroastrians, Christian Ministers, Clerics and Bishops, to whom registered letters have been sent to the effect that Islām alone is the true religion and all other religions have drifted far away from the truth. These letters also contained an offer that if anyone of our opponents doubts my statement, he should come and stay with me for one year and witness the signs of Islām at my hands. If I turned out to be wrong, he would be paid compensation at the rate of two hundred rupees a month. And if I am proven right I would demand nothing from him except that he should become a Muslim. I even offered to deposit the amount of compensation in advance, but no one paid any attention to my offer....

The validity of my statement might be determined by inquiring from some Christian minister whether he has received such a registered letter conveying the message of Islām or not....Letters and announcements containing the message of Islām have also been despatched to the members of British Parliament and Prince of Wales.... as testified by postal receipts I have in my possession.

[Shahādat-ul-Qur'ān, Rūḥānī Khazā'in, vol. 6, pp. 369-371]

I have been informed categorically that if any opponent of Islām confronts me, I will be supreme and he will be humiliated. Why then do those who call themselves Muslims and doubt my truth not arrange for some Christian minister to stand up against me. Let them tell some Christian minister or a Hindu pundit that I am an impostor and assure him that no harm will come to him if he confronts me. Then God Almighty will Himself decide between us. If I am proved to be wrong I will transfer all the property that I have inherited to such Christian minister or Hindu Pundit. If he turns out to be false, I will require nothing from him but that he should become a Muslim.

I make this offer in full sincerity and affirm in the name of Allah the Glorious, that I am ready for such a contest. I have issued twelve thousand announcements to this effect but no pundit or minister has come forward in good faith. What greater proof can there be of my truth than that I am always ready for such a contest? If the opposing pundit or minister is not ready to show any sign, he can simply announce through some newspaper that he is ready to witness such a sign and that if such a sign does appear and he is not able to match it, he will immediately accept Islām. I will be more than willing to abide by such a plan. Let someone from among the Muslims step forward with the courage to test, in this manner, the truth of a person whom they denounce as a disbeliever and irreligious person. Then witness the resulting drama.

[Ā'īna-e-Kamālāt-e-Islām, Rūḥānī Khazā'in, vol. 5, p.348]

Manifestation of the Power of the Living God, Honour of the Holy Prophet[sa], and Truth of the Holy Qur'ān

One of the powerful qualities of the Holy Qur'ān is that its true follower is able to work miracles and manifest extraordinary signs in such large numbers that no one can match him in this respect. I too claim that if all my opponents from east and west come together and compete with me in the matter of signs and miracles, I will, by the grace of God Almighty, and through the power bestowed by Him, be supreme over all of them. This supremacy will not be due to any superior spiritual power of mine, but because God has desired that I should furnish proof of the great power of His Holy Word, the Qur'ān, and of the spiritual power and high rank of His Messenger Muḥammad, the Chosen One (peace and blessings of Allah be upon him.) He has of His grace, and not on account of any merit of mine, enabled me to follow His Glorious Prophet and His Supreme Word and to love them both. I believe in the Word of God, the Holy Qur'ān, which is a manifestation of Divine power. God Almighty has bestowed all this upon me in accordance with the promises held out in the Holy Qur'ān:

لَهُمُ الْبُشْرٰى فِي الْحَيٰوةِ الدُّنْيَا [248]

اَيَّدَهُمْ بِرُوْحٍ مِّنْهُ [249]

يَجْعَلْ لَّكُمْ فُرْقَانًا [250]

[Chashma-e-Ma'rifat, Rūḥānī Khazā'in, vol. 23, pp. 409-410]

---

[248] 'For them are glad tidings in the present life.'—Yūnus,10:65 **[Publisher]**

[249] 'Whom He has strengthened with inspiration from Himself.'—Al-Mujādalah, 58:23 **[Publisher]**

[250] 'He will grant you a distinction.'—Al-Anfāl, 8:30 **[Publisher]**

If all nations of the world should unite against me and a test were made to whom God reveals the unseen, whose prayers does He accept, whom does He help and for whom does He manifest great signs, I affirm, in the name of God, that I would emerge supreme. Is there anyone who will step forth against me for such a trial? God has bestowed thousands of signs upon me to let my opponents know that Islām is indeed the true faith. I seek no honour for myself, but only the honour of that for which I have been sent.

[Ḥaqīqat-ul-Waḥī, Rūḥānī Khazā'in, vol. 22, pp. 181-182]

A living faith is one through which we can find the Living God, and the Living God is He Who sends revelation to us directly or, at least, enables us to meet a person who is the recipient of direct revelation. I, therefore, convey to the whole world the good news that the God of Islām is such a Living God. Those with whom no one can now converse, and whose signs no one can see, are dead, not gods.... A true religion can never become a mere tale, and Islām is a true religion. I intend to demonstrate the truth of Islām to every person, whether he is a Christian, Āryā, Jew or Brahmu. Is there anyone who wants to see the Living God? We do not worship the dead. Our God is Living and helps us with His revelation, His converse and His heavenly signs. If there is a single Christian in the world who is a sincere seeker after truth, let him compare his dead god with our Living God. I affirm truly that forty days would be enough for such a test....If I am found to be false I will accept every punishment. But this test will be through prayer. The person whose God is True will doubtlessly emerge truthful. God will certainly make me supreme in such a contest....I am willing to agree to any reasonable condition for such a test. I stand in the field of contest and proclaim that the God of Islām is the only Living God. The Christians have only a dead god in their hands. Let the person who wishes to test this, come forward and stand up against me.

[Majmū'ah Ishtihārāt, vol. 2, pp. 311-313]

One method with which I have fulfilled my duty vis-à-vis all opposing religions, is that I have proclaimed publicly that heavenly signs, Divine blessings and God's powerful works are found only in Islām and that there is no religion which can stand up to Islām in respect of such signs. God Almighty has sent me forward for the purpose of refuting all opponents. I know for certain that there is no one among the Hindus, Christians and Sikhs who can compete with me in respect of heavenly signs and blessings and acceptance of prayers. Obviously, the only living faith would be the one which is supported by heavenly signs and is distinguished by the light that shines upon it, and that faith is none other than Islām. Is there anyone among the Christians, Sikhs or Hindus who can challenge me in this respect? It is enough proof of my truth that **no one can stand up to me.** Now you can satisfy yourselves in any way you want.

[Tiryāq-ul-Qulūb, Rūḥānī Khazā'in, vol. 15, pp. 248-249]

Refutation of the Āryās' False Doctrines

This book, *Surmah Chashm-e-Āryā*, has been written for the purpose of the debate with Lāla Murlīdhar Ṣāḥib, drawing master, of Hoshiārpur, and it utterly refutes the false doctrines of the Vedas. It has been written with the certainty that no Āryā can refute it, as falsehood can never withstand the truth. If any Āryā gentleman still considers the principles and doctrines of the Vedas which have been refuted in this book to be true, and believes in the Vedas and their principles as Divine revelation, I call upon him, in the name of Ishwar, to write a refutation of my book and receive five hundred rupees as an award. This award will be made on the certificate of an arbitrator who should be a Christian minister or a Brahmu.

I would even agree if, after the publication of the refutation of my book by such an Āryā, Munshī Jīwan Dās Ṣāḥib, Secretary Āryā Samāj, Lahore, who is the most respected gentleman from among the Āryās of our neighbourhood, would attend along with his sons a public meeting of the Muslim, Āryā and Christian divines, and affirm on oath that all the criticism raised in my book *Surmah Chashm-e-Āryā*, which he has read carefully and understood, has been totally refuted in the reply of the Āryā writer, and that if his affirmation is not made in full sincerity and truth, may he and his sons, who are present with him, be called to account in this very life. If this is done, the writer of the refutation would be awarded five hundred rupees in cash simply on the testimony of the said Munshī Ṣāḥib. If the Munshī Ṣāḥib does not suffer from any ill effects within one year in consequence of his oath, the Āryās would be entitled to claim that he had made his affirmation sincerely according to his knowledge and understanding.

Peace be on him who follows the guidance.

Announced by:
Ghulām Aḥmad
Qādiān,
Distt. Gurdāspūr, Punjab.

[Surmah Chashm-e-Āryā, Rūḥānī Khazā'in, vol. 2, pp. 321-322]

Announcement for a Forty Day Prayer Vigil

گــرچــه هــر کس زرهِ لاف بیانے دارد

صــادق آنست که از صدق نشانے دارد [251]

Those who have read my previous announcements will be aware of my announcement that if a respectable Āryā gentleman, Christian minister or some other gentleman out of the opponents of Islām were to come and stay with me at Qādiān for one year, and did not witness any heavenly sign during that time, I would pay him two thousand four hundred rupees by way of compensation.

I despatched this offer by registered post to all the principal Christian ministers and leading Āryā gentlemen, but none of them came to Qādiān. In the case of Munshī Inderman Ṣāḥib, I sent that amount in cash to Lahore to satisfy him that the money would be available for the award, but he slipped away to Farīdkot. One gentleman by the name of Lekh Rām of Peshawar did come to Qādiān, and he was repeatedly invited to stay here for one year on payment of his expenses at the rate of twice the salary which he received when he was a government servant at Peshawar; and in the end it was even suggested that if he could not stay at Qādiān for a whole year he should at least stay for forty days. He rejected both propositions, and yet made several false allegations in his announcements. In *Surmah Chashm-e-Āryā,* he has again been invited to come and stay at Qādiān for forty days. Everyone can read it there.

The the purpose of this announcement is to carry the

---

[251] *Anyone can issue a statement by way of boasting,*
But truthful is the one who produces a true sign. **[Publisher]**

matter to its limit vis-à-vis Munshī Jīwan Dās Ṣāḥib who, from among the Āryās, appears to be a most decent and gentle person, and Lāla Murlīdhar Ṣāḥib, drawing master, of Hoshiārpur, who I also believe to be one of the better type of Āryās, and Munshī Inderman Ṣāḥib of Murādabad who is, as it were, the joint founder of the Āryā Samāj and Mr. 'Abdullāh Ātham, formerly Extra Assistant Commissioner from Amritsar who is a decent and gentle minded Christian, the Reverend 'Imād-ud-Dīn of Amritsar, and Reverend Thākar Dās Ṣāḥib, the author of *Iẓhār-e-'Īswī.*

I now reduce the period of one year to forty days on the condition that the gentleman who is willing to take up the challenge should stay with me throughout the period of forty days at Qādiān or at any other place where I may be residing. If, during that time, I put forward no extraordinary prophecy, or the prophecy proves to be wrong, or, if it is not proved wrong but the gentleman is able to match it, he will immediately be awarded five hundred rupees. But if such a prophecy is fulfilled, the gentleman making the trial would have to accept Islām…. If the gentleman has doubts about the prophecy, or if he thinks it is only a matter of guess work, he may himself make such a prophecy within forty days and prove that it has been fulfilled. If he fails to do so and my prophecy is fulfilled, then he will have to accept Islām. All this will be committed to writing and attested to by both sides.

These gentlemen are granted three months from the date of the publication of this book, i.e., 20th September 1886, within which to respond to this invitation. If no fair response is received from any of them during this time, it will be understood that they have evaded the contest.

Peace be on those who follow the guidance.

Announced by: Ghulām Aḥmad From Qādiān,

Distt. Gurdāspūr, Punjab.

[Surmah Chashm-e-Āryā, Rūḥānī Khazā'in, vol. 2, pp. 309-310]

محال است سعدی که راه صفا

تواں یافت جز در پئے مصطفےٰ[252]

For the Careful Attention of Sardār Rāj Indar Singh

I have received your pamphlet which you have entitled '*Remedy for the Obsession of the Qādiānī*'. Not knowing what to do in answer to your abuse, insult, and all the calumnies you have directed against our lord and master, Muḥammad Muṣṭafā, Aḥmad Mujtabā (peace and blessings of Allah be upon him), I commit this matter to the Mighty and Powerful One, Who is protective of the honour of his loved ones. I feel all the more sorry for you in view of the fact that my book *Sat Bachan* was couched in terms of extreme respect and courtesy, and I had described Bābā Nānak in reverent terms, for which you have ill requited me....

You have heaped vile abuse upon the Holy Loved One of God who, for the sake of the honour and glory of God, did not value his own life as more than the life of an insect and endured a thousand deaths in that cause, and you have denigrated him in various ways. I had not imagined that there were such people among the Sikhs. The sun, in your estimation, appears as a thing of no value. O ignorant one, you have slighted the light that illumined the

---

[252] *Sa'dī, it is impossible that the right path;*
Be obtained except in the footsteps of the Muṣṭafā[sa]. **[Publisher]**

world at a time when it had sunk in darkness, and revived it after it was dead. All Prophethoods were established through him.... Hearken! I bear witness that Islām is the bright religion that manifests Divine support all the time. How great is the Messenger from whom we receive light afresh, and how exalted is the Prophet for whose love we perceive the holy spirit dwelling within us. That is how our supplications are accepted and we are able to work wonders. We experience the Living God in this faith. All other faiths are but the worship of the dead.

Where are the worshippers of the dead? Can they speak? Where are the worshippers of creatures? Can they stand up against us? Where are those who claimed mischievously that no prophecy of the Holy Prophet (peace and blessings of Allah be upon him) was ever fulfilled, and that he did not show any sign? They will all be put to shame and will seek to hide themselves but will find no place to hide; for the time has come when the light of the truth of Islām will strike the faces of the disbelievers.

I have seen Bābā Nānak Ṣāḥib twice in my visions. He acknowledged that he had obtained light from the same source. Vain talk and falsehood are the characteristics of those who swallow carrion; I have stated only that which I have seen. That is why I hold Bābā Nānak Ṣāḥib in high esteem, as I know that he drank from the same spring from which we drink. God Almighty knows that I speak out of the comprehension which has been bestowed upon me.

If you deny that Bābā Ṣāḥib was a Muslim and insist that the Holy Prophet (peace and blessings of Allah be upon him) was—God forbid—a wicked person, I will not attempt to persuade you through reason and logic, but I put forward another method of settlement through Divine intervention....

I propose that you should state on oath, in a public gathering, that Bābā Nānak was disgusted with Islām and esteemed the Prophet of Islām an evil man and that in truth he was (God forbid) wicked and vicious and was not a true Prophet. You should then supplicate:

> 'If these two statements of mine are false, then do You, O Mighty Kartār, inflict severe punishment on me for this impertinence within one year.'

Once you have made this statement and supplication, we shall deposit five hundred rupees wherever you may desire. If you are true in your affirmation, you will suffer no harm whatsoever within one year and the amount of five hundred rupees will be paid over to you, and I will be disgraced and humiliated. But, on the other hand, if some punishment does come down upon you, all Sikhs will be guided to the truth.

[Majmū'ah Ishtihārāt, vol. 2, pp. 394-399]

Announcement on the Death of Lekh Rām

I affirm truly and on oath that I bear no enmity towards any people; I only desire to correct them in their beliefs, as far as it is possible for me. If someone insults me, my complaint is addressed to God and not to any court. I am inspired with sympathy for all men. I do not know how and in what words to satisfy Āryā gentlemen that recourse to mischief is not my way. I am distressed by the loss of human life but I am also pleased with the fulfilment of a Divine prophecy. I am pleased only because I desire the good of mankind. I would wish them to reflect that it is not possible for a human being, on his own, to predict such an event so clearly years in advance.

My heart is both distressed and pleased at this moment. I am distressed that if Lekh Rām had, at least, restrained himself from vilification, I would have supplicated on his behalf and would have hoped that, even if he had been cut to pieces, he would have survived. Nothing is impossible for the God Whom I know. On the other hand, I am happy that the prophecy has been so clearly fulfilled….

If anyone still entertains doubts and considers me a party to the conspiracy of slaying Lekh Rām, as some Hindu papers have alleged, I have a very effective way of settling the whole matter: Such a person should state on oath in my presence that:

> I am certain that this man was party to the conspiracy of murder, or the murder was committed under his direction. If this statement of mine is not true, may You, O Mighty God, afflict me within the period of one year with such terrible torment as should not proceed from human hands nor be suspected of having been brought about by human design.

If thereafter such a person should survive for a whole year without being afflicted, as mentioned in the supplication, I may be deemed guilty and condemned to suffer the punishment of murder. If there is any Āryā who is brave enough to try and relieve the whole world of its suspicions, let him adopt this method, which is quite simple and straightforward.

[Sirāj-e-Munīr, Rūḥānī Khazā'in, vol. 12, pp. 28-29]

Real Test between Islām and Christianity

Both Christians and Muslims claim that they possess faith and live righteous lives. The question is, which of the two claims is true in the eyes of God, i.e., whose faith is acceptable to God and whose life is truly righteous, and, on the other hand, whose faith is mere satanic illusion and whose claim of righteous life is a blind fantasy. I believe that only that faith is true and acceptable to God which is supported by heavenly testimony and which shows signs of its acceptability to God; and only a life that is marked by heavenly signs can be accepted as righteous. If a mere claim were to be accepted, all people claim that many righteous ones have lived among them in the past and are present among them even today, and they cite examples of their works and miracles, the reality of which is difficult to ascertain. So if the Christians imagine that belief in the atonement of Jesus bestows holy faith and a righteous life, they should come forward and compete with me in the matter of acceptance of prayer and the manifestation of heavenly signs. If their lives are proven to be righteous by the testimony of heavenly signs, I then deserve every punishment and every type of disgrace.

I declare emphatically that, according to spiritual standards, the life of the Christians is utterly vile, and the God of Holiness, Who is the Lord of heaven and earth, is as disgusted with their beliefs as we are disgusted with decomposed carrion. If I am false in this assertion, and do not have the support of God in making it, then let them settle with me in a gentle and courteous manner. I affirm again that the Christians certainly do not enjoy that righteous life which descends from heaven and illumines the hearts. It is true, as I have already stated, that some of them are good by nature, as indeed are some people from other faiths, but such natural decency is not what I am talking about now; because such people are to be found among every people, including the low castes. What I am speaking of here is the heavenly and righteous life which is achieved through God's loving Word and descends from heaven and is accompanied by heavenly signs. Such life is not to be found among the Christians.

[Sirāj-ud-Dīn 'Īsā'ī ke Chār Sawāloń kā Jawāb, Rūḥānī Khazā'in, vol. 12, pp. 342-344]

I have repeatedly invited Christian ministers, not by the sword, but with courteous words, that they should come and settle with me which of the two, Jesus or our Holy Prophet Muṣṭafā (peace and blessings of Allah be upon him) is alive by virtue of his spiritual blessings and grace. If it were proved that Jesus is the son of God, I would, in the words of the Holy Qur'ān, be the first to worship him. O Ye Christian clerics of Europe and America, why do you raise such clamour? You know that I am known to millions of people. Come forward and compete with me. If, within one year, Divine signs and such prophecies as illustrate the Might and Power of God are manifested at your hands, and I am not proven to be your match, I shall acknowledge Jesus, son of Mary, to be God. But if the True God, Whom I know and you do not know, makes me supreme and your religion is proven to be bereft of heavenly signs, it will be incumbent upon you to accept Islām.

[Tiryāq-ul-Qulūb, Rūḥānī Khazā'in, vol. 15, p. 160]

I say with full confidence, and God Almighty knows that I am true in my claim, and my truth has been established by experience and a great number of signs, that if Jesus is the living God and is the redeemer of the bearers of his cross, and accepts their prayers (although his own prayer was not accepted), then let a Christian priest or monk come forward and exhibit some extraordinary sign with the help and support of Jesus. I stand in the field of contest and affirm truly that I can behold my God. He is always before me and with me. I proclaim that Jesus has no superiority over me as I represent the light of Muḥammad[sa], which always exhibits the signs of life. What more is needed?

[Malfūẓāt, vol. 3, pp. 124-125]

An Invitation to All Good People

The manner in which the Christian clergymen have raised varied objections against Islām, have changed their theories about, and have retrieved their earlier statements in great humiliation, is well known to anyone who has made a comprehensive review of the discussions between them and Muslim scholars. Their objections are of three types. One, such as are altogether false and are baseless calumnies; there is nothing to support their authenticity. Two, such as are based upon matters that are authentic, but are not open to objection or criticism; they have been made a target of criticism out of simple-mindedness, lack of reflection, or inner blindness. Three, such objections as are a mixture of that which is true and unobjectionable, and of that which is false and slanderous.... Some Āryās are also in the habit of presenting criticism based on a defective translation of some verse of the Holy Qur'ān, or based on some meaningless tale heard from some ignorant or hostile person....

It is in view of such criticism that I hereby make this announcement. All the principles and teachings set out in the Holy Qur'ān are replete with wisdom, insight and truth and not the least part of any of them is open to criticism. As the principles and teachings of every religion comprise hundreds of details and a discussion of all of them would take a long time, I would make this suggestion in good faith to those who deny the principles set out in the Holy Qur'ān. They should, after careful study, set forth two or three basic objections, derived from the verses of the Holy Qur'ān, which in their estimation are objections of the strongest, firmest and the highest grade, and which they believe cannot be refuted or dispelled. Those objections should be treated as the basic test, which would be decisive of all other objections. If the basic objections are totally refuted, smaller objections would automatically fall. If we are unable to reply in a satisfactory manner to those objections, and fail to establish that the principles and teachings which the opposite party upholds in contrast to the principles and teachings that are objected to are, in comparison, of much lower standard and are bereft of truth, then the opposite party will be paid the sum of fifty rupees in respect of each such objection. But if our opponent is proved false and fails to establish that the principles and teachings that he believes in possess all those qualities that are possessed by the principles and teachings of Islām, and which we shall set forth, he will have to become a Muslim. He will first have to agree to this condition on oath. Thereafter we shall publish a pamphlet refuting his objections. He would also be obliged to publish a pamphlet refuting our objections to the principles and teachings in which he believes. After the publication of both these pamphlets, a decision shall be arrived at, either through an umpire or by oath, whichever method is agreed upon. It is, however, necessary that the opposite party should be a well known cleric who is well versed in the scripture of his faith and should be capable of writing a reply based on that scripture, so that our time may not be wasted....

We shall await a response from some Hindu pundit or Christian cleric to this announcement for three months after the 20th September 1886. If no one from among the Āryās or Christians comes forward within that time, their silence will be a proof of their defeat.

[Surmah Chashm-e-Āryā, Rūḥānī Khazā'in, vol. 2, pp. 312-314]

A Proposal to Seek Divine Settlement

We have learnt from long experience that, despite failing repeatedly, our opponents have not abandoned their campaign of vilification....They stage foul and painful plays which are derogatory of the Holy Prophet (peace and blessings of Allah be upon him) and represent him as a person of evil character.

How, then, should this matter be settled? We can of course issue effective refutation, but how can we stop them from offending again? How can we tie up their foul tongues and how can we put a lock upon their reviling mouths?...These heartless Christian ministers have wounded our hearts by hurling millions of vile abuses on our Holy Prophet (peace and blessings of Allah be upon him)....

How then can these contentions, which increase daily, be settled? We have despaired of anything good coming out of debates and discussions. These have only led to an increase in rancour and hatred. In this state of affairs, there is, in my estimation, only one easy way to reach a settlement, if the Christian ministers were to agree to it: It is to seek a decision of these disputes from God Almighty.

I wish to state that I am most eager to seek a Divine settlement of this affair, and I wish most sincerely that these daily contentions may be set at rest in this manner. If God does not render a decision in my favour, I will hand over all my property, moveable and immovable, the value of which is not less than ten thousand rupees, to the

Christians. I am prepared to deposit up to three thousand rupees in advance for this purpose. This would be a sufficient penalty for me. I also promise that I shall, in such case, make an announcement bearing my signature that the Christians have been victorious and I have been defeated. This announcement will not be subject to any explicit or implicit condition.

The method of settlement will be as follows: One of the respected Christian ministers, whose names are mentioned below, should declare his willingness to come forward against me at a place to be agreed between us. Both of us should present ourselves on the appointed day at the appointed place along with a number of our followers. We should seek a decision from God Almighty through the prayer that God Almighty may, within one year, afflict one of us, who is a liar and deserving of His wrath, with such torment as, out of His sense of Honour, He has always imposed upon false and disbelieving people, including Pharaoh, Nimrod, the people of Noah and the Jews. The Christian ministers should note that this supplication does not call down a curse upon anyone. Its only purpose is the chastisement of a false person who is not willing to abandon his falsehood. The death of one man is a small price to pay for the revival of the whole world.

[Anjām-e-Ātham, Rūḥānī Khazā'in, vol. 11, pp. 38-41]

Conclusive Arguments for Reverend Whitebrecht

...Miāń Fateḥ Masīḥ, a Christian preacher, had claimed that he too was a recipient of revelation, and could set forth revealed prophecies in advance of their occurrence. Monday, the 21st of May 1888, was the day appointed to test his claim at my residence. Many respectable Muslims and Hindus of standing came to my residence to witness the presentation of prophecies by Miāń Fateḥ Masīḥ, who arrived accompanied by a number of Christians after 10:00 am. But, instead of setting forth his prophecies against me...he only said that he did not claim to be a recipient of revelation and that whatever he had said was merely to counter my claim....

The purpose of this announcement is that if a respectable European Christian should claim to be a recipient of revelation, he will be at liberty to set forth his revealed prophecies in a meeting to be held at Batāla, where I intend to remain till the end of Ramaḍān, provided he has no intention of running away after acknowledging his falsehood, as Fateḥ Masīḥ did. Reverend Mr. Whitebrecht, who is a respectable European missionary in these parts, is especially invited. If the reverend gentleman would acknowledge in a public meeting that Christians are no longer capable of receiving revelation, I shall not require him to set forth his prophecies against me. In such case, I shall, in a meeting to be called as desired by him, present such revealed prophecies in advance as will not admit of any doubt whatsoever. If I am not able to present any such definite prophecy as may be considered by the average Hindu, Muslim and Christian to be beyond human power, I shall immediately present two hundred rupees in cash to the reverend gentleman as compensation for his trouble. If he so desires, I can deposit this amount with a respectable Hindu. If the revered gentleman should acknowledge that the prophecy presented by me is truly beyond human power, then it would be obligatory on him to stand firm to test the truth or falsehood of the prophecy. He should arrange for the publication of the prophecy in *Nūr Afshān*, which is a Christian religious newspaper, along with his affirmation that he has acknowledged the prophecy to be beyond human power, in all respects; because, if it is proven to be true, it must have proceeded from the spring of Divine acceptance and love, and not from any doubtful source like guess work or speculation. Moreover, if this prophecy is truly fulfilled, he would immediately accept Islām, since a prophecy that proceeds from the spring of Divine love is enough proof of the truth of the religion by following which a person is blessed with Divine love, and obviously, a person blessed with the love of God has certainly achieved salvation. If the prophecy does not prove to be true, the deposited amount of two hundred rupees will be handed over to the reverend gentleman.

[Majmū'ah Ishtihārāt, vol. 1, pp. 147-149]

Miāń Fateḥ Masīḥ has announced in the 7th June, 1888, issue of *Nūr Afshān* that he is willing to hold a meeting for the purpose of testing the truth of my revelations. He proposes that a paper containing four questions, enclosed in a sealed envelope, should be handed over to someone present in the meeting, and then I should disclose the text of these questions to him. With reference to this announcement, it is necessary to point out, as I have mentioned in my announcement of 24th May 1888, that Miāń Fateḥ Masīḥ, whose nature consists of falsehood upon falsehood, is not worthy of being addressed by me. To address him and to hold a meeting with him is unworthy of a righteous person. But if Reverend Whitebrecht should make this request, which is published on page 7 of *Nūr Afshān* of 7th June 1888, I would readily accept it. We have the support of the Almighty and the All-Knowing God of Whom the Christians are unaware. He knows all my secrets and helps His sincere servants, but does not approve of His name being made a subject of sport and jest. Therefore, let Reverend Whitebrecht hold a public meeting in Batāla and state on oath that if I disclose to him, within ten weeks, the contents of a sealed envelope which will be presented by him he will immediately discard the Christian faith and become a Muslim. If he fails to do so, the amount of one thousand rupees, which he shall deposit in advance with a third party to be agreed upon, will be paid over to the Anjuman Ḥimāyat-e-Islām, Lahore, as penalty. After this public announcement and its publication in *Nūr Afshān*, if I disclose the contents of the sealed envelope within ten weeks, the reverend gentleman will be under obligation to carry out his promise. Failing to do so, he will lose his deposit of one thousand rupees. On the other hand, if I fail to disclose the contents of the sealed envelope, I will renounce my claim of being the recipient of revelation and will submit to whatever punishment may be imposed upon me.

Announced by,
Ghulām Aḥmad of Qādiān, 9 June 1888.

[Majmū'ah Ishtihārāt, vol. 1, pp. 150-152]

Lack of Righteousness among Christians

Is any Christian cleric blessed with the Holy Spirit? I am tired of calling upon Christian clerics of the whole world to come forward, but not one of them has responded. Some Christian clerics published a challenge in *Nūr Afshān* requiring the disclosure of the contents of a sealed envelope which they would present in a meeting, but when this challenge was accepted on condition that, upon such disclosure, the challenger or challengers would accept Islām, they forgot all about it. The Christian clergymen have long put a seal on the possibility of revelation. Now that the seal has been broken and the grace of the

Holy Spirit is proven to be descending upon the Muslims, the hollowness of the Christians' belief has been fully exposed.

[Majmū'ah Ishtihārāt, vol. 1, p. 156]

In this meeting I suggest an easy method of settlement to Deputy 'Abdullāh Ātham Ṣāḥib and all the other Christian gentlemen.... I shall pray to the Living and Perfect God for a sign and you gentlemen should pray to Jesus. You believe that he is the almighty; if that is so, you will certainly succeed. I announce in the name of Allah that if I fail to manifest a sign against you, I shall willingly submit to any punishment, and equally so if you succeed in manifesting a sign in opposition to me.

[Jang-e-Muqaddas, Rūḥānī Khazā'in, vol. 6, p. 138]

How can the Torah and the Gospels stand against the Holy Qur'ān? Even if people try to discover and set forth the countless verities, spiritual insights and wisdom comprised in the seven brief verses of *Sūrah Al-Fātiḥah*—in a natural sequence and firm order—from the Book of Moses[as], or from the few pages of the Gospel of Jesus they can never succeed, even if they spend their whole lives trying....If they believe that the Torah or the Gospel is perfect in setting forth Divine verities, insights and spiritualities of the Word of God, I am prepared to award them five hundred rupees in cash. If they consider this amount too little, I am prepared to increase it as much as they may suggest, provided it is within my means. What they have to do is set forth from their voluminous books—which number about seventy—truths and insights of the law and well-arranged pearls and jewels of the unique characteristics of the Divine Word, like those that I shall set forth from *Sūrah Al-Fātiḥah* and shall present to them in print. It will be the duty of Christian priests to present, from the Torah, the Gospel and all their other books, truths, insights and characteristic qualities of the Divine Word, which match the ones I will present from *Sūrah Al-Fātiḥah*. The attributes referred to must be extraordinary wonders that cannot be found in any human composition. If they do so, and if three umpires, chosen from among followers of other religions, certify that the qualities that have been established in the case of *Sūrah Al-Fātiḥah* are also contained in the passages presented by the Christian missionaries, the amount of five hundred rupees, which shall be in deposit to their satisfaction, shall be handed over to them.

Now does any Christian minister have the courage to come forward for such a contest?

[Sirāj-ud-Dīn 'Īsā'ī ke Chār Sawāloń kā Jawāb, Rūḥānī Khazā'in, vol. 12, pp. 360-361]

Open Challenge to All Christians

There is nothing in the Gospel that establishes the godhood of Jesus.... If his godhood can be established by the words of the Gospel, then the revelations vouchsafed to me connote my godhood to a greater degree than do the revelations of Jesus in his case. If the Christian ministers are not capable of determining this matter by themselves, then let them submit the revelations and words of Jesus set out in the Gospel, which are supposed to establish his godhood, to three umpires who may be mutually agreed upon from among non-Muslims and non-Christians, and if they decide and state on oath that the godhood of Jesus is established more clearly from his reported words, I would hand over one thousand rupees to the Christian ministers as a penalty. The umpires should state on oath, in the name of God Almighty, that they have made the truthful decision, and also state that that if it be otherwise, may God Almighty afflict them, within one year, with such torment as should involve their ruin and disgrace. But I am convinced that the Christian ministers will not agree to this method of settlement.

[Kitāb-ul-Bariyyah, Rūḥānī Khazā'in, vol. 13, p.106]

It is also my claim that my prophecies and signs are stronger than those of Jesus. If any Christian minister can establish that the prophecies and signs of Jesus are stronger than mine, I shall hand over one thousand rupees to him.

Mirzā Ghulām Aḥmad

[Majmū'ah Ishtihārāt, vol. 2, p. 314]

Invitation to Christians for *Mubāhalah*

As the religious rancour of the Christians keeps mounting, it has become necessary that, in order to put an end to this daily conflict, they should enter into a *Mubāhalah* [prayer duel] with me on the question of the truth or falsehood of Islām and Christianity. Should the Christians be averse to the use of the word 'curse', I will not insist on it, and will propose that both sides should pray in the following words:

> 'Lord of the world, Islām teaches that the doctrine of Trinity is altogether false and a satanic device, and that son of Mary was not God but only a human being and a Prophet, and that Ḥaḍrat Muḥammad Muṣṭafā (peace and blessings of Allah be upon him) was a true Prophet and Messenger of God, and was the Seal of the Prophets, and that the Holy Qur'ān is the Word of God which is free from all error and misguidance. The Christian teaching, on the other hand, is that Jesus, son of Mary, was the true God who created the heaven and earth and through whose blood the world was re-

deemed, and that God is made of a Trinity: the father, the son and the holy ghost; and that Jesus, a combination of the three, is the perfect God. Almighty God, may You judge between the two parties who are present before You, in the following manner: May the one who professes the wrong doctrine be destroyed in a great torment within one year, because the destruction of a few would provide deliverance for the whole world.'

One of the parties should make this supplication and the other should say Āmīn; and then the other party should make the same supplication and the first party should say Āmīn; and both should await God's Judgement for one year. I promise that I shall deposit two thousand rupees to pay over to Christians who participate in this *Mubāhalah*. This is a necessary method of settlement as we claim that the Living and Mighty God is with us, and the Christians claim that He is with them.

From the result of the *Mubāhalah* the public will learn which party has God's support. If the Christians do not agree to this method of settlement, they will build for themselves a store of curses in heaven, and people will know that they are false. My invitation is addressed to Dr Clark, Reverend 'Imād-ud-Dīn, Ḥissām-ud-Dīn (Editor of *Kashf-ul-Ḥaqā'iq*), Munshī Ṣafdar 'Alī Bhandārah, Reverend Fateḥ Masīḥ and to every Christian minister who is an enemy of Islām and may wish to join in. This is a good way of settlement so that the world may be rid of these daily conflicts and the false ones may be humiliated. *Peace be on those who follow the guidance.*

Mirzā Ghulām Aḥmad
Qādiān.

[Anjām-e-Ātham, Rūḥānī Khazā'in, vol. 11, p. 33]

I state on oath that Allah the Glorious, has clearly conveyed to me through revelation that Jesus (peace be upon him) was a human being like all others, and that he was a true Prophet and Messenger of God and was His chosen one. I have also been told that, through following the Holy Prophet (peace and blessings of Allah be upon him), I have been given whatever Jesus[as] was given, and that I am the Promised Messiah, and that I have been furnished with a weapon of light which shall dispel all darkness and will break the cross. It is, therefore, necessary that within one year of the *Mubāhalah*, a sign should be manifested in my support. If no such sign is manifested, it would be established that I am not from God and that I deserve to die. Accepting all this, I call upon Dr. Martin Clark to announce that if, after the *Mubāhalah*, a sign is manifested within one year in support of Mirzā Ghulām Aḥmad and no sign is manifested in his support, he would accept Islām, failing which he should transfer half of his property to me for purpose of propagating Islām and should never again stand in opposition to Islām.

Doctor Ṣāḥib should appreciate that I have imposed much harder conditions upon myself than I have proposed for him. For instance, if both of us are able to show a sign, he will be the winner, and if neither of us is able to manifest a sign within the period specified, even then he will be considered the winner. My truth will only be proved if I am able to manifest a sign, within the specified period, which Doctor Ṣāḥib is unable to match. If, after the publication of this announcement, he does not publish an announcement as I have intimated above, he will be deemed to have evaded the challenge. I would still be ready for a logical debate with him, provided he publicly acknowledges that he and his people are unable to manifest any sign, as heavenly signs are a characteristic of Islām alone and Christianity is bereft of such blessings.

[Ḥujjat-ul-Islām, Rūḥānī Khazā'in, vol. 6, pp. 49-50]

Prophecy about Ātham and its Fulfilment

The prophecy which was made at Amritsar on 5th June 1893, at the conclusion of the debate with the Christians, was supposed to be fulfilled by 5th September, 1894, at the latest. And it has, according to the design and command of God Almighty, been fulfilled so clearly before the expiry of that date, that a just-minded and sane person cannot help but acknowledge it....

If the Christians rely upon their cunning devices to dispute this, or anyone else has any doubts about it, I am prepared to enter into a *Mubāhalah* to determine whether the Muslims have been victorious, as is the case, or if the victory goes to the Christians, as they unjustly imagine. If they do not desist from falsehood and trickery, the *Mubāhalah* will take place in the following manner. On a day to be agreed upon, both parties will present themselves at the appointed place, and Mr. 'Abdullāh Ātham shall make the following affirmation three times:

> During the period of the prophecy I have not for a single moment stood in awe of Islām, and have throughout considered Islām and the Prophet of Islām (peace and blessings of Allah be upon him) to be in the wrong and still so consider. The idea of their being true has never crossed my mind. I have always believed and still believe that Jesus is the son of God and is God Himself, as is the belief of Protestant Christians. If my affirmation is not true and I have concealed the truth, then, O Mighty Lord, may You afflict

me with death within one year."

We shall say Āmīn to this supplication. If the supplication is not fulfilled within one year, and Mr. 'Abdullāh Ātham is not afflicted within that period in the manner in which the false ones are afflicted, I shall pay him one thousand rupees as penalty.

[Majmū'ah Ishtihārāt, vol. 2, pp. 23-30]

I do not wish to trouble Mr. 'Abdullāh Ātham to come to my place of residence in Amritsar. On his invitation, I shall go to his residence with one thousand rupees.... He will have to take no trouble whatever. I will also not require him to make his affirmation standing up or sitting down. He may keep lying on his bed and simply make his required announcement three times.

[Majmū'ah Ishtihārāt, vol. 2, p. 52]

If some bigoted and senseless people should still entertain doubts, I hereby make this second announcement, offering an award of two thousand rupees. If Mr. Ātham affirms on oath three times, in a public meeting, that his heart has not in the least been affected by the greatness of Islām during the period of the prophecy, and he has throughout remained an enemy of Islām, having a firm faith in the sonship and divinity of Jesus and in the doctrine of atonement, I shall immediately pay him two thousand rupees, according to the conditions laid down in my announcement of 9th September, 1894....

If Mr. Ātham should still refuse to take the proposed oath, everyone should then note that he has concealed the truth out of his fear of the Christians and that Islām is supreme and victorious....

Our opponents should keep in mind that Mr. Ātham will never make the affirmation on oath. Why would he not do it? Because he is a liar. To those who say that he might be afraid that dying within a year is a possibility, we reply: Who will cause him to die? His god Jesus or someone else? This is a contest between two gods; the True God Who is our God, and the false god set up by the Christians. If Mr. Ātham believes in the divinity and power of Jesus, and has personal experience of it, he should pray to Jesus to keep him alive during this period. Man is mortal; Mr. Ātham is now sixty-four and I am about sixty. We are equally subject to the law of nature. If I were called upon to make an affirmation on oath in order to test the truth, I would affirm not just that I will survive for one year but even ten years; this is because of my certainty that God Almighty will help me in a contest about religion....This is a contest between two gods. Only He, who is the True God, will now be victorious. I affirm that the Might of our God will surely be manifested in this manner, and I shall not die within the appointed period of one year; but if Mr. Ātham makes a false affirmation on oath, he will certainly die within that period. The question is: what will befall Mr. Ātham's god, if that god is not able to save him. Will he resign from his function as the redeemer? There is no way of escape for Mr. Ātham. He should either stop calling Jesus, 'God Almighty' or should make the required affirmation on oath. What is more, if he acknowledges publicly that his Messiah, the son of God, does not have the power to keep him alive for a year but does have the power to keep him alive for four months or even three days, I shall, after his confession to this effect, agree to a period of four months or even three days.

[Majmū'ah Ishtihārāt, vol. 2, pp. 57-63]

From the servant of the One God, Aḥmad, may Allah

grant him forgiveness and success, to Mr. 'Abdullāh Ātham. I have read your letter, which is on page 10 of the 21 September 1894 issue of *Nūr Afshān*. I regret to say that you have done your best to conceal the truth in this letter. Through revelation, I have obtained from God Almighty certain and definite knowledge, which is as clear as the rising sun, that you were deeply affected by the greatness and truth of Islām during the period appointed in the prophecy, and that is why you were terrified of its fulfilment. I affirm on oath, in the name of Allah the Glorious, that what I am saying is true; this is what I have been told by God Almighty, Who is aware of the perceptions of a human heart and has the knowledge of a man's most secret thoughts. If this statement of mine is not true, may God cause me to die in your life. This is why I wanted you to make an affirmation on oath, in a public meeting, in the words and manner that I have suggested, so that the matter may be decided between us, and the world may not remain in the dark anymore. If you so desire, I can make an affirmation on oath for a period extending, in my case, to one, two, or even three years, because I know that a truthful person is not destroyed, but only the person whom falsehood has already ruined will be destroyed. If I am called upon to make an affirmation on oath concerning the truth of my revelation, or the truth of Islām, I will not require a penny from you, but if you make the required affirmation on oath, you will be handed bags containing three thousand rupees in advance.

[Majmū'ah Ishtihārāt, vol. 2, pp. 86-87]

It is incumbent upon Mr. Ātham…to satisfy us by the simple and easy means of a statement on oath that he did not stand in awe of my prophecy, rather he was only afraid because he considered me to be a blood thirsty person and imagined that he would become a victim of my sword. He is required to do no more than to make the statement mentioned in my announcements of 9th and 20th September 1894, at which point he will be paid four thousand rupees. It is idle for him to pretend that Christians are forbidden to take an oath. Were Peter and Paul and many righteous Christians of earlier ages unaware of this prohibition, or were they not Christians?...

If Mr. Ātham makes the required statement on oath, he will inevitably die within one year, and there are no conditions whatsoever. Even if he fails to make the required statement on oath, God Almighty will not leave unpunished an offender who is trying to deceive the world by concealing the truth.

[Majmū'ah Ishtihārāt, vol. 2, pp. 103-106]

About redemption, Allah Almighty has said in the Holy Qur'ān:

وَقَالُوا لَنْ يَدْخُلَ الْجَنَّةَ إِلَّا مَنْ كَانَ هُودًا أَوْ نَصٰرٰى تِلْكَ أَمَانِيُّهُمْ قُلْ
هَاتُوا بُرْهَانَكُمْ إِنْ كُنْتُمْ صٰدِقِيْنَ ۝ بَلٰى مَنْ أَسْلَمَ وَجْهَهُ لِلّٰهِ وَهُوَ مُحْسِنٌ
فَلَهُ أَجْرُهُ عِنْدَ رَبِّهِ وَلَا خَوْفٌ عَلَيْهِمْ وَلَا هُمْ يَحْزَنُوْنَ ۝[253]

' And they said: No one but Jews and Christians will enter heaven, i.e., achieve salvation. These are only their vain desires. Tell them: Set forth your proof if you are truthful; i.e., show us what kind of salvation you have achieved. Indeed, the truly redeemed is he who hands himself over to Allah, that is, who has devoted his life in the way of Almighty God and spent it in His way and, after devotion, continuously performs good deeds and all

---

[253] Al-Baqarah, 2:112-113 **[Publisher]**

kinds of good actions. Such a person will receive his reward from his Lord. These people will have no fear nor shall they grieve, i.e., they will be fully redeemed.'

In these verses, Allah the Glorious has said that the claim of the Jews and Christians that they are redeemed is only a vain desire, and they do not possess the true spirit of life. Real salvation is something which can be experienced in this very life. Such a person is able to devote himself wholly to God Almighty, so that his life and his death and all his actions are entirely for the sake of God. He is wholly lost to his own ego, and God's will becomes his will. This is not just the desire of his heart; rather, all his faculties, reasoning, and thinking are dedicated to God. It is only then that he truly deserves to be called a *Muḥsin*, i.e., one who carries service and obedience as far as is possible for him. Such a person is truly redeemed, as is said at another place:

قُلْ اِنَّ صَلَاتِيْ وَ نُسُكِيْ وَمَحْيَايَ وَ مَمَاتِيْ لِلّٰهِ رَبِّ الْعٰلَمِيْنَ ○
لَا شَرِيْكَ لَهٗ ۚ وَبِذٰلِكَ اُمِرْتُ وَاَنَا اَوَّلُ الْمُسْلِمِيْنَ ○[254]

(Part 8, Sūrah An'ām, Rukū' 20)

'Proclaim: My prayer and my sacrifices, my life and my death are all for Allah, the Lord of the worlds, Who has no associate. I have been commanded to work to attain that status and I am the foremost of those who submit wholly to Allah.'

Allah the Glorious mentions further signs of such redemption in His Noble Book. Although what has already been mentioned clearly distinguishes those who are truly redeemed, God has, nevertheless, set out the signs of the

---

[254] Al-An'ām, 6:163-164 **[Publisher]**

redeemed. This is because the worldly minded are unable to perceive this inner redemption and closeness to God and the distinction between the redeemed and the unredeemed remains in doubt. The followers of every religion claim to be redeemed. God Almighty has, therefore, appointed signs for the true believers who attain salvation in this very life, whereby they can be distinguished, and no doubt remains. Some of these signs are:

أَلَآ إِنَّ أَوْلِيَآءَ اللّٰهِ لَا خَوْفٌ عَلَيْهِمْ وَلَا هُمْ يَحْزَنُوْنَ ۝ اَلَّذِيْنَ اٰمَنُوْا
وَكَانُوْا يَتَّقُوْنَ ۝ لَهُمُ الْبُشْرٰى فِي الْحَيٰوةِ الدُّنْيَا وَفِي الْاٰخِرَةِ لَا
تَبْدِيْلَ لِكَلِمٰتِ اللّٰهِ ذٰلِكَ هُوَ الْفَوْزُ الْعَظِيْمُ ۝[255]

(Part 11, Rukū‘ 12, Sūrah Yūnus)

This means that:

‘Hearken, the friends of Allah shall certainly have no fear, nor shall they grieve. They are the ones who truly believe, i.e., they became subservient to Allah and His Messenger and then became pious. For them are glad tidings from God Almighty in this world and in the hereafter, i.e., God will continue to give them glad tidings through dreams, visions, and Divine discourse. There is no changing the words of God. This is the great triumph which is destined for them, i.e., through such success they will be distinguished from the disbelievers, who are not truly redeemed and who will not be able to stand against them.’ At another place it is said:

إِنَّ الَّذِيْنَ قَالُوْا رَبُّنَا اللّٰهُ ثُمَّ اسْتَقَامُوْا تَتَنَزَّلُ عَلَيْهِمُ الْمَلٰٓئِكَةُ أَلَّا
تَخَافُوْا وَلَا تَحْزَنُوْا وَأَبْشِرُوْا بِالْجَنَّةِ الَّتِيْ كُنْتُمْ تُوْعَدُوْنَ ۝ نَحْنُ أَوْلِيٰٓؤُكُمْ
فِي الْحَيٰوةِ الدُّنْيَا وَفِي الْاٰخِرَةِ وَلَكُمْ فِيْهَا مَا تَشْتَهِيْٓ أَنْفُسُكُمْ وَلَكُمْ فِيْهَا مَا

---

[255] Yūnus, 10:63-65 **[Publisher]**

تَدَّعُوْنَ ۝ نُزُلًا مِّنْ غَفُوْرٍ رَّحِيْمٍ ۝ [256]

(Part 24, Rukū‘ 18)

That is: ‘The sign of those who say ‘Our Lord is Allah’ and then remain steadfast, is that angels descend upon them, and reassure them: ‘Fear not nor grieve, and rejoice in the Garden that you were promised. We are your friends and caretakers in this life and in the hereafter. Therein you will have all that you desire, and therein you will have all that you ask for. This is an entertainment from the Most Forgiving, the Ever-Merciful.’

Please note that the signs of the redeemed which are set out in these verses include converse with God, acceptance by Him, His guardianship and providence, the enjoyment of heavenly life in this world and God’s help and His support.

The following verse which I recited yesterday, gives the indication that a truly redeemed one always brings forth good fruit and is bestowed heavenly blessings.

تُؤْتِيْٓ اُكُلَهَا كُلَّ حِيْنٍ [257]

At another place it is said:

وَاِذَا سَاَلَكَ عِبَادِيْ عَنِّيْ فَاِنِّيْ قَرِيْبٌ اُجِيْبُ دَعْوَةَ الدَّاعِ اِذَا
دَعَانِ فَلْيَسْتَجِيْبُوْا لِيْ وَلْيُؤْمِنُوْا بِيْ لَعَلَّهُمْ يَرْشُدُوْنَ [258]

(Part 2, Rukū‘ 7)

‘O Prophet, when My servants inquire from thee concerning Me, tell them I am near.’ This means that when the Muslims enquire what are the bounties in respect of

---

[256] Ḥā Mīm Al-Sajdah, 41:31-33 **[Publisher]**

[257] It brings forth its fruit at all times, Ibrāhīm, 14:26 **[Publisher]**

[258] Al-Baqarah, 2:187 **[Publisher]**

which we are distinguished from others, they should be told that the distinction is that they are close to God and the others are far from Him. 'I respond to the call of the supplicant when he calls on Me. So they should respond to Me and have firm faith in Me, that they may be rightly guided.' That is, God responds to those of them who pray to Him and talks to them and accepts their supplications. 'They should, therefore, carry out His commands and have firm faith in Him so that they may attain righteousness.'

The signs of the redeemed are set at various other places, but it would take too long to rehearse them all. One of them is:

يٰۤاَيُّهَا الَّذِيْنَ اٰمَنُوْۤا اِنْ تَتَّقُوا اللّٰهَ يَجْعَلْ لَّكُمْ فُرْقَانًا [259]

(Part 9, Rukū' 18, Sūrah Anfāl)

'O Ye who believe, if you fear God, He will bestow a mark of distinction between you and the others.'

Now I respectfully ask Mr. 'Abdullāh Ātham: If the Christian faith prescribes any path to salvation which you consider to be right and true, and by following which you believe salvation can be achieved, then the signs of such salvation and the signs of those who are delivered from the darkness of this world through such salvation, must surely be recorded in the Gospels. Please tell me briefly whether those signs can be found in your own person, or in those whom you consider holy among you, or your leaders, or those among you whom you consider to be of a higher order? If these signs are found in them, kindly furnish proof thereof; and if such signs are not found in

---

[259] Al-Anfāl, 8:30 **[Publisher]**

them, then please consider the following: If there is no discoverable sign of the truth and correctness of something, is it possible to have confidence and certainty about it? For instance, if a medicine fails to produce the effects which it is supposed to produce, can it be considered genuine and effective? When we look at the path to salvation which you gentlemen have presented and compare it with that of the Holy Qur'ān, your path clearly seems to be artificial and unnatural; and it has also been established that no true way of salvation has been taught in your religion. The path which Allah the Glorious has set out in the Holy Qur'ān is that when a person dedicates himself and his whole life to the cause of God Almighty, he makes a true sacrifice of his self and becomes worthy of being bestowed new life in return for the death which he has accepted.

If you consider that this way of salvation which is set out in the Holy Qur'ān is not true, then you should produce, in the words of Jesus, a well reasoned way of salvation as an alternative; and you should also set out its signs in the blessed words of Jesus so that those present in this meeting may be able to decide upon the issue immediately.... No verity can be proved without its signs. One of the criteria of distinguishing verities is to test them by their signs. We on our side have set out the signs of the way of salvation taught by Islām, supported by my claim that those signs are found in me. Now you are under obligation to do the same on your side. If you fail to prove the truth and perfection of the way of salvation attributed to Jesus, your claim cannot be accepted. On the other hand, whatever the Holy Qur'ān has set out, is true and correct; it is not a mere claim, but is supported by proof, which I have set forth. You should not stop at making a mere claim of salvation without any proof. One of you gentlemen should stand up and announce that he has attained salvation according to the teaching of Jesus, and that the signs of salvation and perfect righteousness appointed by Jesus are to be found in him. We would be ready to examine such a claim, for our only purpose is to seek the truth. No one is prepared to accept mere words. I have already submitted to you that I have experience of the salvation that the Holy Qur'ān promises, and I am prepared to affirm once more on oath, in the name of Allah Almighty, that I am ready to prove my claim. What I require is to know whether true salvation can be achieved together with its signs in your religion or not. If it can be achieved, then demonstrate it and compare it with the proof that I am ready to offer. If such salvation, together with its signs, is not to be found in your religion, you have only to say so and I will furnish proof of my claim unilaterally.

[Jang-e-Muqaddas, Rūḥānī Khazā'in, vol. 6, pp. 143-149]

Mr. Ātham will never make the required affirmation on oath. Even if the Christian clerics should continue to urge him to the extreme limit, he will never make the affirmation against me because he knows in his heart that my prophecy concerning him has been fulfilled. It is enough proof of my truth that Mr. Ātham will never make the required affirmation on oath in opposition to me, however much the Christians might urge him to do so. If he does make the affirmation, the second aspect of the prophecy will doubtlessly be fulfilled. The word of God can never be averted.

[Majmū'ah Ishtihārāt, vol. 2, p. 204]

An Easy *Mubāhalah* for the Christians

On 2nd May 1906, I received the announcement of Aḥmad Masīḥ, the blind Christian of Delhi, in which he has challenged me to a *Mubāhalah* for the purpose of arriving at a final Judgement between Islām and Christianity. I accepted his challenge in my announcement of 5th May, on condition that the Bishops of Lahore, Calcutta, Madras and Bombay should also join in the *Mubāhalah*. It will not be necessary for them to take the trouble of coming together at one place. The *Mubāhalah* can be held in writing….It has occurred to me today that further facility may be provided to the Christian gentlemen so that they should have no excuse left. I, therefore, announce that I am ready to enter into *Mubāhalah* with Aḥmad Masīḥ himself, and all that I require from the four Bishops is that they need not present themselves for the *Mubāhalah*, but should announce over their signatures, in the newspapers *Pioneer* or *The Civil and Military Gazette*, that the defeat of Aḥmad Masīḥ will be considered the defeat of the four Bishops also. I suggest this because Aḥmad Masīḥ is an unknown person, and unless the reverend Bishops appoint him their representative, the result of the *Mubāhalah* cannot produce much effect. After this clarification, I trust that the reverend Bishops would, after full deliberation, agree to this form of the *Mubāhalah*.

Further, if my suggestion does not find favour with all four Bishops, it would be enough if the Bishop of Lahore alone were to make the suggested announcement. *Peace be on him who follows the guidance.*

Mirzā Ghulām Aḥmad, The Promised Messiah
Qādiān, 11 May 1906.

[Majmū'ah Ishtihārāt, vol. 3, pp.556-557]

Invitation to Her Majesty the Queen of England

It is enough proof of my truth that the signs shown at my hands are beyond human power. If Her Majesty, the Empress of India, Queen of Britain, should be interested, my God has the power to manifest a sign for her which would be indicative of joy and good fortune; provided that after witnessing the sign she would accept my message, and that the effect would be given throughout the country to the mission that I hold on behalf of Jesus. But the sign to be manifested would be according to the design of God and not according to any human design. It will, however, be extraordinary and will be reflective of the majesty of God.

[Toḥfah-e-Qaiṣariyyah, Rūḥānī Khazā'in, vol. 12, p. 276]

If Her Majesty the Queen should desire to witness a sign as proof of my claim, I am certain that such a sign will be shown within one year and I will pray that she spend this period in health and security. If no sign is manifested and I prove to be false, then I am willing to be hanged in Her Majesty's capital. All this entreaty is out of my desire that our benign Queen should turn to the God of heaven, of Whom the Christian faith is unaware in this age.

[Toḥfah-e-Qaiṣariyyah, Rūḥānī Khazā'in, vol. 12, p. 276, footnote]

A Test for Disclosing the Unseen

It is a good opportunity for any seeker after truth, be he a Hindu, Jew, Christian, Āryā, Brahmu, or any other, to come forward and test the truth of my claim. If he can stand up to me in the matter of the disclosing of the unseen and the acceptance of prayers, I call God to witness that I shall hand over to him all my immovable property, which is valued at around ten thousand rupees. I am ready to furnish any guarantee to this effect to the satisfaction of such a seeker. God is my witness that I shall not default, and will be ready even to suffer death in such a case. Allah Almighty knows that I am sincere in this offer. If anyone entertains any doubt in this respect, he should put forward a better plan, which I shall accept without objection. If I am false it would be better that I were destroyed by means of some severe punishment. If I am true, then I desire to save those who have destroyed themselves.

I call on all Christian clerics, who are respected and distinguished among their own people, in the name of God, to listen to me. Gentlemen, if you have in your hearts even a particle of love for that righteous one whose name is Jesus the Messiah, I call on you to stand up against me. I call you in the name of God, Who caused Jesus to be born of the righteous Mary, Who sent down the Gospel, Who caused Jesus to die a natural death and revived him spiritually and exalted him to heaven and put him in the living company of Abraham[as], Moses[as], Jonah[as] and other Prophets who had been revived spiritually before him, that you should stand up against me. If the truth is on your side and Jesus is truly God, you will be victorious. If he is not God and is a humble and helpless person, and Islām is true, God Almighty will hear me and will manifest at my hands that which is beyond your power.

[Ā'īna-e-Kamālāt-e-Islām, Rūḥānī Khazā'in, vol. 5, pp. 276-277]

There was a time when the Christian ministers alleged, out of their bigotry, that there were no prophecies in the Holy Qur'ān. Muslim divines tried to answer them, but the truth is that, in the matter of prophecies and extraordinary signs, an effective reply can be given only by one who can himself make a prophecy. This matter cannot be settled by verbal debate. When the false denials of the Christian ministers transgressed the limits,

God sent me to furnish proof of the righteousness of the Holy Prophet (peace and blessings of Allah be upon him) and the truth of Islām. Where are the Christian ministers now? Let them stand up to me. I have not come out of time. I have come at a time when the Christians have trampled Islām under their feet. O Ye blind Muslims, who has taught you to oppose the truth? Islām has been ruined; all its limbs have been wounded by external attacks and internal innovations, and twenty three years of the fourteenth century have passed; millions have renounced Islām and have become the enemies of God and His Messenger, but you keep insisting that no one has come from God and only dajjāl has appeared. Show me any Christian cleric who now alleges that the Holy Prophet (peace and blessings of Allah be upon him) made no prophecy. That time has passed. Now the time has come when God desires to make it manifest that His Messenger, **Muḥammad of Arabia** (peace and blessings of Allah be upon him) who has been reviled, whose name has been dishonoured and who has been declared false by unfortunate Christian ministers in hundreds of thousands of books published in this age, **is true and the Chief of the righteous**. He has been extensively denied but in the end he has been bestowed the crown of honour. I am one of his servants to whom God speaks and in whose support the gates of the unseen and of heavenly signs have been opened wide. O Ye ignorant ones, you may denounce him as a blasphemer, but what value can your denunciations have in the eyes of one who is occupied with the service of the faith under God's command, and sees Divine bounties descending upon Him like rain? The same God, Who descended on the heart of the son of Mary, has also descended on my heart, but in greater glory. He was a human being and so am I. The light of the sun falls on a wall but the wall cannot claim to be the Sun. The True Sun can say: Depart from me; and then see whether you have any honour.

[Ḥaqīqat-ul-Waḥī, Rūḥānī Khazā'in, vol. 22, pp. 285-287]

God has bestowed upon me strength from Himself so that no Christian cleric can withstand me in debate. God has so impressed the hearts of Christian divines with awe that none of them has any strength left to stand up against me. God has sent me the support of the Holy Spirit and has appointed His angels to keep me company, and no Christian cleric can challenge me. These are the people who used to say that the Holy Prophet (peace and blessings of Allah be upon him) performed no miracles and made no prophecy; and now, despite being challenged, they fail to come forward. This is because God has put it in their hearts that they will experience nothing but defeat when they stand up against me.

[Tohfah-e-Golarhviyyah , Rūḥānī Khazā'in, vol. 17, pp. 149-150]

I proclaim in the name of God Who has sent me, that if any hard-hearted Christian, Hindu or Āryā should deny the bright and clear signs that I have manifested in the past, and should make a simple straightforward announcement in a paper, that on witnessing a sign, whatever it may be, so long as it is beyond human power, he would accept Islām, I am sure that within one year of making such an announcement he will witness a sign. This is because I draw light from that illumined life which was bestowed upon the Holy Prophet (peace and blessings of Allah be upon him) whom I follow. No one can stand up to it. If there is a seeker after truth from among Christians or Hindus or Āryās, let him come forward, and if he believes in the truth of his religion, let him compete with me in the manifestation of heavenly signs. But I tell you beforehand that no one will come forward. They will try to evade my challenge by presenting dishonest and complicated conditions. This is because their religions are dead and they have no one alive from whom they can receive spiritual grace and from whom they can obtain a life shining with signs.

[Tiryāq-ul-Qulūb, Rūḥānī Khazā'in vol. 15, pp. 140-141]

Divine Permission for *Mubāhalah* against Maulavīs

In the early days I had thought that I was not at liberty to challenge Muslims to a *Mubāhalah*, because *Mubāhalah* involves calling down a curse on each other, and it is not permissible to call down a curse on a Muslim; but my opponents from among the Muslims persist in denouncing me as a disbeliever, and, under the Islamic dispensation, he who denounces a true Muslim as a disbeliever himself becomes the subject of such denunciation. I have, therefore, been commanded to challenge to a *Mubāhalah* those who denounce me as disbeliever and possess sons and daughters and are the originators of the denunciations directed at me.

[Ā'īna-e-Kamālāt-e-Islām, Rūḥānī Khazā'in, vol. 5, p. 332]

In the beginning I avoided the *Mubāhalah*, because I believed that a curse should not be called down on a Muslim. But now I have been told that he who denounces a Muslim as a disbeliever, and does not desist, even though his opponent faces the Ka'bah when he prays, professes belief in the Unity of God, the Prophethood of Muḥammad (peace and blessings of Allah be upon him), and other Islamic doctrines, such a person is himself excluded from Islām. I have, therefore, been commissioned to enter into a *Mubāhalah* with those who claim to be Muftīs and Maulavīs and Muḥaddathīn who have sons and wives and have led the campaign denouncing me as a disbeliever. I have been directed that I should set forth before them, in a public meeting, a detailed explanation of my claim and should refute all the objections and doubts which disturb their minds. If they still do not desist from denouncing me as a disbeliever, I shall call them to a *Mubāhalah*.

[Ā'īna-e-Kamālāt-e-Islām, Rūḥānī Khazā'in, vol. 5, pp. 256-257]

I wish to inform all the Maulavīs and Muftīs who denounce me as a disbeliever because of minor differences or through their own ignorance, that God Almighty has commissioned me and I invite them to a *Mubāhalah* in the following terms. I will first set before you, in a meeting called for the purpose of *Mubāhalah*, the reasons in support of my doctrines derived from the Holy Qur'ān and Aḥādīth. If you still persist in denouncing me as a disbeliever, I shall challenge you to a *Mubāhalah* in the same meeting. My first addressee is Miāń Nadhīr Ḥussain of Delhi; should he decline my invitation, my next addressee would be Sheikh Muḥammad Ḥussain of Batāla, and should he also decline, all those Maulavīs would be my addressees who denounce me as a disbeliever and occupy a leading position among the Muslims. I grant all these gentlemen a period of four months from today, 10th December 1892, within which to enter into a *Mubāhalah* with me under the conditions set out above. If they fail to do so and persist in denouncing me, they will be held responsible before God. I had desired in this book to refute all the false charges which they have levelled against me as the basis for denouncing me as a disbeliever, but, on account of the illness of the scribe and some other reasons, that part has not yet been printed. All the same, I shall read out the contents of the paper in the meeting called for the purpose of *Mubāhalah*, whether or not it has been printed by that time. It is a necessary condition that I should refute whatever has been written against me by those who have denounced me as a disbeliever, and that I should put forward convincing arguments which will leave no room for them to denounce me. If they still continue to do so, the *Mubāhalah* supplication shall be made in the same meeting. The revelation that has been vouchsafed to me in this context is as follows:

نَظَرَ اللّٰهُ اِلَيْكَ مُعَطَّرًا۔ وَ قَالُوْا اَ تَجْعَلُ فِيْهَا مَنْ يُّفْسِدُ فِيْهَا قَالَ
اِنِّى اَعْلَمُ مَا لَا تَعْلَمُوْنَ۔ قَالُوْا كِتَابٌ مُمْتَلِئٌ مِّنَ الْكُفْرِ وَ الْكِذْبِ۔
قُلْ تَعَالَوْا نَدْعُ اَبْنَآئَنَا وَ اَبْنَآئَكُمْ وَ نِسَآئَنَا وَ نِسَآئَكُمْ وَ اَنْفُسَنَا
وَ اَنْفُسَكُمْ ثُمَّ نَبْتَهِلْ فَنَجْعَلْ لَعْنَةَ اللّٰهِ عَلَى الْكَاذِبِيْنَ۔

'God Almighty has looked at you with a fragrant look. Some people have said in their hearts: Lord will you establish someone in the earth who will create disturbance therein? And God replied to them: I know that which you know not. They said: His book is replete with disbelief and falsehood. Say to them: Come, let us call our sons and your sons, and our women and your women and our own selves and your own selves and call down the curse of Allah on the liars.'

This is the permission that I have been granted for *Mubāhalah*.

[Ā'īna-e-Kamālāt-e-Islām, Rūḥānī Khazā'in, vol. 5, pp. 261-266]

O Ye Maulavīs and custodians of shrines who oppose

me, the contentions between us have exceeded all limits. My Community is much smaller in number than yours, and at the moment does not exceed four or five thousand. Nevertheless, be sure that this tree has been planted by the hand of God Who will not let it be destroyed. He will not be pleased till He carries it to perfection. He will water it and enclose it within a compound and will foster it in a wonderful manner. Have you spared any effort in trying to destroy it? Had it been a human project, it would have been destroyed long ago.

It is He Who commanded me to invite you to a *Mubāhalah* so that the enemy of truth may be ruined and the lover of darkness may fall into the abyss of chastisement. Hitherto I had not wanted to call for *Mubāhalah*, nor did I wish to pray for anyone's ruin. Mr. 'Abd-ul-Ḥaq of Ghaznī, presently of Amritsar, desired to hold a *Mubāhalah* with me, but I put him off for a long time. At last, on his insistence, a *Mubāhalah* was held, but I made no supplication for his ruin. But now things have come to such a pass that I have been called dajjāl, I have been named Satan and I have been accounted a liar and an impostor. My opponents have cursed me in their public announcements and in their meetings I have been mentioned with contempt. Now you seem to be intent upon denouncing me as if you have not the slightest doubt in my being a disbeliever. Everyone of you considers reviling me as an act of great merit. You have declared it the way of Islām to call curses on my head.

In the time of all this bitterness and distress, God was with me; He comforted and consoled me throughout. Can an insect stand up against a whole world? Will a particle set itself against the universe? Can the soul of a liar possess such steadfastness? Can a low impostor possess such power? Be sure, therefore, it is not me you are fighting, but you are fighting God. Can you not distinguish between fragrance and foul smell? Can you not observe the majesty of truth? It would have been much better for you if you had shed tears before God Almighty and had sought guidance from Him concerning me with a trembling heart, and had then followed a certainty and not pursued doubts and delusions.

Now get up and be ready for *Mubāhalah.* You know that my claim is based on the authority of the Holy Qur'ān and Aḥādīth and on Divine revelations vouchsafed to me. You rejected the authority of the Qur'ān and the Aḥādīth and disregarded altogether the Word of God, as if it were no more than a broken reed.

This leaves the second basis of my claim, so I call upon you in the name of the Mighty and Jealous God—and no faithful one can reject a call in His name—to come for a *Mubāhalah* for a Judgement on the basis of the revelation vouchsafed to me.

The procedure will be as follows: After the date and place of the *Mubāhalah* have been agreed upon, I will present myself with a paper on which all the revelations, which I have set out, will be written, and I shall supplicate:

> Lord, if these revelations that I hold in my hand are my inventions and You know that I have made them myself, or if they are the result of the incitement of Satan and are not Your Words, may You then cause me to die before the end of one year from this date, or afflict me with such torment as may be worse than death, and do not grant me deliverance until I die, so that my disgrace may be known and people may be delivered from the mischief of my design, as I do not

> desire that Your creatures should be mislead on my account, and it is better that such an impostor should die. But, O All-Knowing and All-Aware God, if it is in Your knowledge that all these revelations which I hold in my hand are from You and are Your Words, then may You afflict these opponents of mine who are present here, within one year of this date, with a severe torment; afflict some with blindness, some with leprosy, some with paralysis, some with lunacy, and some with epilepsy. Make some of them the victims of snakebite, or the bite of a mad dog; destroy the property of some and afflict some with calamity and some with disgrace.

When I finish my supplication, both parties should say Āmīn. Everyone of the opposite party who is present for *Mubāhalah* should then supplicate:

> O All-Knowing and All-Aware God, we account this person, whose name is Ghulām Aḥmad, a liar, an impostor and a disbeliever. If he is truly a liar and an impostor and a disbeliever and a faithless one, and his alleged revelations are not from You but are his own invention, then may You, as a Benefactor of the Muslims, destroy this impostor within a period of one year so that the people may be saved against his mischief. But if he is not an impostor and is from You and all these revelations are Words of Your Mouth, then may You afflict us, who consider him a disbeliever and a liar, within the period of one year, with painful and disgraceful torment by making some of us blind, some leprous, some paralytic, some lunatics, and some by being bitten by a snake or a mad dog. May You afflict with a calamity the wealth and life of some and the honour of others.

At the end of this supplication, everyone should say Āmīn. If anyone considers me a liar and an impostor, but wishes to avoid the use of the expression 'disbeliever', he will be at liberty to employ only the term 'liar' and 'impostor', concerning which he is certain.

After the *Mubāhalah*, if I die within a year or am afflicted with some torment from which I am not expected to be delivered, the people will be secure from my mischief and I shall become accursed forever. I proclaim here and now, that in such case I should be considered a liar and accursed. I will not mind being called dajjāl or the accursed or Satan, and will deserve always to be mentioned with a curse and will accept the Divine Judgement without reservation. In this case, anyone who follows me or considers me to be good or truthful will be subject to God's chastisement. Thus my end would be vile as is the end of all disgraceful liars.

But, if God safeguards me for a year against death or physical calamity, and my opponents are afflicted with Divine wrath and each of them becomes the subject of some misfortune, and my prayer against them is manifested in a shining manner, the world will recognize the truth and this daily conflict will come to an end. I repeat that up to now I have never prayed against anyone who professed to be a Muslim, and have endured everything with patience; but on that day I shall seek the Judgement of God and shall hold to His Holiness and Honour, so that by destroying the party that is in the wrong and is committed to falsehood, He may safeguard Islām against the mischief of the wicked.

I also agree that my prayer should be regarded as having been answered only if each one of those who come into the field for *Mubāhalah* is afflicted, one way or another, within one year. If even a single one of them is spared—

out of a total of one or two thousand—I shall consider myself to be false and I shall repent at their hands. If I die within one year, the world will be restored to peace and security by the death of an evil one.

But one of my conditions is that at least ten of those whose names are mentioned below should be present at the time of the *Mubāhalah*. If more of them can be present, so much the better, inasmuch as the affliction of a large number with Divine torment is such a clear sign as no one can doubt.

Bear witness, O earth and O heaven, that the curse of God lies on him who, having received this book, neither comes to *Mubāhalah* nor desists from denouncing me as a disbeliever and defaming me, nor keeps away from the company of those who mock at me. O Ye believers, say Āmīn to this in the name of God. I have to record that up till now these wicked Maulavīs have not paid any heed to this straightforward manner of Judgement, so that if I am a liar, as they imagine, I may be chastised by God Almighty Who is the Judge of judges.

[Anjām-e-Ātham, Rūḥānī Khazā'in, vol. 11, pp. 64-67]

Open Invitation to All who Seek a Sign

After issuing several invitations to *Mubāhalah*, I have for my part given up making any further attempts in that connection, but everyone who considers me a liar, hypocrite, or an impostor, and rejects my claim of being the Promised Messiah, and regards the revelation vouchsafed to me by God Almighty as my invention, whether he is a Muslim, Hindu, Āryā or follower of any other religion, he is at liberty to come forward and publish a written statement of *Mubāhalah* against me. He should announce in some newspapers, taking oath in the name of God Almighty, that he is fully convinced that I, who claim to be Promised Messiah, am an impostor and liar and dajjāl, and my supposed revelations, some of which are entered in this book, are not the words of God but are all of my own making. This statement should conclude with the supplication:

> O God Almighty, if in Your estimation this person is true and not a liar, impostor, disbeliever and faithless, then may You on account of my rejecting him and slandering him, send down some severe punishment upon me, otherwise may You chastise him, Āmīn.

This method of seeking a sign is open to everyone. If, after the publication of this prayer in at least three well-known newspapers, such a person should still escape heavenly punishment, everyone will be free to conclude that I am not from God. No period will be fixed for the manifestation of such a sign. The only requirement will be that something should occur which can be appreciated by everyone.

[Ḥaqīqat-ul-Waḥī, Rūḥānī Khazā'in, vol. 22, pp. 71-72]

Ever since God has named me the Promised Messiah and Mahdī, those who call themselves Muslims and call me as a disbeliever, have been greatly agitated against me. I have proved my claim clearly on the basis of the Holy Qur'ān and Aḥādīth, but they deliberately ignored what I said. Then God manifested many heavenly signs in my support but they derived no benefit from these either. Thereafter many of them came forward for *Mubāhalah* and some of them, who claimed to be recipients of revelation, predicted that I shall be destroyed within a specific period during their very lives, but they were themselves destroyed while I lived. Alas, even then the Muslims did not reflect that if all my claims had been of my own making, my opponents would not have been defeated in each and every case. They have been condemned as false by the Holy Qur'ān. The Aḥādīth describing the spiritual ascension of the Holy Prophet[sa] and the Ḥadīth which predicts that the Promised Messiah would be one of the Muslims, proves that they are liars. The results of the *Mubaḥalahs* proclaim their falsehood. Then by what authority do they so daringly oppose and reject me, who has been sent by God, and has continued to call them to the truth for nearly twenty-six years? Have they not experienced the warning conveyed in the verse:

يُصِبْكُمْ بَعْضُ الَّذِي يَعِدُكُمْ [260]

Where is Ghulām Dastgīr who supplicated for my destruction in his book *Faiḍ-e-Raḥmānī*, and prayed for the death of whichever of us was false? Where is Maulavī Charāgh Dīn of Jammu who stood up for *Mubāhalah* against me and predicted my death on the basis of a revelation he was supposed to have received? Where is Faqīr Mirzā who had a large following and who predicted my death with great enthusiasm. He even announced that God had informed him from His throne that I was an impostor and would die during his own lifetime in the following month of Ramaḍān. But when Ramaḍān came, it was he himself who died of the plague. Where is Sa'd-ullāh of Ludhiāna who stood up for *Mubāhalah* against me and predicted my death? He died of the plague in my lifetime. Where is Maulavī Moḥy-ud-Dīn of Lakhoke who called me the Pharaoh and predicted my death in his lifetime and pub-

---

[260] 'Some of that which he threatens you with will *surely* befall you.'— Al-Mu'min, 40:29 **[Publisher]**

lished several of his supposed revelations concerning me? He too passed away in my lifetime. Where is the accountant Bābū Ilāhī Bakhsh of Lahore, the author of *'Aṣā-e-Mūsā,* who described himself as Moses and called me Pharaoh and predicted my death by the plague in his own lifetime, and published several other prophecies about my ruin? He too died of plague within my lifetime, thus bearing witness that his book *'Aṣā-e-Mūsā* was false and a bundle of impostures. All these people had hoped that I would become an illustration of the verse:

اِنْ يَّكُ كَاذِبًا فَعَلَيْهِ كَذِبُهٗ [261]

But they themselves illustrated this verse by their ruin. By destroying them God also made me an illustration of the second part of the same verse:

وَاِنْ يَّكُ صَادِقًا يُّصِبْكُمْ بَعْضُ الَّذِيْ يَعِدُكُمْ [262]

Have not all these events fully established the design of God Almighty? Yet it was necessary for my opponents to have rejected me because of the Divine prediction published 26 years ago in *Brāhīn-e-Aḥmadiyyah*:

> A Warner came to the world and the world did not accept him, but God will accept him and will establish his truth with powerful assaults.

I am certain that God will not stop His signs till my truth is made manifest to the world.

Today, 15th May 1908, it has occurred to me that there is

---

[261] 'If he be a liar, on him will be *the sin of* his lie.'—Al-Mu'min, 40:29 **[Publisher]**

[262] 'But if he is truthful, then some of that which he threatens you with will *surely* befall you.'—Al-Mu'min, 40:29 **[Publisher]**

another method by which a God fearing person may perchance emerge from the dangerous whirlpool of denial. It is as follows: Someone out of my opponents who deems me a disbeliever and a liar should obtain the attention of at least ten reputed clerics, or of at least ten well known leading personalities, and should come out against me in order to carry out a test of our truth or falsehood. We should select two persons who are critically ill and each of them should, by the drawing of lots, be allocated to each of us for prayer. Thereafter, the one whose patient recovers completely or lives longer than the other patient, will be considered true. All this is in the hand of Allah Almighty, and, relying on His promise, I predict that God will either bestow full health on the patient allocated to me or will grant him longer life than the other patient; and this will be the testimony of my truth. If this does not happen, it may be concluded that I am not from God. But it will be necessary that the person who stands up against me, and the ten Maulavīs or leading personalities who support him, must announce in three leading papers that, in the case of my triumph, they will accept me and join my Jamā'at. I shall also be bound by similar conditions.... One benefit resulting from such a contest would be that God Almighty would bestow new life upon someone dangerously ill, who has lost all hope of life, and would thus manifest a sign of reviving the dead. Secondly, the contention between us will be judged peacefully and easily. *Peace be on him who follows the right path.*

Announced by:

Mirzā Ghulām Aḥmad Qādiānī, The Promised Messiah. 15 May, 1908.

[Chashma-e-Ma'rifat, Rūḥānī Khazā'in, vol. 23, pp. 2-4]

I have steadfastly endured vilification at the hands of

Maulavī Nadhīr Ḥussain Ṣāḥib of Delhi and his disciples. Now, in my capacity as a commissioned one of God, I invite him and his followers to God's Judgement in the confidence that He Himself will decide between us. He is aware of what goes on in the hearts and what transpires in the minds, and does not approve of any hurtful activity or needless bewailing. Truly virtuous is he who fears Him. I am not demeaned by anyone calling me a dog or a disbeliever or dajjāl. Man possesses no honour on his own. Honour is bestowed only by the reflection of God's light. If He is not pleased with me and I am evil in His estimation, then I am worse than a thousand dogs.

[Persian Poem]

If God is not pleased with man;
Then no animal is more to be pitied than him.
If we keep feeding the dog of the mean self;
Then we are worse than dogs of the streets.

O Allah! O Guide of all seekers;
O Ye, Whose love is our life.
Make our end upon complete reconciliation with Your will;
So that our desires relating to both the worlds may be fulfilled.

The world and its people are busy making hue and cry;
But Your seekers are in another world.
There is one, whom You have granted the light of the heart;
And there is another struggling in the mud;
The eye, the ear, and the heart, all receive light from You;
Your are the Fountainhead of guidance and grace.

In short, God, the Mighty and Holy, is my refuge and I

commit the whole of my affair to Him. I do not wish to return abuse for abuse, nor do I wish to say anything on my own. It is only He Who has the final say. It is a pity that my opponents have complicated a simple matter. They do not believe that God Almighty has the authority to do what He wills and to appoint whosoever He may please, as His chosen one. Can man fight Him? Does man have the right to ask Him: Why did You do this or why did You not do that?

[Āsmānī Faiṣlah, Rūḥānī Khazā'in, vol. 4, pp. 334-335]

Fie on these people, for they do not honour that which God and His Messenger have said. Seventeen years of the century have passed, but their reformer is still hiding in some cave. Why are they so miserly towards me? Had God so willed, I would not have come. At times it comes to my mind that I should supplicate Him to relieve me of this office and to appoint someone else in my place. But, at that very instant, it occurs to me that there can be no greater sin than to lack the courage to perform the service that God desires of me. The more I wish to retire, the more God Almighty pulls me forward. There is rarely a night during which I am not confronted with the words: "I am with thee and My heavenly hosts are with thee." The pure of heart will see God after death, but I swear by His countenance that I behold Him here and now. The world does not know me but He Who has sent me knows me. Those who seek my ruin are utterly mistaken and totally unfortunate. I am a tree planted by the Hand of the True Master. He who seeks to cut me down only desires to partake of the fate of Korah, Judas Iscariot and Abū Jahl. My eyes shed tears daily for someone to come forward and seek Judgement concerning me, according to the standard of prophethood, and then see on whose side

God is; but coming forward for such a test is not the business of every characterless person. There was one Ghulām Dastgīr, one of the disbelieving hosts of the Punjab, who laid down his life in this attempt. It is now impossible for someone like him to come forward.

O Ye people, be sure that I am supported by the Hand that will be faithful to me till the end. If your men and your women, your young and your old, your small and your great, should all come together and supplicate for my ruin until their noses are rubbed out by their repeated prostration and their hands are numbed, even then God will not hear their supplication and will not desist till He has fulfilled His design. If not even a single person remains with me, God's angels will be with me, and if you conceal the true testimony, stones will well nigh bear testimony in my support. Do not, therefore, wrong your souls. The false and the true have different countenances. God does not leave any matter without judgement. I curse a life of falsehood and imposture, and the failure to serve the Creator for fear of His creatures. It is not possible for me to be lax in performing the service which God Almighty has appointed for me at its appropriate time, though the sun and the earth may join hands to trample me down. What is man but an insect and what is a human being but a lump of flesh? Can you then expect me to disobey the command of the Ever-Living and Self-Subsisting One for the sake of an insect or a lump of flesh? In the end God has always judged between His commissioned ones and their opponents; He will do the same now. There is a season for the coming of God's commissioned ones and a season for their departure. Be sure, therefore, that I have neither come out of season nor shall I depart out of season. Do not fight God. It is not within your power to destroy me.

[Tohfah-e-Golarhviyyah , Rūḥānī Khazā'in, vol. 17, pp. 49-50]

Peace is Best

O Ye Muslim divines who denounce me as a liar and a disbeliever or are in doubt concerning me, it has occurred to me that I should approach you once more for a settlement. This does not mean that I shall compel you to accept my beliefs or modify them in any respect contrary to the comprehension that God has bestowed upon me. What I mean is that we should make a firm agreement that neither side, including our respective supporters, will indulge in any kind of offensive language against the other, nor attack the honour of the other in speech or writing or by way of innuendo. If anyone from one side visits anyone on the other, he should be treated with due courtesy….

If my enterprise is not authorised by God, it will be destroyed; but if it is so authorised, no enemy can destroy it. To go on slighting this Community because its numbers are small is inconsistent with good morals. This is the time when our opposing divines should display their good manners, for when the membership of the Aḥmadīyyah Movement grows into millions and people of every standing, including some sovereigns, come into its fold, as God Almighty has promised, all this rancour and hatred will naturally disappear. But the courtesy and politeness that will then be extended to the members of the Movement will not be for the sake of God, and the gentle behaviour of the opposing divines will not be considered as part of good manners. Now is the time to show good manners when the membership of this Movement is no more than a few thousands.... For the present there is no better plan for the settlement of these differences. Hereafter, whichever side has the support of God will gradually achieve supremacy. Truth first appears in the shape of a small seed and gradually grows into a big tree, which bears fruits and flowers among which birds which seeks the truth can relax.

Announced by:
Mirzā Ghulām Aḥmad, From Qādiān
5 March, 1901.

[Majmū'ah Ishtihārāt, vol. 3, pp. 398-400]

Six Signs of Divine Support

I announce once more, for the sake of those who seek the truth, that if they have not even now realized that I am true, they can satisfy themselves again through any of the following six signs which God Almighty has bestowed upon me.

One: Any arrogant person who desires to compete with me in proficiency in Arabic, is at liberty to produce the match of this Arabic writing both in poetry and in prose; and if some Arabic speaking person testifies that his work is equal to mine, I shall be accounted false.

Two: Failing this, my opponents can compete with me in writing an Arabic commentary on any seven verses of the Holy Qur'ān which are randomly selected, and if I am not acknowledged as being clearly superior to them, I am to be accounted as false.

Three: One of my well-known opponents should stay with me for a year. During this time, if I fail to manifest some sign which is beyond the power of man, I may be accounted false.

Four: Some of my well-known opponents may announce

publicly that if they witness a sign within one year of the date of the announcement, they will repent and acknowledge my truth. If, within that time, no sign is manifested by me which is beyond human power, whether by way of prophecy or otherwise, I shall acknowledge that I am false.

Five: Failing all these, Sheikh Muḥammad Ḥussain of Batāla and other well-known opponents of mine should come forward for *Mubāhalah* with me. Thereafter, if even a single one of them escapes the consequences of my supplication in the *Mubāhalah*, I shall acknowledge myself to be false.

I invite every opponent in the name of God Almighty to make a trial by any one of the methods that I have suggested: They should either write and publish a reply to this writing in fluent Arabic within two months, before 10th March 1897; or they should compete with me in writing an Arabic commentary on any seven verses of the Holy Qur'ān in my presence; or anyone of them can come and stay with me for one year for the purpose of witnessing a sign, or he can await a sign for one year, after making a unilateral announcement; or he can enter into *Mubāhalah* with me.

Six: If none of these methods appeals to them, they should enter into a truce with me and my Community for a period of seven years on the condition that they will not denounce me as a disbeliever and a liar, will not revile me, will meet everyone of us with courtesy and goodwill, will generally behave towards us like good Muslims in fear of God, and will refrain from every kind of mischief and misconduct. And if during this seven year period, I am not able to perform, with the support of God Almighty, outstanding service in the cause of Islām, for instance, if the destruction of false religions, which has been predicted at the hands of the Promised Messiah, is not manifested through me, and God Almighty does not manifest those signs at my hands which should make Islām supreme and whereby people should begin to accept Islām from every direction, and the false god of Christianity should be destroyed, and the world should enter a new epoch, I will acknowledge myself a liar. I call God Almighty to witness that I shall be bound by this declaration. God Almighty knows that I am not a liar. The period of seven years is not long, and it is not within human power to work such a revolution in such a short time. As I offer to make this agreement sincerely, in the name of God Almighty, and call all of you to make this truce, you should fear God and respond to me. If I am not from God, I am bound to be ruined. Otherwise no one can ruin a commissioned one of God.

[Anjām-e-Ātham, Rūḥānī Khazā'in, vol. 11, pp. 304-319]

Prayer for a Divine Decree

The controversy between my opponents and me has now reached the limit. He Who has sent me will now judge between us. If I am true, heaven will surely bear strong witness for me, which will set people atremble. But if I have offended God by inventing lies against Him over a period of twenty-five years, how can I escape His wrath? In such case, even if all of you should become my friends, I will still be a ruined person because God's hand would be against me.

O Ye people, keep in mind that I am not a liar but am oppressed, I am not an impostor but a righteous man.

[Ḥaqīqat-ul-Waḥī, Rūḥānī Khazā'in, vol. 22, pp. 189-190]

The treatment that my own people have accorded to me is well known and the hostility of other people towards me is natural. All of them have done their utmost to destroy me. They have contrived every project for doing me harm and have carried it to its limit. They have omitted nothing—prayers, declarations of the merit of slaying me, slander and defamation. Then which is the hand that safeguards me? Had I been a liar, God would Himself have furnished the means of my ruin and it would not have been necessary for people to devise methods for my ruin and be frustrated by God. Is it the sign of a liar that the Holy Qur'ān should bear witness for him, heavenly signs should be manifested in his support, reason should uphold him, and those who desire his death should themselves die? I do not believe that after the age of the Holy Prophet (peace and blessings of Allah be upon him), any opponent of a godly or true person has suffered such clear defeat and disgrace as my enemies have on account of their opposition to me. When they attacked my honour they were themselves disgraced, and when they announced that I was a liar and I would die before them, they ended up dying before me.

[Tohfah-e-Golarhviyyah , Rūḥānī Khazā'in, vol. 17, pp. 45-46]

How can God, Whose powerful hand supports heaven and earth and all that is between them, be frustrated by the designs of men? The day is near when He will announce His Judgement. It is a sign of the righteous that the end is always in their favour. God descends upon their hearts with His manifestations. How can that structure be demolished in which the true King has His abode? Revile me as much as you like, and devise whatever means of persecution you can think of, and make every plan for my ruin, but remember that God will soon prove that His hand is supreme. A foolish one thinks that he can win with his devices, but God rebukes him: 'O accursed one, I shall frustrate all thy designs.' Had God so willed, He would have bestowed sight upon these opposing Maulavīs and their followers, and they would have recognized the time and the season of the advent of God's Messiah; but the prophecies of the Holy Qur'ān and of the Ḥadīth were bound to be fulfilled, which had predicted that the Promised Messiah would be persecuted by the Muslim divines who would denounce him as a disbeliever, condemn him to death, slander him and account him as being outside the pale of Islām and a destroyer of the faith.

[Tohfah-e-Golarhviyyah , Rūḥānī Khazā'in, vol. 17, p. 53]

God Almighty has not yet exhausted His support and His signs, and I declare on oath in His name that He will not desist till my truth is manifested throughout the world. O Ye people who hear my voice, fear God and do not transgress. Had all this been a human project, God would have destroyed me, and not a trace would be left. But you have seen how the help of God Almighty has supported me all along, and numberless signs have been manifested in my support. How many of my enemies have perished as a consequence of holding *Mubāhalah* with me. O servants of God, do reflect, does God Almighty accord such treatment to liars?

[Ḥaqīqat-ul-Waḥī, Rūḥānī Khazā'in, vol. 22, p.554]

INDEX OF REFERENCES OF THE HOLY QUR'ĀN

1:1-2 72
1:2 286
1:3 72
1:4 72
1:5 72
1:6 98,99
1:6-7 73,136,142,144,165
1:7 73,100,101
2:40 150
2:63 117
2:84 19
2:88 150
2:94 36
2:112-113 423
2:113 58,59,64,117
2:156-158 31
2:166 40
2:178 29
2:180 24
2:187 426
2:201 58,61
2:208 58
2:224 317
2:229 322
2:234 315
2:265 27
2:283 33
2:284 33
3:32 108,116
3:56 194,200
3:65 117
3:98 113
3:111 143
3:119 40
3:135 20
3:140 343
3:145 198,205,206,208
3:174 29
4:6-7 16
4:10-11 16
4:20 311,315,322
4:35 323
4:47 309
4:129 18
4:136 34
4:142 343
4:151-152 118
4:157-158 215
4:158 259
4:165 153,154
4:166 153
5:4 128,148,205
5:9 34
5:25 134
5:33 24
5:52 40
5:118 192,193,195,205,207,208
6:83 98
6:101 96
6:153 33
6:163-164 424
7:15-16 279
7:26 376
7:27 81
8:2 18
8:30 395,427
8:48 29
8:62 18
9:24 74
9:119 158
9:128 39
10:63-65 425
10:65 395
12:25 85
12:54 2
13:18 164

13:23....29
13:32....165
14:26....426
15:10....162,164
15:49....182,210
16:21-22....199
16:29....194
16:33....194
16:44....188
16:91....24,26,41,56,57
17:16....165
17:37....19,374
17:82....70
17:94....183
18:84....295
18:85....295
18:86-89....296
18:87....302
18:90-92....298
18:93-103....299
18:100....306
18:101....306
18:102....306
19:32-33....201
20:75....159,355
21:9....199
21:35....199
21:97....283,309
22:31....33
23:2-3....78
23:9....80,88
23:10....82,84
23:15....81,99,224
23:45....150
23:51....137,264
24:31....330
24:56....155,165
25:3-4....224
25:64....18
25:73....18,34
26:4....39,112,136
27:35....87
27:45....220
29:50....163
29:70....113,165
30:3-4....308
32:12....194
33:36....34
33:40....234
33:41....139,140,180,205
33:73....88
36:27....182
39:54....237
40:29....444,445
40:58....285
41:31-33....426
41:35....18
42:41....20,26
49:8-9....70
49:12-13....19
56:80....160
58:23....69,395
60:9....41
60:10....41
61:7....204
62:3....160
65:11-12....186
68:5....9,12
72:27-28....141, 147,357
75:3....2
76:9-10....58
89:28-31....3,68
89:31....182
90:18....39
91:10-11....4
97:2....186
103:4....34
113:5....286
114:6-7....286

SUBJECT INDEX

'Abdul Karīm
admonition to treat women kindly 313
Abū Bakr
affirmed that all Prophets had died 208
Afghanistan
Jesus Christ in, ... 266
Aḥādīth
about latter days 280
about the descent of Messiah...... 171
Dajjāl will prevail in latter days according to 280
mention of Dajjāl in 279
Ajīj
defined 305
Angels
repudiation by philosophers 44
Antichrist
misguidance about Jesus caused by 184
Arabs
claim of literary excellence refuted 366
Arabic
mastery of the Promised Messiah of 366
Āryās
appeal of the Promised Messiah to establish veil 328
false doctrines refuted 398
Ascension (of Jesus)
difference between the Christian and popular Muslim beliefs 169-171
falsity according to Gospels 248
no mention of physical in Holy Qur'ān 129
popular beliefs about Jesus' 169
true meanings of 179-180
Ātham, 'Abdulllāh
prophecy about, and its fullfillment 419-423
Atonement
cannot purify from sin 54
Baker, Reverend Mr.
on Indian conversion to Christianity 291
Baqā
compared with revival after death 100
defined 60
Benares
Jesus Christ in 266
Benevolence
as third quality for doing good 26
Blessings of Allah
of certainty 46
of full comprehension (of God) 54
Brāhīn-e-Aḥmadiyyah
challenges to those who deny the truth of Holy Qur'ān 392
reward offered in 391
Brahmus
Believe in God, but not in Prophets 119
Bravery
Holy Qur'ān on 29
Buddha
similarity with Jesus in the events of life 268
Buddhism
scriptures provide evidence of Jesus' travels 267
Burūz
Promised Messiah as 131
Celibacy
controlling oneself during 331

Certainty
faith a ladder towards 49
faith, and insight 43
grades of 77
Challenges
of Promised Messiah to
opponents 337-454
Charity (*ṣadaqāh*)
defined 27
Chastity
as first quality for discarding
evil 14
five methods of maintaining 14
means of attaining 330
Children
proper upbringing of 335
Chitral
Jesus Christ in 266
Christian missionaries
as true Dajjāl 280-281
Christians
lack of righteousness in 414
encountered by Dhulqarnain 296
a sincere appeal to 231
Christianity
as manifestation of Satan 279
doctrines doomed to be crushed . 247
Indian conversion to 291
mention of Dajjāl in Book of
Daniel 279
missionaries as Dajjāl 280-281
real test between Islām and 405
review of 229
Companions of the Holy Prophet
devotion of 157
Converse with God
and complete surrender 66
signs of 356
Creation
and morals (*khulq*) 8
Cross
biblical evidence of deliverance
of Jesus from 255-261
broken by Promised Messiah 272
deliverance of Jesus from 252-261
description of 252
doctrines doomed to be crushed .. 247
Curse
Christian belief about 247
meaning of 247
Dajjāl
as enemy of Islām 287
Christian priests as 280-281
creation of religious mischief by
.... 309
defined 279-280
description in Holy Qur'ān and
in Aḥādīth 279
meaning of circuiting the
Ka`bah 287
mention of, in Book of Daniel 279
slaying of, by Promised Messiah
.... 285
to prevail in latter days
according to Aḥādīth 280
Death of Jesus
death of, according to Holy
Qur'ān 193-208
evidence in the Holy Qur'ān of ... 376
plead to Maulavī Nadhīr
Ḥussain for a debate on 372
Demascus
relationship with Promised
Messiah 188-189
Descent (of Jesus)
Aḥādīth on 185
correct meanings of 186
deeper meanings and spiritual
difference between the Christian
and popular Muslim beliefs
.... 169-171
mystery of 185
true meanings of 179-180

Dhikr
defined.. 163
Dhulqarnain
equipped with comfort................ 296
Holy Qur'ān on.................... 295-299
people at the time of.................. 296
prophecy about courses followed by Promised Messiah 299, 303
three kinds of people faced by.... 298
to rescue the people from Gog and Magog 453
Divine Decree
prayer for................................... 453
rejection by philosophers............ 276
Divine Settlement
proposal to seek.......................... 409
Divine Support
knowledge of Holy Qur'ān as sign of................................. 360,451
types of, for the righteous........... 338
Divine Blessings
evidence in the form of,............. 353
Dreams
types of people who experience 75-76
Elia(s)
meaning of descent of................ 181
Equity
as second quality for doing good.. 26
Europe
abolishing veil in 327
Evil
spread in latter days.................... 288
Faith
and unseen.................................... 43
demands belief in unseen............. 43
salvation depends on 50
signs of true,.............................. 387
stages of progress in 52
steadfastness in............................ 73
three categories of the faithful...... 55
Fanā
defined 60
Fire
use made by Gog and Magog 305
Forgiveness
as first quality for doing good.......20
Full comprehension (of God)
bestowed by God Alone................52
Galilee
Jesus travelled to.........................251
Gentleness
as fourth quality for discarding evil 19
Ghaḍḍ-e-Baṣar
meaning and significance of 332
God Almighty
creation a sole attribute of...........225
does not punish without sending guidance.....................................151
Recognition a blessing of *Raḥīmiyyat*....................................52
true belief of Jesus same as taught by Holy Qur'ān 245
Gog and Magog
characteristics of.........................307
Europeans powers as...................307
experts in use of fire....................305
Holy Qur'ān on 306
times of.......................................305
Gospels
imperfect teaching of 24
Graciousness
as fourth quality for doing good....26
Guidance
belongs to God Almighty alone ..335
Ḥadīth
description of Promised Messiah as Prophet in 343
Ḥāfiẓ Muḥammad Yūsuf
misguided assertions challenged 377
Heavenly signs
people who partake in 75

Heedlessness of the heart
remedies for.................................. 32
Ḥidāyatullāh
response to the critique of........... 216
Holy Prophet
Abū Bakr affirmed his death 208
account of spiritual descent (*Me'rāj*)..................................... 191
ascent is spiritual phenomenon... 187
blessing of *khilāfat* after............. 166
blessings of Divine understanding for believers in...... 50
cleared Jesus of false charges..... 274
contradictory popular beliefs about, being the last prophet....... 178
exalted moral station of................. 9
love for Allah 157
meeting with Jesus...................... 191
noble example of the wives of,... 324
obedience makes one a beloved of God 116
on distinction between two Messiahs.................................... 176
on Gog and Magog..................... 307
on *iḥsān* 61
on kind treatment of wife 314
resemblance with Jesus 275
respect for women shown by,..... 312
the first teacher and true heir of the Holy Qur'ān.......................... 160
Holy Qur'ān
about confirmed disbelievers...... 118
about deceit practised by jews.... 281
authority to last till day of judgment..................................... 125
belief taught about God 245
brought perfection to imperfect teachings.................................... 128
confirmation of Torah by,........... 149
deeper meanings revealed to perfect believer.......................... 339
designation of Christian priests as Dajjāl..................................... 282
does not close door of prophethood...............................126
Holy Prophet the best teacher of,..159
knowledge of, as sign of Divine support......................................360
knowledge of, granted to the Promised Messiah.......................358
meanings revealed only to the righteous 159
not a book of old stories..............295
on Dajjāl and Satan.....................279
on *dhikr*......................................163
on disobedience of Moses companions................................134
on exercise of moral quality..........21
on mischief of Christians 309
on *Nafs-e-Ammārah*........................2
on *Nafs-e-Lawwāmah* 2
on obedience of Muslims 120
on spiritual states 68
on tidings of permanent *khilāfat*.166
promise of successors among Muslims 148
provides for all needs..................355
safeguarding requires appearance of spiritual teachers 162-163
teaches to love virtuous...............39
testifies that Jesus is dead 136
two types of verses......................118
use of word Allah in....................119
will preserve forever 163
Holy Spirit
and perfect believers 90
does not move from station in heaven...66
during stage of 'baqa' 66
Honesty
second quality for discarding evil...15
Human Rights
and polygamy.............................318
in marriage.................................322

Human states
three sources of.............................. 1
Humanity
seal of Prophethood as perfection of.............................. 129
Husband
as manifestation of Divine for wife.. 312
guardian of wife 315
importance of kind treatment to women....................................... 313
responsibility for providing the wife.. 315
right to divorce 314
Ibn-e-'Abbās
belief that Jesus had died............ 194
Idolatry
relationship between decoration and ornaments and women......... 324
Immorality
unbridled freedom root of........... 329
India
conversion to Christianity in 291
Islām
about sacrifice of wealth lives and honour.................................. 157
and its blessings.......................... 152
and obedience to the Holy Prophet 157
corruption during the middle centuries 154
defined... 59
freshness brought by buruz of Holy Prophet 138
great signs in support of, ... 337
real test between Christianity and,... 405
Istighfār
remedy for heedlessness 32
Jahūl
Defined.. 88
Jesus Christ
belief about creating real birds false and polytheistic 226
belief about God same as taught by Holy Qur'ān...........................245
belief of Promised Messiah about 212
Buddhist scriptures confirm travels of....................................267
companions of, vs. companions of Holy Prophet...........................134
compared with Rama 241
confession of human weaknesses by,...........................234
critique of fictitious miracles of, .226
death clearly mentioned in Holy Qur'ān...192
death of.......................................169
death of, according to Holy Qur'ān.................................200-208
did not claim to be God...............231
divine mystery of re-advent 273
Holy Qur'ān proclaims as not accursed.....................................246
in Chitral, Afghanistan, Tibet, Nepal, and Benares 266
in Kashmir 263
in search for the lost tribe............249
life and circumstances of 238-240
miracles of 218
misguidance caused by Antichrist 184
no claim of Godhead by..............232
ointment of.................................261
perverted account in Christianity 211
popular beliefs about ascension of..169
possible use of Mesmerism.........222
proofs of the death of..................193
Prophecy of a Great Prophet after him.......................................25
refutation of two principle charges against...........................215

royal treatment accorded to 265
similarity with Buddha in he events of life 268
spiritual meanings of the miracles of 221
status of the disciples of 242
testimony of Gospels about deliverance from cross 255
true claim and teachings of 228
true status of 210
truth affirmed by Holy Qur'ān 214
visit to Punjab 265

Jews
conspiracy against Jesus 213
mistreatment of Jesus by 232
Jesus and 248
sign of 248

Ka'bah
as center of Islām 287
meanings of the Dajjāl circuiting the 287
safeguarding by Promised Messiah 287

Kashmir
Jesus in 263
journey of Mary and Jesus to 137

Khulafā'
belief required in, ... 155

Khātam-ul-Anbiyā'
perfection of humanity 129

Khilāfat
promised for Muslims 148-149
reflection of Prophethood 166

Khulā'
permission to women to seek divorce 316

Knowledge of Unseen
a test based on, ... 431

Laghv
Defined 19

Latter Days
advent of Messiah in 169
religious disputes in 305-307

Liqā
as love of God 61
defined 60
miracles of Holy Prophet as examples of 59

Lost tribe
Jesus in search for the 249

Love
reality of 36
to Satan forbidden 38

Mahdī
Aḥmadiyyah belief on the advent of 171
contradictions in the popular beliefs 174
none other than 'Īsā 172

Manū Shāstar
on divorce 314
permission of divorce by husband in 314

Marriage
purpose of 316
taqwā in 321

Maulavīs
as branches of *Dajjāliyat* 284
contradictions in belief about Mahdī 175

Maulavī Muḥammad Ḥussain Bāṭālvī
challenge on the knowledge of Arabic 362
instigation by Miāń Nadhīr Ḥussain 340

Maulavī Thana'ullāh
challenges to 367

Men of God
excellences of 93

Mesmerism
evil characteristics of 222

Messiah
second advent 277

Metteyya
a prophecy applicable to Messiah 270
prophecy of Buddha about..... 269
Miāń 'Abdūl Ḥakīm
finding fault in Holy Qur'ān and Holy Prophet 117
outrageous misinterpretations of .....
Miāń Fateḥ Masīḥ
challenges to..... 412
Miāń Nadhīr Ḥussain
challenge to 340
instigation to Batālvī by 340
Miracles
according to spititual faculties.... 220
Moral state
distinction between natural and 5
Morals
and creation (*khalq*) 8
and use of reason 11
bravery as 7
change in 35
development of..... 10
generosity as, ... 7
Holy Prophet as possessing all 7
mercy as 7
patience as 7
retribution as..... 7
Mosaic Dispensation
parallelism with Muḥammadī dispensation..... 146
Moses
converse of Allah with 153
follower Prophets of..... 130
many Messengers in support of.. 150
***Mubāhalah* (prayer duel)**
Divine permission for..... 435
invitations to Christians for 416-430
Mudd
Promised Messiah ode on the debate in 367
Muḥaddath
as reformers who uncover true spiritual teachings 149
Muḥaddathīn
in support of Torah 152
need for..... 154
Muḥammad
symbolism of name..... 139
Muḥammadī Dispensation
parallelism with Mosaic dispensation 146
Muḥkamāt
defined..... 118
Muslims
commanded to seek refuge with God against Dajjāl 286
contradictory popular beliefs 178
conversion to Christianity by 291
Mutashābihāt
defined..... 119
Nadwah
challenge by Promised Messiah to, ... 335
challenges to the scholars of 355
Nafs-e-Ammārah
and fulfillment 85
dominates man before moral state takes over..... 2
Nafs-e-Lawwāmah
and human reform..... 8
and morality..... 11
compared with a growing child..... 3
Divine wisdom for calling it to witness 2
Nafs-e-Muṭma'innah
and human reform..... 8
and love of God 4
and success 4
highest spiritual state 68
not separate from moral state..... 6
Natural aptitude
and attainment of exalted spirituality..... 107

Natural conditions of man
distinction between moral and.. 6, 10
Natural Love of God
increases love for Holy Prophet.. 107
signs to those who have............. 108
Nepal
Jesus Christ in............................ 266
New Testament
imperfect teaching of.......................
Paradise
no expulsion from............... 182-183
Patience
Holy Qur'ān on............................ 31
Peace
invitation to 450
Peacefulness
as third quality for discarding evil... 17
Perfect Believer
acceptance of prayers of............ 281
deeper meanings revealed to 339
impact of the prayers of............. 339
qualities of................................ 338
Peter
desertion of Jesus by.................. 242
Philosophers
and concept of soul...................... 47
lower grade, vs. superior 47
need to reflect on meaning of faith 47
repudiation of angels by 49
Physical conditions
effect on soul 5
examples of 3
Pig
true meaning of the slaying of, ... 176
Pīr Mehr 'Alī Shāh
invitation of Promised Messiah to, ... 357
Plato
parable about change in morals 35
Polygamy
and human rights 318
response to critique of,................317
Prayer(s)
a lovely 72
as remover of calamities 105
by wives of Holy Prophet 324
impact of the prayers of the Promised Messiah.......................345
Promised Messiah
and Gog and Magog....................305
and revival of faith......................174
apprehending Dajjāl....................287
approach to upbringing of children 335
as exactly identical to spirit of Holy Prophet..............................145
as follower of Holy Prophet........145
as Muḥammad and Aḥmad 145
as proof of perfection of Holy Prophet.......................................132
as Seal of *Auliyā'*.......................146
challenges to opponents..............337
claim in his own words...............173
close relationship with Jesus.......185
cross broken by 272
Dajjāl's supremacy during appearance of,............................284
declaration of Islamic beliefs by 354
description by Holy Prophet of, .. 176
evidence in the form of Divine Blessings...................................353
extreme care about treatment of wife 313
frequent converse with God the only claim of 146
functions of................................190
impact of the prayers of 345
knowledge of Holy Qur'ān granted to 358
prayers for heavenly signs and decree...348
proclamation of his truth to disbelievers 320

prophecy about, in *Sūrah Al-Kahf* 295
reason for harsh language against Christians 213
relationship with Demascus 188
similarity with Jesus Christ 264
supplication to God to prove his truth 322
times of 301
to propagate through light of faith 172
trumpet as symbol of 284

Prophet(s)
as being necessarily a Messenger 140
as demonstrator's of God's existence 114
as sole means of belief in Unity of God 111
as teachers of Unity of God 111
continuation of mission through successors 164
defined in Arabic and Hebrew 126
faith in unseen taught by 43
meanings and significance of seal of 128-131
no independent, after Holy Prophet 125
two types of miracles 219
why essential to believe in 116
why have needs like others 122

Prophethood
special characteristics of 357
subtleness of 150

Punjab
visit of Jesus Christ to 265

Qādiān
Maulvaī 'Abdul Laṭīfs visits 130

Qarn
Arabic term for century 302

Queen of England
invitation to 431

Raḥīmiyyat
rescues from passion and leads to faith 52

Raḥmāniyyat
demands guidance before punishment 151

Rama
compared with Jesus Christ 241

Reason
and Prophets 43
leads towards God 114

Reform
requires reformation of women 324
three methods of 8

Reformers
reflectively invested with qualities of Prophets 160

Relationship with God
personal merit and 75

Religious disputes
During times of Gog and Magog 305

Religious wars
Promised Messiah to put an end to, ... 172

Revelation
challenged to those who claim 387
Subtleness of, ... 150
types of people who experience 75-76

Righteous
Divine support for 338

Righteousness
as motive for actions 322

Ṣāḥibzādah 'Abdul Laṭīf Ṣāḥib
discussions with Promised Messiah 130-131

Ṣalāt
remedy for heedlessness ....

Salvation
and cleansing of heart 109
depends on faith 50

Sardār Rāj Indar Singh
response to ... 401
Satan
Manifested in corrupted form of Christianity ... 279
Seal of Prophethood
Holy Qur'ān on ... 140
meanings and significance of ... 128-131
not broken by complete devotion Holy Prophet ... 142
principle connotation of ... 128
Seekers
calamities as source of progress . 107
God's polishing hearts of ... 108
Self
source of moral state—self reproaching self ... 2
source of physical state—self that incites to evil ... 1
source of spirituality—soul at rest ... 3
Self-improvement
through improvement of women 323
Self-reproaching self
as source of moral condition ... 2
Holy Qur'ān on ... 2
Signs
invitation of Promised Messiah to show ... 339
Sin
ridding of, through certainty of faith ... 43
Son of God
true meaning of ... 236
Soul at rest
as source of spiritual condition ... 68
defined ... 3
Spiritual fulfillment
abandonment of vain pursuits and ... 78
discarding ego and ... 80
humility and ... 78
restraint of passion and ... 79
spending wealth in cause of Allah and ... 79
stages of ... 78
Suffering
and spiritual progress ... 100
as necessity for Divine favor ... 100
Ṣūfīṣ
different orders of ... 175
on two types of spiritual progress ... 107
Sūrah Al-Fātiḥah
challenge to write a commentary on ... 359
clearly implies Christians are Dajjāl ... 279
meanings and significance of ... 72-73
on mischief of Christians ... 309
perfect guidance towards nearness and comprehension of the Divine ... 94
Sūrah al-Kahf
prophecy about the Promised Messiah[as] in ... 295
Ṣūrāḥ Yūsuf
prophecy about Holy Prophet[sa] in ... 304
Taḥdīth
and unseen ... 142
Taqwā
in marriage ... 321
Tawaffī
meanings of ... 376
true connotation of ... 196-198
Tibet
Jesus Christ in ... 266
Tomb of Jesus
as evidence of death of Jesus ... 267
Torah
Holy Qur'ān on ... 149
many Messengers in support of .. 150
muḥaddathīn in support of ... 152

on followers of Moses as disobedient 134
on training of children 335
Transmigration of Souls
critique of 210
Trinity
absurdity of the doctrine of......... 244
Trusts
wide connotation of discharging... 88
Truthful
defined....................................... 158
exhortation to keep company of . 158
Truthfulness
as moral quality 33
as natural condition 33
Unchastity
remedies for,............................... 330
Unitarian Sect
renunciation of Trinity by........... 241
Unity of God
cannot be attained without following Holy Prophet.............. 121
Holy Prophet as highest example of................................. 135
Vedantists
refutation of 95
Veil
extreme attitudes about............... 332
Islamic system of........................ 328
response to critique of 327
Whitebrecht, Reverend
conclusive argument for 411
Wife
right to divorce 316
Williams, Sir Monier
on the travels on Buddha's disciples...................................... 267
Wives
equal treatment of....................... 320
influence of Husband on............. 323
Wives of the Holy Prophet
noble example of........................ 324
Woman
kind treatment of.........................311
Women
inculcating piety in......................323
respect shown by Holy Prophet to 312
Wrath of Allah
Holy Qur'ān on,..........................355
Wujudis
refutation of 95
Ẓalūm
defined 88

INDEX OF TERMS

Ajīj 305
Auliyā'ullāh 134
Asran Sam 268
Baqā 60
Dajjāl 279
Dajjāliyyat 284
Dhulqarnain 295-303
Fanā 60-65
Ghaḍḍ-e-baṣar 332
Hadab 283
Khātam-ul-Khulafā 210
Khātam-ul-Anbiyā' 205
Liqā' 60
Gog and Magog 283,305-309
Kalīmullāh 356
Mahdī 170-178
Masah 284
Me'rāj 191
Metteyya 270
Mubāhalah 185,387,416,430
Muḥaddathīn 142, 148
Muḥaddath 142
Muḥkamāt 118
Mutashābihāt 118
Nābā 142
Nabī 126,142
Nās 286
Nasal 283
Nūzul 185-186
Qarn 302
Sagpat 268
Sāsta 268
Taḥ dīth 142
Tawaffī 193-198,207,375
Tauḥīd 111
Yājūj and Mājūj 305